T3-BUX-518

CONTEMPORARY PERSPECTIVES ON CHRISTIAN MARRIAGE

CONTEMPORARY PERSPECTIVES ON CHRISTIAN MARRIAGE

Propositions and Papers from the International Theological Commission

Edited by

Monsignor Richard Malone

and

John R. Connery, S.J.

Loyola University Press
Chicago, Illinois 60657

Printed in the United States of America

Library of Congress Cataloging in Publication Data

Contemporary perspectives on Christian marriage.

1. Marriage – Religious aspects – Catholic Church – Addresses, essays, lectures. 2. Catholic Church – Doctrines – Addresses, essays, lectures. I. Malone, Richard. II. Connery, John R., 1913- . III. Catholic Church. Commissio Theologica Internationalis.

BX2250.C6 1984 261.8'3581 84-11262

ISBN 0-8294-0472-4

TABLE OF CONTENTS

FOREWORD

Few will doubt that the institution of marriage is facing critical problems today. To have evidence of this one needs no more than the shocking statistics on divorce in our country; in some parts of the country half as many people are divorced every year as are married, a clear sign of the widespread instability of marital unions. Nor is the crisis only on the level of practice or performance. One can hardly raise a meaningful question about marriage today that has not become controversial. Such uncertainty undoubtedly makes its own contribution to the ongoing corrosion of practice. Even with clear convictions keeping a marriage intact calls for great skill and effort. The absence of such convictions can easily undermine the efforts necessary to maintain a viable marital union.

Vatican II in *Gaudium et Spes* (47) called attention to the many problems with which marriage is confronted in different parts of the world. Many of these problems are linked, at least to some extent, to cultural changes that have taken place. The Council did not, of course, place itself in opposition to change as such. Indeed, it acknowledged the fact that changes that take place in society often bring out the true character of marriage in one way or another. In this respect one can point to the way in which the change from the extended family to the so-called nuclear family has brought out the importance of conjugal love and companionship in marriage. One can also show how the advent of technological reproduction served to sharpen the real meaning of human procreation as an expression of conjugal love. But no one can deny that changes in our society have also produced difficulties. The Council could not be complacent about these.

While upholding the institution of marriage, Vatican II attempted to respond to the needs of our times by taking a more personalist approach. More than in the past the Council pointed to the nature of marriage as a "community of life and love" arising from a personal commitment. Without underplaying other marital goals in any way, it focused on the importance of conjugal love in marriage today. The caution regarding the other goals of marriage was needed to offset the current movement to reverse the priority once given to procreation. The Council set no priorities but maintained a balance between the unitive or personal and the procreative aspects of marriage. An exaggerated personalism is just as unhealthy as an exaggerated procreationism.

The teaching of Vatican II on marriage stimulated a theological and pastoral renewal in this area. At the same time, however, it also became the subject of debate. With the many questions that were being raised, the need for reflection that would be both constructive and critical impressed itself on the members of the International Theological Commission set up by the Holy See to study theological issues. The Commission decided to deal with some of these questions in its winter 1977 session. A subcommission was appointed and went to work on them. The matter to be discussed was broken down into five different problem areas dealing with (1) marriage as an institution, (2) marriage as sacrament, (3) the relation between marriage as contract-covenant and marriage as sacrament, (4) indissolubility, and (5) remarriage.

Working papers, or *relationes*, were drawn up to cover these areas and to serve as the basis for the discussions. W. Ernst dealt with the issue of marriage as an institution. He traced its origin to the sexual differences with which humankind was endowed by the Creator Himself. The institution of marriage was reaffirmed by Jesus and restored to its original indissolubility. In the New Testament marriage also became a "sign" of the love of Christ for His Church. Given this meaning, even though the Church at the beginning did not enter actively into the marriage ceremony, marriage was never regarded simply as a secular institution. The participation of the Church in the actual ceremony was a gradual development, but in no sense a usurpation. Differences in this development are detected in the eastern and western Churches. Such differences are consistent with an essential unity, and should be allowed for in any canonical regulation. Also, following Vatican II (GS 26), the subcommission agreed that the common good to be protected is not something apart from the persons who make up the community but the facilitation of their own personal development and perfection.

The meaning of marriage as specifically Christian and its relation to baptism were discussed under the direction of K. Lehmann. It is the sacramental character of marriage that makes it specifically Christian. It also gives it the kind of indissolubility that characterizes the relation of Christ to His Church. The question under much discussion today is whether the baptized Christian who no longer believes receives the sacrament when he marries. A basic Christian intention is required for marriage, as for any sacrament, and it is difficult to see how this can be present where there is unbelief. The mind of the subcommission is that the absence of faith casts doubt on the presence of a sacramental intention, and therefore on the validity of the marriage. Implied here is the identity of the sacrament with the contract in the case of the baptized, a question which is taken up more in detail in the next discussion. According to the subcommission the practical problem arising from the case of a person who is baptized but no longer believes should be resolved by restoring the person's faith, not by compromising basic sacramental doctrine.

The identity of the marital covenant or contract with the sacrament for Christians is explored further under the guidance of C. Caffarra. More specifically, the question raised concerns the possibility for a Christian of intending to enter marriage without receiving the sacrament. The question raises such issues as what constitutes the sacrament, and who is the minister of the sacrament. In its conclusion the subcommission espouses the traditional position that for the Christian sacramentality is not something accidental to the marriage which can be present or absent. It is something essential. It would be contradictory for a Christian to turn back to a nonsacramental marriage. He might by reason of invincible ignorance or error think that he could enter marriage without receiving the sacrament. He might even make an irrevocable commitment which would go far beyond a transitory relationship with a partner. While this relationship might have all the appearances of marriage, the Church could not recognize it as such. It would be a mistake, then, to initiate a practice that allowed a choice of sacramental or nonsacramental marriage, or for a priest or deacon to assist or say prayers at a nonsacramental marriage.

The problem of indissolubility was discussed under the guidance of E. Hamel, S.J. The teaching on indissolubility goes back to the New Testament and the early Church. It was affirmed even in regard to adultery, although the Matthean text is difficult to interpret and there are instances of indulgence in very difficult cases. Although the teaching is certain, it has never been clearly defined. The indissolubility of the sacramental marriage that has been consummated is based on the indissolubility of the relation of Christ to his Church, which Christian marriage is meant to symbolize. The power of the Church to dissolve other marriages cannot be extended to these. But the subcommission did not want to rule out the possibility of further refinements of the notion of sacramentality and consummation in regard to indissolubility.

The discussion of the status of the divorced and remarrried was led by J. Medina-Esteves who relied on a document that came from the Pontifical Commission on the Family under E. Gagnon. The subcommission agreed that legislation against divorce is based on the judgment of Christ himself and is an expression of the relation of marriage to the love of Christ for his Church. Also, since the state of the divorced is incompatible with the mystery of love expressed in the Eucharist, the sign of unity with Christ which the Eucharist expressed could not be verified in the case of the remarried. This does not mean that these people are entirely removed from the Church or that they should be excluded from all pastoral care. They still have obligations and need help to fulfill these obligations. Also, to prevent marriage failures programs are needed that will be aimed at developing an awareness and understanding of the meaning of marriage "in the Lord."

The above material represents a distillation of the reflections of the subcommission. The conclusions of these reflections were formulated into propositions at the end of the sessions and submitted to the whole Commission for a vote. An ablsolute majority voted in favor of them.

In 1978 Monsignor Philippe Delhaye, Secretary of the International Theological Commission, began publishing the papers of the 1977 ITC discussion of Christian Marriage in the magazine *Esprit et Vie.* We began translating the papers for the use of the Bishops Conference in the United States. Later on, Monsignor Delhaye collected them in a volume *Problèmes Doctrinaux du Mariage Chrétien (Louvain-la-Neuve, 1979).* The French volume includes the Propositions of the ITC grouped into five headings, a special commentary on each group of propositions, the essays on marriage as institution, sacrament, reality in the order of creation and grace, and indissolubility, a study of the pastoral care of the divorced and remarried by Archbishop Gagnon, and a note on the relationship of nature and grace in Vatican II.

We present the propositions of the ITC on Christian Marriage with Monsignor Delhaye's commentary. This captures key points of the oral discussion. Since we began by translating the earlier papers, we compared the early papers with the texts of the book. We kept

Professor Ernst's paper as published in *Esprit et Vie* since there were no major differences from the text of the Delhaye volume. We have added three other essays to Delhaye's note on nature and grace: an article on indissolubility in the gospels by the late Bishop Descamps, published in *Revue Théologique de Louvain,* Father Martelet's christological theses, published in *La Documentation Catholique,* and Monsignor Martimort's study of the role of liturgical history in the development of our theology of marriage published in *Esprit et Vie* in 1978. We chose the last three because, linked with the major articles, they provide scriptural and historical bases for points made in the essays and in the propositions.

We have assembled this valuable collection of material for the English speaking world. In effect, our nine theologians, representatives of different schools and cultures, summarize a great deal of the theological reflection that developed in the creative post-conciliar period. In their syntheses they present a mosaic of the major trends in the theology of marriage and will provide an updated enrichment of Catholic pastoral and theological reflection on this most basic of all human institutions, Christian marriage.

In his "Apostolic Exhortation on the Family," Pope John Paul II said:

> . . . I feel it is my duty to extend a pressing invitation to theologians, asking them to unite their efforts in order to collaborate with the hierarchical magisterium and to commit themselves to the task of illustrating ever more clearly the biblical foundations, the ethical grounds and the personalistic reason behind this doctrine [of Christian marriage and family life].
>
> * * * *
>
> A united effort by theologians in this regard, inspired by a convinced adherence to the magisterium, which is the one authentic guide for the people of God, is particularly urgent for reasons that include the close link between Catholic teaching on this matter and the view of the human person that the church proposes: Doubt or error in the field of marriage or the family involves obscuring to a serious extent the integral truth about the human person in a culture situation that is already so often confused and contradictory. In fulfillment of their specific role theologians are

> called upon to provide enlightenment and a deeper understanding, and their contribution is of incomparable value and represents a unique and highly meritorious service to the family and humanity.[1]

In these essays we find theologians already representing and applying the basic themes of church teaching to our modern problems. Their work serves as a model of the kind of response the Pope expects of the theological community. The reasons the Pope gives for this work are deeply pastoral and so, in this case, the theological response assumes an almost immediate pastoral influence on the life of the Church.

We wish to thank those who prepared the translations and in a special way, Father Roger Balducelli, OSFS, who translated the greater part of the texts and Mr. David Byers who edited the volume. Gratitude also must go to the staff persons who at various moments helped launch and organize the project: Edward Horan, Theresa Purcell, Ann Pasternacki, and Patricia Boman.

Last, but not least, we must report that the Chairmen of the NCCB Committee on Doctrine, Cardinal William Baum and Archbishop James Hickey, encouraged the initiative and pressed for its completion. They saw the volume as filling a gap in our English speaking world by introducing theologians who are not familiar to our public and who do theology in a way slightly different from what is the common approach here. They felt that this volume would be a valuable tool for all kinds of theological formation, such as seminaries and adult education classes.

Monsignor Richard Malone

John R. Connery, S.J.

Part I

STATEMENTS OF THE INTERNATIONAL THEOLOGICAL COMMMISSION

CHAPTER 1

Propositions on the Doctrine of Christian Marriage:

with Introduction and Commentary

by Monsignor Philippe Delhaye

INTRODUCTION

Even though the teaching of Vatican II on marriage and the family is scattered through several documents such as *Lumen Gentium, Gaudium et Spes,* and *Apostolicam Actuositatem,* it has provided the incentive for theological and pastoral renewal in this area, giving new impetus to the sort of inquiries which paved the way for these documents.

The need for reflection both constructive and critical has thus become clear to members of the International Theological Commission. With the approval of its President, His Eminence Cardinal Seper, these men decided in 1975 to include in their program of study some doctrinal problems relating to Christian marriage. A subcommission soon set to work and made preparations for the session of December 1977. The members of the subcommission were Professors B. Ahern, C. P.; C. Caffarra; Ph. Delhaye [President]; Wilhelm Ernst; E. Hamel; K. Lehmann; J. Mahoney [Moderator]; J. Medina-Estevez; and O. Semmelroth.

The subject matter was divided into five large themes. The themes were prepared for by producing working papers and "reports." The reports were in turn supplemented by documents. Prof. Wilhelm Ernst was given charge of the first day which was devoted to marriage as an institution. The sacramentality of marriage, and its relation to faith and baptism, were studied under the guidance of Prof. K. Lehmann. Before Fr. Hamel guided the study of the indissolubility of marriage, Prof. Caffarra contributed new views on the old "contract versus sacrament" problem by examining it from the standpoint of the history of salvation, especially in terms of its relation to creation and redemption. The situation of divorced and remarried persons pertains primarily to pastoral theology, yet it has a bearing on the question of indissolubility and the question of the Church's powers in this area. Mgr. Medina-Estevez conducted the discussion of this problem with the help of a document issued by the Pontifical Committee on the Family.

At the end of each session, the subcommission formulated a number of propositions which were submitted to all the members of the ITC for a vote. As expected, many amendments were suggested and certain revisions were proposed. The ITC now publishes the final version of these propositions, collected under five headings suggested by the way in which they originated. These propositions have received the absolute majority of the votes of the members of the ITC. This means that the members approved not only their basic orientation, but also their wording and the form in which they are now presented.[1]

INTERNATIONAL THEOLOGICAL COMMMISSION

Propositions on the Doctrine of Christian Marriage

1. MATRIMONY AS AN INSTITUTION

1.1 The Human and Divine View of Matrimony

The marital covenant is founded upon preexistent and permanent structures which constitute the difference between man and woman. It is "instituted" by the spouses themselves, even though in its concrete form it is subject to different historical and cultural changes as well as to individual personalities. Thus marriage shows itself to be an institution of the creator himself, both through the mutual help in conjugal love and fidelity that the spouses offer one another, and through the rearing of children within the heart of the family community.

1.2 Marriage in Christ

As is easily shown in the New Testament, Jesus confirmed this institution which existed "from the very beginning" and cured it of its previous defects (Mk 10:2–9, 10–12) by restoring all its dignity and its original requirements. He sanctified this state of life (GS 48,2) by including it within the mystery of love which unites him as redeemer to his Church. This is the reason why the task of regulating Christian marriage (1 Cor 7:10 ff.) has been entrusted to the Church.

1.3 The Apostles

The epistles of the New Testament say that marriage should be honored in every way (Heb 13:4); in response to certain attacks, they present it as a good work of the creator (1 Tm 4:1–5). They exalt the marriage of the faithful by noting its insertion into the mystery of the covenant and the love which unites Christ and the Church (Eph 5:22–33; GS 48,2–3).

They ask, therefore, that marriage be contracted "in the Lord" (1 Cor 7:39) and that matrimonial life be lived in accordance with the dignity of a "new creature" (2 Cor 5:17), "in Christ" (Eph 5:21–33), putting Christians on guard against the pagans' sins (1 Cor 6:12–20;

cf.6:9–10). On the basis of a "right deriving from faith" and in their desire to assure its permanence, the Churches of apostolic times formulated certain moral orientations (Col 3:18 ff.; Ti 2:3–5; 1 Pt 3:1–7) and juridical dispositions that would help people live matrimony "according to the faith" in different human situations and conditions.

1.4 The First Centuries

During the first centuries of church history, Christians contracted marriage "like other men" *(Ad Diognetum* v.6) with the father of the family presiding, and only with domestic rites and gestures, as, for example, joining right hands. Still they did not lose sight of the "extraordinary and truly paradoxical laws of their spiritual society" *(ibid.*, v.4): Christians eliminated from the home liturgies every trace of pagan cult, and placed special importance on the procreation and education of children *(ibid.*, v.6); they accepted the bishop's vigilance over matrimony (St. Ignatius of Antioch, *Ad Polycarpum* v.2); they showed in their marriages a special submission to God and a relationship with their faith (Clement of Alexandria, *Stromata*, iv, 20); and sometimes at the marriage rite they enjoyed the celebration of the eucharistic sacrifice and a special blessing (Tertullian, *Ad Uxorem*, ii, 9).

1.5 The Eastern Tradition

From very early times in the Eastern Churches, the shepherds of the Church took an active part in the celebration of marriages, either in place of the fathers of the family or along with them. This change was not the result of a usurpation, but came about as a response to requests made by the family and with the approval of civil authority.

Because of this evolution, the ceremonies formerly carried out within the family were little by little included within liturgical rites. As time passed, the idea took shape that the ministers of the rite of the "mystery" of matrimony included not only the couple, but also the shepherd of the Church.

1.6 The Western Tradition

In the Western Churches, the problem of what element constituted marriage from a juridical point of view arose with the encounter between the Christian vision of matrimony and Roman law. This was resolved by considering the consent of the spouses as the only constitutive element. The fact that, up until the time of the Council of Trent, clandestine marriages were considered valid is a result of this decision. Still, the blessing of the priest and his presence as witness for the Church, as well as some liturgical rites, had been encouraged for a long time. With the decree *Tametsi*, the presence of the pastor and witnesses became the ordinary canonical form necessary for the validity of marriage.

1.7 The New Churches

In line with the desires of Vatican Council II and the new rite for celebrating matrimony, one hopes that new liturgical and juridical norms will be developed under the guidance of ecclesiastical authority among peoples who have recently come to the gospel, to harmonize the reality of Christian marriage with the authentic values of these peoples' own traditions.

This diversity of norms, due to the plurality of cultures, is compatible with basic unity and therefore does not go beyond the limits of legitimate pluralism.

The Christian and ecclesial character of the union and of the mutual self-giving of the spouses can be expressed in different ways, under the influence of the baptism which they have received and in the presence of witnesses, among whom the competent priest occupies a very important place. Today various canonical adaptations of these various elements may be opportune.

1.8 Canonical Adaptations

The reform of canon law should be guided by a global view of matrimony according to its various personal and social dimensions. The Church must realize that juridical ordinances are meant to promote and develop conditions that are progressively more attentive to the human values of matrimony. Of course, such regulations cannot reflect the total reality of matrimony.

1.9 Personalistic View of the Institution

"The beginning, the subject and the goal of all social institutions is and must be the human person, who by its very nature stands completely in need of social life." (GS 25). As an "intimate partnership of life and conjugal love" (GS 48), matrimony is a suitable place and an apt means of promoting the welfare of persons in line with their vocation. Therefore marriage can never be thought of as a way of sacrificing persons to some common good extrinsic to themselves, since the common good is "the sum of those conditions of social life which allow people, whether as groups or as individuals, to reach their fulfillment more fully and more easily" (GS 26).

1.10 Structure and Not Superstructure

While marriage is subject to economic realism at its beginning and for its entire duration, it is not a superstructure for private ownership of goods and resources. Certainly the concrete ways in which the marriage and the family subsist may be tied to economic conditions. But the definitive union of a man and a woman in a conjugal covenant corresponds primarily to human nature and the needs which the creator put in them. This is the reason why matrimony is not an obstacle to the personal maturation of couples, but rather is a great help to them.

Commentary

1. INSTITUTION

(Propositions 1.1–1.10)

The first set of propositions is not particularly polemical in either import or intent. All the same, it was meant to respond to the objections formulated today against marriage as an institution. What are these objections? There is a great variety of them. Some people say that a man and a woman make of their union what they please, independently of any preestablished structure, or that if love is present there is neither need for rites meant to negotiate the way into marriage, or for any models of married life. Others say that marriage sacrifices the good of persons to the good of an oppressive society external to the persons themselves, or perhaps even to more or less disguised economic imperatives. Finally, there are those who reproach the Church for having usurped an authority over marriage that properly belongs to families or the state, and that here too the drive toward secularization must have its way. We hear that according to the *Epistle to Diognetus,* "Christians marry just as other people do," or that only in the 11th century did ecclesial authority prevail and succeed in regulating marriage and the rites which constitute the celebration of it.

How does the ITC meet these objections? It was no easy task to condense into ten propositions the working paper and presentation[2] prepared by Professor Wilhelm Ernst, together with the documents appended to them.[3] The complete meaning of the propositions will be accessible only to those who read his commentary and the final report. Here we can only indicate the directions in which thought and discussion moved.

There are two essential areas: on the one hand, the person, the human couple before God, creator and redeemer; on the other, the specific role played by the church as the guardian responsible for promoting in marriage the goals which faith aims to achieve.

Preconciliar theology would have responded by stressing the necessity of a juridical contract. It would have referred to "pure nature" as the basis of a natural law to which a sacrament of the faith was added as an extrinsic element. The ITC did not ignore anything of value in such approaches, yet it chose to address the issue from the perspective of salvation history and personalist philosophy.

Anthropology, psychology, and sociology (Propositions 1.1; 1.9; 1.10) enlighten us on marriage as founded on sexual differentiation (Proposition 1.1), which creates the possibility of an interpersonal relation of a specific and particularly enriching type (Proposition 1.10). For the believer, however, marriage derives its meaning above all from what God, the creator and redeemer, has done. One cannot ignore the distinction between nature and grace,[4] but in the history of salvation a very special continuity exists between marriage as willed by God, the creator for "nature as created" and marriage as restored by the redeemer and his grace for "nature as redeemed." This is indeed the reason why Matthew (19:5) and Paul (Eph 5:31) remind us that God willed to bring marriage back, through grace, to what it had been "at the beginning" (Propositions 1.1 and 1.2). The Lord God created human beings in his image. He made them male and female in order to give them to each other, in the joy of complementarity. Isolation could thus be overcome. Another purpose was to lend them the almost divine capacity to transmit and give life (Proposition 1.1).

The apostolic writings (Proposition 1.3) have well perceived the importance of this gift, and the summons it implies. Paul sums it up well when he proclaims that Christian marriage takes place "in the Lord" (1 Cor 7:39), in keeping with the logic of faith and grace that institutes a new creation (2 Cor 5:17). Materially considered, sexual intimacy between the spouses who have become one "in Christ" is the same as in the fornications and adulteries of pagans (1 Cor 6:12–20; 6:9–10), but it differs from these in its human and divine reality.

This union can be taken up into the love which Christ bears for his Church (Eph 5:22–23). This human covenant thus takes its place within the covenant between God and his people. As the spouses relate to each other, they are no longer objects but subjects, that is, persons (Proposition 1.9). Marriage is not meant to enslave one of the spouses. Marriage is not the outcome of an arrangement about property and possessions, or the product of economic society (Proposition 1.10). "The definitive union of man and woman" (Proposition 1.10) is a response to God's grace, to the call which God himself has located in people at all levels of their being, in order to help them grow and transcend themselves through the strength of his grace (Proposition 1.10).

Thus, when the Church formulates moral and canonical directives and plays a role in the celebration of marriage, we should not see in this only the exercise of an authority or a response to the wishes of families or the state (Proposition 1.5). The purpose of the Church's intervention is above all to make more specific, and to apply, the requirements emerging from the new creation in Christ and from faith. Here, too, much can be learned from history,[5] or from comparing the traditions of the West with those of the East and of the Third World concerning the celebration of marriage and the orientations which are consequent upon it. One of the more paradoxical results of this comparison has been that the elements which are essential to the act of entering the state of Christian marriage, characterized by its two-fold relation to Christ and to the Church, have come clearly to the fore (Proposition 1.7, par. 2).

On the one hand, the deliberate and free gift of the spouses to each other and their mutual commitment are made under the influence of their baptism (Proposition 1.7, par. 2) and are a manifestation of their "royal priesthood" (LG 34). On the other hand, this quite personal and intimate mutual gift must of necessity be witnessed by the representatives of God's people. Among these witnesses, a special place undoubtedly pertains to the pastor, for reasons that differ from tradition to tradition.

However, it was not the primary purpose of the ITC to stress this fact. Its inquiries were intended to answer the objection of clerical usurpation (Proposition 1.5) and to ascertain how pastors have come to play an increasingly large role in the celebration of marriage. The commission did not intend, of course, to write a short history of the liturgy of marriage, nor to pretend that during the early centuries this liturgy must have exibited a clerical character, or still less to discover a primitive canon law of marriage. Yet the commission could not overlook the very clear convergence of two things. On the one hand, pastors took pains to eliminate pagan elements from wedding celebrations and to discern how faith affects both the act of entering married life and married life itself. On the other hand, families wished to have the community witness the transition to a new state in life, to have the blessing of the priest, and to conjoin the human interpersonal gift to the gift of Christ to his church in the holy Eucharist. It is not at all surprising that pastors have participated in the past (Propositions 1.5 and 1.6) and can still do so in the present (Proposition 1.7) within a coherent pluralism. This shows that, while safeguarding the substance of the sacrament, the church can work out a synthesis between the immutable reality of Christian marriage and the genuine traditions embedded in various cultures and in various moments of history. Because of this capacity, we can hope that changes will be made in the norms that regulate marriage among people recently converted to Christianity (Proposition 1.7). Canonical reforms are, of course, implied in these changes. With regard to the reforms now being prepared, the ITC has expressed resignation rather than enthusiasm (Proposition 1.8)

2. SACRAMENTALITY OF CHRISTIAN MARRIAGE

2.1 Real Symbol and Sacramental Sign

Jesus Christ redisclosed in a prophetic way the reality of matrimony as it was intended by God at man's beginnings (see Gn 1:27; Mk 10:6; Mt 19:4; Gn 2:24; Mk 10:7–8; Mt 9:25) and restored it through his death and resurrection. For this reason Christian marriage is lived "in the Lord" (1 Cor 7:39) and is also formed by elements of the saving action performed by Christ.

Already in the Old Testament, marital union was a figure of the covenant between God and the people of Israel (see Hos 2; Jer 3:6–13; Ez 16 and 23; Is 54). In the New Testament Christian marriage rises to a new dignity as a representation of the mystery which unites Christ and the Church (see Eph 5:21–33). Theological interpretation illuminates this analogy more profoundly: the supreme love and gift of the Lord who shed his blood, and the faithful and irrevocable attachment of his spouse, the Church, become models and examples for Christian marriage.

This resemblance is a relationship of real sharing in the covenant of love between Christ and the Church. For its part, Christian marriage, as a real symbol and sacramental sign, represents the Church of Christ concretely in the world and, especially under its family aspect, it is rightly called the "domestic church" (LG 11).

2.2 Sacrament in a Real Sense

In this way matrimony takes on the likeness of the mystery of the union between Jesus Christ and the Church. This inclusion of Christian marriage in the economy of salvation is enough to justify the title sacrament in a broad sense.

But also it is both the concrete condensation and the real actualization of this primordial sacrament. It follows from this that Christian marriage is in itself a real and true sign of salvation which confers the grace of Jesus Christ. For this reason the Catholic Church numbers it among the seven sacraments (see DS 1327, 1801).

The relationship between marriage and its sacramentality is unique because they are reciprocally constitutive. Indissolubility makes it easier to understand the sacramental nature of Christian marriage; from the theological point of view, its sacramental nature constitutes the preeminent, although not the only, grounds for its indissolubility.

2.3 Baptism, Real Faith, Intention, Sacramental Marriage

Just like the other sacraments, marriage confers grace in the final analysis by virtue of the action performed by Jesus Christ and not only through the faith of the one receiving it. However, this does not mean that grace is conferred in the sacrament of marriage outside of faith or in the absence of faith. It follows from this – according to classical principles – that faith is presupposed as a dispositive cause of the fruitful effect of the sacrament. The validity of marriage, however, does not necessarily depend on whether or not it has the fruit of the sacrament.

The existence today of baptized nonbelievers raises a new theological problem and a grave pastoral dilemma, especially when the lack of faith, or even the rejection of faith, seems clear. The intention of carrying out what Christ and the Church desire is the minimum condition required before consent is considered to be a real human act on the sacramental plane. The problem of the intention and that of the personal faith of the contracting parties must not be confused, but they must not be totally separated either.

In the final analysis, the real intention is born from and feeds on living faith. Where there is no trace of faith (in the sense of *belief*—being disposed to believe), and no desire for grace or salvation, then a real doubt arises as to whether there is the above mentioned general and truly sacramental intention and whether the marriage is validly contracted or not. As was noted, the personal faith of the contracting parties does not constitute the sacramentality of matrimony, but the absence of personal faith weakens the validity of the sacrament.

This gives rise to new problems for which a satisfactory answer has yet to be found, and it imposes new pastoral responsibilities regarding Christian matrimony. "Priests should first of all strengthen and nourish the faith of those about to be married, for the sacrament of matrimony presupposes and demands faith" (OCMP 7).

2.4 Dynamic Interconnection

For the Church, baptism is the social basis and the sacrament of faith through which believers become members of the Body of Christ. The existence of "baptized nonbelievers" implies problems of great importance in this respect as well. A true response to practical and pastoral problems will not be found in changes which subvert the central core of sacramental doctrine and of matrimonial doctrine, but only in a radical renewal of baptismal spirituality.

We must view and renew baptism in its essential unity and in the dynamic articulation of all its elements and dimensions: faith, preparation for the sacrament, the rite, profession of faith, incorporation into Christ and into the Church, moral consequences, and active participation in church life. The intimate connection between baptism, faith, and the Church must be stressed. Only in this way will it be clear that matrimony between the baptized is in itself a true sacrament—that is, not by some kind of automatic process but by matrimony's own internal nature.

Commentary

2. SACRAMENTALITY OF CHRISTIAN MARRIAGE

(Propositions 2.1–2.4)

The very meaning of the institution of marriage is based on its sacramental character (second set of propositions) and implies a difference between the competencies and the identity of the societies involved (third set of propositions). A book bent on patching up the differences between Catholicism and the Reformation is even forced to acknowledge that on this question a "special controversy"[6] exists. In Catholicism, the institution of marriage is grounded on the insertion of conjugal love into the paschal mystery. Thus the church, faithful to her Lord, plays a primordial role in that institution. "Protestant doctrine, on the contrary, does not grant this. In keeping with a famous saying of Luther, it regards marriage as a 'worldly affair.' The Church concerns herself with marriage only in her proclamation of the Word of God. She does not need to worry about it any more than she worries about the profession a Christian might choose to pursue."[7]

The advances in ecumenical understanding, today's sacramental crisis, and the fact that there are now "baptized persons who do not believe," converged to induce members of the ITC to rethink, under the guidance of Prof. Karl Lehmann,[8] a certain number of problems. What is meant when we say that Christian marriage is a sacrament? What role does faith play in sacramental actions? Specifically, what are we to think of people who have no personal faith and yet do come and request a religious wedding?

Let us speak first of marriage as a sacrament (Propositions 2.1; 2.2). Books have been written by the dozen on the meaning and evolution of the word *sacrament*. The members of the ITC were aware of this. They knew that, under the influence of Aristotelianism, this term was assigned in the 12th century a more precise definition centered on the two notions of sign and efficient causality.[9] Marriage was included among the seven sacraments, and it became possible to draw a sharper distinction between the efficacious signs of Christ himself and of his grace and a variety of sacred things and symbolic signs which came to be called *sacramentals*. It would all the same be a mistake to believe that we are dealing here with a novelty. The seven sacraments, marriage included, are found also in the Eastern Churches, and even in the non-Chalcedonian Churches which were lucky enough to be spared the "Aristotelian invasion."

On the other hand, while it is true that the formulae were less precise prior to the 12th century, the classic definition of Isidore of Seville (A.D. 636) coupled the notion of sign (*signum*) with that of force (*virtus*) before the scholastic theologians of the 12th century substituted cause (*causa*) for force in order to remain true to Aristotelian categories.[10] It was from this perspective of efficient causality and of causality efficacious in inself[11] that the Council of Trent defined the sacramentality of marriage (session 24, canon 1; DS 1327; 1801), as recalled in propositions 2.1 and 2.2.

But we also understand the word *sacrament* in keeping with its biblical origins and its patristic dimension, namely, as *mysterion* (Propositions 2.1; 2.2). In this sense LG 1 presents the Church as a "kind of sacrament or sign of intimate union with God, and of the unity of all mankind." In this perspective, we emphasize less the causality which causes a force to pass from one person to another through the performance of a rite than the union between a human and a divine reality.

What is this *mysterion*? Col 1:26 and many other texts say that what is involved here is essentially the incarnation of the firstborn Son, himself God the creator, head and body of the church, firstborn from among the dead, who wills to unite humans to his own divinizing image (Col 1). This takes place above all through baptism, which the Epistle to the Romans presents as an assimilation to the *mysterion* of Christ. Christ has died, he has been buried, he has arisen from the dead. This he has done for us, which means both "for our sake" and "in our place." Our faith, then, induces us to repeat this ritual gesture of entry into the baptismal stream, burial within it, and emergence from it. But since we are dealing here not only with a symbol, but also with a communion, our ritual death and resurrection became divinization. We die to sin, and we return to life to live for God.

The text of Ephesians 5 places Christian marriage within the framework of the paschal *mysterion*. For this reason the death and resurrection of Christ for us (Rom 4:25) are presented here in keeping with another biblical category: the conjugal love of the Lord for his people. However, it is the same *mysterion* of the saving love of Christ and of the Church (Eph 5:32). It is into this paschal *mysterion,* under its conjugal dimension, that the conjugal love between a Christian man and a Christian woman is inserted. This union is rich in gifts and moral demands, to be sure, but it is linked above all to a love redeemed according to the wish of God the creator (Eph 5:31) and enhanced by his grace. This has been stressed in clear language in GS 48: "Authentic married love is caught up into divine love and is governed and enriched by Christ's redeeming power and the saving activity of the Church. Thus this love can lead the spouses to God with powerful effect and can aid and strengthen them in the sublime office of being a father or a mother." LG 11 says that the spouses "signify and partake" of the great mystery. It so identifies conjugal love with the *mysterion* of the love between Christ and the Church that it describes the family with the patristic expression "the domestic church." (See Proposition 2.1.)

If Christian marriage is a sacrament in a double sense, that is, as "efficacious sign" of Christ's grace and as specific insertion into the *mysterion* of salvation, a problem emerges about people who do not have Christian faith. How can they contract such a marriage? The ITC decided to deal with this problem primarily because it represents a new development and therefore demands attention.[12] Another reason was that the problem offers an opportunity to come to grips with the relationship between faith and sacrament, which were examined by Vatican II in a new–indeed, a renewed–perspective.

If we read scripture in harmony with tradition, it is a simplification but not a falsification to say that the teaching office of the Church has always maintained both that sacramental signs owe their efficacy to the fact that they perpetuate, through her ministers, the deed of Christ, and that the graces offered must be accepted by the persons who are to benefit from them. This primary condition of personal acceptance must be fulfilled if the sacrament is to be efficacious–*a fortiori* if it is to be fruitful. If faith cannot be personal (as in the case of infant baptism), it at least finds a substitute in the faith of the Church, of godparents and parents. Once the age of reason has been reached, faith can be personally accepted by a fundamental option or in a ceremonial profession of faith, which has taken a variety of forms throughout history.

No use denying it: if the dispositive importance of personal faith became somewhat blurred in sixteenth century Catholic theology and in the Council of Trent (session seven, canons 5–7; DS 1605–08), this was due to reaction against the doctrines of the reformers. The Reformation had maintained that in the sacraments there is no action of Christ or of the Church independent of the personal faith of the Christian. The sacramental gestures of the Church were regarded only as nourishment for, or as the sign of, the faith of the people, not as the sign of God's action through the Church.

Vatican II transcended polemics and even still extant opposition, and undertook to bear a more irenic witness to the traditional faith of the Catholic Church. It affirmed that sacraments confer grace (thus paying homage to the traditional formula, *ex opere operato*), but also that they presuppose faith, and nourish, strengthen, and express it (see SC 59).

This is what the ITC intended to express in its turn. In Christian marriage, grace is communicated ultimately by virtue of the work of Christ. On the other hand, the faith of the baptized man and woman who want to marry "in the Lord" is not an adventitious element. Grace is not given outside faith and without faith (Proposition 2.3).

Proposition 2.4 goes even further. It seeks to make explicit the normal dynamic involved in the origins and development of all Christian life on the basis of faith. The commission did this in the spirit of the discourses attributed to Peter and Paul in Acts. It adopted a schema which survived many literary transformations from the Fathers of the Church and the medieval theologians, and found expression again in chapter 6 of the sixth session of the Council of Trent (DS 1526), where it served to illustrate the theme of faith as the root of justification. Man hears the word of God as proclaimed and believes that Jesus is his redeemer. He makes ready to be baptized, and at his baptism professes his faith. Thus he is incorporated into Christ, accepts the ethical condition annexed to justification, and comes to play an active role in the Church. When a man and a woman marry, they do this obviously in the light of their faith, or their link to Christ. They ask him to lend their conjugal love the strength and the unconditioned quality of redemptive agape.

But what happens when this dynamism is disturbed, if not completely shattered? The prospective spouses have received baptism, the sacrament of faith. However, they have not lived this faith; they have rejected it. After long discussion, summarized here to some extent, the ITC came to the conclusion that two questions need to be answered. The first of these is located at the level of facts: when and how anyone can know whether the young man and the young woman who ask for a church wedding really have faith or have lost it. The second question is more doctrinal in nature: can one say, as some writers do, "No faith, no wedding"? Or can one engage in an automatic processing, and say "There has been a baptism, hence the only possible marriage is a sacramental one"?

The first question has been answered in several different ways in different contexts, but the answers have not always been free of that astounding antisacramentalism which certain Catholic circles have expressed since the council. Is it all that easy to serenely assess the existence or nonexistence of faith? Who is truly competent to make such a judgment? Is it not wiser to let oneself be guided by intentions and motivations? Yet when we examine intentions and motivations, we notice that the majority of cases fall into two large categories. Quite paradoxically, some candidates ask for a Christian marriage only for worldly reasons: the couple want a beautiful ceremony, and their parents think that a church wedding is proper. In spite of their baptism in infancy, these people are totally indifferent to or even hostile to Christ and the Church. Because faith is blocked, their intention is blocked. They have no intention of entering into the sacramental mystery, and committing themselves "according to the rite of holy mother Church." One need only be honest to deny these people a ceremony which, all things considered, would be a theatrical pageant, if not a parasacramental parody. The absence of faith and intention would render such a marriage invalid.

But there are other cases as well, and they are more numerous than the elitists assume. Here the prospective spouses are certainly open to learning. True, their faith and knowledge of religion are not much in evidence; yet they possess a desire for the divine and for the higher dimensions of marriage. With the help of pastors and the Christian family, this simple disposition to faith can develop, and grow stronger and clearer. Why not take advantage of this opportunity and engage in a catechetical instruction which will add clarity and vigor to their faith, and at the same time will encounter the dynamic of personal intention and reinforce it?

This line of reasoning leads to the middle course which the ITC has chosen to follow on the second question. We should resolve these cases on the grounds neither of baptism received long ago, nor of the absence of faith with an automatic appeal to principle; nor, on the contrary, should we denigrate the reality of the sacrament. The key to the solution of the problem lies in the intention to do what the Church does when she offers a permanent sacrament which entails indissolubility, fidelity, and the procreation of offspring. Both baptism and explicit faith are required for a valid sacramental marriage. Together they nourish the intention of incorporating human conjugal love into paschal love of Christ. If an explicit refusal to believe, in spite of baptism in infancy, entails the refusal to do what the Church of God does, a stable sacramental marriage is out of the question. Are these young people then excluded from any marriage? This question, among others is considered in the third set of propositions.

3. CREATION AND REDEMPTION

3.1 Marriage as Willed by God

Since all things were created in Christ, through Christ, and for Christ, marriage as a true institution of the creator becomes a figure of the mystery of the union of Christ the bridegroom with the Church his bride and, in a certain way, is directed toward this mystery. Marriage celebrated between two baptized persons has been elevated to the dignity of a real sacrament, that is, signifying and participating in the spousal love of Christ for the Church.

3.2 The Inseparability of Christ's Actions

Between two baptized persons, marriage as an institution willed by God the creator cannot be separated from marriage the sacrament. The sacramentality of marriage between the baptized is not an accidental element which could either be present or absent; this sacramentality is so tied to the essence of marriage as to be inseparable from it.

3.3 Every Marriage Between Baptized Persons Must Be Sacramental

As a result, between baptized persons no other married state can really and truly exist which differs from that in which the Christian man and woman, giving and accepting one another freely and with irrevocable personal consent as spouses, are radically removed from the "hardness of heart" of which Christ spoke (see Mt 19:8) and, through the sacrament, are really and truly included within the mystery of the marital union of Christ with the Church, thus being given the real possiblity of living in perpetual love. Consequently, the Church cannot in any way recognize that two baptized persons are living in a marital state equal to their dignity and their life as "new creatures in Christ" if they are not united by the sacrament of matrimony.

3.4 The "Legitimate" Marriage of Nonchristians

The strength and greatness of the grace of Christ are extended to all people, even those beyond the Church, because of God's desire to save all mankind. They shape all human marital love and strengthen created nature as well as matrimony "as it was from the beginning." Therefore, men and women who have not yet heard the gospel message are united by a human covenant. This legitimate marriage has its authentic goodness and values, which assure its consistency. But one must realize that these goods, even though the spouses are not aware of it, come from God the creator and make them share – in an inchoate way – in the marital love which unites Christ with his Church.

3.5 Union of Christians Who Pay No Heed to the Requirements of Their Baptism

It would thus be contradictory to say that Christians, baptized in the Catholic Church, might really and truly step back and content themselves with a nonsacramental state. This would mean that they could be content with the shadow when Christ offers them the reality of his spousal love. Still we cannot exclude cases where the conscience of even some Christians is malformed by ignorance or invincible error. They come to believe sincerely that they are able to contract marriage without receiving the sacrament.

In such a situation, they are unable to contract a valid sacramental marriage because they lack any faith and lack the intention of doing what the Church does. On the other hand, they still have the natural right to contract marriage. In such circumstances they are capable of giving and accepting one another as spouses because they intend to contract an irrevocable commitment. This mutual and irrevocable self-giving creates a psychological relationship between them which by its internal structure is different from a transitory relationship.

Still, this relationship, even if it resembles marriage, cannot in any way be recognized by the Church as a nonsacramental conjugal union. For the Church, no natural marriage separated from the sacramental exists for baptized persons, but only natural marriage elevated to the dignity of a sacrament.

3.6 Progressive Marriages

It is therefore wrong and very dangerous to introduce or to tolerate within the Christian community the practice of the couple's celebrating successive wedding ceremonies in different stages, even though they be connected, or to allow a priest or deacon to assist at or read prayers on the occasion of a nonsacramental marriage which baptized persons attempt to celebrate.

3.7 Civil Marriage

In a pluralistic society, the public authority of the state can impose on the engaged a public ceremony through which they publicly profess their status as spouses. The state can furthermore make laws which regulate in a precise and correct manner the civil effects deriving from marriage, as well as rights and duties regarding the family.

The Catholic faithful ought to be adequately instructed that these official formalities, commonly called civil marriage, do not constitute for them a true marriage. The only exception occurs in cases when – through dispensation from the canonical form or because of the very prolonged absence of a qualified church witness – the civil ceremony itself can serve as an extraordinary canonical form for the celebration of the sacrament of matrimony (see Canon 1098). For nonchristians and often even for noncatholic Christians, this civil ceremony can have constitutive value both as legitimate marriage and as sacramental marriage.

Commentary

3. CREATION AND REDEMPTION

(Propositions 3.1–3.7)

In order to find our way through the very intricate doctrine contained in this third set of propositions – the doctrine was studied under the guidance of Prof. Caffarra[13] – we need to start from two indispensable points of reference: the specificity that marks Christian marriage[14] and the diversity that obtains among the various types of marriage because of the different ways in which persons relate to Christ, creator and redeemer.

It has been said that the proper framework for the discussion of the doctrine in question is the theology of nature and supernature. Today, many tend to disagree with this position. They believe that Vatican II ignored the distinction between the natural and the supernatural,[15] or absorbed grace into nature.[16] We can, I believe, still use this terminology, at least for the purpose of showing a little more easily exactly how the two aspects of marriage differ.

When Greek philosophers (Plato, Aristotle, the Stoics) speak of *physis*, they refer above all to the cosmos as it exists before the spirit (*pneuma*) brings its action to bear upon it. This cosmos is not amenable to knowledge; it escapes providence and is not created by the gods, the demiurge, the "prime mover." Obviously, this is not the notion of nature adopted by church fathers or the scholastics, but it is the one which was brought back to life in Averroism as well as in Grotius's theory of natural law. Grotius was bent on building ethics on the supposition that there is no God–*quasi Deus non daretur*. True, this theory was not universally adopted, yet political theorists and the philosophers of the Enlightenment did eliminate at least Christ from their perspective and were content to speak of a Supreme Being. The royalist jurists of the *ancien régime* and the revolutionaries of 1789 paradoxically allied in agreeing to regard marriage as a purely worldly institution, exclusively dependent on the state. If Catholics wished to have an additional ceremony, just as Protestants did who paid a visit to their church to receive a blessing, this could be allowed, but with the understanding that the marriage had already been contracted.

An even stranger alliance was concluded between the royalist jurists and some theologians who favored *pure nature* terminology. Of course, they did declare that this, pure nature[17] which is not oriented toward grace, was only hypothesis; but, in this as in many other areas of morality, they soon forgot the hypothetical quality they credited to pure nature and made that nature the foundation of their doctrine. Thus marriage was described as a legal contract, a civil institution which the church had usurped. The sacrament was an extrinsic factor–the golden frame around a painting which existed apart from the frame. The one can be separated from the other. Upon inspection, this was not a quarrel about competencies, but about the very meaning of being a Christian. The many popes, especially Leo XIII, who rejected this separation (Proposition 3.2) took a doctrinal position which was linked to the views of the church Fathers and scholastic theologians.

The Fathers and the theologians maintained, in effect, that the hypothesis of a pure nature is not needed for us to affirm with revelation, and especially with St. Paul, that divinization is unmerited. Nature and grace do exist as the two dimensions of the being of a Christian, but both are the work of God, creator and redeemer. They constitute a continuum. It goes without saying that one cannot ignore nature or the human and civil aspects of marriage. Yet with Augustine, the Victorines, Albert the Great, Thomas, and Bonaventure – and Vatican II – we must locate nature within the history of salvation. Human nature is always connected to a particlur moment in the history of salvation. Nature as created (*natura condita*; Proposition 3.4) is linked to the creation of all things at the beginning. Then there is sinful nature, characterized by stubbornness of the heart, which explains why divorce exists (Proposition 3.3). Finally there is redeemed nature, which receives from grace the strength to overcome the difficulties of married life (Proposition 3.3) and to ground conjugal love on the agape of Christ. Once we adopt this perspective, it is not difficult to understand why, due to an ontological necessity rather than the existence of a law, Christians who are aware of their commitment to Christ may not revert to earlier stages of salvation history and contract a nonsacramental marriage (Proposition 3.3) or make a purely natural union into a legitimate preparatory stage to the insertion of their love into Christ's agape.

But what about Christians who, because of ignorance or error, are not aware that they are to insert conjugal love into the agape of Christ? How are we to assess the other types of marriage? The ITC felt that it should take a position on these issues in order to draw useful contrasts, and also to show more clearly that the human values of marriage ought not be misprised.[18]

Let us first consider the case of Christians whose conscience is malformed by invincible error or ignorance (Proposition 3.5). They have a natural right to marry. Because they lack faith and intention, they are incapable of being married in the way their baptism requires that they should (Proposition 2.3). They nevertheless have the natural right to marry. The ITC did not feel it could follow the view of some jurists who speak here of another type of legitimate marriage. However, the commission did wish to acknowledge the reality and consistency of this union at the psychological level. It draws a distinction between it and a mere liaison.

With regard to the marriage of unbaptized persons in relation to which canonical terminology uses the term *legitimate* the ITC acknowledges their consistency, their value, and the goods they offer (Proposition 3.4). Had the ITC operated within the perspective of pure nature, it could have been blamed for indulging in a contradictory regression to an earlier age. What we have here instead is a logical unfolding of a dialectic which proceeds from the work of creation to the work of redemption. Christ the savior did not limit himself to divinizing human marriage. By defeating the hold of sin, he also restored the dignity of that marriage which, together with the Father and the Spirit, he willed as one of the components of his own deed of creation.

We still need to speak of civil marriages. We cannot forget for a moment that civil marriage has been in the past, and sometimes still is, a weapon in a war. However, in a secularized and pluralistic society, it is at times difficult, as regards all its members, to make the civil effects of marriage contingent on the reception of the sacrament. At any rate, the ITC has no opinion of its own to voice with regard to concordats or revisions of concordats. In Proposition 3.7 it merely intends to acknowledge that the state has indeed the right to regulate the civil recognition of marriage by way of demanding that certain formalities proper to civil marriage be observed.

There remains, of course, a danger: some Christians might think that a civil cermony takes the place of the sacramental celebration. In countries where the Napoleon-Caprara concordat more or less survives, experience shows that, as far as the faithful are concerned, it has been possible to ward off this danger.[19] Paradoxically, today the danger comes from clerics who yield to fashionable antisacramentalist sentiment. If we prescind from the extraordinary cases mentioned in Proposition 3.7, how can anyone wish that the sacrament of marriage be celebrated by the magistrate of a state which is secular if not downright atheistic?

4. INDISSOLUBILITY OF MARRIAGE

4.1 The Principle

The early Church's tradition, based on the teaching of Christ and the apostles, affirms the indissolubility of marriage, even in cases of adultery. This principle applies despite certain texts which are hard to interpret and despite examples of indulgence – the extension and frequency of which is difficult to judge – toward persons in very difficult situations.

4.2 The Church's Doctrine

The Council of Trent declared that the Church has not erred when it has taught and teaches in accordance with the doctrine of the gospel and the apostles that the marriage bond cannot be broken through adultery. Nevertheless, because of historical doubts (opinions of Ambrosiaster, Catharinus, and Cajetan) and for some more or less ecumenical reasons, the council limited itself to pronouncing an anathema against those who deny the Church's authority on this issue.

It cannot be said then that the council had the intention of solemnly defining marriage's indissolubility as a truth of faith. Still, account must be taken of what Pius XI said in *Casti Connubi*, referring to this canon: "If therefore the church has not erred and does not err in teaching this, and consequently it is certain that the bond of marriage cannot be dissolved even on account of the sin of adultery, it is evident that the other causes of divorce, which are usually brought forward, have even less value and cannot be taken into consideration" (DS 1807).

4.3 Intrinsic Indissolubility

The intrinsic indissolubility of marriage can be considered under various aspects and be grounded in various ways:

– From the point of view of the spouses: their intimate conjugal union as a mutual self-giving of two persons, just like their very marital love itself and the welfare of the offspring, demands indissoluble unity. From this is derived the spouses' moral duty to protect, maintain and develop the marital covenant.

– From God's vantage point: from the human act by which the spouses give and accept each other there rises a bond which is based on the will of God and inscribed in nature, independent of human authority and removed from the sphere of power of the spouses, and therefore intrinsically indissoluble.

– From a Christological perspective: the final and deepest basis for the indissolubility of Christian matrimony lies in the fact that it is the image, sacrament, and witness of the indissoluble union between Christ and the Church that has been called the *bonum sacramenti*. In this sense indissolubility becomes a reality of grace.

– The social perspective: indissolubility is demanded by the institution of marriage itself. The spouses' personal decision comes to be accepted, protected, and reinforced by society itself, especially by the ecclesial community, for the good by the offspring and for the common good. This is the juridico-ecclesial dimension of matrimony.

These various aspects are intimately tied together: the fidelity to which the spouses are bound and which ought to be protected by society, especially by the ecclesial community, is demanded by God the creator and by Christ who makes it possible through his grace.

4.4. Extrinsic Indissolubility and the Power of the Church over Marriages

Hand in hand with practice, the Church has elaborated a doctrine concerning its powers over marriages, clearly indicating the scope and limits of that power. The Church acknowledges that it does not have any power to invalidate a sacramental marriage which is contracted and consummated (*ratum et consummatum*).

For very grave reason and out of concern for the good of the faith and the salvation of souls, all other marriages can be invalidated by competent Church authority or – according to another interpretation – can be declared dissolved. This teaching is only a particular application of the theory explaining the evolution of doctrine in the church. Today it is generally accepted by Catholic theologians.

Neither is it to be excluded that the Church can further define the concepts of sacramentality and consummation by explaining them even better, so that she can present the whole doctrine on the indissolubility of marriage in a deeper and more precise way.

Commentary

4. INDISSOLUBILITY

(Proposition 4.1–4.4)

The indissolubility of marriage is bound up in a very special way with the sacramentality of marriage (Proposition 2.2). It is made possible by the fact that human love is inserted into the agape that binds Christ to his church (Propositions 3.1; 3.2; 3.3, etc.), in spite of any stubbornness of the heart. We now need examine indissolubility in its own terms and attend to the problems it raises in our time.

When we submit to a close scrutiny the fourth set of propositions, prepared under the direction of Fr. E. Hamel,[20] we notice that we are indeed dealing with the traditional church doctrine which has recently been reaffirmed by Vatican II. However, there is a large difference between *Gaudium et Spes* in 1965 and these 1977 propositions. This is the difference that separates what used to be called a doctrine "in tranquil possession"[21] from a doctrine exposed to challenges that call for response.

The 1965 text does not even mention the "Zoghby affair,"[22] which called in question the meaning of the statements of the Council of Trent on the basis of the hesitations we note in the early centuries of the Church and of the doubts expressed by some theologians. Since 1965 many studies, books, and articles have appeared. Some theologians believe that these supply overwhelming evidence in support of the historical dissolution of some marital bonds. Others refuse to grant that, with one or two exceptions, there has been any hesitation. The ITC could not undertake to resolve these historical questions. It wisely acknowledged that the questions are difficult. It has expressed the hesitations of the fathers of Trent better than Vatican II did. It is not possible to speak of indissolubility as a dogma of faith in the strict sense of the phrase, but neither can it be denied that we are dealing here with Catholic doctrine[23] endowed with all the solidity implied in that theological note. In taking this position, the ITC finds support both in the teaching of Pius XI and in the tridentine clause which mentions the "fidelity to evangelical and apostolic doctrine" (Proposition 4.2).

The postconciliar discussion has also induced the ITC to use the distinction between extrinsic and intrinsic indissolubility, a distinction unknown to Vatican II. Extrinsic indissolubility is involved when an authority intervenes and annuls a marriage or declares with authority that a particular union is null and void (Proposition 4.4).

Consonant with the general phenomenon of "the development of doctrine" (Proposition 4.4), the Church has claimed certain powers over the nonsacramental marriages of pagans (Proposition 4.4), in line with what is known as the "Pauline Privilege" or the "Privilege of the Faith."[24] But the Church does not claim any power to dissolve consummated sacramental marriages. We can avoid being scandalized by any apparent contradiction if we perceive that in the former case we are dealing with a human covenant and in the latter with a union grounded in Christ. This does not mean, of course, that progress cannot be made

(Proposition 4.4, at the end). As we learn more about the way in which the conjugal bond comes to be constituted, the consummation theory of medieval canonists may well turn out to be too inadequate to be tenable any longer. According to this theory, marriage is consummated by one act of sexual intercourse, no more, no less. However, no one has yet elaborated another acceptable theory. The theory which has been some times suggested, that consumation ought to be equated with a long process of psychological maturation, contains the problem of seeming to promote trial marriage.

The intrinsic indissolubility of marriage concerns not the level of authority bearing on marriage from outside but the level of the very realities involved. The bond which unites in Christ a man and a woman who have given themselves to each other, or accepted each other, is inherently indestructible. It escapes the reach of every authority. "Let no man separate what God has joined!" (Mt 19:6). Read Proposition 4.3 over and over again, and note how it insists upon the arguments which, convincingly and forcefully, lead to the conclusion that Christian marriage is indissoluble. We are a long way from the serenity displayed by Vatican II in 1965. There, the position was taken for granted; here, we notice an anxious concern with defending church doctrine against criticism leveled at it from all directions. Yet this indissolubility emerges from exigencies intrinsic to the conjugal union itself, from the will of God the creator, from the love of the redeemer, as well as from considerations relative to the good of society and the well-being of the offspring.

Instead of summarizing these clear and powerful texts, let us follow the example of Proposition 4.4 and coordinate all the arguments into a dynamic dialectic. The wish that marriage should be permanent and faithful resides above all in the will, the affectivity, and the desire of the spouses who give themselves to each other in the totality of their own selves – what they are and what they are going to be. Each spouse expects to be able to count on the other for better or for worse. They both build their lives and activities on the basis of this expectation, so much so that when one is away the other feels lost.

Alas! Just as much as any other human value, this beautiful ideal is threatened by weakness, boredom, egoism, and aggressiveness. The other may be in danger of being made into an object or an instrument for the attainment of self-centered pleasure, or even a scapegoat. This is the reason why, even before a crisis occurs, the grace of Christ undertakes to heal conjugal love from its faults, to transform desire into gift, to elevate eros to the level of agape, which does not seek its own good but cares above all for the good of the other.[25] Love shifts from the key of desire to that of gift. These are the graces which Christ gives his faithful by means of a permanent sacrament.

This sacrament is constituted by a communion which is ontological as well as psychological and moral and includes its own *mysterion* of love. If the spouses suffer in their fidelity, or for the sake of it, they must remember that Christ has already traveled that road. If he asks much of them, he himself has given them much more. The indissolubility precept could not have made sense–the sense which, in the Old Testament, sinful nature failed to perceive because of stubborness of heart–if Christ had not brought grace and light. Here, too, we may repeat what is said in John 1:17: ". . . though the law was given through Moses, grace and truth have come through Jesus Christ' (JB), or in Ephesians 4:32: "Be friends with one another, and kind, forgiving each other as readily as God forgave you in Christ" (JB). Perhaps those scholastic theologians were not so far wrong who maintained that the fidelity and the indissolubility of marriage hinge on the precept that prescribes forgiveness and appeals to the example of the universal forgiveness which has come to us in and through Christ.

5. THE DIVORCED WHO HAVE REMARRIED

5.1 Gospel Radicalism

Faithful to the radicalism of the gospel, the Church cannot refrain from stating with St. Paul the Apostle, "To those now married, however, I give this command (though it is not mine; it is the Lord's): a wife must not separate from her husband. If she does separate, she must either remain single or become reconciled again. Similarly, a husband must not divorce his wife" (1 Cor 7: 10–11). It follows from this that new unions following divorce under civil law cannot be considered regular or legitimate.

5.2 Prophetic Witness

This severity does not derive from a merely disciplinary law or from a type of legalism. It is rather a judgment pronounced by Jesus himself (Mk 10:6 ff.) Understood in this way, this harsh norm is a prophetic witness to the irreversible fidelity of love which binds Christ to his Church. It shows also that the spouses' love is incorporated into the very love of Christ (Eph 5:23–32).

5.3 Nonsacramentalization

The incompatibility of the state of remarried divorced persons with the precept and mystery of the paschal love of the Lord makes it impossible for these people to receive the sign of unity with Christ in the Eucharist. Access to eucharistic communion can only come through penance, which implies detestation of the sin committed and the firm purpose of not sinning again (see DS 1676).

Let all Christians, therefore, remember the words of the apostle: "Whoever eats the bread or drinks the cup of the Lord unworthily, sins against the Body and Blood of the Lord. A man should examine himself first; only then should he eat of the bread and drink of the cup. He who eats and drinks without recognizing the Body eats and drinks a judgment on himself" (1 Cor 11:27–29).

5.4. Pastoral Care of the Divorced Who Have Remarried

While this illegitimate situation does not permit a life of full communion with the Church, Christians who find themselves in this state yet are not excluded from the action of divine grace and from a link with the Church. Therefore they must not be deprived of pastoral assistance (see the address of Pope Paul VI, Nov 4, 1977).

They are not dispensed from the numerous obligations stemming from baptism, especially the duty of providing for the Christian education of their children. The paths of Christian prayer, both public and private, penance, and certain apostolic activities remain open to them. They must not be ignored, but rather helped like all Christians who are trying, with the help of Christ's grace, to free themselves from the bonds of sin.

5.5 Combating the Causes of Divorce

The need for pastoral action to avoid the multiplication of divorces and of new civil marriages of the divorced seems ever more urgent. It is recommended that future spouses be given a vivid awareness of all their responsibilities as spouses and parents. The real meaning of matrimony must be ever more adequately presented as a covenant contracted "in the Lord" (1 Cor 7:39). Thus Christians will be better disposed to observe the command of God and to witness to the union of Christ and the Church. That will redound to the greater personal advantage of the spouses, of their children, and of society itself.

Commentary

5. THE REMARRIAGE OF DIVORCED PERSONS

(Propositions 5.1–5.5)

When we deal with the indissolubility of Christian marriage, we inevitably raise the urgent and distressing problem of Catholics who are divorced and remarried. When we deal with this problem in turn, our concern is both doctrinal and pastoral in nature, for we should never separate the two domains of doctrine and pastoral practice.[26]

We also examine the effect upon the faith of the church and her fidelity to the Lord Jesus of practices which call in question the impact of his teaching and his will to deliver humankind from sin. It is not possible to do justice to the precept and the demands of the Lord by announcing, "A sacramental Christian marriage contracted and consummated is indissoluble," and then going on to accept remarriage as normal and legitimate. To admit remarried divorcees to the Eucharist amounts to abandoning the apostolic rule which declares that we should not partake of the Body and Blood of the Lord Jesus unless we have relinquished a situation which, objectively considered, implies sin, and unless we are determined not to dwell within the situation any longer. Of course, this determination is a human one, and so it is fragile. All the same, it must be genuine.

Having said this much, note how the text of the propositions makes it clear that the ITC had no trouble parting company with a rigoristic pastoral practice which, even if it did not go as far as advocating formal excommunications (as was the case until very recently in some countries), did all the same ostracize divorced and remarried Catholics and left them pretty much to their own devices as sheep without a shepherd. Throughout the preparatory phase, the ITC greatly appreciated a document issued by the Pontifical Committee on the Family under the title "Pastoral Care of Divorced and Remarried Catholics" and written by His Excellency Bishop Gagnon, the Committee's President, with the assistance of Fr. Diarmuio Martin.[27]

Between the time this document was issued and the time the ITC held its meeting, the Holy Father Paul VI had also gone on record in favor of a pastoral practice that stresses benevolence and charity. For reference, see the end of this article, note 28.

In light of what has just been said, it is easier to understand the meaning of the propositions in this fifth set, especially those which relate to the civil remarriage of divorcees, as well as the impossibility of admitting these individuals to eucharistic communion. The members of the ITC were aware that exegetes have been debating – even very recently – the clause "lewd conduct is a separate case – *nisi fornicationis causa*" in Matthew 19:9. This is why they chose to anchor their position on Mark 10:6–12 (Proposition 5.2), which is clear cut and justifies the last words in proposition 5.1. They were aware that specialists in biblical moral theology wonder whether Jesus' interdiction of divorce is a law, or a norm, or only an ideal to which we are being summoned. They refer to 1 Corinthians 7: 10-11, where Paul, on the basis of his authority and charism as an apostle, certifies that a command is at stake (*paraggello*). At a lower level no doubt, and yet ineluctably, the theologian is here what St. Paul was: a witness who is not entitled to evade the radicalism of Jesus (Proposition 5.1). The Lord has issued a verdict (Proposition 5.2) which has nothing to do with legalism or with a will to repress and oppress. That verdict is a prophetic sign of the extent of the agape of Christ and its all-encompassing demand.

The rigor of this demand led Christ to surrender his life for us. In the Eucharist, we relive this mystery. If Christians do not follow Christ to the end, what could possibly entitle them to partake of the sacrificial meal which the Lord has renewed? How could they participate in the offering which the faithful make through the mediation of the priest acting in the person of Christ (*in persona Christi*)? When conjugal love assumed into agape is ruptured, a break with the sacrament of agape follows as a consequence. St. Paul mentions this (Proposition 5.3) in relation to all sinners to be sure, but certainly without excluding divorced and remarried persons who were numerous in the Greek and Roman society of his time. Doesn't Paul prescribe, as the Church does, that in sexual matters Christians should conduct themselves in a manner totally different from the pagans (Proposition 1.3)?

Objections will no doubt be raised. Some could object that Paul recommends that the faithful should examine their consciences and ascertain whether they are worthy to eat the Body of Christ. Paul speaks about conscience, not about the Church. This objection forgets that, while conscience passes judgment, this judgment is ruled by the judgment of the Lord himself. Conscience is not a valid guide unless it be an echo of God's own voice. The Apostle to the Gentiles says this often. Suffice it to quote here another passage of that same epistle: "Mind you, I have nothing on my conscience. But that does not mean that I am declaring myself innocent. The Lord is to judge me" (1 Cor 4: 4).

Another possible difficulty: why exclude from the Eucharist those who commit serious sins in the area of sexuality and not those who commit serious sins in the area of justice? True, the collective conscience of Christians has now grown more sensitive to sins against justice, solidarity, and charity. This is genuine progress. But can this be a good reason to throw overboard all the demands of Christian morality in matters of family life and sexuality, as if they were long dead taboos? The objection reveals the need for greater severity towards public sinners in matters of justice, not for permissivenes in matters of sexual morality. However, two remarks are in order. It is not easy to ascertain whether a charge of injustice is justified. There is the risk of being swayed by one's own interests. In the second place, the situation of divorced and remarried persons has an element of tragedy, insofar as divorce creates a perduring situation difficult to escape. Since it is grounded on juridical acts, it is verifiable and public.

This is precisely why, although objectively we must accept the impossibility of admitting such persons to eucharistic communion, we should strive for a pastoral practice which will make a return home possible. Contempt, rejection, and insults neither are called for by the gospel, nor are effective. There is room here for a new kind of pastoral ministry that would follow the directives of Pope Paul VI in his allocution of November 6, 1977 (Proposition 5.4).[28] Is not this valid for many other areas as well? In a Christian environment, the moral life of the large majority of Christians can be assumed not to fall below that minimum degree of adherence to Christ which is indispensable for eucharistic life. When needed, the sacrament of penance sets things right. But in our secularized world which everywhere projects a vision of man and of the world in which God no longer has a place, one is not a disciple of Christ unless one knows and wills oneself to be. This does not mean that we are succumbing to the temptation of elitism. Can there really be an elite in the ordinary sense of the word if every Christian value is a gift of grace? Yet we must accept the fact that not all of those who believe in Christ respond equally to this grace, as we well know from the parable of the sower. Thus forbearance toward the weak is in order, but vigilance also. We must help them so that the deeds they do as Christians be more mature and more deliberate (Propositions 2.3; 2.4).

It is in this sense that Proposition 5.5 advocates preventive action. If there are so many divorced persons, is it not because so many hurry into marriage? Some marriages are, in fact, null and void for lack of commitment and maturity. But in many other cases, young people have freely, and hence validly, engaged in a venture which turns sour. Here there is room for a new form of family apostolate. The successes already achieved give hope that we are not merely expressing here a pious wish.

It is time to bring to a close this commentary, already too long and yet still too short. The publication of the volume announced earlier will no doubt allow for deeper reflection. In the meantime, the members of the ITC dare to hope that readers of this commentary will display, in reading it, as much good will, as much concern for theological methods, and as much commitment to Christ as the members themselves have tried to use in preparing the propositions here commented upon.

Part II

POSITION PAPERS BY MEMBERS OF THE INTERNATIONAL THEOLOGICAL COMMISSION

CHAPTER 2

Marriage as Institution and the Contemporary Challenge to It

by Professor Wilhelm Ernst

Theological language today employs many names and definitions in speaking of marriage. Marriage is called a community of the sexes, community of life and love, community of existence, conjugal union, matrimonial contract, sacred bond, sacrament, the image of and participation in the union of love between Christ and the Church, and institution.[1]

Precisely this last notion of institution – taken in its application to marriage – has for some time been submitted to fiery criticism. The present discussion will study very closely the problem of "marriage as institution" by examining its anthropological, sociological, and theological foundations and components, as well as its historical development and its present meaning.

After a brief introduction concerning the idea and the essence of the institution, the first part will deal with marriage as institution by examining its foundations, the lines of its development through history, and its traditional theological interpretation.

The second part will examine the contemporary questioning of "marriage as institution" against the background of the recent conception of marriage as a personal community of love and life. At the same time I will propose a critical evaluation of current objections to marriage as institution and from it will draw some consequences for church doctrine on marriage. Our goal is not merely to refute errors, but to isolate the germ of truth which these errors might contain.

A. Marriage as Institution

I. The Idea and Essence of Institutions in General

Etymologically, *institution* refers to an established reality resulting from an act of formation or creation.

1. FROM THE POINT OF VIEW OF SOCIAL PHILOSOPHY

The foundation of institutions is the social and historical nature of the human being. In general, institutions are stable social entities which arise to bring together and organize individuals into a whole. The institution is a specifically human reality, marked by an inter-human, trans-individual, and social character. Because any institution objectively restricts human behavior, the institution always appears as an organization with a durable and stable character, objectively preformed and imposed from outside the person. Every institution has its own meaning and purpose. On the basis of a guiding idea, it aims at the steady and lasting achievement of definite ends and results. If one submits to the guiding idea of a particular institution, one accepts this idea as normative and the rules of conduct which further its realization. Thus institutions make their members the subjects of relations (of both a social order and juridical order) with other persons and with the community. In conformity with the nature of each institution, these relations assume a character qualified for a particular realm of existence.

The problem with this concept of institution is that, to a certain extent, it gives the institution an ontological priority over the individual and therefore may not sufficiently recognize the being and value of the person.

2. FROM THE ANTHROPOLOGICAL AND SOCIOLOGICAL POINT OF VIEW

In order to understand institutions and account for their origins, research in physical anthropology takes as its starting point the special biological condition of man, that is, both the indeterminate nature of his instincts and the openness which distinguish the human subject. The drives bound to the biological constitution of the human person are largely undifferentiated (nonspecific) fundamental requirements; precisely because of their indeterminate nature and their biological plasticity, they need to be shaped and to receive direction from the intervention of social norms and of a stabilization process which focuses them on concrete and lasting interests in the cultural superstructure of institutions.

In an analoguous way, sociology underlines the human being's need for the help and recognition of one's fellow humans because that need constitutes a permanent datum, and calls for institutions which sustain the individual and at the same time provide space where the concrete subject can develop one's self. Concerning the place and function of the individual in the institution, the notions of role and role expectation take on such great importance, that, from the sociological point of view, one can define *institution* as *an organized demand for roles.* A complete descriptive definition would be as follows: *a relatively durable structure consisting of models of behavior, roles, and relations that persons regularly employ in a definite, sanctioned, uniform way in order to satisfy their social needs.*[2] It is necessary to complete this description by a discussion of the character of the obligation, because norms of conduct – precepts and prohibitions about one's manner of acting – determine clearly how one must behave as a member of a community, in order that the objective or objectives of the institution be realized. The question arises likewise of knowing whether the concept of institution developed on the basis of physical anthropology can account sufficiently for the historicity of the human being. Institutions result not from the poverty of nature, but from the aptitude of man to give form and meaning to nature and history.

3. FROM THE HISTORICAL POINT OF VIEW

Considered from this point of view, institutions present themselves in the realms of law and religion, where they originated and are truly "at home" as bodies of fundamental norms and as knowledge or intiation into the knowledge of these norms. With respect to the history of religion and theology, one recognizes on the one hand institutions established by God, and on the other hand those established by the Church, both of which are often bound to definite rites.

Institutions lie at the heart of the history of law, for they are constitutive elements of order in diverse areas of existence – indeed, of the entire juridical order. In the course of evolution, different concepts of institutions have developed. With some adaptation, they can be applied to any particular institution. The historical development of institutions is closely bound to social and political evolution, for this evolution spurred the formation of a dense network of institutions. At the present time, along with a strong need for security and a flight to institutions, there is a manifest tendency to question their values and course of development, so that one often speaks simply of a crisis of institutions.

II. Notion and Essence of Marriage as Institution

Under the heading of institution, can one consider marriage as traditionally understood and as it is understood today? In order to examine the question as closely as possible, we must discuss its different aspects.

1. MARRIAGE AS INSTITUTION FROM THE POINT OF VIEW OF ANTHROPOLOGY AND SOCIOLOGY

Anthropological and sociological research on marriage generally begins – based on the global findings of these disciplines – with an effort to state precisely the specific nature of human sexuality as opposed to animal sexuality. In the eyes of the physical anthropologist, the specific marks of human sexuality are the reduction of the role of instinct and the fact that the corresponding pleasure is not necessarily bound to reproduction as its biological end. The indeterminateness and plasticity of instinctual drives represent for mankind simultaneously a danger and an opportunity for cultural development. There is for man an indication and an invitation that moves him to establish norms in the realm of sexual activity which serve to safeguard the character of his drives and to channel their exercise. In this way, on the whole, there is no development of natural sexual behavior in the sense of behavior whose correction would be assured by instinct, as with animals; rather, natural development will always be the product of cultural norms.

The cultural regulation which is imposed upon the sexual drive belongs, according to H. Schelsky, "to the products of culture and to the vital needs of man as well as tools and language. One does not contradict this in seeing in this regulation of human sexual and reproductive functions the primary social form of human behavior." There exists an interdependence between, on the one hand, the influence exercised in every area and on every level of cultural and social life by the duality of the sexes as the primary principle of structuring and, on the other hand, the cultural and social – as well as religious – influence on the exercise of sexual functions. It is precisely this latter influence that affects not only the primary elements of sexuality but equally the domain of eros – something often neglected by physical anthropology.

Empirical demonstration of these general views may be found in the comparative study of civilizations. In all known civilizations we can recognize some rules and models imposed by society on sexual relations and the distribution of sexual roles.[3] The tenor of these norms is not the same everywhere, and from the ethnological and sociological points of view sexual instinct is not the primary factor in the formation of the institution of marriage.[4] According to recent ethnological and sociological findings, the primary factors in this formation reside in the effort to insure one's own posterity. As a result marriage has taken form especially as an institution and as a community of the social and economic order; it derives its stability and durable character from the need to provide for the education of children and from the cooperative relationship of the spouses.[5] Only indirectly (and therefore secondarily) do the institutions of marriage and of the family require the regulation of sexual activity.

It is equally necessary to stress that while the institution of marriage – from the perspective of the comparative study of civilization – always includes norms for sexual life, it does not reserve to marriage every form of sexual activity and does not govern just the latter. The institution of marriage is bound in a general way to privileged sexual relations, but rarely are licit sexual activities limited to marriage alone. According to F.X. Kaufman, it is "problematic to assert that by reason of his sexual instinct man is naturally oriented toward marriage; for in most civilizations this instinct can be licitly satisfied outside of marriage."

However, among peoples and civilizations that have undergone a more sophisticated social development, one can find the tendency to submit the sexual activity of spouses to a body of norms. Monogamy seems to appear more and more the norm as the social integration of humanity progresses. In European civilization it does not seem to be seriously questioned, even if some sociologists pose questions with regard to Africa.

If, on the basis of these considerations, which are surely incomplete, one is looking for an answer to the questions posed by marriage as an institution, one can propose in the socio-anthropological perspective, by way of a working definition beyond the specifically anthropological point of view, the following description:

> Under the term 'institution of marriage' we understand this complex of norms which govern the establishment and the rupture of the bonds which join, in a durable way and in view of procreation, partners of different sexes, and which are characterized by economic cohabitation. These norms determine the reciprocal rights and duties of the spouses as well as of their relatives and their descendants.[6]

Given an accurate understanding of the notion of natural, one can accept this definition proposed by P. Adnès: "Marriage is a society, a stable union of a man and a woman; it is a natural arrangement."[7] This definition implies neither a reference to the history of civilization nor an assertion concerning the essential elements and ends of marriage. It takes a simple position: marriage as an institution is a stable union between man and woman whose foundation is found in human nature.

2. MARRIAGE AS INSTITUTION IN SACRED SCRIPTURE

In this perspective the question is now posed: how, in the course of history, have marriage and its norms been understood and lived in the light of the revelation of the Old and New Testaments? What significance have revelation and theology had for marriage, its structure, and its reform?[8]

a. The Institution of Marriage in the Old Testament

The development of the concept of marriage in the Old Testament tradition has many aspects. It contains social, juridical, ethical, and theological elements which make it difficult to achieve a coherent synthesis.[9]

The Old Testament teaches essentially that marriage is a divinely-established, preexistent institution. It is woven into the general nature of the human race in order to maintain it. In Old Testament tradition – all primitive societies, particularly those of the ancient Orient – the rules concern not all sexual activities, but only those which, in a social perspective, concern the procreation of offspring with a view to maintaining the race.

This purpose of marriage elucidates, for patriarchal times, the common law of levirate, polygamy, and the different ethical demands made on husband and wife regarding sexual behavior.

A new adaptation to the development of economic and social life appeared with the codification of Mosaic law. Incest was prohibited in order to protect the family by regulating sexual relations with close relatives in the restrictive sense of the word (Lv 18:6–23; 20:10–21). Further insights on this matter are offered by the comparative study of civilizations. Bigamy and sexual relations with foreign women taken in war are sanctioned (Dt 21:15–17; 21:10–14). A legal procedure for divorce is provided (Dt 24:1–4). In this phase of its development, sexual ethics enjoyed only a subordinate role; the primary concern was to defend the institution of marriage on the social plane. Social life was the determining factor behind the moral norms imposed on sexual and conjugal life.

A new development of the concept of marriage begins in the post-exilic period. The legal stipulations are not changed, but there begins to appear an ideal image of marriage which, in contrast to the sole emphasis on social and institutional factors that characterized the primitive period, included personal considerations as well in its understanding of marriage, and began to stimulate a development of a sense of monogamy. One can find significant indications of this in the prophet Malachi, in the wisdom books, and in the ideal representation of marriage by Tobit (see Mal 2:10–16; Prov 5:15–19; Eccl 19:9; Jdt 8:2–8; 16:25; Tob 8:6ff.). The primary purpose of the institution, the preservation of the race, remains the same, but juridical and moral reflections give attention to other aspects of marriage also. The mutual help and care of the spouses as well as conjugal love and fidelity have never been totally neglected.

Toward the end of the Old Testament period, Israel was a monogamous society for all practical purposes. Polygamy was the exception. Certainly, according to the law which was developed by Israel throughout its history, the possibility of polygamy and divorce was recognized. But the ideal of monogamy and of interpersonal relationships uniting husband and wife took on more significance, even if the ancient structures were not modified juridically. On the whole, one can say with W. Molinski:

> The Hebraic conception of marriage was naturalistic; it assumed nature with all its implications as a gift and task which come from God. It conveyed a positive attitude toward marriage, children, and sexual relationships, within forcibly imposed limits.[10]

The lines of development briefly indicated here show that the Old Testament viewed marriage essentially on the social plane and elaborated the conditions which were imposed for the best possible realization of the matrimonial institution. This understanding of marriage, and especially its development toward the end of the era, cannot be understood apart from revelation and the theology of the Old Testament. Faith in the Lord and in the covenant shaped in a decisive way the historico-cultural development of Old Testament ideas on marriage and sexuality.

In light of this faith, one can see the accounts of the creation of man and woman as the theological development of the fundamental relationship between the Lord and Israel in the history of the people of God under the old covenant.

The creation accounts, as theological interpretations of created reality and of the likeness of God, culminate in the presentation of man as created in the very image of God. The deepest core of this likeness resides in man's capacity and call to be a partner of God and to enter into a covenant with him. To this corresponds, on the level of created reality, both the complementarity which orders the two sexes one to the other in view of human fulfillment and the mutual assistance present in the union and encounter between partners (Gn 1:27; 2:18,24). As man and as woman the human being is the image and likeness of God."[11]

The likeness of the human being to God and the duality of the sexes are then inseparable. Different from all other ancient conceptions, this theological interpretation of sexuality and of its exercise nevertheless excludes sacralization and divinization of sexuality. On the contrary, it lends itself to a demythologization and a desacralization. This results also from the fact that the order to increase and multiply that accompanied the creation of man is not mentioned in relation to the affirmation of the divine likeness; it is announced apart from that and in connection with the mission to subdue the earth (Gn 1:28ff.).[12]

In this context, a particular importance is attached to the "symbolism of marriage" in the Old Testament. The relationship between God and his people is symbolized by marriage (Hos 2; Jer 3:6ff.; Ez 16; 23; Is 54).

By reason of its symbolic content which refers to the covenant between God and His people, the matrimonial convenant, as a reality of the created order, takes on a great value in the theology of the Old Testament. The institution of marriage is presupposed as a reality deriving from creation. But it is not only an institution; in its most intimate core it is a covenant. This is precisely why it can be an image of the covenant between God and his people.

This significance attached to marriage has consequences for our understanding of sexuality and marriage. Fertility cults and sacred prostitution are signs of the infidelity and apostasy committed for strange gods. For the Lord, homosexual acts are an abomination because they appear in Canaanite religion as a means of divine service. God exacted from Israel his spouse unconditional confidence and fidelity; Israel followed him in the desert (Jer 2:2). For the people of God, fertility is both a mission stemming from creation and a blessing ordered to the promises to be fulfilled in the future.

Surely, the legislation and practice of Israel throughout its history (which by reason of the covenant is not mere history but salvation history), continually remained in arrears of the original plan. In fact, Israel was on the whole fixated in institutional statutes based on patriarchal structures. Nevertheless, under the influence of the theology of the covenant and the teachings of the prophets, Israel developed in history and bred an idea of sexuality and of marriage in which, besides social and institutional elements, the personal dimensions of the conjugal community gained significance.

b. The Institution of Marriage in the New Testament

The New Testament texts on marriage offer no complete treatise on marriage, particularly on marriage as an institution. Whatever position the New Testament does take on marriage is based both on the new situation that Jesus himself inaugurated with new authority, and also, from a pastoral point of view, on the life lived according to faith within the existing structures.

The institution of marriage, like other institutions, is assumed and respected inasmuch as it is firmly established in society. Its meaning – in juridical structures – is in no way contradicted or damaged; yet, as a way of life pertaining to this world, marriage is evaluated in an eschatological perspective, and this ambivalence is clearly expressed (Lk 24:20; 17:27; Mt 24:38ff.; Mk 12:25). The New Testament does not specifically address the hierarchy of the ends of marriage or the forms in which it is entered, but it presupposes the structures and norms of the cultural milieu of antiquity. Further, in its entirety, in its theological aspect (its faith in the salvific activity of God) and in its anthropological aspect (according to a theological concept of man) it provides an interpretation of Christian life which influences the way one understands institutions, particularly marriage.

The Old Testament understanding of marriage was given a new interpretation of Jesus himself when, beyond Mosaic law, he invoked the original will of God announced in Genesis and proclaimed it:

> In the beginning God made them man and woman. So then a man will leave his father and mother and the two will become one flesh. Thus they are not two, but one flesh. Therefore, what God has united, man must not separate (Mk 10:6–9; cf. Mt 19:4–6).

For Jesus, it is the will of God that a marriage, once contracted, not be dissolved. By his reference to the beginning of creation, he treats monogamous and indissoluble marriage as an institution of the creator. God himself is the author of marriage, and his will cannot be disregarded by man. Through this proclamation on marriage by Jesus, the historical legislation of Israel and its interpretation vanished in the gospel. The created order is closely connected with the order of salvation. At the same time, hardness of heart (Mt 10:5) is condemned as a retreat from God's demands. From the moment that man is freed by faith from this hardness of heart, he is capable of understanding and living the original will of God. From then on this hardness of heart will always be an offense and subject to condemnation since it is a refusal of grace.

With good reason Cardinal Ratzinger has emphasized:

> Jesus offers a new teaching on marriage which renders possible in faith the commandment intimated at the begin-

ning and inserted into the context of the faith, so the marriage can become an element of the rule of faith inasmuch as, seen in faith, it receives its structure and its meaning.[13]

In a fundamental text, the Epistle to the Ephesians (Eph 5:21–33) in the context of a teaching on marriage and the mystery of the Church also points to the text from Genesis which the synoptic pericope on divorce invokes to establish the indissolubility of marriage (Mt 29:4ff.; Mk 10:6–8). Here is recalled, like a response to the order established by creation, the singular relationship uniting husband and wife in marriage, and at the same time the relationship uniting Christ and the Church. Much emphasis is placed on this relationship, which is drawn from the interpretation of Genesis 2:24. *Mystery* (v. 32) primarily refers to the bond of love uniting the Church and Christ, but it presents an analogy with the union of love between husband and wife in marriage. Marriage becomes the image of the union of love which is superior to it. Exegetically, one should not see here a direct argument from Scripture in favor of the sacramentality of marriage. The latter indeed appears more as a guarantee of the Christian outcome of salvation. Because of this it surpasses every other union between human beings.[14]

How did the communities of the primitive Church understand the interpretation that Jesus and Paul gave to marriage? Did they see there a moral directive, a precept expressing either a point of reference or an ethical model, a prophetic call, a law?[15]

In current exegesis of the different texts on marriage there is little agreement. The methods of form criticism and redaction criticism can surely shed new light on thinking regarding marriage by discovering a development in the presentation of Jesus' words and by placing them in the context of the Sermon on the Mount and the entire ethical teaching of the gospel. But up to this point no consensus has been reached.[16] R. Schnackenburg is right in emphasizing that there are many gaps in our knowledge of the primitive Church and that the texts upon which we rest our case are uncertain and debated.

One can, however, attempt to see, in summary fashion, how the original and strict directive of Jesus is understood by the synoptics and by St. Paul. Luke (16:18), who sought to place his community on guard against the sexual license of the pagan world, understands the teaching of Jesus as an ethical directive and takes a rigorous view of marriage. The supposedly primitive logion of Jesus, "Whoever divorces his wife commits adultery and whoever marries a divorced woman commits adultery," is presented by Luke in these terms, "Whoever divorces his wife and marries another commits adultery, and he who marries a woman divorced by her husband commits adultery." This does not alter the original meaning.[17]

Mark interprets the original logion of Jesus, for the sake of Christians converted from paganism, in light of Roman law which accorded the right to divorce to each of the two spouses. He understands the word of the Lord as a strict precept.[18]

Apart from the exception clause "in the case of fornication," the statement which invokes the logion of Jesus is directed against the sending away of one's spouse "for any reason whatsoever" in Matthew's gospel. Insertion of the exception clause (5:32; 19:9) is intended to take into account the special situation of the Judeo-Christian community. In the case of fornication, according to many researchers (including Catholics), Matthew would allow an exception to the prohibition against divorce. According to Schnackenburg – who refers to Bonsirven and to several contemporary Catholic exegetes – the "case of fornication" would not refer to adultery but to "illegitimate Jewish marriages, notably the marriages of persons who are related . . . , marriages which are forbidden by the Jews but permitted by the Greeks and Romans." Others understand *fornication* as *adultery*. However the Matthean addition ought to be interpreted, one cannot infer the existence, in the Matthean community of the Judeo-Christian community, of a practice permitting divorce and remarriage in the case of adultery.

In the First Letter to the Corinthians, Paul takes an unambiguous position on divorce by recalling the teaching of the Lord. He directs the prohibition of divorce to the wife as well as the husband, an addition in which one can see the influence of the Roman law. On his own authority ("As to the others, it is I who say this, not the Lord"), Paul outlines particular directives on mixed marriages between pagans and Christians (7: 12–16). If the nonbelieving spouse wants to leave, the believing spouse is not bound (7:15). Paul does not expressly mention authorization for a new marriage. Does he permit separation only, or a new marriage? One cannot determine this with certitude from the context;[10] but the apostle does not explicitly exclude remarriage.

These few passages let us see clearly that the primitive Church consciously adhered in principle to the requirements of the Lord who demands from the living the conjugal commitment of irreversible fidelity which faith makes possible. At the same time the primitive Church – immersed in the historical reality of its times – could consider different circumstances and situations when searching for pastoral dispositions and practices. We know too little about the actual progress of this search to conclude that the primitive Church soon instituted a new juridical casuistry, although one cannot deny that Paul gave specific interpretations which approximated casuistic and juridical norms.[20]

On the other hand, it is necessary to keep in mind that Christian marriage itself remained intact. One can begin to understand more deeply its particular reality, which involves marriage's reference to the Church, the reciprocal relationships of spouses, and the relativization of the value of marriage *vis-à-vis* the parousia. These are the first elements of a spirituality of marriage. Already there appear the lines of a sexual ethic, in that premarital and extramarital sexual relations are excluded and love in its sexual form is related exclusively to marriage. The reasons for this are: the equal status of the husband and the wife, the rejection of fornication and a deep understanding of the mutual gift, even if all of this was not yet fully realized in the institution of marriage of that time.

c. *Summary*

If we wish to summarize in a few propositions the biblical statements and their development, we have the following points:

1) The Old Testament and the New Testament consider marriage as an institution rooted in creation. In different civilizations, its demands must be specifically expressed through a complex of norms and directives.

2) In old testament history, a concept of marriages developed on the basis of patriarchal structures, in which its social and institutional aspects, that is, the role of marriage in the life of the race, predominate. Marriage is the subject of norm and laws: marriage is seen as a contract, and divorce is subjected to laws. One can see the naturalism of the notion of sexuality in the emphasis on *procreatio prolis*, and the frank account of extramarital sexual relations. Yahwistic faith and the thought of the Old Testament pervade the growing tendency toward monogamy; they inspire appreciation of the feminine condi-

tion as well as an understanding of sexuality: sexuality was freed of myths rooted either in the fertility cults or the fear of incubus demons.

3) The New Testament accepts the existing institutions with their culturally conditioned structures, but it addresses the teachings of Jesus to the persons living within these structures. His teaching goes beyond the law and invokes the original order of creation (Gn 2:14); it assumes that order into the order of salvation (reciprocity of the one and the other). This teaching proclaims an ethical requirement based on the law and teaches that faith makes possible the understanding and realization of it.

4) The Pauline theology of marriage (Eph 5) finds the meaning and foundation of the relations between husband and wife in the relationship uniting Christ and the Church. In this way it points toward an understanding of the conjugal bond and the irrevocable fidelity pledged by the spouses (unity and indissolubility) which, in the notion of marriage subsequently developed by the Church, will contribute to the elaboration of doctrine regarding the sacramental character of marriage.

5) The synoptics and St. Paul attest and proclaim unequivocably the teaching of Jesus forbidding divorce. However, by considering different situations in the community and certain concrete cases, they give the original teaching of Jesus an interpretation which concretizes it (for pagans, Mark and Paul; for the Jews, Matthew; concerning marriage between Christians and pagans, Paul; on the subject of a wife who leaves her husband, Mark and Paul; concerning "fornication" on the part of the wife, Matthew). This interpretation takes on great importance in later doctrinal development.

6) Differing from the Old Testament understanding of sexuality and marriage, which is institutionalistic, legalistic, and naturalistic, the New Testament presents, in the historico-cultural framework and on the basis of a theological anthropology, a humanization of sexuality and of marriage (the dignity of the wife, a marriage account indicating the sexual and total gift of self, insertion of the duties of marriage into the precept of love, the definitive and irrevocable character of the pledge of fidelity in marriage as an ethical requirement and not as an extrinsic, rigid law). In the primitive Church this humanization and the understanding of it were not sufficiently developed to be the object of a general consciousness to be realized in practice, except in an inchoate way.

III. Marriage as Institution in the Development of Theological Teaching

The development of the doctrine of marriage throughout the history of theology is extremely complicated; it involved the overlapping domains of ethics, dogma, juridical procedure, and pastoral practice. This development over the centuries of the teaching made the institution of marriage into a vast, closed, and inviolable system.

a. Conjugal Ethics and the Institution of Marriage

Throughout the history of Christianity, extensive efforts have been made to translate the message of faith into life animated by faith and to propose firm positions and directives for Christians which would be valuable in a variety of situations. These efforts underwent developments which, especially in matters of sexual and marital ethics, gave rise both to correct theological interpretations and to a series of aberrations. For the most part these latter have not yet been fully removed. Rather, they have perhaps produced excesses and reactions in the opposite direction.

The development of sexual and conjugal morality has been influenced in a decisive way by the double doctrine of Augustine on the deep-seated goodness of marriage as an institution and on the malice of concupiscence in sexual matters. In his view, the objective ends of marriage are: procreation (*proles*) and the healing of concupiscence (*remedium concupiscentiae*).

To the question of the moral lawfulness of conjugal relations, Augustine gave two response. According to the first, the spouses make good out of the evil–disordered pleasure and desire–only if they have procreation in view in the conjugal act. The other response adds that because of the *remedium concupiscentiae* the spouses cannot refuse each other (*debitum reddere*), but it is a sin to demand this duty (*debitum petere*) beyond what is necessary to bear children. It is venial sin by virtue of the concession allowed in 1 Corinthians 7:5ff., which Augustine sees as a matter of toleration, not of law.

Thus sex in marriage, which remains extrinsically an evil by virtue of the pleasure inherent in it, can be tolerated from the moral point of view or considered only venial sin. However, it needs to be balanced by the threefold good that Augustine proposes: the good of fidelity, the good of procreation, and the good of the sacrament (*fides, proles, sacramentum*). This concept of the ethos of marriage is based on the Augustinian notion of order, behind which is the Stoic doctrine of ataraxia, as well as speculation on marriage in paradise.[21]

This teaching on the goods of marriage considered as a counterbalance led in early scholasticism to what became known as the theory of indulgence. According to this theory, the spouses are "excused" from sin when their intention involves procreation (*proles*) or the fulfillment of their conjugal duties (*fides*). If the motive of conjugal relations is to protect the spouses from misconduct or to appease their sexual desires, they are exempt from grave fault but not from venial sin.

In high scholasticism, despite a positive evaluation of sexual pleasure by Albert the Great (by reason of its conformity to nature) and despite the consideration, introduced by St. Thomas, of a new objective secondary end of marriage, namely the community of life of the spouses (*mutuum obsequium*), sexuality remained the object of strong distrust. At the same time, thanks to reflection on natural law and the Aristotelian doctrine of degrees, a change came about in the interpretation of sexuality and the morality of the conjugal act. Its point of departure was the notion of man as belonging to a species. The human being has, along with the animals, a desire for sexual union. Animals and human beings are anxious, by nature, to maintain their species and human sexuality is exclusively in the service of the propagation of mankind. The sexual act is, by its nature, ordained to procreation, and from this arises a moral obligation to realize the sexual encounter in such a way that it respects biological nature and tends toward procreation.

For the period extending from late scholasticism until the middle of the twentieth century the aforementioned understanding underwent, in turn, a change in meaning in which the moral liceity of conjugal relations called for respect of physiological normality. Because the act is necessarily *actus per se aptus ad generationem*, one does not have the right to alter its nature.

This development represents a clear orientation toward a pure morality of the act considered separately, as is often the case with casuistry.

With good reason, Cardinal Ratzinger states concerning this:

> From then on, it was no longer possible to explain why the moral form of the exercise of sexuality required marriage,

> which is without doubt held as the best guarantee possible for the education of the children, but the necessity of which in reality can no longer be deduced from natural criteria that one has taken for granted.[22]

Let us summarize: traditional sexual and conjugal ethics, as developed from the patristic age – particularly since St. Augustine – until the twentieth century, is determined in a one-sided way, on the one hand by the goods of marriage which serve to excuse the spouses from the subjective point of view and on the other hand by its objective ends and the hierarchy of those ends (*fines primarius, fines secundarii*). In marriage as institution, this ethic attributes to the function of procreation an exaggerated primacy *vis-à-vis* marriage. On the whole, procreation is at the service of the social and institutional dimension of the conjugal reality more than at the service of its personal aspect. Consequently, this evaluation of conjugal relations arrives at an interpretation determined by the criteria of nature and of physiological order. Ultimately, the evaluation – marked as it is by a finalist vision centered on generation, institution, and nature – tends to reduce more or less to the status of a pious overlay that which in reality is the proper theological and Christocentric foundation and the center of Christian marriage: its sacramentality.

b. Sacrament and the Institution of Marriage

The doctrine of the sacrament of marriage constitutes the proper center of the teachings of the Church on marriage as institution and as covenant, since the sacrament is the Christian foundation of the matrimonial institution. Even in the teachings of the Old Testament, marriage possessed a religious dimension as an institution established by the creator and anchored in the order of creation. Its sacred character derived from the fact that it was instituted by God and guaranteed by divine law.[23]

In the New Testament, as we have seen, marriage, which pertains to the order of creation, is assumed into the order of redemption; St. Paul sees its significance in reference to the relationship between Christ and the Church. Marriage is the concrete arena where the spouses must realize their following and their imitation of Christ (*sequela Christi*).

At the beginning of the patristic era, marriage was conceived as *res sacra*, but there was still no theological reflection on its sacramentality in the strict sense of the word. Augustine inserted marriage into the whole of salvation history and related it to Christ, whom he considered *sacramentum* in the proper sense; and even for St. Bonaventure, the concept of sacrament in the precise sense was still to come.

In the eleventh century, the number of the sacraments was fixed at seven, but two more centuries passed before theology developed a complete doctrinal formulation of the sacramentality of marriage. Marriage was often considered a peculiar sacrament.

From then until the twentieth century, theology constantly renewed its effort to deepen the doctrine of marriage. Scholastic theology concentrated on the following points: the notion, origin, sacramentality, finality, and properties of marriage; its exterior sign; its effects; the minister; the subject; and the authority of the Church over marriage.[24] This research developed in close connection with the discipline which is the object of moral theology and ecclesiastical law, and found expression in certain decisions of the magisterium (from the Council of Florence in 1439 and the Council of Trent to the encyclicals of the nineteenth and twentieth centuries), without arriving at a perfect and definitive clarification on the theological plane. Theological discussion encountered difficulties, especially regarding the following questions: of what does the exterior sign or the interior grace of the sacrament of marriage consist? When did Christ institute this sacrament? What is its matter and its form? Theologically, these elements pertain to the notion of sacrament.[25]

In order to determine the relationship between marriage as sacrament and marriage as institution, there is no need to go into its doctrinal development. It suffices to say that, according to traditional Catholic doctrine, the marriage of baptized Christians possesses the dignity of a sacrament; that is to say, for the baptized, the conjugal contract of the spouses is a sacramental reality.

According to traditional Catholic doctrine and terminology, there is a real identity between marriage as institution in the created order and marriage as sacrament. We must not, however, understand this identity in such a way that the validity of each of these two aspects of Christian marriage – institution and sacrament – is exempt from every condition. Inasmuch as it is an institution, marriage presupposes the following conditions: the capacity of the partners to contract marriage (that is to say, the practical absence of diriment impediments); the will on the part of both to contract marriage in view of establishing a concrete conjugal community (lasting and exclusive);

and an official notification of their will in response to the social dimension of marriage. The real conditions of marriage as sacrament are: the aptitude (or disposition) to contract a sacramental marriage (for all practical purposes, the baptism of the partners); the intention (at least virtual) to do what the Church does; the absence of diriment impediments; and the intervention of the Church (which will be determined more precisely according to different circumstances).

The other teachings of traditional theology on sacramental marriage can be summarized as follows:

1) The sacrament of marriage consists in reality in the contract itself (the actual identity between sacrament and contract). It does not need to be supplemented by a rite of its own. The mutual consent of the parties to establish a concrete conjugal community and to live up to the obligations inherent in it is the efficacious sign of the grace of the sacrament. The contract and the sacrament are inseparable; therefore, every valid contract marriage is *eo ipso* a sacrament.

2) The matter of the sacrament of marriage consists of the words of the contract inasmuch as they express the mutual giving of conjugal rights. The form consists of the words of the contract inasmuch as they express the acceptance of these rights. Both matter and the form reside in the contract itself, not in the blessing of the priest.

3) The spouses themselves, not the priest assisting at marriage, are the ministers of the sacrament of marriage.

4) The marriage contract (*contractus*) creates a conjugal bond (*vinculum, matrimonium in facto esse*) by which the spouses are bound morally and juridically to each other. This bond has two properties: the intrinsic and extrinsic indissolubility of a contracted and consummated marriage and the unicity of marriage.

In this theology, the sacrament of marriage is totally bound to the contract. This results–as can be understood from the historical context in which marriage is formed–in a juridical conception which more or less loses sight of or insufficiently considers the religious, personal, and properly sacramental elements of Christian marriage.

In the juridical act (the contract of marriage) that we have said is the constitutive element of the sacrament, the personal faith of the contractants is not at issue. The state of being baptized is of value to the person seeking marriage only as the necessary and sufficient condition, from the moment that the will to validly conclude the contract is present.

Moreover, according to this doctrine, the institution based on the sacrament remains outside of the personal encounter. The properties that are attributed to the sacramental institution exist on the objective level; they are not the immediate expression of a meaning derived from the encounter of love.

Finally, this doctrine should better illuminate that which constitutes the "interior space" of the sacrament: the property that Christian marriage possesses, seen by faith, of realizing in a lasting way the union of Christ with his Church.

Here still the institutional aspect enjoys an absolute priority over a global vision of the sacrament.

c. *Law and the Institution of Marriage*

aa. Ecclesial Power to Legislate in Matrimonial Matters

According to current law, the Church demands in matters pertaining to its members a *protestas propria et exclusiva* in defining the impediments to marriage and regulating the different juridical consideration touching on the conjugal bond.

This legislative and judicial competence is the result of a long and sinuous history. The primitive Church did not deal with juridical structure, but accepted the structure of its time. It abstained from exercising a canonical authority on marriage and followed the principle stated by the unknown author of the Letter to Diognetus: Christians "marry just like the whole world." The Church was not aware of juridical power which would make it possible to establish impediments to marriage or to impose a definite form on the celebration of marriage.

On the other hand, there developed relatively soon the beginnings of an ecclesiastical discipline shaped principally by theological and pastoral considerations. With the increase in the number of the faithful and the diffusion of Christian communities in various cultures, the need for fixed rules became clearer. Starting from the teaching of the faith, there began to be outlined a few features of a kind of "law of the faith," which was critically different from the juridical practice of the surrounding culture and which sought to give currency to the Christian message with its specific requirement concerning the sanctity of marriage, even though the first centuries knew few official formulations.[26]

The evolution which led ecclesiastical discipline to establish a law of marriage—on which its competence regarding the sacramental character of marriage was to be based–was tortuous and beset with problems. During the first ten centuries, one cannot speak in precise terms of the sacramentality of marriage. During this time the legislation of the state was accepted as a reality and fact; Christianity developed moral directives for the use that Christians made of civil norms. The Church progressively assumed a subsidiary role in order to make up for the state's failure to carry out its responsibilities. At the same time, the Church's influence penetrated more and more deeply into public and private life. Thus, new juridical situations were created. In the West (unlike the East, which knew only the law of the empire) this process led the Church, in putting its discipline into practice, to assume little by little a juridical authority (in the proper sense of the word) and, finally, to exercise an exclusive legislative power of its own and to form a system of ecclesiastical law.[27]

The Church was in *de facto* possession of this competence until the seventeenth century. At that point, Protestantism, Gallicanism, and Josephinism, as well as modern theories of the state, began to challenge what they called the totalitarian pretentions of the Church. A new definition of the competence of the Church *vis-à-vis* that of the state was set forth in the Code of Canon Law of 1918, which defined the *potestas propria et exclusiva* of the Church over the marriages of Christians and the competence of the state for the purely civil dimensions of marriage.

From Trent to the Code, the doctrinal development passed through several stages. The Council of Trent defined the power of the Church to establish impediments and to legislate on the different questions relating to the conjugal bond.[28] The Syllabus of Pius IX and the Code declared that this power of the Church is a Catholic truth.[29] Pius VI and the Code affirmed the exclusive competence of the Church in the aforementioned matters.[30]

This teaching draws upon several arguments. Already sacred scripture (Acts 15:20; 21:25; and 1 Cor 15:1–5: cf. Lev 18) witnesses to some legislative interventions by the Church. In practice, the Church of the first centuries–often in opposition to civil law–claimed and maintained the right to legislate in this way as a power that it received from Christ and possessed on its own. Theological reflection recognizes in the Church a legislative and judiciary power, proper and exclusive, by virtue of its competence concerning the administration of the sacraments, including the sacrament of marriage which is identical to the contract of marriage.[31]

bb. Material Domain of Matrimonial Law

Just as no culture can ignore the existence of the institution of marriage, or refrain from regulating it in its normal course, so the Church cannot fail to establish norms and laws that protect and promote Christian marriage. Now and throughout history, different and complementary foundations have supported the justification of this legal system. History can show variations in the understanding of the competence thus claimed. The Church today, by virtue of its legislative and judiciary competence, exercises this power in three particular areas: the capacity to contract marriage, the will to do so, and the form of the celebration.

According to current canon law, the capacity involved requires mental and physical aptitude and the absence of diriment impediments. Both outside Christianity and within it, it has been necessary throughout history to identify impediments in order to guarantee and to protect the matrimonial institution. Religious and civil mores play an important role in the development of ecclesiastical law. Thus, Old Testament law (Lev 18 and 20), the law and custom of Rome, and, in the ninth century, Germanic law were conflated to determine which degree of blood relationship constitute an impediment; the consequent extensive system was acceptably reduced only by the fourth Lateran council.

Moreover, during the early centuries, the practice termed the Pauline privilege and – especially in the East – remarriage after separation posed delicate problems in the context of biblical teaching on the unity and indissolubility of marriage.

For theological considerations, the Western Church adopted the posture of defending the matrimonial bond in establishing juridical norms. But it also strove to do justice to different circumstances and situations by interpreting the biblical teachings in such a way as to make explicit the power of the Church and to develop an extensive system of dispensations. While remaining constantly attentive to situations and their changes, the Church both had to avoid or to soften unnecessary rigor for the spouses and had to safeguard the theological doctrine of the indissolubility of marriage between two baptized persons. This evolution continued until our time, as the changes in the Code of Canon Law show. Moreover, one should note that several questions remain open precisely in the matter of impediments.[33]

With regard to the will to contract marriage, the second condition of validity, current law requires that marital consent be exempt from all illegitimate pressure regarding all its essential elements, especially the unicity and indissolubility of the bond. The will to contract is defined as the voluntary act by which the two parties mutually give and accept the exclusive and irrevocable right *in corpus* with respect to acts directed toward procreation.[34] The essential object of matrimonial consent is the full right to the conjugal act.[35] Juridical determinations on this matter affirm this; the expression of consent binds the baptized with a bond whose conditions are not defined by the partners themselves but are born from the meaning and the finality of marriage.[36]

Because the bond created by consent[37] is raised to the dignity of a sacrament, the baptized receive the sacrament (intrinsic indissolubility) through the very exchange of consent. Nevertheless, extrinsic indissolubility is acquired only through the consummation of marriage. In order to understand this determination of ecclesiastical law, it is necessary to explore its historical development. In the milieu in which it grew, the primitive Church first encountered the Roman concept, according to which marriage was a social state existing as long as the partners desired to be married. Christianity assumed the idea of consent, but before the year 600 it introduced the notion that marriage is constituted by mutual consent and does not demand continued accord in order to subsist.[38] In this way, consent, once given, has a permanent effect on the marriage of the partners.

Much later, Christianity expanded to come in contact with the Germanic understanding of marriage, according to which the validity of marriage requires consummation in the conjugal act. In the ninth century, Pope Nicholas I taught the theory of consent; at the same time, Hincmar of Reims defended the theory of *copula*.[39] The controversy of the Middle Ages between the School of Bologna (Gratian) and that of Paris (Peter Lombard) ended in a decision that the validity of marriage (essence) is insured by consent while its integrity (indissolubility) is insured by *copula*. The Council of Florence applied the concept of efffficient cause of marriage to the exchange of consent. The Council of Trent confirmed this doctrine and recognized that clandestine marriages also had been valid marriages.[40]

The codification of ecclesiastical law in the Code of Canon Law set the doctrine on consent for the time being. It underlined the indispensable necessity of mutual consent, but drew attention to the needs of the institution by imposing certain norms of law. These norms seemed to award priority to the institution and the objective dimensions over the personal order; thus the code eliminated the tension between the personal component and the institutional component of marriage in a one-sided way.

Historically, the question of the will to contract marriages has intimately involved the question of public notification of that will. Since the fourth or fifth century, the Roman Church has attested to the practice of priestly benediction and the celebration of a nuptial mass. The Church called for some kind of official manifestation of the will without making the validity of the marriage depend on it. The adoption by the Church of the theory of consent gave rise in the Middle Ages to a grave problem concerning clandestine marriages. The Council of Trent declared that, in the future, the baptized would be unable to contract secret marriages and that marriages not contracted in the form prescribed by the Church would be invalid.[42] The new legislation instituted by the Code of Canon Law allowed the impediment of clandestinity to fall by the wayside, and introduced as the form of marriage a ritual prescribed under pain of nullity for all marriages concluded between couples in which at least one party was baptized.[43]

This law has undergone a new modification in the legislation concerning mixed marriages. The drafting of a new law provides that the observation of the canonical form of marriage is "in the future, obligatory for Christians baptized in or converted to the Catholic Church, but no longer for Catholics who are formally or publicly separated from the Church. In excluding this last category of persons, the intention is to permit them to contract a valid marriage outside the Catholic Church, since as a general rule they are not disposed to contract marriage according to ecclesial form."[44]

In its juridical practice, the Church has moved away from an earlier attitude which proposed a legal regulation as a moral norm. It deduced the power to do this from its responsibility to administer the sacraments and from the social character of the community that it forms. Since the Council of Trent, it has held to the position that the sacramental sign (the promise of fidelity) is given in its full sense only if the consent is expressed publicly in the way prescribed by the Church. Whether the norm of ecclesiastical law on the obligation of canonical form conveys a strict requirement of the ecclesial dimension of marriage or whether it is a matter of positive prescription of ecclesiastical law is a moot question.[45]

Reflection in light of the current understanding of the sacraments and of ecclesiology on the need for reform of marriage law has led the Church to recognize both that the manner in which it must establish such norms derives from positive ecclesiastical law, and yet that certain limits are imposed on the dispositions of the Church because the reality of the sacrament taken in its totality requires an explicit ecclesial concern for marriage. Perhaps one can see in the new juridical dispositions of marriage the primary response of the Church to the criticisms that it values only the institution and not the person, that it emphasizes juridicism to the detriment of pastoral care, that it is backward in all of its doctrine on marriage, and that it fails to take into account contemporary thought, sensitivities, and life. These developments and the current questioning of the institution of marriage will be the subject of the following section.

B. The Current Questioning of Marriage as Institution – First Critical Evaluation

I. Changes in Perspective and Clarification of the Theology of Marriage

1. IN THE UNDERSTANDING OF MARRIAGE FROM THE PERSONALIST POINT OF VIEW

As the result of a long historical development, contemporary anthropology and theology have changed so that they associate the notion of marriage more with personalist categories. Juridical, institutional, and biological aspects are deemphasized or better integrated into a global vision of marriage. This change has not come readily, but is the result of a complex process.

a. Economic and Social Factors of Change

In preindustrial society, the economic, social, juridical, and ethical norms of the bourgeoisie of the sixteenth through nineteenth centuries, and the stable reign of the extended family largely defined marriage and the family. With increasing industrialization, urbanization, and mobility, the image and the function of marriage and family underwent a structural change that one can summarize in the following way: the extended family was reduced to the nucleus of parents and children, with a small number of children; a system of personal savings replaced the consumption economy; the place of work was separated from home; the wife was emancipated to assume professional tasks even if she had several children; people became free in choice of spouse; an egalitarian concept of the couple replaced the patriarchal regime in which the authority of the husband dominated the household; and marriage was conceived of as a private institution rather than as a unit of society.[46]

b. *Anthropological Elements Contributing to a More Profound Interpretation of Marriage*

Founded on the economic and social changes mentioned above and following from data furnished by the experience of the natural sciences, there has developed in the twentieth century, especially on the basis of transcendental philosophy and of dialogical personalism and in critical discussion of the traditional concept of sexuality and marriage, a more profound vision of both.

Anthropologists stress the fact that the human being is entirely characterized and influenced by sexuality and marriage. The husband and the wife develop their human personalities inasmuch as they are sexual beings. Thus the totality of the human being–in its fulfillment or its failure–is here at stake. The impact of the sexual is expressed by the need to find one's complement and one's orientation toward the "Thou" of the partner. The encounter of husband and wife in the love of a couple is, in the eyes of interpersonal personalism, the highest form of the I-Thou dialogue which constitutes the human being. This love of the couple in total and lasting commitment takes hold of the individuals involved and insures a singular dignity to them, to their conjugal life, and to their going beyond themselves by bearing children as an expression of their love.[46]

This idea of sexuality and marriage completes the traditional view of the goods and ends of marriage by reference to a concept which relates to the dignity of the person and that of marriage. A principally finalist concept of marriage yields place to a personalist view founded on the community of love and life. At the same time the ethical force of the naturalist and physiological notion of the conjugal act for the community of spouses is questioned and, taking into account the recent findings of biology and medicine, the problem of responsible parenthood and of birth control is reconsidered. The sovereign norm of the conjugal act is no longer sought, according to a prevalent understanding, in the "nature of the act" but in the "nature of the person *and* of his acts." The prudent and responsible decision of the spouses becomes a real condition of the morality of the act.

It would be incorrect to consider a vision of marriage and sexuality based on the idea of personal love and conjugal community as a pure and simple rejection of the institutional element. Only a narrow and one-sided view of the situation could cause such an exclusion; we will speak of this later. Certainly the personalist vision of sexuality in marriage is a reaction against the exaggerated institutionalizing tendency of the past, but it does not attack the institution itself. In a global view of personalism, it is impossible to reject the very notion of institution. The foundation of the possibility of passage from the I to the We, from one person to another, is based on the fact that the individual always exists in society and is constituted by society. Thus passage of persons to Us results not in the isolation of the Us in a private circle, but opens upon the whole community, which is constitutive for the existence of the individual as well as for the existence of the community of Us.[48]

Because this conjugal community of Us goes beyond itself to take in the Us found in the child or children, marriage is not a private intimacy between two persons, but is oriented toward a larger community of the family and is supplanted by the community which renders it possible: the community of the whole, that is to say, society.[49] In this way the personal aspect and the social aspect of sexuality in marriage are indissolubly bound by a reciprocal relationship. Each of the two aspects is constitutive of marriage. For this reason, sexuality and marriage are susceptible to being regulated by the norms of a personal and social character and need this regulation.[50]

What is in question today is not the necessity of regulation but its character and scope. The norms established by the community cannot be arbitrary but should be designed, in different historical situations and circumstances, so as to respect both the personal development of the individual and the requirements of the common good. Ethical and juridical norms must also permit sexuality and marriage to be realized as expressions of the relationship which directs man beyond society toward the absolute – the personal Absolute.[51]

This vision of human existence, of sexuality, and of marriage gives profound meaning to the indissolubility of marriage. The indissolubility of marriage is not considered primarily from the point of view of the institution and of exterior law but from the point of view of fidelity, which is an intrinsic aspect of love and not something added or juxtaposed from the outside. Fidelity is rather the very means by which love holds to itself and assures the permanence of its unconditional acceptance. Through this fidelity lived as unconditional love the spouses participate in the mystery, that no one can fully comprehend, of the divine fidelity which is promised to humanity in Christ.

In this perspective, K. Lehmann, concerning the relationship between personal fidelity and the institutional character of marriage, remarks:

> Every representation of a "conjugal bond" understood in an objectivized way, which considers marriage itself as an objectively pre-established thing and which metaphysically hypostasizes the institutional character of marriage separated from the fundamental personal relationship, dislocates the essence of marriage and breaks the natural and irreducible tension between the personal and the institutional.[52]

c. *Marriage in Light of Church Doctrine*

Contemporary theology and the teaching of the Church confirm and deepen the contributions of anthropology to the interpretation of sexuality and marriage. The texts of Vatican II on marriage and the family reflect a consciously personalistic and existentialistic way of thinking. The teachings of *Gaudium et Spes* on these subjects undoubtedly represent a number of compromises. Yet one should note that, in comparison with prior declarations and even with the first draft of the document itself, these teachings are distinguished by their emphasis on the idea of the dignity of marriage as a profound community of life and love, established on the covenant of the spouses, that is to say, on their irrevocable consent.[53] The "spouses themselves establish" by the personal and free act by which they mutually give and receive, a community which is an institution and which divine law confirms for the good of the spouses, the children, and society.[54]

GS also goes beyond the perspective of the Code which speaks only of the transfer and acceptance of "the right to the body for acts which are *per se* directed toward procreation." The Augustinian hierarchy of the ends of marriage is no longer referred to (see CIC, canon

1013,1), and we read *covenant* in place of the word *contract.*[55] Fidelity founded on mutual love signifies irrevocable fidelity. In contrast to the traditional teaching, GS relates the fruitfulness of marriage to Genesis 2:28: "it is not good that man be alone"; only in connection with this does it mention the couple's participation in the work of creation by citing Genesis 1:28.[56] The meaning of all these expressions and all these changes in emphasis is of great significance; they spring from a theological evaluation which until now had not appeared with such clarity in the teachings of the Church. The personal and social character of marriage is clearly revealed. The juridical and institutional elements are not denied, but they are put in their proper place. This profound and human view of the conjugal community is opposed to every type of dualism, injurious separation of spirit and body, or opposition in principle of person and institution.

2. NEW PERSPECTIVES IN THE SACRAMENTAL CONCEPTION OF MARRIAGE

Corresponding to this personalist vision of marriage which Vatican II, expressed as the official teaching of the Church is a deepened understanding of the sacramentality of marriage, as recent dogmatic research shows.[57]

While the different approaches taken to this question differ in nuance, they tend to converge. They begin with the concept of sacrament in general. One wishes to go beyond the limited and abstract notion of a certain post-Tridentine theology. The notion which harmonizes best with the whole of salvation history and the life of the Church is that which understands the sacraments as rendering present the teachings and actions of Christ by signifying them. Through the sacraments we are, in a mysterious way, incorporated into the body of Christ and brought in contact with his death and resurrection. The Church is a global sacrament, and the particular sacraments are the ways in which the Church—that is to say, the operative presence of Christ—is active among us. According to this view, the sacrament of marriage should be presented as the actualizing sign of the fidelity of the love of the Christ toward his Spouse, the Church.

It is precisely in accord with this view that one must take into consideration the human aspect of the sacrament of marriage. Man today knows that he is no longer bound to a metaphysical understanding of the universe; he no longer lives his life only in the even flow of time.

Rather, there are throughout human existence some high points, some critical moments in which one's entire life is concentrated and is entirely at stake. At these moments the human person decides the direction and meaning of his life. Some examples are birth and death, grave sin, the choice of a spouse, the creation of a conjugal community. These moments produce a "symbolic experience," and one must look to them to find the point of contact with a concept of sacrament adapted to the current way of thinking. On the one hand, humanity finds itself immersed in the world and in the community. On the other hand, it experiences in its liberty and responsibility something of the inaccessible, a transcendence over the purely biological. The expression of "critical moments" of human existence, which are ambiguous and admit of diverse interpretations, attains through the sacrament an unequivocal meaning; the sacrament concretizes fundamental human situations. Through the sacrament, a human situation comes to be perceived as the locus of a decision; it receives its qualification from the proclamation made by the sacrament (*forma sacramenti*), and the sacrament confers on the decision of the person the clear character of a decision for or against faith.

> The sacrament is in essence a concentration, expressed in a sign and in a corporal way, of the Word of God who calls for man's participation and promises him grace, who encounters man in his concrete human situations and places his hand upon him.[58]

Starting from this notion of sacrament, as from the anthropological angle, one must say that marriage signifies all human existence in a specific way, under the particular aspect of the individual's insertion into the system of human exchanges and the reciprocal relationships of spouses. According to this point of view, the pledge of fidelity can be the locus of an experience of transcendence, where individuals surpass themselves and penetrate into the sphere of mystery. This orientation toward transcendence remains ambiguous and risky, and makes an additional demand on mankind.[59] One finds here an initial movement in the direction of the sacrament whose fact and meaning are given to us by revelation alone. Revelation makes visible for us the fact that the order of creation is assumed by the order of salvation. In this way, marriage in its created nature is a sign of the promise by which God pledges his fidelity and which is fully declared in

Christ. This is why conjugal fidelity and love, in all kinds of marriage–not only in Christian marriage–are always supported by the fidelity and love of God. For inasmuch as human fidelity suggests an inaccessible mystery, it is the mystery of the immanent fidelity of God. Only divine fidelity makes it possible for the spouses to remain faithful to their commitment.

Walter Kasper sees here "the reason why, in the final analysis, the uniqueness and indissolubility of marriage can be recognized only in Christianity and lived only in Christian faith."[60] In Christ is revealed, beyond the entire created order, the ultimate essence of marriage, perceptible only by faith: that of an actualizing sign of the fidelity and love vowed, in Christ, by God to his Church. As every type of Christian community implies an actualization of Christ and the Church, so in a specific way does marriage as the smallest unit of community in Christ. Thus, when the spouses' exchange of promises of fidelity is grounded in faith, the personal and free act by which they mutually give and accept each other is the sacramental sign of the fidelity binding Christ to the Church.[61]

The primary consequences of this understanding of the sacrament of marriage is that in good theology one can no longer adopt the simplistic distinction between "natural marriage" and "sacramental marriage."[62] Creation itself is referred to Christ (Col 1:16), and every form of love and fidelity between spouses can then be an event of grace. The distinction between what is called "presacramental marriage" and "fully sacramental marriage" consists in the fact that it is the latter to which God infallibly guarantees his grace and into which he introduces the baptized, in this critical moment of their existence which is marriage, according to his definitive will of grace.[63]

> When two baptized persons, in a fully responsible love, exchange their "yes" before God and humanity–in the sense explained above–God unconditionally guarantees them His grace in view of their decision. This–and nothing else–is a sacrament.[64]

Another consequence of this wider concept of sacrament is a deepened view not only of the personal dimension but also of the social and institutional dimensions of marriage. If the promise of fidelity given in faith is the sacramental sign of the union of fidelity which binds Christ to the Church, this sign "is given in its full and intimate sense only if, in a certain way, it is 'posed' publicly in society and in the Church."[65] If one considers precisely the personal character of matrimonial commitment as a donation of self to one's spouse, the will to unite in marriage is manifested as serious only when it is a publicly declared commitment. That is why K. Lehmann states

> The public nature of this act of will does not constitute only its manifestation or objectivization; it does not serve merely as a societal and concrete sign of the existence of an intimate love. Rather, the yes becomes fully real only through this pronouncement which renders its importance and its consistency visible. Intimate love constitutes a marriage in the full sense when it declares itself responsibly before an Us and commits itself to the other freely and publicly.[66]

A vision of marriage where the commitment of fidelity toward the partner is the sacramental sign nullifies the objection that the institution based on the sacrament remains exterior to love. The institution does not express the verdict of a law imposed from outside, but is the social and official dimension of the personal pledge of fidelity toward the partner. The very dynamic of faithful love demands that one render the social dimension of the covenant visible. The juridical form of its social recognition is of secondary importance.[67] This perspective also places in better light the indissolubility of marriage as "unconditional fidelity." According to the teachings of Vatican II, marriage – in the very interpretation of the Epistle to the Ephesians – is the image of and participation in the covenant of love between Christ and the Church. This sacrament represents the unconditional fidelity of God. Thus, the possibility of the unconditional fidelity of the spouses is ultimately founded in faith.

This way of understanding sacramental marriage does not prevent the unconditional pledge of fidelity from encountering tensions and difficulties, but these cannot justify the cancellation of a commitment which consciously founds its hope on the death and resurrection of Christ.

3. CHANGE IN THE JURIDICAL UNDERSTANDING OF MARRIAGE

It would be wrong to say that in the past ecclesiastical law did not take into account the personal aspect of marriage. The fact that it held unshakeably to the consent of the spouses as a fundamental and constitutive element of marriage (*consensus facit matrimonium*) shows that for church doctrine, every law relative to marriage is based on the spouses' pledge of fidelity.

However, in order to justify the existence and scope of matrimonial law as well as the institutionalization of the conjugal contract, today one must rely less on the juridical concept of contract than on the concept of marriage as illuminated by contemporary anthropology and theology.

There are various ways to justify the existence of a law regulating matters concerning marriage. First of all, if one starts from consent considered as the "yes" of the partners which is constitutive of marriage, this resolute and unconditioned "yes" implies an opposition to every subjective limitation and condition. The commitment that the partners exchange, which is unconditional and fundamentally exclusive of every condition, deprivatizes and desubjectivizes their decision and objectifies it to some extent without detriment to its personal character and without ending in an exteriorized and objectivist bond. Thus, the unconditional *yes* which is exchanged forms the basis for a requirement and (in a broad sense) a law and an ordination of law – a sort of institutionalization, which involves a guarantee and a release, and therefore, also a liberation, in the double meaning of the term. The partners are no longer free to drift with their changing wishes and desires. At the same time, they are set free because of the full realization of their community of love and life. In this approach, all law applying to marriage has a functional character. It is clear that this law founded on a personal basis, which introduces an institutional element guaranteeing personal liberty, must indeed be permanent in its fundamental structure, yet must respond in its concrete development to the historical condition of man and marriage. It must be equally clear that the law has limits and can never embrace the total reality of human existence.

According to another attempt at a new presentation on the intervention of law in matrimonial matters, one must start with the very nature of man. For Ratzinger, human existence is necessarily public and involves "so to speak, a relationship to law and to its formulation":[68]

> It is a property of human nature not to be a pure nature, but to have and to have obligatorily, a history and a law in order to be able to obtain its 'natural' being. Such is the

> immediate anthropological reason why human sexuality is subject to regulation by society, which establishes the law, and why sexual morality is bound to its insertion in the normative structure that human society imposes on it.

This anthropological justification can point to the fact that no society has treated sex and eros as private matters left to the good pleasure of each person; all have submitted them to social regulation. This is confirmed, we have shown above, by cultural anthropological research. If, with Ratzinger, one moves from this anthropological justification to a theological justification, then, in the light of faith, the true form of the regulation of marriage is that which the latter has received from the covenant of God with man in Jesus Christ in which "the person is no longer dominated by the community and reduced to the state of an object, but where the articulation of the personal and of the social is truly restored to their intimate identity."

Law and its formulation pertain to the essence of marriage and are not simply adventitious. Since the fact of being human and of existing in society are not based on themselves but on transcendence, the law is truly law only "where it appears as positive reality corresponding to the very idea of law and also to transcendence."[69]

II. The Questioning of the Institution of Marriage

The changes that have occurred in our understanding of man and his relationships to the community and to society, to the world and to God, have led in our time – both within the Church and outside it, by virtue of a prevalent mistrust of every type of institution – to an attitude of scepticism toward the institution of marriage. The criticisms aim at everything from the radical exclusion of marriage as an institution to particular challenge concerning the necessity or legitimacy of the ethical and legal norms which have developed throughout history.

The character, modes, and principles of the argumentation are very complex, making it hard to find a single unifying theme. Rationalistic considerations play a decisive role in many ways. It is not uncommon that idealistic representations and affective and emotional factors are involved. Often enough, these objections are grounded in an ideological bias.

At the present time, this school of thought is not yet fully developed. It would, moreover, hardly be possible to present clearly every detail of it. One can nevertheless note, for purposes of theological discussion in the church, several principles and tendencies from which a series of critical questions can be raised.

1. THE INSTITUTION OF MARRIAGE AS ALIENATION OF MAN

a. In Marxist-Leninist Teaching

Modern Marxism-Leninism, as represented by the socialist camp, does not question the necessity of marriage (and of the family) as an institution. Its critique focuses upon a non-socialist understanding of marriage and the family, the ideal type of which is called *bourgeois marriage.* According to this analysis, the proper bond of marriage is not conjugal love, but the interest of the class to which the spouses belong. In capitalist society, the choice of spouse and of marriage itself is determined by economic ends.[70] The structures of marriage and the family are the result of the relationships of ownership and production. From this arises oppression of the wife, who "belongs" to her husband. Only the liquidation of capitalism will permit the development of more human structures and assure the moral dignity of the individual. It is only through a socialization of the interplay of ownership and of production (already present in socialism) that "the love of husband and wife can blossom in companionship, with equal rights and obligations, between free and responsible persons."[71] That is why socialism does not question the institution of marriage. The new socialist society has eradicated the causes of the institution's degradation. "Only the marriage and the family founded on love are moral, and it is only there that love continues to exist."[72]

Yet this understanding of marriage also admits, with regard to morality and law,[73] a softening of the norms of sexual and conjugal life. Divorce is allowed when a marriage fails. Abortion (until the end of the third month) is the exclusive decision of the mother. Homosexuality is not held to be a perversion, but is seen as a variation of sexuality "inasmuch as it does not exclude mental and physical communion with another human being in reciprocal and full satisfaction."[74] Premarital sexual relations are exempt from moral reproach when the couples are motivated by reciprocal love. Criticism of the institution of marriage, which appears among the young – as in other countries – nevertheless clashes with the reality of problems in the home.

b. The Contemporary Critique of Society and Civilization

Certain elements of this critique hold that the institution of marriage as it is encountered in highly developed civilizations today is the result and expression of a repressive social order.[75] According to this view, monogamy stands at the base of current norms of marriage. Now, monogamy does not correspond in any way with human nature; it is developed within the framework of a civilization built upon personal ownership. The channeling of sexuality into marriage has gravely injured its orignal vitality. Marriage itself has been degraded to the level of a pure institution, in which all that is living is condemned to death. As long as the husband and wife found in the religious faith of their union a guarantee of the indissolubility of marriage, monogamous marriage was not a rigid institution. Now that it lacks this security, it has become an oppressive constraint.

In order to confirm their theory, the proponents of this criticism of civilization point to statistical data which reveal a wide divergence between current practice and norms. They see there evidence that the norms are repressive and for this reason ought to be abolished. It is necessary to find some other norms which are better suited to nature. This new morality would by no means lead to the dissolution of morals or to pure chaos, as many people fear; rather, it would allow a real reconciliation between the individual and society. It would not be a morality in which full sexual license constitutes the norm, but an ethos of love, assuming the totality of human nature and situated beyond the good and evil. Such an ethics would not propagate values, but would be based on the notion that human nature, left to itself, would develop by its own dynamism a form of behavior that corresponded best to the reality of the individual and community. An institution which would respond to integral human nature would be "group marriage like the form of the family in backward civilizations."

A good number of the critics of civilization and society say that this class of new structures can be built up only after the radical abolition of the current repressive structures; that is to say, when society itself has been transformed. Since this will not come about rapidly, they say, it is necessary for people to gather in small communities in order to anticipate the future forms of life and thus create a new consciousness. In fact, on the basis of such theories, communities or communes that practiced group marriage arose in many places in Western countries during the 1960s. They disbanded after short periods of time, but the ideas developed by the critics of civilization and society about the obsolete character of the institution of marriage have survived – particularly among the young – especially as the mass media find these ideas interesting and have propagated them widely.

The critique of society and civilization does not exclude marriage purely and simply – as the explanation below will demonstrate – but rather the kind of marriage which is current in present-day society. This critique of the form which until now has characterized marriage emphasizes (in a one-sided way) the social dimension of marriage. The diagnostic and prognostic method derives a qualitative evaluation from quantitative data: from the statistics on divorce to the bad constitution of marriages, from the frequency of premarital or extramarital sexual relations to the general desuetude of ethical norms, from existing social institutions to the universally repressive character of institutions.

2. THE INSTITUTION OF MARRIAGE AS CONTRARY TO THE COMMUNITY OF LOVE

While the critique of society, insofar as it is a critique of marriage, condemns the matrimonial institution in its present form, criticizing it for being historically obsolete, others speak of a crisis of marriage and maintain that this institution no longer corresponds to anthropological data and the science of our time.

a. Marriage and Sexuality

A good number of authors go so far as to see in a new conception of sexuality a criterion justifying the condemnation of marriage. There is a strong tendency to value sex and pleasure in themselves to the point of neglecting emotional and personal relations with one's partner. Confined to the plane of the pure satisfaction of needs and drives, sexuality becomes the object of consummation and finds itself limited by the constraints of consummation. From this point of view marriage must be considered an inappropriate means for achieving the lasting satisfaction of needs.

At the same time, according to this perspective, marriage is undergoing a "reversal of function." If in the past it was oriented especially toward procreation, now it ought to serve only pleasure. This exclusive focus distorts sexuality and prevents one from taking into account the full scope of sexuality and marriage.

b. Marriage and Intimacy of the Couple

Nature is taken much more seriously by the argument which questions the institution of marriage by starting from a personalist conception of the relationship between partners and by putting love – not the institution – in the foreground as the motive of marriage. It is the young especially who pose a list of questions of this sort: Why do sexual relations always involve the entire person and his or her total and irrevocable commitment? Why cannot any couple in love have sexual relations? Why must premarital relations of this type always be immoral? Why is it necessary, in order to make the exercise of sexuality morally permissible, to surround it with the rigid constraints of an institution that was established in view of procreation? What has the civil or ecclesiastical celebration of marriage to do with intimate and private sexual behavior, which is entirely confidential and concerns only the partner?

Underlying these questions is a development that one can describe as the "emancipation" of marriage. It leads from the institutionalization of marriage in the sacred order, through its secularization in recent decades, to its privatization and, finally, to its deinstitutionalization. This evolution does not exclude the fact that many people today still see marriage as an important institution, to which they give their assent to the extent that it is not a normative system preconceived and imposed from without, a repressive constraint imposed by society or by the Church. Marriage is – to quote Vatican II – a "community of life and of love" which rests on the personal commitment of the partners. From this one can draw the following conclusion: when two partners are in love, they have this "community of love," and consequently they can establish also a "community of life." This latter is effected without the civil or ecclesiastical celebration of marriage, the celebrations being only an exterior and official notification or a formality of registration required by society. The ecclesiastical celebration is simply an addition.

On the basis of this line of reasoning, some speak of *pre-forms* or *new-forms* for life together and for marriage:

1) "Going steady" relationship, entered into after puberty, which are not oriented, at least in the beginning, toward marriage but which constitute a preparation for marriage. From such "apprenticeships" arise erotic contacts (necking and petting) and occasionally complete sexual relations.

2) "Going all the way" during adolescence: currently, complete sexual relations are valued by the young. Youths claim that these experiences further the development and shaping of sexuality as well as its integration into the overall development of the person. Such experiences are considered a normal way to prepare for marriage.[76]

Some young people see in a relationship of this sort, especially if intercourse is involved, a progression toward marriage and an anticipatory form of marriage, even if the relationship does not result in marriage or if it is abandoned. They emphasize that the Catholic doctrine of marriage attributes too much importance to the sexual act by making it legitimate only in marriage. This implies that marriage is principally based on the allowance of the sexual act. But to confer a supreme value upon the sexual act is not proper given the general context of sexuality and of marriage. The sexual relation within the framework of a premarital encounter supplies its own motivation, so that it is not its presence but its omission that ought to be suspect.

Because many modern young people cannot bear the responsibilities of marriage and family, it is necessary to avoid the conception of new life. Thus the practice of birth control is seen to be morally legitimized, since it permits passage through the period during which the partners are neither mature enough for nor capable of handling the responsibilities inherent in the obligations of marriage and the family.

3) Marital relations between engaged couples with the firm intention and pledge to contract marriage: in this case the partners find themselves facing circumstances that delay their marriage (residence, studies, temporary separation). In some countries where the law separates the civil celebration from the religious celebration, it is not uncommon that the spouses contract a civil union sometime before their religious marriage, in order to benefit from certain rights (in matters concerning residence, financial exemption, educational aid, compensation in the case of separation, etc.). Many couples consider this situation as already being a marriage or at least a form of marriage. They say they find Catholic moral teaching, which permits conjugal relations only in marriage, unintelligible.

The arguments of the young purport to draw support from theories of the human sciences which describe these anticipatory marriages as part of an evolutionary process toward integration into the conjugal life that has existed throughout human existence.[77] Also, concerning premarital relations, they expect from the Church a nuanced evaluation which goes beyond the position held until now.

4) A lasting sexual partnership with the exclusion, as a matter of principle, of a civil or religious marriage: here the institution of marriage is totally rejected. This life together inaugurated by lasting right needs no sort of legitimation. The personal relation is simply an intimate community of purely private character. It can be stable and lasting but should not necessarily be indissoluble. The community of life is maintained as long as the community of love prospers. There is here a distrust not only of the institutionalization of the community, but also of absolute monogamy.

5) Marriages for profit, especially in the second half of life: in this case there is established a community of life or of residence which has not been regularized by a civil union or by a religious marriage, and which is directed toward protecting the right of each of the partners to some civil advantage such as a pension. The partners do not exclude the institution of marriage on principle, but consider its application unprofitable.

All these challenges to marriage – including intermediate premarital or para-marital forms – are based on a new idea of love, sexuality, and marriage. Moreover, they question both the ethical norms in force and the juridical norms of the institution.

All of the aforementioned types of relationships without doubt do violence to the social and juridical dimensions of the relationship between partners. It is of no help to invite theology to reflect on the pastoral situation of the time. Theology is able neither to yield to every modern tendency nor to content itself with simple refutations. Rather, it must consider from the proper perspective the tension existing between the personal dimensions and the institutional dimensions of marriage.

If love alone is insufficient to constitute marriage, so the institution alone is insufficient as the norm of marriage. If pleasure and instinct are incapable by themselves of morally justifying sexual relations, so the institution is incapable by itself of being the norm of all sexual conduct. Shortlived sexual encounters, stable dating relationships, and the relations between fiancés cannot, from the anthropological point of view and in an ethical evaluation, be grouped together, even though sexual relations, as a total gift of love, call for the guarantee of the conjugal covenant in order to attain their full meaning.

3. THE INSTITUTION OF MARRIAGE AND INDISSOLUBILITY

More and more often, most recently, through changes in the worldwide understanding of marriage, the indissolubility of marriage as an institutional norm is challenged. Is indissolubility a necessary element of marriage as institution or required by marriage as an intrinsic law? Must the requirement of unconditional fidelity which has developed from the personal aspect of marriage agree with the traditional doctrine of the indissolubility of marriage as institution, or should it be reinterpreted and modified?

According to the present-day conception of the sacramentality of marriage, is it necessary to maintain the traditional doctrine according to which the marriages of the baptized are *eo ipso* sacraments and for this reason indissoluble? Is sacramental marriage always indissoluble once it is *ratum et consummatum*? Is not the power of the Church able to be extended *in favorem fidei* to sacramental marriage themselves?

These are only a few examples of the questions raised about marriage. They arise not only among believers, but are widely and passionately discussed in publications of every sort.

The Second Vatican Council confirmed the traditional teachings on the indissolubility of marriage without delving into concrete problems. GS presents divorce as a misfortune, declares the matrimonial consent irrevocable by virtue of its divine institution, and considers conjugal love to be sanctified by the sacrament of Christ and anchored in an unbreakable fidelity.[78]

In order to build a firm basis for indissolubility, recent theology starts from the personal dimension of unconditional fidelity. This fidelity is not simply a law of the institution which is imposed from without upon the matrimonial covenant. It is above all a perseverance in the *yes* of the "I" and the "Thou" exchanged in love and pronounced before the "We." The institution can never take the place of the personal commitment of the partners; it cannot create love and fidelity.

If marriage does not exist as a new structure of the "Us," it remains an empty structure of lifeless existence.

Let us briefly mention here a few questions about the indissolubility of marriage:

a. Indissolubility as Law of the Institution

In discussing the biblical teachings on the prohibition of divorce, their application in the primitive Church, and the practice of the Eastern Church, the objection is raised that the Latin Church has raised a requirement of the gospel to law. Without doubt, this law is concretized and softened by the Pauline and Petrine privileges, but for sacramental marriage (*ratum et consummatum*) and it alone, the law keeps its absolute value. That which Jesus wished to suggest as a possibility to be grasped in faith, unconditional fidelity as a sign of the fidelity of Christ, has become an alienating feature in Church life by being transformed into the indissolubility of the institution. Thus the nonbaptized and the baptized who have never accepted the faith are subjected to the law. The sacrament has been institutionalized.[79]

b. Indissolubility and the Capacity to Contract Marriage

At present, the human sciences allow us to see that the process of personalization and the progressive acquisition of the aptitude for total commitment are restrained and hampered in the contemporary world by many internal and external factors. Many persons who get married quickly may not be able to grasp the importance of their decision. They are not capable of contracting a marriage. This is why there is an extraordinarily high proportion of divorces in the marriages of young people. Nevertheless, according to current law, one has to deal with indissoluble marriages, stable institutions, removed from "the good pleasure" of human beings. In the minds of many persons, the personal and institutional aspects of indissolubility reach here an unbearable level of tension.

c. Indissolubility and Dead or Shipwrecked Marriages

The questions of believers and the literature on the subject frequently emphasize, with reference to the personal dimensions of marriage, that the church ought to take seriously the fact that some marriages can actually be broken and cease to exist. But if it is determined that a marriage is dead, then it is necessary to give the parties–however great their responsibility for the death of the first marriage–a chance to try again.[80] Surely, such reasoning on dead or shipwrecked marriages gives no consideration to the possibility of unlimited indulgence of one's partner or an extreme willingness to give oneself totally. The impossibility of reconciliation and beginning anew together is rather too quickly invoked. On the other hand, we cannot deny that there may remain, from the initial love and even from a firmly resolved will, only an institutional bond. In this case, does unconditional fidelity require the permanence of the bond; is it absolutely impossible for marriage to die?[81]

In this context, many authors insist on the necessity of clarifying, according to sacramental theology, whether the permanence of a sacramental marriage, in the case of irreparable failure, is more than a juridical entity which must, for the common good, prolong marriage as a social institution, but to which no personal or sacramental reality corresponds. The Church has taken into account the break-up of certain marriages by considering as justified, indeed as obligatory in some circumstances, the *separatio mensae et tori*. In this case the conjugal community of life is suspended while the matrimonial bond remains.

With the Pauline and Petrine privileges, the Church sees itself authorized, for the sake of the faith, to consider as legitimate an attenuation of the indissoluble character of the matrimonial institution. Now, if sacramental marriages break up, there often arises the danger of the parties' becoming separated from the Church and from the faith. This is why many authors pose the question: is it possible for the Church's power over nonconsummated sacramental marriages to be extended to consummated sacramental marriages? In such circumstances, would a remarriage be valid?[82] A quick glance at the wide debate on this topic shows that there is no agreement among theologians, even if the position of the magisterium remains firm.

All these challenges to marriage are not due to a desire for novelty, but to a profound solicitude for the persons involved and for their conjugal community of life. But the opinions reported here also reveal a tendency to accentuate the personal elements of marriage, with less attention to the social, institutional, and juridical structures. The personal and institutional dimensions of marriage have not yet been adequately reconciled.

4. THE INSTITUTION OF MARRIAGE AND MARRIAGE LEGISLATION

Several of the arguments treated above which question the institution of marriage also refer from various points of view, to ecclesiastical marriage law. Today the most severe critics of marriage strike at the way this law has been defined historically and in the present. It is necessary to keep this in mind whenever one deals with these schools of thought.

Since we have already shown the fundamental meaning and necessity of juridical regulation, we will treat here only a few questions which seek to obtain a fundamental reform or revision of the legislation.

a. Usurpation by the Church of Competence in Matrimonial Matters?

A primary criticism focuses on the Church's claim to establish *potestate propria et exclusiva* impediments to marriage and to take cognizance of matters concerning the bond of marriage. The representatives of this criticism make a case from the historical development of Church law. Until the tenth century marriage was not highly structured. Either the family, the clan, or the head of the family regulated its provisions. During the first centuries, the Church accommodated itself to this sort of regulation and, for its part, gave only directives of an ethical nature, which did not always touch on the validity of marriage. In the eleventh and twelfth centuries the Church exercised an exclusive juridical competence, and in the course of the following centuries it developed that competence. In today's secularized world, some think, the Church ought to desist from such legislation and limit itself exclusively to helping the faithful through ethical and religious directives. The Church is not a legal organization but one of faith and the life of faith.

This reasoning fails to see, as we have already shown many times, that the Church – in accord with current anthropological, sociological, and theological notions – cannot abandon the law that properly belongs to it. Sacramental marriage, inasmuch as it is an institution of Christian faith participating in the law of the faith, includes *eo ipso* social and institutional dimensions that the Church, as a social reality, has had to regulate. Vatican II rightly situated the community of life and of love at the center of marriage and did not emphasize as before the preeminence of the institutional dimensions. However, it in no way renounced the principle of juridical regulation. An opposition between the community of love and the community of law cannot be reconciled with the social constitution of the Church.[83]

This does not mean that ecclesiastical law in its concrete determinations should fail to adapt to circumstances that change with the times or, taking into account the present situation, should fail to recognize the legitimacy of certain claims of civil power to regulate certain temporal and profane aspects of marriage. The Church should recognize that many aspects of marriage fall under the domain of civil authority while others possess a clearly religious and ecclesial dimension.[84]

b. The Scandal of Positive Legislation and the Procedure of the Church

Among the faithful, as in the course of theological debate, scandal is occasioned by provisions regarding the nullity of marriages in which personal consent is not lacking but which a defect renders invalid. In such cases, a religious remarriage is permitted after civil divorce. The faithful and the pastors themselves hardly understand certain juridical dispositions. A presumption in favor of the validity of marriage likewise gives rise to scandal. Many persons see this as a way of favoring the institutional dimension to the detriment of the personal dimension of marriage.

c. The Obligation of Canonical Form

Projected marriage law does not impose any obligation of canonical form on Catholics who are formally or publicly separated from the Church. A number of authors anticipate, as the next step, a modification of the current law which would allow the contractants to choose between a civil celebration and an ecclesial celebration. We do not see any objection in principle to the recognition of the civil form as valid for Catholics. It is simply on the pastoral and practical plane that reservations are expressed. Nevertheless, given the current understanding of marriage in its personal and sacramental dimensions as well as today's ecclesiology, the suitableness of having the spouses exchange their pledge of fidelity in a visible community of believers is clear.

In speaking of these questions we have addressed only a few areas of ecclesiastical law. Other questions remain open to examination, as for example those which concern procedure in matrimonial cases or the relationship between *consensus* and *consummatio*. In the study of these problems, theology ought to remain conscious of the fact that law and legislation must keep in mind the service of human and Christian reality, that they must play a protective but not a dominating role, and that if in our earthly condition it is necessary to establish a law, the latter cannot be imposed in an absolute way.

5. CRITICAL EVALUATION OF THE OBJECTIONS; CONSEQUENCES FOR THE CHURCH'S DOCTRINE ON MARRIAGE

In the preceding sections we have already mentioned the essential elements for a critical evaluation of the objections currently made against Catholic doctrine. Therefore, it will suffice to draw attention to a few central points which occupy the current debates.

a. Marxist-Leninist Doctrine

The Marxist-Leninist theory of marriage represents, on the essential points, a gross simplification of the real data of the problem. It does justice neither to the doctrine of the Church on consent nor to historical and present realities. In respect to modern industrial states it ought to be considered completely outdated.

Although in principle the theory claims to uphold the necessity and stability of the institution of marriage, it nonetheless destroys this institution through the laxity of its norms and its moral and juridical laws.

The affirmation that marriage is moral only to the extent that love persists therein undermines the concept of perpetual fidelity and at the same time, the indissolubility of marriage. The Marxist conception implies first the reduction of being to consciousness, since a reality exists only as long as it is present to consciousness. One therefore falls back into pure phenomenology and to the pre-Christian Roman understanding, according to which marriage ceases to exist from the moment that the consent is lacking. Also, the conception depends on the reduction of being to time, so that for marriage what is permanent is made subject to the shifting feelings.

Moreover, the ethical and juridical norms of Marxism concerning homosexuality and pre-marital relations relativize *de facto* the assertions bearing on marriage as institution.

b. Critique of Society and Civilization

Certain forms of this critique which are influenced by Marxism, such as behaviorism or research on behavior, hold that the indissolubility of monogamous marriage results from a repressive development of civilization and society which contradicts the nature of human sexuality. Some find support for this thesis in statistical data which reveals the deviation of practice from the norm (divorces, premarital and extramarital relations).

One cannot dismiss statistical studies with a sweep of the hand. Even within the framework of theological discussion many people ask today if the high proportion of infractions against the current norms do not indicate, on the ethical plane, a change in convictions which requires the rethinking of these norms.

However, one cannot simply make actual behavior as established by statistics into a valid norm. The manner in which people conduct their lives does not lead to sound conclusions as to the real conviction of the parties concerned or as to the normative value of these convictions. Monogamy has been presented as the simple result of the evolution of civilization. Rather, should not one consider monogamous marriage, in the global perspective of human sexuality, as the most adequate form of sexual encounter in the human condition, where nature calls for culture? From the point of view of both cultural anthropology and theology, the restoration of any form of polygamy would be a regression from the highest type of marriage.

c. Relationship Between the Institution of Marriage and the Community of Love

aa. Relationship Between Marriage and Sexuality

Present-day ways of thinking attribute to sexuality a great importance in the realm of conjugal relations. The many forms of sexual encounter serve the interpersonal relation between the spouses as well as the development of the personality and the family itself. One has gone far beyond a Manichaean depreciation of pleasure and the notion that sexuality is primordially ordained toward procreation.

Nevertheless, putting a premium on sexuality in many ways has introduced a new separation of sexuality and marriage. According to a very widespread opinion, the “right to pleasure” becomes the primary norm of sexual behavior. Marriage is an inadequate means of assuring the satisfaction of this desire for gratification.

In this understanding of sexuality, the pendulum swings back to hedonism. Marriage is reduced to a utilitarian function, limited to time. Its personal value is simply lost sight of and the ambivalent character of sexuality is totally overlooked.

The Church's preaching will be able to counter this widely prevalent attitude, propagated by the mass media, only if it offers a positive vision with the appropriate justifications instead of insisting anew on prohibitions.

bb. Relation Between Marriage and Living Together

According to the doctrine of the Church, as a document of the SCDF reminds us once again,[85] sexual relations are reserved exclusively for marriage. Partners who contract a shortlived or lasting liaison, even one which resembles marriage, on the basis of love or of specific interests (for example, marriage for financial gain), even if they have privately exchanged a promise of fidelity (the secret marriages of students), may not claim this right.

For the most part, this teaching of the Church encounters only discontent, incomprehension, or rejection. In most people's eyes it attributes to sexual relations an exaggerated importance which does not correspond to the proper character of the relation established between the partners. A critical evaluation of such affirmations cannot ignore the fact that, in the concrete behavior adopted by many individuals before marriage or in the unions which resemble marriage, a change in conviction is evident. The parties concerned do not conceive of their conduct as violating a norm recognized as just. This evolution of thought has been confirmed by a number of confessors: in sacramental confessions admission of guilt in these areas is becoming relatively rare.

In contemporary publications on moral theology one often encounters the idea that while marriage attains its full form only at the time of its public celebration (civil or ecclesial), there can exist certain inchoate forms of marriage, to which some persons find themselves compelled by the general evolution of social life or by particular circumstances (for example, in the case of student marriages). There is a lack of convincing theological, pastoral, and juridical arguments in support of this position. If one starts with the assumption that between the personal dimension and the institutional dimension of marriage there is a tension but not a hiatus or opposition, it would be difficult to construct convincing reasons in favor of the legitimacy of forms of marriage preceding or imitating marriage properly so called, whatever pastoral directives the Church might be able to conceive in order to meet concrete needs.

d. Objections Against the Indissolubility of Marriage

In our day, the Church must confront the fact that, in almost every country in the world, the number of divorces – even in Catholic marriages – has risen rapidly. On the doctrinal plane and on that of pastoral practice the Orthodox and Protestant churches treat the problem of divorce and remarriage with less severity than the Roman Catholic Church. The latter appears today as the sole bulwark of the indissolubility of marriage. It maintains that by virtue of its divine institution matrimonial consent is irrevocable and therefore gives rise – precisely in the personalist conception of marriage – to a permanent bond of fidelity which, when the marriage is sacramental, cannot be broken by the partners (intrinsic indissolubility) nor dissolved by any authority in this world (extrinsic indissolubility).

On the other hand, one cannot lose sight of the fact that in many respects marriage is today more vulnerable and more fragile than formerly, when it was fully integrated into the extended family, a more closed society, and was protected by this collectivity. The conviction that in every circumstance marriage must be maintained and that one can, at most, allow separation from bed and board tends to be much weaker, even among Catholics.

A good number of objections against the doctrine and discipline of the Church recognize that the Church is bound by the radical demands of Jesus. Therefore, critics abstain from asking for a modification of the ecclesial doctrine on the absolute indissolubility of marriage; rather, they want a change in practice. In their minds, an ecclesial "economy" would have to admit the divorced and remarried to the sacraments, after an extensive examination of the case and without recognition of the second civil marriage. This raises the question: would not such authorization lead to a pure and simple toleration of the marriage of divorced persons? Other authors introduce a distinction between the recognition of such a union after divorce and the toleration of it by the way of pardon, when the second marriage is civilly valid and when, by reason of new responsibilities, the situation has become irreversible.[86]

According to current discipline, the Church in fact tolerates such a common life but requires that the parties live as brother and sister. Does the Church conceive this new life together as a pure cohabitation or as a community of life from which only sexual relations are excluded? Starting from a personalist conception of this community of life, many authors see in the prohibition of sexual relations an unbearable demand. They consider the community a real marriage, even if not ecclesial or sacramental.

Others go still further by affirming that the change they recommend on the level of pastoral practices (admission of the divorced and remarried to the sacraments) necessarily implies a change in the doctrine of absolute indissolubility, and that the Church must approve such a change.[87] For a good number of them, this change involves expanding grounds for dissolution. Such grounds would include not only physical death but also moral death, which destroys the marriage. Once this is recognized by the Church, a second union could be contracted, even as a sacramental marriage.[88]

These questions and requests show that today, in theology as on the practical level, there reigns a great uncertainty and people seek broad solutions. Thus there is in theology and in pastoral practice a process that one wishes to see continued in an analogous way throughout the history of the Church and not to be terminated at the present time. The Church still claims the right to look again at scripture and its own teaching in the light of the faith of the time. In its current teaching, the Church does not simply go back over the teachings of scripture. This is evident, for example, in that which concerns the doctrine of the indissolubility of sacramental marriage, the broadening of the Pauline and Petrine privileges, and the distinction between indissoluble sacramental marriage and natural marriage susceptible to dissolution.[89] Raising the question of the indissolubility of marriage is a legitimate pursuit of a deeper interpretation, according to some authors. This process asserts that the Church, in the exercise of its doctrinal and pastoral responsibility, is elaborating doctrinal and pastoral decisions.

e. Objections Against Current Ecclesiastical Law

It has become commonplace to assert that current matrimonial law can no longer adequately respond to the realities and requirements of the present day. A fundamental reform is demanded, not just a reordering of the legislation. The critics of the legalization of the institution of marriage, of the Church's claim to exclusive authority in this matter, of the Church's discipline and procedure in this matter, as well as of many other current norms are still very insistent in calling for new solutions and aids. Until now, the Church has responded in two ways: first, it has revised some particular norms and the body of norms governing certain areas (*e.g.*, the law relative to mixed marriages); and second, it has named a commission for a revision of all canon law, including marriage law.

One cannot escape the difficulties that exist with respect to marriage:

1) in determining the relationship between the institution and the personal bond;

2) in the interpretation of the biblical prohibition of divorce (as a moral directive, as a precept imposing a direction, as a precept requiring execution, as a law) and its concretization from the primitive Church until now;

3) in determining the moral and juridical competence of the Church with regard to marriage as community of persons and as institution.

In connection with these theological problems some social and psychological difficulties are encountered:

1) regarding objective and subjective factors which in the post-industrial era imperil marriage and render it more fragile (e.g., decreasing involvement in the family and society; the breaking up and mobility of the family; the influence of environment and personal failure);

2) in ascertaining the personal capacity to contract marriage. Psychological aptitude and the fixing of a minimum age (sixteen for the husband, fourteen for the wife) tell us nothing about personal capacity;

3) with respect to the divergence between juridical categories and personal categories concerning the consummation of marriage. A single *copula perfecta* renders marriage juridically valid in the full sense. It does not give assurance as to personal consummation;

4) from the fact that conviction concerning the indissolubility of marriage has weakened. The high proportion of divorces precisely among prematurely concluded marriages makes one think that many young persons contract a sort of trial marriage and that in case of failure they no longer hold themselves bound but move on to a new union;

5) from the fact that the will to contract marriage is affected by social constraints and also, more and more, by psychological deficiencies (psychopathologies, neuroses, psychoses);

A revision of canon law cannot neglect a clarification of all these points. The urgent tasks today are, it seems:

1) anthropological, theological, and sociological justification of the relationship between the personal dimension of marriage and its institutional and juridical dimension – a relationship which rightly expresses a tension but not an opposition;

2) renewed reflection on the juridical competence of the Church in matrimonial matters, including its justification, its nature, and the scope of its purpose. Which of these aspects must submit to inquiries based on anthropology and on "the rule of faith"?

3) deepened investigation of the biblical and theological foundations of the indissolubility of marriage and of pastoral assistance for couples who are the victims of a failed union. In this area the teaching of Jesus forbids laxity. The Church must do its best to affirm and protect marriage. But the Church must also show itself to be minister of the merciful love of the Lord.

Conclusion

These reflections do not end in proposals for concrete solutions. Nor do they pretend to embrace completely the entire complex of questions concerning the relationship between "marriage as personal community of love and of life" and "marriage as institution." They simply intend to point out a few fundamental problems of which further clarification is rendered necessary by current debates in the Church on marriage.

CHAPTER 3

The Sacramentality of Christian Marriage:

The Bond between Baptism, Faith, and Marriage

by Karl Lehmann

A host of problems must be addressed when we undertake to situate Christian marriage within the framework of ecclesiology and sacramental theology.[1] Here we shall examine two of these problems.

The first relates to scriptural exegesis and biblical theology. It addresses the foundations of the ecclesial and sacramental dimensions of Christian marriage and seeks to ascertain what consequences are to be drawn in elaborating a systematic theology of marriage.

The second problem explores which relations are to be posited between what has been ascertained concerning Christian marriage, with baptism as the constitutive element for a Christian marriage. We hope that, in this way, we can throw some light on the connections among baptism, faith, intention, and conjugal commitment.

1. THE SACRAMENTALITY OF CATHOLIC MARRIAGE

A note on method is required at the outset. As we explore the foundations of marriage at the level of ecclesiology and sacramental theology, it is well not to start from a general and classic notion of sacrament (example: external sign instituted by Jesus Christ, signifying and effecting an inner grace) and procede to show how this notion might apply to the sacrament of marriage. Likewise, it would be methodologically inappropriate to approach the sacramentality of marriage from the vantage point of its specific grace of state and to move from there to further statements. If we are to make a theologically valid statement, we must begin by interrogating the New Testament and refrain from defining the particular case of Christian marriage according to sacramental theology in general. As we adopt this approach, we are of course aware that, here as elsewhere, the Church is the framework within which the interpretation and explication of Scripture must take place.

Specific exegetical issues need not be discussed in detail. We seek rather a synthesis that would pave the way to systematics. The basic witness of the synoptic gospels in this matter is as follows: in his preaching, Jesus rejected juridical stipulations which had taken shape in Israel in the course of its history. Jesus appealed to the original will of the creator against the practice of divorce, which the Old Testament and Judaism admitted. Thus the novelty of Jesus' position consists in the fact that he resisted the downgrading of God's will that had occurred in history. He proclaimed God's unconditional summons and the radical and all-encompassing quality inherent in that summons. We thus perceive the inner contradiction which mars Jewish casuistics: the historical forms of the law and the various interpretations of it bespeak a flight from what God demanded at the beginning.

In Jesus' bold reaffirmation of the original order of creation we may further isolate two elements:

1) Only the disciple who adheres to Jesus by faith, wills to follow him, and rests his hope in him can be sufficiently freed from stubbornness of the heart and return to the authentic origins.

2) The justification that comes to us from Christ is present here by implication in this sense: indirectly, justification carries the mark of the Christ who, above and beyond the stipulations of the law, delivered humankind from stubbornness of the heart and enabled it to do what God willed at the beginning. (See in particular Mk 10:1–11; Mt 19:1–12).

After the paschal event the christological dimension in the conception of marriage comes openly to light: elements appear in that notion which are explicitly christological. As far as the earliest Church is concerned, the crucial text is 1 Corinthians 7:39, where Paul recommends that marriage be contracted "in the Lord." This expression may at first seem rather insignificant, yet it is important, as important here as in its other contexts throughtout the Pauline writings. (See the justification of the apostolic ministry or ministries in 1 Thes 5:12; Rom 16:2; 1 Cor 15:38.) The expression shows that Christian marriage is not merely a "worldly affair." For "the new man in Jesus Christ" marriage takes on a new dimension. Thus it is no accident that, in the New Testament, marriage and the family appear as the privileged place where Christian values are to be safeguarded. We can begin to surface implications that will make a difference in a systematic theology of marriage: nature and grace, creation and covenant, are not two orders merely juxtaposed one to the other. They entail each other. Or, to say it differently, the reality of redemption which the new covenant brings forth makes it possible for marriage to recover a genuine conformity with the order of creation. Thus marriage takes the fullness of its normative character from the history of salvation. This is why marriage does not appear in the New Testament as a "natural phenomenon." It is always thought of within the historical perspective of the covenant, which makes it possible for marriage to achieve conformity with the will of the creator.

It is in this context that Ephesians 5:21–32 takes on its true meaning and import.[2] Especially because of verse 32, this text was later interpreted as containing a reference to the sacramentality of Christian marriage: "This mystery (μυστήριον–*sacramentum*) has many implications; but I am saying it applies to Christ and the Church" (JB). The Greek term μυστήριον had been rendered as *sacramentum* in the Vulgate. This translation invited in turn an interpretation directly contingent on the notion of sacrament. From an exegetical point of view,[3] it is obvious enough that we are not entitled to read into the word μυστήριον the technical concept of sacrament which emerges only later. But particular exegetical questions aside, we are still entitled to so understand the text as to see expressed in it the relation that obtains between Christ and the Church. The μυστήριον is above all the eternal design of salvation, conceived by God, historically carried out by Jesus Christ, and made present by the Church. Μυστήριον means, then, the fundamental framework upon which Christian salvation is grounded. Marriage is incorporated into this all-encompassing reality of salvation.[4] Even if μυστήριον does not primarily refer to marriage, the meaning of marriage is clarified decisively by the relation that exists between Christ and the Church. Marriage becomes the "image of a loftier covenant of love: the gift which a man makes of his own self to his wife becomes the image of the gift which Christ makes of his life, while the gift the wife makes of herself to her husband becomes the image of how the Church relates to Christ."[5]

In its own way, then, marriage is a means by which the eternal love of God, revealed in Jesus Christ, achieves presence in the world. More than an extrinsic similarity exists between the love that unites two human beings and the union of Christ with his Church. The words *image* and *comparison* often used in this connection can be ambiguous and create problems, for they may indeed denote a merely extrinsic relation. What we see in the covenant of marriage actualizes the relation that binds Christ to the Church in the history of salvation. Rahner speaks of "a relationship between the two unities such that they condition one another: the former exists *precisely because* the latter exists. Their mutual relationship of similarity is not subsequent to the two but is a genuine relationship of participation since the unity between Christ and the Church is the ultimate cause and origin of the unity of marriage."[6]

Marriage is a sharing in the fundamental sacrament of Christ and the Church. To use the language of M. J. Scheeben, it is an articulation of the great mystery of Christ and the Church.[7] For God's love and fidelity, irretrievably offered in Christ and actualized in the Church, are not merely signified by the union of man and woman. This union is the real symbol that makes God's love and fidelity present in the world. That which constitutes the mystery of the Church the union of Christ with his people – is realized in the community of life that obtains between husband and wife. Our understanding of the word μυστήριον must, therefore, precede the distinction – entirely correct, to be sure – between the ecclesiological and the sacramental dimension of marriage. Fundamentally, the term μυστήριον does not refer only to the formal content of the concept of sacrament in general. It refers to the very reality of salvation in its entirety, the reality within which Christian marriage is located, from which it emerges, and which it also brings to expression. We know that the Council of Trent itself did not infer the sacramental character of marriage only from Ephesians 5:32. The council sees in this text an indication of, a suggestion of, or an allusion to sacramentality (*quod Paulus Apostolus innuit*). Contemporary exegesis likewise accents only indirectly the *sacramentality* of marriage in the strict sense, yet it does offer an ecclesiological and sacramental context of far greater richness because it has achieved a deeper understanding of this sacramentality. If we were to consider this text in isolation, we would fail to recognize the much richer hermeneutical possibilities it offers.

2. THE FUNDAMENTAL RELATIONS BETWEEN THE INDISSOLUBILITY AND THE SACRAMENTALITY OF MARRIAGE

The sacramentality of marriage is not to be established merely by appealing to a few isolated texts from the Bible. We can construct a convincing justification of sacramentality by means of a carefully articulated argument that shows its appropriateness. This applies in particular to the unity and indissolubility which are characteristic attributes of marriage.

When, for example, Ephesians 5:21ff. focuses attention only on the unity between husband and wife, it does not dwell on all the attributes that mark the relationship between Christ and the Church.[8] "Nothing prevents us from also including in this comparison the element of irrevocable fidelity to the covenant. We thus ground conjugal fidelity by comparing it with fidelity to Christ."[9] In order to recast this argument in a more cogent form, we may follow H. Volk, who has outlined it succinctly and in a way which, I believe, remains fundamentally valid.

> The total surrender of the self which is to be realized in marriage implies a relationship to God as to its ground and goal. Christ has inserted the whole reality which marriage is into the Christian order. By virtue of baptism, the being of a Christian has a sacramental character impressed upon it. There is here a relationship that differs from all other interpersonal relations. When signs are given which represent the realities of grace, and belong fundamentally to Christian and ecclesial life, it is not possible that these signs should be, in the new covenant, nothing more than empty and depleted symbols of grace. . . . From a biblical perspective, every community of Christians united in Christ implies an actualization of Christ's presence, and therefore an actualization of the Church (Mt 18:20). This can be applied in a special way to marriage, which is a total community in Christ, albeit the smallest of them all. These presuppositions permit us also to understand historically both the fact that marriage was recognized to be a sacrament, and the fact of its institution. Christ instituted this sacrament

> . . . by establishing the new covenant as the eternal sign of victorious grace. He thus lent a sacramental efficacy to this sign that, from the beginning, represents and brings to fruition the graced unity between Christ and the Church.[10]

This may be a sufficient indication of how, in connection with the main scriptural texts, an argument emerges which makes a case for the appropriateness of the sacramentality of marriage.[11]

When we seek to ground the unity and indissolubility of marriage on its sacramental structure, we need to refer first to the unbreakable unity between Jesus Christ and the Church, a unity which is signified and embodied in marriage.[12] In any case, indissolubility is not to be accounted for as if it were an exigency imposed upon marriage from outside marriage itself. It cannot be understood as a legal obligation which sets aside personal love. The unique character of Jesus Christ and of the Church, and the exclusiveness that marks the relationship between them ultimately bespeak an irrevocable fidelity. Volk appeals also to the person's wholeness and to marriage in its quality as a community of persons.

According to Volk, the wholeness of the human person, as well as the personal community of marriage, can provide the foundation for conjugal fidelity.

> Since to be a person is to be in charge of oneself, personhood embraces the whole of the human being in its uniqueness and difference from all others. This wholeness, however, becomes possible and actual only in a face-to-face encounter with other persons. But every time persons encounter each other, a relationship to God is also implied as ground and condition for the possibility of the encounter itself. Hence love, in its quality as total surrender of the self to another, always includes God as its presupposition, for only because of God is total surrender inwardly necessary and even possible at all. Apart from God, a person runs the risk of suffering the loss of his own self. God restores marriage to its pristine condition, not only by sharpening the ethical demands to which it must submit but also by enhancing the wholeness of the person through victory over sin. Because of that victory, the person now has the possibility of being in charge of himself in a freedom restored by

> grace. If one does not consider the person in his totality, the state of marriage could not be sacramentally assumed into the relationship between Christ and the Church.[13]

What has just been said about total surrender on the part of the person[14] can be explicated further through a phenomenological analysis of fidelity among humans, at least in its quality as postulate. The free yes which is expressed in the consent given and received before God and the community is an unconditional promise that is unaffected by the passing of time. This look at things from below, this uncomplicated analysis of the promise of fidelity has some relevance since, more than any other sacrament, marriage is bound up with a natural reality. After all, marriage as sacrament is not something located to one side of marriage as a real-life reality. It is also in this sense that we should understand the well-known statement of Schlier: "In earthly marriage the relationship of Christ to the Church comes to fruition."[15]

The grace of the sacrament relates to marriage as a total and permanent union of persons. Grace takes it into the mystery of salvation, together with everything which its reality entails. The particular character of this sacrament also exemplifies in a special way the concept of grace. For grace is always God's covenant with human beings, a covenant which involves a close union with him, mysterious and undeserved. Sacramentality means that the reality of marriage is taken up into the mystery of salvation–Christ in relation to the Church. This is why the love that marks this relation between Christ and the Church becomes a norm and the inner form of marriage itself.

"Just as Christ loved the Church and sacrificed himself for her," (Eph 5:25; JB) so, too, husbands and wives must love each other in Jesus Christ. Marriage participates then in the manifestation in history of God's unmerited and unconditional commitment which establishes the Church as fundamental sacrament.

> When a marriage takes place between baptized people in the Church it constitutes an element in the Church's role as basic sacrament, so that the parties actively share in and contribute to the Church's role as basic sacrament, for both give manifest expression to the unifying love of the grace of God, and a marriage of this kind between them achieves this precisely as an element in the social unity of the Church herself. Now because of this the marriage as an

> event of grace gives rise to a sacramental event of grace in which this sign actively contributes to the irrevocable manifestation of God's pledge of grace to mankind, that pledge which is constantly in force and of which God himself never repents. And this manifestation is nothing else than the Church herself.[16]

Naturally, God's grace in the sacrament of marriage does not operate unless the spouses cooperate with it. Even in a sacramental marriage, God's grace may be crippled by unfaith and lack of love between husband and wife. And yet the basic statement remains true: in the act of instituting marriage, God promised his grace and attached it to marriage when contracted by baptized Christians. This he has done irrevocably. There is, however, one more step that must be taken:

> . . . the sign function of a particular marriage can sinfully be degraded into a lie when that which it is intended to manifest and to render present is not present in itself, namely the love that is grace-given and unifying. In the Church as a whole the intrinsic connection between sign and signified reality can no longer radically be destroyed because of the eschatological victory of grace in Christ. Nevertheless the basic parallelism between marriage and the Church continues to exist. The following proposition applies just as much to the Church as it does to marriage: she is the sign, at the palpable level of historical and social human life, of the fact that the love which is made effective and victorious throughout the whole of humanity is precisely the love of God for us and of us for God, the love which comprehends and unifies all so long as no one sinfully denies it.[17]

This is why, no matter which anthropological indications might converge to suggest the sacramentality of marriage, in the last analysis it is only if we start with the irrevocable fidelity of Christ to the Church that we bring this sacramentality fully to light. It is precisely because covenant and grace are the ultimate foundation of Christian marriage and the condition for the possibilty of its total realization that this marriage, taken up as it is into the reality of salvation in Jesus Christ, is placed under the sign of the cross and resurrection.

Sacramentality may well have the ring of an abstract theological formula, yet it bespeaks something that proves decisive for marriage as lived in a Christian way. It is only here that a spirituality of marriage can discover its foundations. The sacrament of marriage, just like the other sacraments, exists only within the mystery of God's forgiveness and justification through grace. Because marriage is placed under the sign of the cross, it always thrives on forgiveness, on undeserved giving, and on a love which lets itself be crucified and whose determination to give itself cannot be overcome. The hours of suffering, mutual dissatisfaction, doubts in the presence of the indifference of the other, and the need to be forever forgiving: all these belong to the reality of sacramental marriage. Thus Christian marriage does not refrain from talking things over when this becomes indispensable; it does not withdraw from suffering when suffering cannot be avoided; it is not discouraged by rejection. The yes which constitutes marriage is always surpassed by God's own and sturdier yes. This is a God who did not succumb to the scandal of his own death. On the contrary, out of death he brought forth new life. It is only through the folly of a total gift that God delivered the world from "stubbornness of the heart."

In light of the preceding remarks, we may note that the sacramentality of marriage is not restricted to the moment in which it is contracted. Of course, we do not intend to relativize that moment; but, precisely because marriage is a permanent sacrament, its sacramentality affects it as it is in real life, and even sustains that reality.[18] This uncomplicated insight allows us to discover the strength of the grace promised by God, a grace which makes it possible to overcome the temptation to lapse into an outlook purely human, and so give up life in community.

No doubt the actualization of sacramental marriage depends entirely on the free will of the spouses. However, there are other realities which also condition the quality of the sacrament. The spouses do not act merely as private persons, but as members of the Body of Christ. In the act which constitutes marriage they are joined by Christ, the Head of the Body, and by the Church, the true Body of Christ. These constitutive elements of marriage are closely connected to each other, even if we have not analyzed them with equal depth under the precise aspect of their connectedness.

We have referred from the outset to the connection between the indissolubility and the sacramentality of marriage. It now appears with greater clarity that the indissolubility and sacramentality of marriage constitute a circle. They stand related one to the other in reciprocal causality, in the sense that indissolubility is the foundation which allows us to recognize the sacramentality of marriage, while the sacramentality of marriage constitutes the intrinsic foundation of its indissolubility.[19] The sacramentality of marriage encompasses the natural reasons which converge to ground its indissolubility. The result is that every marriage is indissoluble. However, the indissolubility of Christian marriage is of a special kind, because in their deepest foundation Christian marriages are signs and symbols of the definitive covenant that unites Jesus Christ to his Church.

Because marriage is a sacrament, indissolubility is a duty for Christian spouses. Here we discover the reason why the Church is pastorally solicitous toward spouses. Together with the spouses themselves, the Church is obliged to guarantee and shelter the sign of the covenant in marriage. Ultimately, this is the basis, together with the pastoral responsibility of the Church, for the juridical competence which allows the Church to issue legislation relative to marriage.

3. THE BOND BETWEEN FAITH, BAPTISM AND THE SACRAMENT OF MARRIAGE

Before examining the other repercussions of the sacramentality of marriage on the internal structure of the indissolubility of the same, we need to explore the connection between baptism and the act which is constitutive of marriage. As noted in the CIC, canon 1012, par. 1, Jesus Christ raised the marriage contracted by baptized persons to the dignity of a sacrament (see also DS 860; 1327). In paragraph 2, canon 1012 announces this doctrine and this consequence: no marriage between baptized persons is valid unless it be also a sacrament. Consent and sacrament coincide in reality and in time. The real identity between the human contract and the sacrament (GS 48) is the object of another study in this book.[20]

In the last few years, these theological assertions have been resisted in several ways, especially on the grounds of pastoral considerations. An encroaching secularization has made a considerable change in the religious consciousness of many Christians. Because their faith is now weak or entirely lost, they are no longer in a position to contract a valid Christian marriage in the customary way, unless new pastoral initiatives be brought to bear upon them. Think, for example, of people who come and request a church wedding without being convinced that the Christian conception of marriage is true. There are also people who refuse to make any concession in this regard, and prefer to give up what looks to them to be nothing more than a conventional ceremony. They choose to omit the religious wedding; a civil wedding will do as far as they are concerned. Many theologians have been induced by these circumstances to devise a solution which, in their opinion, confers a Christian value on the civil marriage by dispensing from the canonical form.[21] It is not part of the task assigned to me to assess the value of the various suggested pastoral solutions. But, obviously, the seriousness of the questions at issue here cannot be ignored. It is important to ascertain how theology ought to face them.

We must be on guard here against a twofold temptation. Some might rest content with a very vague notion of sacrament, a notion according to which a sacrament is just something holy.[22] Others might invoke some sort of automatism: since the bride and the groom have been baptized, their marriage must be sacramental. But to have been baptized and to belong to the Church cannot be enough, if this membership means something only extrinsic and circumstantial. The religious structure of marriage must be intrinsically affected by baptism.

Nowadays the connection between sacrament and baptism is a problem that can no longer be handled in the abstract. It is situated within a concrete framework, namely, the problem of baptized persons who have no faith. Many theologians ask themselves: is the mere fact of having been baptized sufficient for a Christian marriage?[23] The question remains perplexing, even if the sacramentality of marriage is not contingent on the depth of the spouses' faith, or the profundity of their love. Many believe that to posit an automatic connection between baptism and marriage as sacrament is out of the question. Can we honestly entertain the presumption that every baptized person is also a believer? Some have suggested for these baptized persons who have no faith a religious nonsacramental celebration.[24] Others favor a celebration of a catechumenal and gradual type, that is, one that would advance progressively by stages, these stages not being preparations for marriage but phases within marriage itself.[25]

In the limited compass of this report, it is not possible to examine all these views. But I believe that some essential notions can be mentioned.

1) With regard to the sacramentality of marriage, the fundamental given is the unity between the order of creation and the order of redemption. After all, it is because of the unity between these two orders that, in marriage, contract is inseparable from sacrament.[26] If we subscribe to the contract–sacrament identity, we must go on to maintain that the consent of the spouses, which is constitutive of marriage, is at the same time the sacramental sign in marriage as sacrament. If, on the contrary, we subscribe to the basic conception that sacrament and contract are to some extent separable, consequences follow as to how nature relates to grace, and creation to covenant.

2) Without a doubt, the sacrament–contract identity cannot be called into question without affecting the foundations on which the sacramentality of marriage rests. The objection that the identity position entails an automatism or a magic notion of sacrament can indeed apply to certain practices, but from the standpoint of dogmatics the objection certainly betrays a misunderstanding, although one widely spread.

It is important not to confuse the different perspectives and dimensions operative in theological reflection. Certainly the good dispositions of the subject are not the cause that make the sacraments effective. Sacraments do not effect grace simply through the faith of recipients (DS 1608).

This does not mean, however, that sacramental life is possible in the absence of faith. As far as the sacrament of marriage is concerned, we must definitely take into account the distinction between the validity and the fruitfulness of sacraments. Faith is a necessary condition for the fruitful reception of a sacrament, but it does not follow that a sacrament validly received is necessarily fruitful. The concept of *opus operatum* inevitably comes into play. This concept does not mean that grace is conferred automatically but that the initiative and the efficaciousness in the sacramental bestowal of grace are traceable to Jesus Christ. This formula never means that a real bestowal of grace can take place apart from the faith or unfaith of the person involved. Thus the phrase *opus operatum* means that since the sacraments are efficacious instruments of Christ, their value and efficacy are objectively guaranteed; in this sense, they are not contingent on the faith of the person concerned (*opus operantis*). But if we consider the whole manner in which the sacraments effect salvation, we must say that the *opus operatum* is, in the manner already indicated, the reason for an *opus operantis*. Hence, to the extent to which the sacrament fruitfully received *also* signifies the faith of the recipient, the *opus operatum* coincides existentially with the *opus operantis*.[27]

With regard to marriage, we need to distinguish carefully the objective reality which results from the administration of the sacrament as such (*opus operatum*) from the fruits of grace, which presuppose a proper disposition on the part of the subject (*opus operantis*). These two realities differ. True, the faith of the subject is a means of salvation in the reception of the sacraments; nevertheless, grace is effected by the instrumental action of the sacrament.

However, a person may receive a sacrament fictively and not disavow the fiction. The phrase *non ponere obicem* (not to interpose an obstacle) is chiefly intended to refer in negative language to the absence of any fiction both in the performance of the sacramental sign on the part of Christ and in the grace of salvation offered in that sign. In this deliberately receptive attitude we should not see some kind of neutrality yielding to the automatic force of a sacrament, but rather a positive passivity of faith which includes the formal will of letting the act of God come to fruition.[28]

3) There is no reason why we should not rediscover in the phenomenon of marriage, as we do elsewhere, the classic principles of sacramental theology, as long as we understand these correctly. From a dogmatic and juridical point of view we begin normatively with baptism in its quality as social foundation of faith in the Church. The internal attitude of any baptized person with regard to this faith is certainly important, yet it cannot be the sole crucial element when it comes to the relation between baptism and marriage. Systematic theology spells out the basic conditions of sacramentality from different perspectives (subject, minister, God, Church and grace). In the pastoral ministry we must, of course, do what we can to make sure that the valid reception of a sacrament also be fruitful. But it makes no sense at all to try to achieve this goal by disrupting the pivotal articulations in the relationship between faith and sacrament.

4) It is imperative to attend also to the question of the intention of those who receive the sacrament of marriage. (As first indication in this regard, see DS 794; 1262; 1313; 1611.) Intention bears a direct relation to the validity of the sacramental act. (See CIC, canons 752 and 754). The question becomes "technical" when we try to decide how conscious a sacramental act must be in order to be also a truly human act (*actus humanus*). If one tries to spell out the commitment and the

express intention, the inclination toward minimalism will of course prevail. In the case of marriage, this is the way we must understand the doctrine and practice of the Church. We are told that the spouses are not required to have an actual intention. An habitual intention, be it implicit[29] or virtually explicit will suffice.[30] This kind of intention exists unless it be directly excluded by a positive act of the will. Concretely, this means that as the spouses contract marriage they are not required to intend to administer and receive a sacrament of the Church, nor to believe in the sacramentality of marriage. It is enough if they will to marry as Christians do. This will to marry includes the intention of receiving the sacrament of marriage, unless this intention be explicitly disavowed.[31]

This minimalistic description of the required intention obviously represents a limit that may not be crossed over if the celebration of marriage is to achieve the quality of a human act. If we hold to this strict and technical interpretation of intention, we need be careful when we bring up the problem of the personal faith of the persons involved. We must always be aware that the basic theological position already mentioned (sacraments achieve their effect *ex opere operato*) may pave the way to a dangerous practice that could lead to automatic sacramentalism. Unless each of the elements involved (for example, baptism, faith, intention, sacrament, etc.) be looked upon together as components of a single whole, we would inevitably lapse into ludicrous notions which, when all is said and done, are theologically indefensible.[32]

At one time it could be reasonably assumed that Christians, living as they did in a relatively homogeneous society, would harbor at least a minimal disposition to believe. It was easier then to understand the required intention in the limited sense mentioned above.

Nowadays this assumption is not valid. And so it is no longer easy to advocate a strictly limited conception of the intention required for a complex act which is premised on faith. Is today's theologian still entitled to stand by this technical and limited concept of intention?

Man's intention and his faith are still distinct realities, to be sure, but they are nevertheless closely connected. We cannot simply place one alongside the other. As a rule, intention stems from faith. This is the sense in which we must understand what is called the *general intention* (*intentio generalis*). It is the act by which one relates to the intention of the Church and has "the intention of doing what the Church does" (*intentio faciendi quod faciunt Christus et ecclesia*).[33] However, we must ask whether, within this global intention and above and beyond it, the person's own faith need not be taken into account. It is all the more urgent to raise this question explicitly about a sacrament received without faith by baptized persons who have no faith.

In this context, we must maintain that a trace of faith[34] is necessary, not only for the fruitful reception of a sacrament, but also for the validity of that reception. Likewise, we would subscribe to the view of Tillard,[35] which, by the way, mirrors the opinion of St. Thomas Aquinas. He writes: "As far as I can see, the intention of the recipient must have at least this minimal reference to salvation if it is to make the rite a valid sacrament . . . . Without this minimal reference to salvation, I doubt that a real sacramental intention exists and that the rite is validly executed for the recipient." In this view, the relation between intention and faith certainly gains greater depth.[36]

Of course, pastoral problems emerge in this connection,[37] and they must be resolved. However, we cannot resolve them by answering the question about intention and its relation to faith in a way different from the one just articulated. It is especially important that we transcend the formal and juridical context within which the connection between intention and faith is sometimes discussed.

The new rules for the celebration of marriage (OCM[38]), issued in 1972, already allude to this pastoral situation when they say: "Pastors are exhorted to nourish the faith of those about to be married. The sacrament of marriage presupposes faith and demands it." (*Imprimis pastores foveant nutriantque fidem nupturientium; Sacramentum Matrimonii fidem supponit atque postulat.*)[39]

5) The pastoral difficulties are undeniable, but we should guard against the illusion that they can be resolved by introducing a basic change in the manner of conceiving the constitutive element of the sacrament of marriage. The pastoral solution can only consist in an increased effort on the part of the Church. Through her preaching, especially at the time when bride and groom prepare for marriage, and within the wedding itself, the Church should strive to elicit a deeper understanding of the sacrament of marriage.[40] The remarks that preface the new rules for the celebration of marriage (OCMP[41]) most clearly stress that, in this area, a renewed catechesis and preaching are needed.

The following solution has been recently suggested. The bride and the groom ask for a church wedding, but they do not fulfil the minimal conditions required. In extreme cases, they would be invited to postpone the wedding. I do not intend to pass a definitive judgment on this position. However, it seems to me that the argument drawn from the parallel case of "delayed baptism" is not to be trusted. Compare the structure of the sacrament of marriage and the situation of the spouses to the case of baptism and you will find a difference. When adult Christians request the sacrament of marriage, that request ought to be taken seriously. We must assume that they have given adequate thought to the matter. The burden of proof (*onus probandi*) rests upon the one who doubts the seriousness of their request. Subjecting this request to rigorous scrutiny is likely to unleash serious tensions on the spot. In any case, an anthropological and pastoral question arises here: whether adults who want a Christian marriage are to be allowed the benefit of the doubt to the point of assuming that their request is seriously meant unless there be conclusive evidence that it is not. Should we not say that, in this situation, it is their natural right to marry that would have to be called in question?

What is certain is that pastoral renewal cannot be secured by turning upside down the foundations of the classic teaching on marriage. What is imperative is a deeper kind of reflection on the theological, juridical, and pastoral significance of what is known as the premarital investigation.[42]

6) The preceding remarks need to be complemented for they do not explore deeply enough the connection between faith, baptism, and the sacrament of marriage. We can be fairly sure that a genuine in-depth renewal is out of the question unless we provide a lucid analysis of how marriage is intrinsically articulated and united with the faith and baptism that constitute the being of a Christian.[43]

Through baptism, a person is incorporated into the Church of Jesus Christ. It will not do to understand this incorporation merely in terms of a moral obligation toward Jesus Christ. It is above all an ontological and existential incorporation into the Body of Christ. In consequence, two baptized persons who contract marriage are not entitled to decide on their own what their union is to mean and what it is to be. As they venture into a life together, they lean on Jesus Christ. He himself intervenes decisively in their marriage. Obviously, these remarks are not convincing unless one takes into account the original structure of baptism. Unfortunately, this structure is sometimes misconstrued by a ritualization of the sacrament, as well as by a doctrinalization of the word, and an externalizing perception which makes of baptism nothing more than a juridical sign of incorporation into the Church. The structure of baptism must be rediscovered precisely at those crucial points where gesture meets cult, and the profession of faith intersects with incorporation into the Church.[44] When this connection between baptism, faith, and Church is more clearly perceived, we can also better appreciate the traditional doctrine according to which a marriage between baptized persons who genuinely profess their faith and take it seriously in their daily lives constitutes a sacrament.

7) The classic conception of how the sacraments are related to one another is not premised on an inconsequential and arbitrary way of collecting the sacraments into a group. Rather, this conception involves a difference among the levels where the sacraments are located and a hierarchy based on the significance proper to each.[45] Thus baptism does not, in and by itself, suffice to insure that a person will belong to the Body in a manner which is complete, living, and active in every respect. There are, it seems, many degrees of belonging to the Church. We can infer this, for example, from the fact that the reality of baptism administered in the various churches and ecclesial Christian communities is being acknowledged, and yet this acknowledgment does not entail a recognition of the church in question and does not make reciprocal admission to the Eucharist possible. It follows that what matters most is for us to unfold the spiritual and sacramental dynamic of baptism, looked upon both as a gift received and a task to complete. Thus we perceive how baptism impinges on the act by which marriage is constituted, just as we ought to perceive the connection between Christian marrriage, confirmation, penance, and the Eucharist. Not without reason Thomas Aquinas declares that baptism marks the beginning of the spiritual life and is the gate to the sacraments, without being their fulfillment.[46] Unless there is a renewal of the pastoral theology of baptism and of its spirituality, we cannot hope to resolve the difficulties we have mentioned earlier with regard to the theology of marriage and the praxis relative to it. It goes without saying that if marriage is taken to be a "permanent sacrament,"[47] as it rightly should, the dynamic and dialectic which are operative among the various sacraments will occupy an even more important place in doctrinal and pastoral theology.

8) Since Vatican II made explicit the conditions for belonging to the Church, the classic conception that posits the unity of contract and sacrament in the marriage of baptized persons has taken on new aspects. If there are various degrees of belonging to the Church,[48] it follows that the sacrament of baptism is, in every case and exclu-

sively, the foundation of this belonging, and that not all baptized persons bring this belonging to fruition in the same degree and with equal depth. The repercussions of this point on the discipline of marriage in the Church are not easily spelled out. A canonist believes he can discern these points of reference: "Thus, for example, we have reason to ask ourselves again questions about the sacramentality of marriage in cases in which the spouses have failed to further develop their membership in the Church."[49] It seems to me, all the same, that we are not entitled to infer dogmatic conclusions from this fact. Only pastoral measures are in order for the benefit of people who find themselves removed from the Church. An example of this is what is known as the "pastoral ministry of concentric circles."[50]

Certainly, a problem arises because the conceptual arsenal at our disposal does not have what it takes to express the complexity and the polymorphous quality that marks the way in which people belong to the Church in general and in particular how they belong at the moment when they get married. This being the case, we should perhaps mention and discuss some ideas which K. Rahner has suggested concerning the way in which grace and sacramental sign are connected in the sacrament of marriage. Rahner writes:

> Marriage does not become an event of grace only at that point at which it acquires the status of a "sacrament". On the contrary the event of grace in marriage becomes a sacramental event of grace as *opus operatum* in those cases where it takes place between two baptized individuals in the Church. The case here is the same as with the faith which justifies of itself even prior to baptism, and which then becomes *opus operatum* in baptism. Up to the present, if I am not mistaken, there has been a strange naiveté among theologians in their approach to marriage in that the distinction and the unity which is familiar to every theologian in the relationship between faith/baptism and between contrition/penance has not consciously been worked out and applied to marriage. In the two former cases the grace-given event of justification is initiated not merely at the moment when the sacrament as such is conferred, but already prior to this at the stage of faith and repentance.[51]

As far as I know, this position has not been truly discussed in the last few years, nor can we discuss it here. But at least this can be retained from it: the relation between a sacramental and a nonsacramental marriage and an entirely profane act (Proposition 3.4). We should compare that relation to the one which exists between the *opus operatum* and the *opus operantis*. The *opus operantis*, in its own way, can constitute an event of grace.[52]

The recognition of the fact that people can belong to the Church in various degrees could have consequences when it comes to assessing marriages contracted by non-Catholic Christians. We should not forget that Vatican II has recognized that separated churches and communities have an ecclesial significance, even though they are not in full communion with the Catholic Church. This is why the confessional status of the spouses can no longer be ignored when we assess the value, as sacramental signs of salvation, of marriages between baptized persons who do not belong to the Catholic Church. Some canonists have drawn conclusions from this: "The juridical discipline of the Church can no longer claim validity for all baptized persons. We should rather agree that the separated churches and ecclesial communities should formulate their own legislation for their own members. To the extent to which the community in question has the character of a church, this legislation defines what Christian life ought to be."[53] W. Aymans takes the position that the Catholic Church should no longer regard as sacramental the marriages of non-Catholic Christians, since we must allow for the fact that many ecclesial communities do not profess the sacramentality of marriage.[54] If this be granted, the scope of canon 1012, par. 2, of the CIC ought to be limited to marriages "between baptized Catholics" (*inter baptizatos Catholicos*). The human covenant which marriage is and the sacrament could be separated when non-Catholic Christians are involved who have no intention of administering or receiving a sacrament, even though they intend to contract a true marriage.

This position is not without value. It does not, however, escape objections which we may not pass over in silence. The position goes against the conviction that baptism entails an incorporation into the one Church of Jesus Christ. If so, can an ecclesial community prevent the existence of a sacrament of marriage if, unlike other sacraments, the constitutive element rests on the foundation of that one "yes" which is marital consent? Does the particular belief of an ecclesial community have the capacity to empty such a fact of its very substance and significance?[55]

These questions, it seems to me, are important enough to deserve consideration. However, it is not possible to resolve them completely and satisfactorily here.

9) The fact that the spouses are baptized is, then, as relevant to the sacramentality of marriage as the word which professes faith is to the whole complex of the other sacraments.[56] However, we should not draw from this the conclusion that the sacrament of marriage must be celebrated according to an ecclesial form or even that the official representative of the Church is the minister of this sacrament. Today, no doubt, the ecclesial celebration is an indispensable means of bringing home to the couple that marriage has the significance of a sacrament. Nor should we forget that, historically, the liturgy has been of great assistance in helping people recognize the sacramentality of marriage. Nevertheless given the unique character of this sacrament, and the most significant role the spouses play in the constitution of it, we should not exaggerate the importance of the qualified assistance rendered by the priest and equate it with the functions which the priest performs in other sacraments such as penance.[57] It is part of the spirituality of marriage that the role of the spouses is not to be curtailed and that their responsibility is to be enhanced. However, this structure must be correctly understood.

People speak of this matter in a way that may not be erroneous in itself, but could lead to erroneous conceptions. It is not quite exact to say that the spouses confer on each other the sacrament of marriage. To speak so is to abridge to some extent the strict dependence of the spouses on the action of Christ. The sacramental character of marriage is not at the disposal of the spouses. What the spouses intend is to receive from Jesus Christ the sanctification of their conjugal union. This is a particularly important consideration.[58] For sacramental marriage does not result from the sole will of the spouses or from that of the community; it depends rather on the sanctifying action of Jesus Christ. Because of baptism, the will of the spouses, who do not act merely in their own name and as private persons but voice their consent as members of the Body of Christ, is intrinsically determined by Jesus Christ. He does not face the spouses only as the Lord who gives orders,[59] but acts in and through them.[60] Only if we bear this in mind can we understand, in the last analysis, the indissolubility of sacramental marriage.

To a degree, these explanations also allow us to show why marriage between baptized persons, and it alone, is sacramental. For only baptized persons belong to Jesus Christ in a way which, under the veil of the sacrament, is truly efficacious. Hence their conjugal community rests upon their faith in Jesus. This is the reason why a close connection exists between baptism and marriage. One could show that this connection is a manifestation of the priesthood which all believers share and which enables them to perform a supernatural action (the sacramental character–*character sacramentale*). This is not, however, the place to prove this point.[61] We must always remind ourselves that marriage between baptized persons bears and must bear an authentic resemblance to the union which binds the Church to Jesus Christ. Naturally, this entails consequences for sacramental marriage: the spouses must love each other as that resemblance demands. Thus, the permanence of their union is for each of them both a right and a duty, and this forever.[62]

From this perspective, it is easy to understand how consistent it is to deny the quality of a sacrament to a marriage between a baptized and an unbaptized person. With good reason this is the position most contemporary writers take.[63] We can well understand that within the Church there cannot be various degrees or stages of sacramentality as far as marriage is concerned. This is certainly true of marriages between baptized Catholics. For the problematic involved, see above, 000, number 8. These explications throw light also on the fact that the Tribunal of the Rota declares null marriages contracted by people who deliberately intend to exclude sacramentality.

4. THE ABSOLUTE INDISSOLUBILITY OF SACRAMENTAL MARRIAGE: HAS THE CHURCH THE POWER TO DISSOLVE IT?

The aspect of the sacramentality of marriage now to be explored does not directly relate to the connection between baptism and marriage. We shall examine the question of the indissolubility of sacramental marriage.

A systematic and complete presentation of the matter requires that we recall at least one fundamental principle. Marriages which are regarded as absolutely indissoluble are those which are not merely contracted through consent but also physically consummated (*matrimonium ratum et consummatum*). No matter by what historical process this precision came to emerge,[64] it is only proper to recognize the profound significance of the fact that the Church did adopt this distinction. The consent itself requires that the community of life just established be also fully actualized. It would be shortsighted on our part to understand the biblical expression "to become one flesh" (Gn 2:24) as referring only to the conjugal union or to sexual intimacy in the strict sense.[65] This phrase refers above all to the act of entering the closest and most intimate sharing of life. It is cohabitation, as primary situation, that both lets sexual intimacy happen and also gives its integral meaning to it. (Note the primary sense of *co-habitatio* and *co-itus*). The bodily fulfillment of a community of life represents in itself a high point and a real symbol of this community. A phenomenology of the body likewise shows how conjugal consent is verified and sealed in sexual intimacy, and so comes to fruition. The very fact that the person is a whole requires this integration and realization. Of all the sacraments, marriage is the one which assumes most deeply and most decisively the reality of our humanness. This is why it is quite appropriate for the Church to hold that sacramental marriage achieves through sexual intercourse full reality.

However, it is not enough to attend to the anthropological dimension. We need add that it is in the sexual union (seen as fulfillment and integration of the new community of life) that the marriage of baptized persons can become a real symbol of the union of Christ with his Church. Because people tend to think of sexual intercourse as something vulgar, this notion is likely to be attacked and demeaned in spite of its loftiness, and yet there is truth in it all the same. As "mystical" analogy, marriage is an image of the unity that binds Jesus Christ to his Church. Just as Christ gives himself totally for his Church, so too the gift which the spouses make of themselves to each other comes to fruition in conjugal intimacy. This is why the concept of consummation (*consummatio*) cannot be understood to refer exclusively to the body.[66] Insofar as sexual intercourse represents the full realization of marriage, in the most concrete form possible, it takes on theological and juridical significance. It follows likewise that the indissolubility of marriage is rooted most deeply in the sacramentality of marriage between baptized persons. Christian marriage is not only a symbol of the irrescindible union between Jesus Christ and his Church; it also participates in this union precisely in its most intimate reality. This is why we are entitled to refer here to the concept of covenant.[67] From this perspective, we understand quite well the reason why the Christian family can be called *the domestic Church* (*ecclesia domestica*).[68]

This is no doubt the reason why it is precisely the indissolubility of marriage which is the supreme expression of the bond connecting the realities of baptism, the Church, and the sacrament of marriage. In the future, this inner bond between baptism and marriage will have to be more insistently stressed in a systematic theology of marriage.[69]

Faith and baptism impact strongly upon the constitution of marriage. No text shows this more forcefully and more clearly than 1 Corinthians 7:12–16,[70] a text which many believe embodies the deepest theology of marriage in the entire New Testament. The Church allows a spouse who has become a Christian to enter a new marriage with a Christian, should the pagan spouse refuse cohabitation. This means that, for a new convert, the orientation of existence as a whole, marriage included, is determined by baptism. It is here that we meet the question: prescinding from acknowledged cases, has the Church the power to dissolve marriages?[71]

We deal with this question only insofar as it concerns the absolute indissolubility of marriage contracted and consummated by baptized persons. Recently, the problem has been raised in the following terms: why not allow for an extension of the power hitherto exercised by the Church to marriages contracted and consummated (*rata et consummata*)?[72] Some theologians maintain that the right of the Church to dissolve these marriages can be grounded on the universal power to bind and to loose which Jesus entrusted to her (Mt 16:19). The Church would not engage in this exercise of power in her own name, but in the name of God.[73] Other theologians look at indissolubility as extrinsically grounded on the relationship it bears to the common good of the Church. Because of that relationship, the Church would have the right to make more flexible the norm which now prescribes indissolubility unconditionally.[74]

These discussions have grown extremely extensive. They bring up many problems with which we cannot deal here, beginning with the fundamental presuppositions of the reasonings themselves. True, history shows that a certain development has taken place regarding the extent to which the Church has exercised her power to dissolve.[75] Note, however, that the marriages concerned are, above all, those contracted by unbelievers.[76] Besides, the reasoning on which these theologians depend is open to serious objections. This is the case, for example, for the concept of vicarious power (*potestas vicaria*) in its concrete application to the matter at hand.[77] Likewise, the position advocated by Gerhartz provokes resistance by the way in which it conceives the correlation between the good of individual persons and the common good of the Church.[78] It is, of course, impossible within the framework of this presentation to meet all these objections or to reexamine the fundamental principles of the treatise *de ecclesia*. Besides, we should also ask ourselves whether, given the circumstances in which we find ourselves sociologically and psychologically, it is reasonable to wish that the Church should extend her power to dissolve Christian marriages. Most likely, such an extension would not bring about an improvement of the situation; it would rather tend to reinforce the prevailing orientation in favor of divorce.

Be that as it may, we want to examine the question from the viewpoint of dogmatics. To begin with, the attempt to legitimate a movement to dissolve sacramental and consummated marriages by extrapolation from the Church's power to dissolve natural marriages would be a methodological error. This would be tantamount to ignoring the essential difference between the two categories of marriages. The dogmatic theologian, if for no other reason than that he is responsible for upholding the principle of the indissolubility of marriage, has no choice but to voice reservations regarding the possibility of extending the practice of dissolving marriages to additional cases and most of all to consummated sacramental marriages. Needless to say, the theologian by no means intends to resist the principle that the Church has power to dissolve in determinate cases. It must certainly be acknowledged that the bond that unites the spouses is a visible reality; it affects both society and the Church. In addition, in each sacramental marriage, the Church engages herself in several different ways. And yet we are not at all entitled to primarily ground the indissolubility of marriage either on the authority of the Church or on her collective interest. Indissolubility has its foundation in Jesus' own will to save and on his will to establish a covenant. The will of Christ, because of what it is in itself, transcends the juridical order of the Church. In view of the basic function of sacramental marriage, namely, to be both a real sign of the indissoluble union between Christ and his Church and a real participation in their oneness, sacramental marriage puts limits to the power of the Church, limits which are determined by what things are in themselves. The Church can do no other than to bear witness to what Christ ultimately wills. This applies also to cases in which, because of human failures, sacramental marriages have suffered shipwreck. "She [the Church] . . . preserves even in the visible order the sign of the covenant which the spouses have broken, but which Christ has upheld. The Church must do this, for she does not intend to betray what she is. Since she is the fundamental sacrament of the saving deed of God, she cannot sacrifice the bond between the invisible reality which faith is and the external structure which can be perceived at the level of law."[79]

This shows once more how directly Christian marriage, taken in the fullness of its meaning, affects the reality of salvation through Jesus Christ. Perhaps even more in the future than in the past, it will be very important for society that no human power (including the power of the Church under certain of its aspects) be entitled to dissolve sacramental and consummated marriages.

CHAPTER 4

Marriage as a Reality in the Order of Creation and Marriage as a Sacrament

by Carlo Caffarra

This presentation is arranged in two parts. I will try in the first part to sketch the history of the problem and in the second to trace the outlines of a systematic reflection on it.

Part One

HISTORICAL SKETCH

In my view, the problem of the relationship between marriage as a reality of the order of creation and marriage as a sacrament has emerged in the Church within four different historical contexts. As one moves from a particular context to another, the problem may seem to be formulated in identical terms, but this does not mean that the question being dealt with is the same.

1. FIRST HISTORICAL CONTEXT: CONDITIONS FOR VALIDITY

The first context is constituted by the debate concerning the conditions required for the validity of the sacrament of marriage.

DUNS SCOTUS (1265–1308)

John Duns Scotus was the first to explicitly address this subject within the framework of an inquiry on the form of marriage. He defined this form thus: "A sign perceptible to the senses instituted by God to signify efficaciously the grace conferred." In his *Oxford Commentary*, he considered various hypotheses concerning marriage.[1] Either the divine institution simply assumes any sign acknowledged by human society as the expression of a contract, or it requires that the consent be specifically expressed through the use of words. In the latter case, it may determine which words should be used, or it may abstain from doing so. In his *Reportata Parisiensia*,[2] Scotus declared that "a sign perceptible to the senses, an audible sign, and the use of specific words" are indispensable to the validity of marriage. Consequently, while mutes can contract a valid marriage, a substantial flaw in the form prevents this marriage from being a sacrament. For the same reason, a marriage between minors contracted by their parents is validly contracted but is not a sacrament. It will become a sacrament when the spouses personally exchange their consent. Le Bras remarks: "This opinion of Scotus was destined to achieve great renown . . . We are not dealing here with a vague remark lost somewhere in the writings of Duns Scotus. . . . Toward the end of the Middle Ages numerous theologians were inclined to concede . . . that without *verba* there is no sacrament, or at least to wonder out loud, and not without embarrassment, whether there could be one. Such is the case with John of Cologne."[3]

CAJETAN (1469–1534)

Scotus had admitted a separation between contract and sacrament in the two cases just mentioned. Thomas de Vio Cajetan added a third case.[4] In his view, marriage is valid when contracted by proxy but cannot be regarded as a sacrament. The reception of a sacrament is a *passio personalis*, a being-acted-upon as a person. Inwardly, a sacrament implies the working of grace; outwardly, it implies an action, or a "passion" perceptible to the senses and involving the person of the recipient. Cajetan takes the position that an active and conscious participation on the part of the persons who contract marriage is indispensable if the conjugal bond between them is to constitute a sacrament. There is no point arguing that the sacrament of marriage pertains to the category of contracts. The sacrament of penance, for example, is constituted by juridical acts, and in juridical matters, as in the matter of contracts, many operations can be performed by proxy – one can be convicted or acquitted by proxy. However, in the case of the sacrament of penance this does not apply. If you maintain that a sacramental marriage can be contracted by proxy, it would follow that the engaged couple who happen to be asleep would receive the sacrament at the moment when their proxies make the contract. According to Cajetan, this is an absurd consequence.

But note a certain lack of coherence in Cajetan's thought, an incoherence of great interest to us here. He maintains that the nonsacramental marriage of two baptized persons invalidates a second marriage, should one take place, "much more," he says, than would a marriage contracted by pagans. It would seem to follow, then, that according to Cajetan the marriage contract of baptized persons possesses a consistency that accrues to it from the quasi-sacramental quality guaranteed to it by baptism. *Radicaliter*, that is, because it is rooted in baptism, that marriage is *ratum; formaliter*, that is, in terms of its form, it is not so, since the form required for a sacramental marriage is absent.

Cajetan's position rests on the contention that "ratification" on the part of the persons concerned is indispensable for the sacramentality of marriage. Thus, a slight yet significant shift takes place in the direction of reflective thought namely, toward the subjective state of the persons contracting marriage. This shift to the subject comes explicitly to the fore in the perspective within which G. Vasquez and F. Rebello undertake their inquiries.

G. VASQUEZ (1549–1604)

In order to understand the theological reflections of Vasquez we need recall his notion of natural law. In fact, his treatise on marriage begins, logically as well as materially, with a definition of marriage "according to natural law."[5] According to this Spanish theologian, natural law refers to the fact that things and human beings are endowed with an "independent" nature – that by reason of which they are what they are. This nature possesses a reality of its own, an intrinsic metaphysical necessity, if you will, which imposes itself even on the very will and intellect of God. Once human beings come to exist, marriage comes necessarily into being as well and is endowed with a nature which does not depend on anyone, God included. On the contrary, the fact that marriage is a sacrament is exclusively contingent on the will of Christ. Christ stipulated that the consent of the two parties which constitutes the marital contract should be a sign that effects their sanctification. This philosophical position entails many serious theological consequences.

To begin with, the sacramentality of marriage has an adventitious quality when seen against marriage as institution. This institution always remains identical in its nature, whether "under natural law" or "under the law of the Gospel." This leads Vasquez to a peculiar interpretation of Ephesians 5. In his view, the marriage of which Paul speaks in this text is not the marriage of baptized persons, but marriage as such. Marriage as such is the *sacramentum magnum*, the great sacrament that signifies the union between Christ and the Church, since marriage "which is established by natural law" expresses that union to perfection. It could hardly be otherwise, since sacramentality neither alters the conjugal contract, nor raises it to a higher level.[6]

This interpretation raises a problem. Unlike any other marriage, the marriage of baptized persons, once consummated, can never be dissolved. How does Vasquez account for this? Not by invoking the sacramentality of marriage, but by engaging in a rather strange piece of reasoning: a consummated sacramental marriage cannot be dissolved even on the ground of heresy. This is because, by virtue of their baptism, the spouses remain forever members of the Church. But the spouse who commits the crime of heresy can be punished and forced to live with the believing spouse without offense to the creator. If the heretic refuses, he can be put to death. This is how the right of the believing spouse can be protected: either the heretic lives with the believing spouse without offense to the creator, or the believing partner regains his freedom. Once the heretic has been put to death, the believing spouse is free to contract a new marriage.[7]

A second consequence of Vasquez's position is that there exists a real identity between contract and sacrament. The sacrament is constituted by the contract itself, to which there accrues, by way of accident and because of a decision on the part of Christ, the capacity to function as an efficacious sign of grace.[8] On this basis, Vasquez feels confident in resolving without hesitation the problems debated by theologians: the sacramentality of the marriage contracted by mutes (Scotus's position), the sacramentality of marriage by proxy (Cajetan's position), the Church's right to demand *ad validitatem* that the contract be entered into according to a particular form, and the repudiation of Cano's position (see below).

The third consequence is that these solutions exact a very high price on two counts.

First, the identity between contract and sacrament must be thought of in real terms, or better still in terms of an adequate identity. Sacramentality is, then, a pure accident; it affects marriage as such in no way. This amounts to radicalizing and stressing to the extreme the partner's intention to perform and receive the sacrament. The mere intention to marry, or even to marry within the framework of the Church, is fundamentally inadequate to raise the contract to the level of a sacrament, since it bears on a reality which is identical whether or not the persons involved are baptized. In the absence of the intention that bears on the sacrament the baptized persons would contract a true marriage. However, it would not be sacramental, since the right to marry is first and foremost a natural right. Thus, the will of the baptized persons is capable of effectively sundering contract from sacrament. Before Vasquez, the possibility of effecting this separation was limited to a number of cases clearly specified. With Vasquez and after him, that possibility exists for any and all marriages. Now it is the intention that tells.[9] If a marriage is to be a sacrament, the contracting parties must have, in a vague way at least, the intention of doing what the Church does. Besides, just as a marriage between pagans does not only persist as *legitimum* once they are baptized, but is *ratum*, so too for baptized persons the marriage contracted without the aforementioned intention, and legitimate as contract, will be *ratum* without being a sacrament. The quality that makes it *ratum* does not depend on the intention of the contracting parties; the fact that we are dealing with baptized persons allows marriage to have this quality.

In the second place, Vasquez resolves the problem of marriages contracted by neophytes prior to baptism, a problem keenly debated in his time. In his opinion, this marriage is not, and can never become, a sacrament. It is, and is bound to remain, a purely natural marriage. Renewing the consent after baptism would produce no effect, since no one can change what is already there.[10]

Note a fourth and last consequence of Vasquez's position. Since marriage is primordially a civil contract and since sacramentality is something that accrues to the contract, the civil power is competent in this area. It is only because Christ so decided by a positive act that this competency is withdrawn from the civil ruler and given to the Church. On the strength of this act, the Church enacts laws "relative to the contract."[11]

F. REBELLO (1545–1608)

The direction taken by Vasquez surfaces even more explicitly in F. Rebello, a Portuguese Jesuit who wrote books on moral theology. His teachings on marriage are presented under the title *De contractu matrimonii*, not *De sacramento matrimonii*, and within the framework of his study *de obligationibus justitiae*. His reasonings revolve around this key assertion: in the last analysis, the nature of the contract is determined by the intention of the contracting parties.[12] Should these want to contract only a nonsacramental marriage, this marriage is wholly valid at the contractual level but is not sacramental. This thesis is stated quite firmly and in the manner of a universal principle. There are certain juridical arguments in favor of it which the author regards as convincing. No positive law annuls these marriages insofar as they are contracts. Nonsacramentality is not a dishonorable (*turpis*) condition. It does not affect the substance of the contract, hence it does not render it invalid. The Church regards as valid nonsacramental marriages contracted with dispensation from "disparity of cult."[13] However, the real foundation of Rebello's position is not constituted by these juridical considerations. That position is ultimately rooted in the conviction that sacramentality is extrinsic to marriage.[14]

THE *INSTITUTIONES MORALES*

The theological position which affirmed the separability of contract from sacrament was later advocated by its adherents in the textbooks of moral theology, and without notable changes. In the seventeenth century, this and the opposite position were even presented in keeping with literary arrangement characteristic of the so-called "moral system." The two positions are first stated, complete with reference to authors and their respective writings. The arguments in favor of each position are presented next. There follows an assessment of the degree of probability to be credited to the two positions *probabilior, probabilis*, and so forth. It will be enough, then, to cite some authors who have been regarded as especially authoritative.

THE *SALMANTICENSES*

The *Salmanticenses* followed the line inaugurated by Vasquez and Rebello. Should a baptized person wish to contract a civil marriage, this marriage would be valid as a contract but not as a sacrament. A new marriage would be impossible nevertheless, for a reason which comes down to this: according to the Council of Florence, the sacrament is constituted by words, things, and the minister's intention as well as the recipient's. Without a formal or a virtual intention, the sacrament cannot be received. In the case presented above, this intention is absent, whereas the conditions for the validity of the contract are present. In marriage, its contractual nature is primary with respect to sacramentality. Therefore, the contract can exist without sacramentality. A comparison: in baptism, the physical ablution is primary with respect to sacramentality. It can even exist without sacramentality when the intention to receive the sacrament is lacking.[15]

P. SPORER (1637–1683)[16]

Sporer maintained that the position which advocates the separability of contract from sacrament "rests on a more solid foundation." In his view, it is the opposite position that must accept the burden of proof. Christ did not annul a contract valid on other grounds. Without altering the nature of the contract, he added to it the dignity of a sacrament. At this point there reappears the comparison with baptism.

R. BILLUART (1683–1757)

Billuart argued in the same way.[17] Consistently enough, he draws from his thesis the conclusion that, if things be considered as they are in themselves, the king's authority allows the ruler to establish diriment impediments. In fact, however, the Church has reserved this power to herself. According to some authors, this came to pass with the consent of the civil rulers, or without their resistance, while others maintain that the Church proceeded by virtue of her own supreme authority.[18]

We notice that the canonists likewise acknowledged the existence of the two contrasting positions without maintaining that either was false. It is all a matter of lesser or greater probability. This is, for instance, the case with Schmalzgrüber (1663–1735), the most renowned canonist of his day.[19] However, Schmalzgrüber decided that the separability thesis "has by far the greater measure of truth" in it.

ST. ALPHONSUS DE LIGUORI (1696–1787)

St. Alphonsus merely mentioned the two postions; he did not assess their respective value.[20] But he did emphasize that the will to separate contract from sacrament is gravely illicit.

From this point on, the debate moved out of the domain of theology within which it had first arisen. Outside the schools of theology, it became part of that larger and deeper confrontation that took place between Church and state, a state which first professed absolutism, then liberalism.

Before going on to explore this new context, we may consider the thought of the three main theologians who defended the inseparability position, and whose position came to exert considerable influence at a later time: R. Bellarmine, F. Suarez, and T. Sanchez.

The Inseparability of Contract From Sacrament Grounded On The Will of Christ

ST. ROBERT BELLARMINE (1542–1621)

Without any doubt, St. Robert Bellarmine's contribution is, historically, the most decisive. His influence is visible in the position the magisterium eventually took and in the formulation of papal teaching. His thesis is clear and explicit: "among Christians, no legitimate marriage can be celebrated which would not be at the same time a true sacrament."[21]

How does Bellarmine structure his argument? He starts out by emphasizing the specific uniqueness of Christian marriage which, in his view, resides in the fact that it is the sign or the symbol of the union of Christ with the Church and the souls of the faithful. The reality which in marriage perfectly signifies this union is the absolute intrinsic and extrinsic indissolubility of the marriage of baptized persons. The efficacy of the sacrament at the level of the grace which bestows sanctification on the spouses is grounded theologically as follows: by virtue of its indissolubility, the marriage between baptized persons is sign and symbol of the union of Christ with the Church and with the soul. It must, therefore, effect the grace which helps the spouses to be symbols in their own lives. Note how the Jesuit theologian conceives indissolubility not in merely juridical terms but as "a union which brings together not only bodies but souls, and is nothing less than the fact of true and divine love."[22] Would God have instituted something so difficult to achieve (namely, a fidelity to the bond that unites one to another individual) without providing the help needed to overcome this difficulty?"[23]

The capacity to express the reality just mentioned is given to Christian marriage not only at the moment in which it is celebrated (*in fieri*) but also all during married life (*in facto esse*). In fact this life itself is the symbol. Bellarmine is the first to maintain that marriage continues to be a sacrament as long as it lasts. The shared life is the external and perceivable symbol which represents the indissoluble union between Christ and the Church. The author even offers this comparison with the sacrament of the Eucharist: after the consecration, the consecrated species continue to be the external and perceivable symbol of spiritual nurture.[24]

Hence, for Bellarmine, the relationship between marriage as contract and marriage as sacrament comes to the fore in the context of this question: what are the matter, form, and minister of this sacrament?[25] In answering this question Bellarmine bases the inseparability of contract from sacrament on the fact that it is theologically impossible to discern in this sacrament any matter, form, and minister of the contract.

Let us try to proceed in orderly fashion. What brings Bellarmine to this conclusion? It is, one could say, an argument from the absurd and distinctly positivistic in structure. We can reduce the argument to this sequence of steps:

1) Marriage is a sacrament. This is a truth of faith defined at the Council of Trent and which no Catholic may question.

2) On the other hand, neither in the sources of revelation nor in the magisterium of the Church do we ever find any designation of the matter, form, and special minister of marriage, even where such designation would be expected to appear.

3) This silence allows only for two basic suppositions: either the matter, form, and minister of the sacrament are identical with those of the contract (which would explain the silence); or marriage is not a sacrament.

4) Two basic consequences derive from the foregoing. The first is that the inseparability position is binding on Catholic theologians as a doctrine of faith (hence Bellarmine's severe repudiation of Cano's view). The second is that the problem should be approached not at the subjective level, namely, the level of intention, but at the objective level.[26]

How are we to understand this inseparability theologically? Bellarmine speaks in this connection of an elevation (*evectio*).[27] The question is whether *elevation* should be understood to be a "complement" added to an incomplete reality or an "addition." Bellarmine's answer seems to favor the second alternative.[28] The result is that newly converted spouses are not sacramentally married simply by virtue of baptism but are required to perform a new act of the will.[29]

F. SUAREZ (1548–1617)

The contribution of F. Suarez seems at first to contrast with Bellarmine's position, for it is framed in terms of the intention required for the celebration of the sacrament, and the possiblity of a separation between contract and a sacrament intentionally effected by the contracting parties. Perhaps this is because Suarez did not leave behind a treatise on marriage; he studied this problem in connection with the whole set of general problems relating to the intention of the minister, which, as we have seen, is the prevailing approach at the beginning of the seventeenth century. However, Suarez did not let himself be controlled by this approach to the problem; he even regarded it as secondary.

Be that as it may, here is his basic teaching. Let us assume that two baptized persons want to contract marriage but do not wish to receive a sacrament. This will to exclude the sacrament may be traceable to an error on their part: they believe that marriage is not a sacrament. But they do want to contract marriage in the manner instituted by Christ. In this case, their error does not exclude the intention required for the reception to do what Christ willed. But there could also be cases in which the spouses want precisely to divorce sacramentality from the contract, or to exclude indissolubility, or perhaps their will is controlled by some other objectionable intent. Here the necessary intention is lacking, and there is no sacrament. The validity of this kind of marriage, based as it is on a contract, is another matter. Contract and sacrament are either separable or they are not. If they are separable, nothing precludes that they be separated in the case under consideration. If contract is not separable from sacrament due to the sacramental institution by Christ, the validity of the contract in the case cited depends intrinsically on the sacrament. The contract is related to the sacrament as the effect to the cause, or as the *res sacramenti* is related to the sacrament. The primary requirement is, then, the intention to receive the sacrament. In the absence of this intention there is no marriage.[30]

Thus, for Suarez, the solution of the problem lies in the answer to the question: is the reality of the contract objectively (*in re ipsa*) separable from sacramentality? There is no point reflecting about intention, for intention is not the heart of the problem. What we need to ask is what properly constitutes the sacrament of marriage, and therefore what relationship the sacrament bears to the contract "after Christ has instituted it." If we are dealing with a contract being raised as such to the level of a sacrament, and thus becoming "a sacred sign which confers and signifies the sanctification of the subject,"[31] it follows that the intention of not performing the sacrament would inhibit the emergence of the contract itself, since the contract does not exist apart from the sacrament.

Suarez's chief contribution to our question consists, I believe, in this: the decisive factor is not the intention of the subject but the will of Christ. Every baptized person has the right to decide to marry or not to marry, but not to choose between a purely contractual marriage and a marriage which is also a sacrament. As soon as we realize that Christ indissolubly bound together contract and sacrament, this position becomes inevitable.

Suarez does not undertake a direct demonstration that contract and sacrament are inseparable, and yet it is clear enough that he follows the line of thought advocated by Bellarmine. For the sacrament of marriage, matter, form, and minister are the same as for the contract.[32] But the way of conceiving the inseparability of contract from sacrament is not always the same. In the passage quoted above, inseparability is conceived in these terms: the value of the contract is a result of the sacrament (*res-sacramentum*). Unless we are mistaken, this means that the conjugal bond (*valor contractus*) is effected by the sacrament. Given this perspective, the case of someone who wills to marry, but not by virtue of the sacrament, is parallel to the case of someone who does not want to administer the sacrament of baptism, but claims all the same to bestow grace on the infant. Elsewhere, Suarez says that "this sacrament presupposes the contract upon which it rests."[33] This discrepancy may be traceable to the fact that in one case marriage is seen *in facto esse* in the other *in fieri*. The difference is one of viewpoint.

T. SANCHEZ (1550–1610)

Sanchez was heavily dependent on the approach adopted by Bellarmine and Suarez. He deserves credit mainly on two counts: on the one hand, his thinking is characterized by an especial exactness; on the other, he fixed with definitive precision the terminology of theology and law.

The greater coherence that marks his discussion comes to the fore in the manner in which he resolves the problem of the marriage of new converts. He does not exclude the probability of the radical solution advocated by Vasquez and Bellarmine, and yet he regards as more probable the thesis that the marriage contracted before baptism becomes a sacrament by virtue of baptism. From the moment of baptism on, marriage represents the union between Christ and the Church and becomes as indissoluble as a marriage *ratum* between baptized persons.[34] When Sanchez undertakes to respond to the objections of Vasquez, his language takes on great theological precision. He argues that we are dealing with a marriage and a bond which are new only in that the natural and nonreligious contract which is open to dissolution becomes indissoluble and sacred, and represents the union of Christ with the Church. In this sense the Council of Trent (sess. 24, can. 1) can say that Christ instituted marriage in the new law. Marriage already existed, of course, but Christ instituted it in the sense that he made of it an indissoluble sacrament.[35]

When Sanchez later dealt with the problem of indissolubility, he followed Suarez both in formulating and answering the question.[36] On this basis, he resolved, as Bellarmine did before him, the classic question concerning the marriage of mutes, marriage by proxy, and the minister of marriage.

As far as terminology is concerned, Sanchez called *ratum* the marriage which is a sacrament and *legitimum* a nonsacramental marriage. After this, there was no terminological vagueness in the matter: canon law adopted this terminology. Moreover, Sanchez was the first to assert that the reality of the sacrament is linked to the conjugal contract by virtue of divine law.[37]

2. SECOND HISTORICAL CONTEXT: THE DEBATE CONCERNING THE MINISTER OF THE SACRAMENT

M. Cano And The Controversy Concerning His Position

The most important position, the one which has exerted the greatest historical influence, is the one advocated by Melchior Cano (1509–60). It is presented at great length in his work *De locis theologicis*.[38]

The fundamental problem for Cano was not to prove that contract is separable from sacrament, but to establish that the priest's blessing is indispensable if a validly contracted marriage is to have the dignity of a sacrament. Obviously, once he felt he had established this necessity, he was bound to declare that among the marriages contracted by baptized persons only those which are blessed by the priest are sacramental. Note that at that time not all marriages were blessed by the priest. The Spanish theologian was undeterred by this fact for he thought that the thesis which asserted the inseparability of contract from sacrament was neither a dogma of faith nor even a teaching agreed upon by theologians, as appears, he says, from the positions of Duns Scotus and Cajetan. Marriage is indeed a sacrament endowed with its own sacred form and deriving its sacredness from the true minister of the Church. Else, how could one account for the position of Duns Scotus who maintained that marriages contracted through wordless signs are not sacramental? Then there was Cajetan who, with the highest degree of probability in Cano's opinion, withheld the quality of sacramentality from marriages contracted at a distance by letter and proxy.[39]

At the basis of Cano's case for the necessity of the priest's ministerial intervention there lies the deep conviction that marriage is a supernatural event of grace. As such, it cannot be reduced only to the elements that constitute a contract (the consent of the contracting parties). It must also include as one of its constitutive elements a sign of its Christian soteriological value. This sign is the form which expresses the supernatural significance and cannot be identified with the words of the contract. This form is spoken by the minister of the Church.[40]

Thus, although Cano maintained that the contract is separable from the sacrament, the thrust of his analysis lay in a different direction. He wished to bring out the soteriological and ecclesial value of the marriage of baptized persons. It is therefore ill-advised, to say the least, to use his position, as some do even to this day, as proof that the Church can regard as true and proper those marriages which are supposed to be nonsacramental. This notion runs counter to the letter and the spirit of his theological reflections.

The position taken by Cano, although relentlessly attacked by Bellarmine,[41] Sanchez, Suarez, and Vasquez, exerted considerable influence because its fundamental insight was so profoundly compelling. His supporters continued to hold that all marriages celebrated without the blessing of the priest ought both to be regarded as marriages in the proper and true sense, and to be denied sacramental value. Among these, G. Estius (1542–1613) is without a doubt the best known. He admitted that the opposite position is "more common" and yet produced a total of fourteen arguments in favor of Cano's position.[42] In his work *De synodo diocesana*,[43] Cardinal P. Lambertini judged that Cano's doctrine was "very probable" and could be adopted without the slightest error.

After Cardinal Lambertini became pope and took the name Benedict XIV, he returned to the question in his apostolic letter *Redditae sunt*, dated September 17, 1744. Unless we are mistaken, this letter represents the first explicit intervention of the magisterium in the separability issue. The case submitted to the pope for adjudication was this: there are Catholics who contract marriage before a civil official or an heretical minister and later fail to renew their consent in accordance with the form prescribed by the Council of Trent. What is one to think of the consent they have expressed? Is it sufficient to constitute a marriage which would have at least the validity of a contract? One opinion answers in the affirmative, another in the negative. No one doubts that this marriage lacks the dignity of a sacrament.[44]

The answer takes shape in two phases. First comes the declaration that, according to the decree *Tametsi*, marriages celebrated under the above conditions are invalid both as contracts and as sacraments.[45] At a later date, Benedict XIV recalled the thesis which affirms the separability of contract from sacrament but made no decision in the matter. A decision would have been irrelevant under the circumstances, since, according to the stipulations of the decree *Tametsi*, the marriages in question are certainly invalid even as contracts.[46]

In conclusion, then, the thinking of Benedict XIV was not identical with the position he took in his work *De synodo*. This is not to say, however, that references to the inseparability debate were henceforth meaningless. They could continue to make sense wherever the decree *Tametsi* had not been promulgated. From the solution advocated it seems to follow that we are dealing here with a mere question of positive law. If we so understand the matter, we are certainly entitled to say that the pope refrained from addressing the separability issue.

All the same the debate persisted, so much so that on July 31, 1751, the Sacred Congregation of the Council declared as "truer and more widely accepted" the view opposed to that of Cano.[47] Cano's position continued to lose ground. In 1785, the last edition of *Theologia moralis* published during the lifetime of the author, St. Alphonsus spoke of the position opposed to Cano's in these terms: "common and, it seems, morally certain."[48]

Note finally that Cano's position then moved out of the field of theological debate and in the works of royalists became one of the arguments used to challenge the competency of the Church in matrimonial matters. We have already remarked that this use of Cano's position does not do justice to its intent.

The Council of Trent and Its Impact on Theology

At the basis of all these discussions we continually find the teaching of the Council of Trent. It is, therefore, imperative that we return to this teaching and examine it explicitly.

The discussions in the Council of Trent developed in two phases. This applies both to the discussions held by the so-called minor theologians and those held by the fathers. We also need to distinguish two decisions concerning the issue at hand: canon 1 of session XXIV, and the decree *Tametsi.*

a) The discussions of the *theologi minores* on the articles concerning marriage began February 9, 1563, and came to a close March 28.[49] The first article of interest to us was submitted to the theologians for examination in this form: *Matrimonium non esse Sacramentum a Deo institutum sed ab hominibus in Ecclesia invectum, nec habere promissiones gratiae.*[50] The discussion of this article lasted until February 22.[51]

The theologians who participated in these discussions had no doubt whatever as to the heretical nature of the proposition before them. Their arguments were always designed to prove that, like other sacraments, marriage contains all the essential elements that pertain to the definition of a sacrament as such.[52]

The discussion among the fathers took place between July 20 and July 31, 1563. The canon which had been presented to them was worded as follows: *Si quis dixerit Matrimonium non esse verum Sacramentum legis evangelicae divinitus institutum sed ab hominibus in Ecclesia invectum . . .* [53]

Three amendments were proposed during the debates:

1) Add *proprie unum ex septem sacramentis legis evangelicae.*[54] This addition was offered by the cardinal of Lorraine (642, 23–24), Cardinal Madrutius (643, 21–22), and many others (see 644, 6; 650, 19–21; 661, 5), and always for the same reason: to repudiate the conception of marriage advocated by Durand of Saint-Pourçain.

2) Add *esse Sacramentum a Christo institutum et conferre grat-*

iam.[55] (651, 47; 652, 2; 653, 40–41). What surfaces here is the abiding concern to assert the sacramentality of marriage in such a way as to shield it against any possibility of doubt or debate.

3) Add *matrimonium christianorum.*[56] This addition was proposed by the bishop of Paris (658, 17) and others (661, 34: *inter Christianos et fideles;* 664, 41: *inter Christifideles*).

The synthesis agreed upon in the end reads as follows: *In primo canone dicatur – proprie unum ex septem sacramentis legis evangelicae. Quod consideretur, quod dixit Durandus, matrimonium esse verum sacramentum sed non univoce cum ceteris. Et addatur – a Christo institutum – ubi sacramentum et quod gratiam conferat.*[57] The Council, then, accepted amendment one and two and rejected amendment three.[58]

b) The debate that preceded the decree *Tametsi* turned out to be one of the most spirited in the whole council. There was agreement that clandestine marriages must be condemned and that parents had no power to invalidate the marriage of their children under legal age, as the heretics had asserted in one of their articles.[59] The problem that did emerge was something else. Experience had shown abundantly that a purely punitive law that forbade clandestine marriages without invalidating them was inadequate. A more radical measure was called for. Here, however, two questions arose: has the Church the power to invalidate these marriages? Once the great majority answered this question in the affirmative, a more specific question followed: how can this authority, and the exercise proposed for it, be justified?

The theologians were almost unanimous in locating the basis of the question in the relation that exists between contract and sacrament. When the Church invalidates clandestine marriages, she does not touch the sacrament; she merely determines the form which the contract is to take.[60] The theologian Luigi di Borgo Nuovo suggested another justification: the power to illegitimate persons (*personas illegitimare*), which is what happens in diriment impediments (406, 29).

The first draft proposal condemned the following proposition: "Clandestine marriages are not true and ratified (*rata*) marriages. Parents have the power to ratify or to invalidate them." But the proposal stipulated that in the future clandestine marriages would be invalid.[61]

Although almost all the fathers condemned clandestine marriages, they worried when it came to establishing the correctness of this decision. In particular, they wanted to avoid giving credibility to the reproach among the heretics that the Catholic Church disposes of the sacraments as she pleases. On the other hand, there was the long-standing practice of erecting diriment impediments. A total of four solutions was proposed:

–The relationship that exists between contract and sacrament enables the Church to invalidate the sacrament *ratione pactionis.*[62]

–The clandestine character of a marriage always bespeaks a flaw in the consent. Suggested by the bishop of Capaccio (644, 36–39; 690, 15–17), this explanation fell on deaf ears. It amounted to regarding as invalid all the clandestine marriages contracted before the Council.

–The blessing of the priest should be declared indispensable for validity (*ad validitatem*), and all clandestine marriages should be declared invalid as a consequence. Some of the fathers even suggested that the priest be declared the minister of the sacrament.[63]

–All persons who contract a clandestine marriage should be declared "incapable" (*inhabiles*), so that the prohibition of clandestinity is equivalent to a *disablement of the person* (*inhabilitatio personae*).[64] This proposal was objected to on the basis that the matter at hand was an *irritatio* of marriage as such, not of people.

A second draft proposal was presented on August 7 and discussed between August 11 and 13 (685–747). Compared to the preceding draft, it included two amendments: 1. canon 1 was inserted into the preamble of the decree; 2. of the four justifications just discussed, the fourth, the disablement of persons, was adopted (683, 1–16).

The discussion brought forth no new elements that had not surfaced earlier. We notice that the four solutions mentioned above arose again. But the discussion grew more complex, since the council was now required to decide whether the problem was one of doctrine or only one of discipline.

A third draft proposal was introduced on September 5 and debated between September 7 and 10.[65] Compared to the second draft, this contained two new elements. The first is of considerable importance. After *rata et vera matrimonia* was added *quamdiu Ecclesia ea rata esse voluit.* This addition would be retained in the final draft (the fourth), but in the negative form, *quandiu Ecclesia irrita non fecit.* This phrase does not mean "even to the moment when," that is to say, "from this moment on" (the fathers rejected the formula *usquequo non sint irritata*; 696, 26–7), but rather "in the periods of time when the Church did not invalidate them." In fact, following the decree of the pseudo-Evaristus, still reported by Gratian (Friedberg, I, 1104), many thought that since the time of Evaristus until Clement III (at the end of the twelfth century) the Chruch had regarded clandestine marriages as invalid (see 709, 9; 772, 41 ff.; 725, 29). It follows from this addition that the nullity in question does not arise *ex natura rei*, but from a decision of the Church. The Church asserts that she has the power to set up the conditions according to which the matrimonial consent does or does not have effect.

The second amendment is the addition of the phrase *anathemate damnat.*

The amended text was voted upon and received 133 favorable and 56 unfavorable votes. The public conference which met on September 13, 1563, at the residence of Cardinal Morone, and at his initiative, to enlist the support of a larger majority achieved no results. In fact, it degenerated into a veritable brawl.[66]

On October 15, the fourth draft proposal was unveiled. Here canon 1 *Super reformatione* dealt with clandestine marriages (888–90). On November 11, the canon was put to a final vote (966–71) and only fifty-five of the Fathers voted against it. The last phases of the debate are very interesting. Lack of consent (*ex defectu consensus*) was rejected outright as a ground of nullity, but some again suggested as grounds the distinction between contract and sacrament, or even the separability of the one from the other. Thus especially the bishop of Granada: "He proved that there can be a marriage apart from the sacrament. This applies to a baptized person who wants to contract marriage, but does not want to receive a sacrament. This person does not receive the sacrament, since sacraments cannot be conferred on persons who do not intend to receive them."[67] (781, 8–10; also, Sforza Pallavicino, *Vera Oecumenici Concilii Tridentini historia*, lib. 22, c. 8 [Milan, 1844], 83).

From the hectic history of the decree *Tametsi* the following conclusions may be drawn:

–The Council of Trent refused to ground and justify the power which the Church exercises in issuing the decree on the distinction between contract and sacrament insofar as this distinction tends to separate contract from sacrament. It chose instead a justification based on the *inhabilitatio personarum*, which, in its opinion, enjoyed stronger support in tradition.[68]

–On the other hand, we should not exaggerate the importance of the fact that this latter justification was preferred by the fathers of Trent. It is unthinkable that, in the context of the canons on reform,

chapter where the problem is addressed comprises two sections. In the first, the author considers the sacramental character of marriage (nos. 1–13) in order to establish that, even if marriage be a sacrament, the only competent authority is that of the state. (Note that in this section the sacramentality of marriage is discussed merely as a supposition, the falsity of which the author will seek to prove in the second section, nos. 24–40). His argument proceeds as follows:

–Marriage is fundamentally a natural contract (no. 3) whose nature is not altered by the sacrament, since the intervention of Christ was merely intended to reinstate its indissolubility.

–Therefore, just as the Church is not competent to analyze the baptismal water, or the eucharistic wine, and to certify their genuineness, but assumes on some other evidence (*ex alio*) that they are genuine and uses them in the celebration of the sacraments, so too she has no competence when it comes to determining the reality or validity of the marriage contract on which the sacrament is grafted (nos. 5 and 22).

–Once the state has juridically defined the contract, there is no longer any need for the Church to legislate, except *quoad usum*. That is, the Church is to provide directives so that the faithful may live saintly lives within marriage (no. 23).

–Besides, the Church has recognized the legislation of the Roman Empire concerning marriage.

In the second part of the chapter (nos. 24–40), the author seeks to prove that marriage is not a sacrament and that it does not, therefore, fall under the competency of the Church. In this way, the more favorable hypothesis is itself eliminated.

J. de LAUNOY (1603–73)

The most important author in this controversy, the one who provided the inspiration for all the others, was J. de Launoy. His fundamental work, published in Paris in 1674, is entitled *Regia in Matrimonium potestas vel Tractatus de jure saecularium principum christianorum in sanciendis impedimentis matrimonium dirimentibus.*[71] Before publishing this book, de Launoy had publicly advocated all his positions, thereby provoking violent controversies.

We shall abstain from examining the historical sections of the book and confine ourselves to the theoretical section, for this is the one which has exerted a decisive influence. De Launoy himself regarded it as "the foundation of all the rest" (268).

In four articles, the author undertakes to establish these points:

–Civil rulers have the power to establish diriment impediments. This right is grounded in the very nature of things and accords with the common opinion of theologians.

–This power has not been undermined by the Church. It is an error to say that the popes have legitimately reserved such power to themselves at the expense of civil rulers who act in this case on the strength of natural law (725).

–The ecclesiastical authority derives no advantage when it deprives secular rulers of this power, nor is it permitted to do so (745).

With regard to our question, it is the demonstration of the first point that is the most interesting. To the arguments from authority (de Launoy lists a large number of theologians, universities, *etc.*)[72] the author adds his own argument.[73] In the last analysis, his position rests on this assertion: marriage is a civil reality, recognized as such both in the Old Testament and the New Testament. Sacramentality superimposed on the civil contract did not bring about any change in that reality. Therefore, marriage is subject to civil legislation (651).[74]

At this point, de Launoy seeks to show that his position accords with the magisterium of the Church. The point of greatest historical importance is made in chapter 15 relative to the decree *Tametsi*. The fathers of Trent grounded the power to invalidate clandestine marriages on the fact that the matter of the sacrament, which until that time had been regarded as valid in the Church, was judged to be invalid by the council, thus making the validity of marriage between baptized persons contingent on the fulfillment of certain conditions. But in order to take this action, the fathers had to have recourse to civil power (since they themselves were not in possession of any such power) on the grounds that civil power has the competence to decide which conditions affect juridical capacity in this area. And, in fact, the council subordinated the efficacy of its own decree to its promulgation by the civil rulers. The council was therefore aware that it was exercising a power which it could not claim as properly its own. However, the council did no wrong, since the legates of the civil rulers were present and raised no objections (664–68).

The second point rests on the confession of the theologians that the Church had acquired the right to reserve to herself jurisdication over marriage through a historical development. The author undertakes to refute this hypothesis by using the same method as that used with regard to the first point (669–709). Bellarmine is the special target of his attacks (692–709).

The third point is less interesting, for it is limited to a historical reflection. The fourth point is demonstrated by appealing again to the basic notion: marriage is a civil matter and consequently falls under the sole competency of the civil ruler. The Church makes laws only with regard to the sacrament. Note especially de Launoy's interpretation of canons 3 and 4 of session XXIV (DS 1803–04). In connection with the word *ecclesia* in canon 4, he explains that the Church "was able to establish, and did establish, diriment impediments through the kings, or through some other person in the Church."[75]

De Launoy returned to this subject in other writings, but added nothing of importance. All the subsequent royalists were content to borrow and repeat his arguments.

Z. B. van ESPEN (1664–1728)

Civil jurists were not alone in advocating these positions. These were also advanced by canonists. Z. B. van Espen was the most outstanding among the latter, particularly because of the enormous influence he had on Josephinism and Febronianism. His fundamental work is entitled *Jus ecclesiasticum universum.*[76] Van Espen raised our question in connection with the debate concerning the impediments to marriage, and more precisely in connection with the competency belonging in this area to civil and ecclesiastical powers.

With regard to merely prohibitive impediments, van Espen has no doubts: Catholic civil rulers are indeed entitled to establish such impediments and to punish offenders (Part II, vol. 2, sect. 1, tit. XIII, chapt. I, no. X, 138).

With regard to diriment impediments, van Espen espouses Sanchez's position: given the nature of the contract, secular rulers are certainly entitled to establish such impediments. Sacramentality is no obstacle, says Sanchez, since marriage is a civil contract by its very nature (no. XI, 138).[77] But van Espen does not add with Sanchez: "The Church is nevertheless entitled to forbid the Christian rulers to use this power; it can reserve this to herself."[78] On this point he prefers Soto, who maintained that secular rulers renounced the exercise of their right out of deference for the Church (no. XI).

In essence, van Espen's position is as follows:

–The Church has the power to establish diriment impediments, but this power cannot exclude that of the state (no. XVIII, 138–39).

–The civil ruler also possesses this power because of the nature of his own authority and the nature of marriage. Out of deference for the Church, the rulers have abstained from using that power, but without ever losing it.

–Should the rulers eventually resume the exercise of this power no serious difficulty would arise, since the two authorities look upon the same reality from two different points of view and pursue different objectives (no. XVIII).

–Canon 4 of the Council of Trent is to be interpreted thus: the council did not intend to define whether the Church receives her competency "from the institution of the sacrament by Christ, or from a tacit or explicit concession at the hands of the civil rulers" (139). Van Espen quotes G. Gerbais (1629–99), but disassociates himself from him at the point where Gerbais traces the competency of the Church to a "right properly her own" (no. XVIII).

B. OBERHAUSER (1710–86)

Still among the canonists, we find B. Oberhauser who radicalizes van Espen's positions by crediting to the secular rulers alone the power to establish impediments to marriage, and by asserting that the Church's legislation in this area results from an usurpation of power. This position he advocated in *Systema historico-criticum diversarum potestatum in legibus matrimonialibus impedimentorum matrimonialium* (Frankfurt, 1771). The arguments herein were derived verbatim from de Launoy and van Espen. After this time, the controversy produced nothing new.

Let us recall the fundamental positions we have encountered:

1) Marriage as contract is separate from marriage as sacrament. Thus the sacramentality of marriage effects no change in natural marriage; it is added to natural marriage "as an accessory is added to the principal thing" (Hannequin).

2) The power of civil rulers with regard to marriage, including sacramental marriage, remains uncurtailed, even if these rulers have abstained for centuries from exercising it out of deference for the Church.

3) For the good of society and the Church, it is imperative that the civil ruler start exercising this power again, and so relieve the Church of a purely temporal task. The Church's sole task is to promote the saintliness of married life.

4) The Council of Trent did not intend to decide how the power of the Church with regard to marriage originated (van Espen); or the term *ecclesia* must be taken to refer to the *societas fidelium*, a society in which the king enjoys a preeminent position (de Launoy); or the word *matrimonii* ought to be taken to imply *sacramenti* (Gerbais); or the Church has been guilty of an usurpation of power (Léridant).

Josephinism and the Synod of Pistoia

The positions just mentioned reappeared in Febronius, a disciple of van Espen, and lie at the roots of the policies which Joseph II (1780–90) inaugurated in his empire regarding marriage. Subsequently, policies were translated into practice and prompted the interventions of the magisterium.

Thus, on September 4, 1781, Joseph II forbade his subjects to petition the Holy See for dispensation from impediments. As the minister Cobenzl explained, marriage is principally a civil matter, and only secondarily a religious one. Hence, the civil courts should make the first decisions as to whether a dispensation is necessary or useful. Once this necessity or usefulness has been recognized, the local ordinary or his consistory are entitled to determine, in accordance with the sacred canons of Rome, whether the dispensation should be resisted on spiritual grounds. In 1783 there came the decision to exclude marriage cases from the ecclesiastical courts in order to reserve them to the civil courts.

In support of these imperial decisions, there emerged a large body of juridico-theological literature which constantly appealed to the positions of de Launoy and van Espen. Let us mention for example J. Le Plat, J. A. Pelzk, J. N. Pehem, L. Litta, P. Tamburini, and G. Silvestri.[79]

In 1786, the Synod of Pistoia took place. On September 26, it turned to the problem of marriage. Tamburini was the promoter of the synod.[80] The basic positions the synod took are these:

–The synod asserted that the contract is distinct, and even separate, from the sacrament. It claimed to infer this separation from the fact that the priest "is the only and true minister" and that therefore his blessing "must be regarded as one of the elements that constitute the sacrament of marriage" (session 5, § V, 182). "From this it can be inferred that the contract does not include the sacrament either essentially or by virtue or its nature" (§ VI, 183).

–However, it is not left "to the free choice of the faithful to separate them" (*ibid.*). The synod even declared that "there is a clear precept to receive the sacrament," since grace is needed in order to meet the obligations of the married state.

–"As a consequence, we assert without hesitation that the supreme civil power has the full right to impose on all contracts, and more particularly on the marriage contract, the laws it deems suitable. . . . We infer from this that the civil power has the original competence to affect the contract" by means of diriment impediments (§ VII, 183). On the other hand, the civil power is requested to abolish certain impediments (§ X, 184–85).

–"Assuming assent or acquiescence (on the part of civil power), we acknowledge that the Church was legitimately entitled to establish [diriment] impediments" (§ XII, 186)

The Intervention of Pius VI

The first intervention of the papal magisterium concerning our question took place in the contest just described.

In the letter *Post factum tibi* addressed to the archbishop of Trier on February 2, 1787, Pius VI had already asserted the exclusive competency of the Church in matrimonial matters, but much more important by far was his letter *Deessemus nobis* of September 16 to Stefano Otriz, bishop of Mottala (Naples). The bishop had consented to act as judge delegated by the king of Naples to hear an appeal against a sentence of nullity issued by the tribunal of the archbishop of Naples (DS 2598). The pope's teaching is set forth, it seems to me, in the following steps.

At the foundation of the whole declaration there lies the assertion that "the marriage contract is truly and properly one of the seven sacraments of the New Dispensation;" and that "it is a dogma of faith that marriage, which before the coming of Christ was merely an indissoluble contract, has become since then one of the seven sacraments." Note how the Pope takes a resolute step beyond tridentine theology: he asserts that the sacrament is the contract. On the strength of this principle, no legislative or juridical competency should be credited to secular rulers. "All these cases fall exclusively within the competence of ecclesiastical judges." This assertion is based on canon 12 of the Council of Trent "the terms of which are so general as to include all cases. The very spirit or purpose of the law are such as to allow for no exception or limitation."

The second and even more important intervention of Pius VI was the bull *Auctorem fidei* of August 28, 1794, which condemned the Synod of Pistoia. Our problem is addressed in propositions 59 and 60 (DS 2659–60).

Proposition 59 labels as "destructive" (*eversiva*) of canons 3, 4, 9, and 12 of Trent, and as heretical, any statement that denies to the Church the power to establish by the exercise of a right of her own (*jure proprio*) impediments affecting the marriage of Christians and the right to dispense from the same. As is apparent from the synodal text to which the bull refers and from the debate in progress at the time, the phrase *jure proprio* means that the Church has this power independently of the consent or acquiescence of secular rulers.

Proposition 60 is a corollary of 59. It asserts that granting the civil power the competency to suppress or curtail canonical impediments and depriving the Church of the power to dispense from such impediments is a consequence "of the heretical principle condemned above."

Obviously, the teaching of Pius VI focused on a controversial issue and was directly meant to assert the exclusive competency of the Church with regard to impediments affecting the marriage contract. This affirmation was aimed both at the position which denies the competence and at the one which traces it to a tacit or explicit concession on the part of secular rulers. This affirmation was based on the contention that the contract itself is (or has turned out to be – *evasit*) one of the seven sacraments of the new dispensation. The pope interpreted the canons of Trent quoted above by repudiating the contention that they are merely disciplinary in nature, as well as van Espen's interpretation followed by Le Plat, and de Launoy's interpretation followed by Tamburini.

Phase Two: The Royalist Conflict in the Nineteenth Century

The Historical Context

The momentous historical event that marked this phase was the advent of the juridical institution of civil marriage. What cultural forces account for the emergence of this institution? In terms of the present inquiry, it will suffice to mention some key points.

There can hardly be any doubt that the controversy stirred up by the royalists and the adherents of Josephinism, even though it was part of a movement apparently confined to the domain of theological debate, did exert a considerable influence on the emergence of civil marriage. This controversy decisively questioned the position that the institution of marriage pertains in its substance to the order of salvation. It thus promoted a decisive laicization of this institution.

Another contributing factor was the very extensive and deep cultural movement which exalted the value of natural law. Already with Grotius, this movement projected the establishment of a social order which prescinded from faith, and appealed to reason as the sole principle of organization in the life of society. Within this perspective marriage was regarded only as a natural law institution. Its religious-sacramental dimension was no longer preeminently important or, at least, no longer a matter of essential interest.

Within this natural law philosophy, this assertion that the freedom of the individual person is a primary and absolute value necessarily led to the conclusion that marriage is but the outcome of the consent exchanged by the parties, as with any other contract. It follows that the consent of the parties was no longer looked upon as the acceptance on their part of an objective state of affairs. Rather, consent freely establishes a relationship between them which can be terminated whenever they choose. The introduction of civil marriage coincided with the introduction of divorce as a civil right.

In essence, then, the creation of civil marriage represents an aspect of the secularization and laicization movement which marks the history of Europe in the modern era. The principle was stated in the French Constitution of September 3–4, 1791, title II, art. 7: "The law regards marriage only as a civil contract."

Civil marriage was introduced for the first time in France in the year 1792, and then definitely sanctioned by the Napoleonic Code (art.

191), which served as a model for the legislation later adopted by other states.

Such is the historical context within which the nineteenth century interventions of the papal magisterium are set. One of the important problems on which the magisterium focused attention is the relationship between contract and sacrament. But note that the papal teaching did not let itself be confused by the polemics; it rather sought to resolve these by clarifying the Catholic doctrine on marriage.

PIUS VII AND PIUS VIII

Under the pontificate of Pius VII there appeared an important instruction of the Sacred Congregation of the Holy Office (July 6, 1817) *ad Praef. Martinicae, Guadalupe, etc. Principia de divortio,*[81] which condemned those who try to justify civil divorce "by a false argument based on the well-known distinction between contract and sacrament." The document quotes canon 1 of the Council of Trent, and continues:

> It is, therefore, heretical to establish a normal and absolute separation between the sacrament and the contract, as if the contract, by virtue of the divine institution, did not enter into to the essence and substance of the sacrament, and as if the sacrament of marriage were only a quality hovering over the contract, analogous to a decorative frame around a painting and external to it . . .

And again:

> Marriage is a sacrament because the contract itself is a sacrament. To say it differently, the contract pertains to the substance of the sacrament, and is part of the definition of it. This is a dogma of the Catholic faith. Even if we assume the possibility of a non-sacramental marriage between believers, it would still remain an article of faith that there never is between believers a sacrament of marriage which would not be constituted in its essence by the contract. According to the new dispensation, there can indeed be a nonsacramental marriage, but never can there be a sacrament in which the contract is no sacrament. This dogma is contained in the canons of the Council of Trent quoted above. . . . It is, therefore, heretical to assert that in

> the new dispensation the marriage contract is normally and by virtue of its essence separate from the sacrament, and that the sacrament is merely a decoration immaterial and external to the value and constitution of the contract.

In the encyclical *Traditi humilitati* issued on March 24, 1829, upon taking possession of Saint John Lateran, Pius VIII impressed upon the bishops the obligation to exhibit a special pastoral concern regarding marriage. It is important to stress

> that marriage should be regulated not only by human law, but also by divine law – that is, it should be ranked among the sacred realities, not the worldly ones, and that, as a consequence, it falls entirely within the competency of the Church. Formerly, the union of husband and wife was intended only for the sake of procreation. . . . Since marriage was raised by Christ to the dignity of a sacrament and endowed with heavenly gifts, the source of happiness in marriage resides less in the procreation of children than in bringing them up for God. This union, which takes its origin from God, signifies the perpetual and supreme union of Christ with the Church. This very intimate association between a man and his wife is a sacrament.[82]

This was one of the most important interventions of the magisterium in the matter at hand. First of all, the sacramentality of marriage was located in the union of husband and wife, a union which owes its origin to God. Presented in this way, the inseparability of contract from sacrament takes on the value of a positive attribute. In addition, the reference to the role played by grace with respect to nature sets the Pope's thesis in its proper context, which is that of the history of salvation.

PIUS IX AND THE *SYLLABUS*

In the teaching of Pius IX the tendency already present in Pius VIII to leave behind the controversy concerning juridical competency and to get at the heart of the problem gained more and more strength. Starting with Pius IX, the key doctrinal point is the contract–sacrament relationship. The implications required to resolve the conflict with the secular power are inferred from this relationship.

The first intervention of Pius IX followed the line taken by Pius VI. His apostolic letter *Multiplices inter* of June 16, 1861, condemned F. G. Vigil's book *Defensa de la autoridad de los Gobiernos y de los Obispos contra las pretenciones de la Curia Romana* (Lima, 1848), and especially the assertion that the secular rulers have in their own right the power to establish diriment impediments.[83]

Soon afterwards there followed an intervention of greater consequence. It concerned the books of N. Nuytz (1800–1874), *Juris Ecclesiastici Institutiones* and *In Jus Ecclesiasticum universum tractationes* (Turin, 1846). The author, professor of canon law at the Royal University of Turin and undistinguished either in talent or scholarship, had repeated the doctrine of the royalists, of Josephinism, and of the Synod of Pistoia. The apostolic letter *Ad apostolicae* of August 23, 1851,[84] condemned as erroneous several of Nuytz's positions: the sacrament of marriage is secondary and separable from the contract; sacramentality is to be reduced to the sole blessing given to the spouses (which was not, by the way, Cano's position); the civil authorities possess the original competency with regard to diriment impediments; the canons of the Council of Trent are to be interpreted as either adopting this conception, or as not dogmatic in nature. The Pope made explicit a teaching of the bull *Auctorem fidei* by interpreting the canons of the Council of Trent as dogmatic in import. The manner in which this position is presented shows that the problem at the root of the debate is theological, not juridical.[85]

Clearly more important still was the intervention occasioned by a piece of proposed legislation meant to introduce civil marriage into the Kingdom of Piedmont.[86] On July 2, 1852, Pius IX wrote to the king: "I merely note that [in the proposed legislation] the contract is being distinguished from the sacrament in accordance with the teachings of Nuytz, teachings which have been presented a thousand times, and a thousand times condemned. What the legislation intends is to strip the sacrament of all the force and efficacy it ought to have in relation to the contract."[87]

Pius IX returned to the question in his letter of September 19, and developed his position further:

> Our intention is only to set forth Catholic teaching with the brevity imposed by the limits of a letter. . . . It is a dogma of faith that marriage has been raised by Our Lord to the dignity of a sacrament. It is a doctrine of the Church

> that the sacrament is not an adventitious quality superimposed on the contract; it pertains to the essence of marriage itself. Apart from the sacrament there is only concubinage. A civil law which supposes that, for Catholics, the sacrament is separable from the marriage contract and on the strength of this supposition dares to regulate the conditions required for validity infringes on the rights of the Church and practically equates concubinage with the sacrament of marriage since it sanctions the one as well as the other as legitimate.[88]

The papal teaching set forth in these private letters reappeared in the consistorial allocution of September 27, 1852, in which the pope condemned, among other things, the introduction of civil marriage in Colombia. He asserted that marriage is one of the seven sacraments; that there can be no marriage between believers which would not at the same time be a sacrament; that a nonsacramental union between Christians, even if contracted in conformity with civil law, is only concubinage; that the sacrament is inseparable from the marriage contract; that the Church is wholly competent to legislate in matters related to the marriage of Christians.[89]

This teaching was later taken up in the *Syllabus* (December 8, 1864) § VII, "*Errores de matrimonio christiano*," propositions 66 and 73 (DS 2966 and 2975).

In sum, the magisterium of Pius IX clearly adopted the following positions:

– In the marriage of baptized persons, there is no separation between contract and sacrament, since sacramentality is not a merely secondary thing compared to the contract.

– Therefore, between baptized persons, there never is a marriage which is not a sacrament. The exclusion of sacramentality renders the contract invalid, and the union is reduced to a concubinage.

– The two preceding positions are set forth as "doctrine of the Catholic Church," and as a consequence of the dogma of faith taught by the Council of Trent in canon 1 of session XXIV.

Theologians

In the nineteenth century our question became the object of a new phase of intense theological and often original reflection. The most important treatises on marriage devote much space to this reflection.

J. MARTIN (1792–1859)

In a work highly praised by Scheeben, *De Matrimonio et potestate ipsum dirimendi Ecclesiae soli exclusive subjecta* (2 vols.; Lyon–Paris, 1844), J. Martin set forth the position announced in the title of the book. The originality of his approach, which Scheeben was to develop later, is traceable to the fact that the competency of the Church is grounded on the relationship between natural marriage and Christian marriage envisaged from the perspective of the history of salvation. Through the mouth of Adam, who was his prototype, Christ spoke a significant and constitutive word which both referred to marriage as it is for all time and to the union to be established one day between Christ and the Church. Every marriage ought to mirror this profound reality and be as it were the carrier of it.[90]

G. PERRONE (1794–1876)

G. Perrone was the first theologian to approach our problem through a critique of Cano's position. According to this Roman theologian, one of the decisive arguments against the proposition that the priest is the minister of the sacrament of marriage is that this proposition results in a most harmful disjunction between contract and sacrament. This is confirmed by the fact that the royalists made that proposition one of their favorite tenets (see above under no. 1).[91]

As Perrone resumed the problem on a larger scale than the problematic of the preceding century, he voiced his conviction that the jurisdictional controversy implies the theological question of the relationship between contract and sacrament. He begins by noting that the contract is the matter of the sacrament not as a civil contract,[92] but as natural contract.[93] The dignity of a sacrament is not added onto the contract; rather the contract acquires its sacramental nature in the very act of being made. Sacramentality is not an addition to an already extant natural contract. It emerges fully in the very act of making the contract, just as the sacramentality of baptism emerges from the ablution.[94] Contract and sacrament are identified in the one and same act. They should not be looked upon as if they were two realities. The distinction exists only between two formalities of the same reality.[95]

M. J. SCHEEBEN (1835–88)

In our view, Scheeben is the theologian who, in the nineteenth century, addressed the problem at hand with the greatest profundity.[96] As we shall see, some theologians had hesitations in the matter, yet Scheeben was convinced that, once the magisterium had spoken, we could no longer doubt that the marriage between Christians becomes a sacrament for the same reasons as those on which its validity rests. On several occasions, Pius IX has solemnly declared that the sacrament of marriage was not an appendage, that it could not be disjointed from marriage as a contract, and that the union between baptized persons could not be legitimate unless it took the form of a sacramental marriage.

In a page remarkable for a depth rarely seen in the theology of marriage in his time, Scheeben gives the reason why sacrament is inseparable from contract.

> Christian marriage is inextricably interwoven with the supernatural fabric of the Church; the greatest damage one can inflict on both is to tear them apart. When such a catastrophe occurs, matrimony completely loses its high mystical character, and the Church loses one of her fairest flowers, wherein her supernatural, all-pervading, transforming power is so splendidly revealed. Nowhere does the mystical life of the Church penetrate more deeply into natural relationships than in matrimony. In this sacrament the Church clasps to her heart the first of all human relationships, that upon which the existence and propagation of human nature depends, so as to make it wholly her own and transform it into herself. The bride of the Son, who as the head of the race has taken possession of the race, makes even the natural generative power of the race serve her purpose, and claims the legitimate use of that power exclusively for her own heavenly end. Nowhere has the truth more strikingly come to light that the whole of nature, down to its deepest roots, shares in the sublime consecration of the God-man, who has taken this nature to Himself. Nowhere does the truth more clearly appear that Christ has been made the cornerstone upon which God has based the preservation of and growth of nature.[97]

The inseparability of contract from sacrament is grounded, then, on the covenant constituted by the incarnation. As Christ takes up the nature of a human being, and makes that nature holy, he transfigures and elevates the human reality of marriage in the Church and through the Church's mediation. On this christologico-ecclesial basis Scheeben speaks of the sacrament of marriage "as an essentially sacred act." He states that it is not possible to separate "sacredness from the nature of matrimony, by holding that it comes in from outside." He rejects Cano's position by remarking that "the assistance of the priesthood is required not to make the marriage holy, but because it is holy."[98] He considers both natural marriage and marriage as a sacrament in relation to the mystery of Christ and the Church.

Natural marriage refers to that mystery only in a symbolic way, while sacramental marriage refers to it in a real way. The former "would only be a figure" which represents a mystery "extrinsic to it," "a figure empty of content," while the latter bears a real, essential, and intrinsic relation to the mystery of Christ and of the church.[99]

D. PALMIERI (1829–1909)

D. Palmieri followed the thought of Perrone, but from the viewpoint of the intention of the contracting parties, a viewpoint which had been forgotten in the royalist controversy, the Synod of Pistoia excepted. After recalling the uncertainties of the past Palmieri states: "Henceforth, the Catholic doctrine is clear enough: these two things are inseparable, not as two realities that must of necessity exist together, but as one and the same reality. There is a duality only with regard to the formalities which are entailed, and indeed necessarily so, by a reality which is one."[100]

Palmieri's reflections proceed in two steps. He first asserts that between baptized persons marriage is the sacrament itself; between baptized persons marriage is necessarily a sacrament. He proves the first part of his argument thus. The efficient cause of marriage *in fieri* (the contract) is the same as the cause of the sacrament: it is the consent of the parties, as taught by Eugene IV (*Decretum pro Armenis*, DS 1327). Hence sacramentality is a modality intrinsic to Christian marriage. Moreover, the sacrament consists in that which signifies the union of Christ with the Church. Now, this signifying reality is the conjugal bond, that is, the contract itself. (Here the position of Bellarmine is adopted.)

On this foundation Palmieri establishes the second part of his position: between baptized persons there can be no marriage which is not a sacrament; the basis of this is not *ex natura rei* but *ex divina institutione* (*ibid.*, 76). It follows that we need to ascertain what Christ willed rather than to ask questions about the intention of the contracting parties. (One recognizes here the argument of Suarez.) Palmieri offers this demonstration: since the sacrament, when it exists, is the contract itself, the institution of the sacrament consisted precisely in the act of conjoining the one with the other; we must assume that this conjunction-institution has been effected through the absolute will of God, independently of the will of human beings (76). The reason is that the institution of a sacrament is an act of God's will, not subordinate to human freedom. Therefore, since Christ raised to sacramentality not a particular marriage, but marriage as such (see Mt 19), and since he did not institute some rite to which one could have recourse if one so chose, it follows that marriage is always a sacrament. The human will can decide "that there is no sacrament" but cannot choose between a purely natural marriage and a marriage which is also sacramental. (See 77–78).

Note, however, that toward the middle of the nineteenth century the interventions of the popes had not yet brought about a consensus among theologians. Thus, A. Berlage in his book *System der katholischen Dogmatik*[101] did not yet see a convincing reason why the sacrament should be inseparable from the contract. Perrone himself mentions many theologians who credited Church and State with a competency *ex aequo* with regard to the conjugal bond.[102]

LEO XIII

Leo XIII returned several times to the teaching of his predecessor. He even lent this teaching a notably greater degree of profundity and explicitness giving it an extremely precise formulation.

In his first encyclical *Inscrutabili* (April 21, 1878) he denounced the fact that certain legislation had entirely ignored the religious character of marriage and demeaned it to the level of a merely civil contract, which is tantamount to treating what is only legal concubinage as marriage.[103]

The first extensive intervention of Leo XIII came in his letter to the bishops and archbishops of the ecclesiastical provinces of Turin, Vercelli, and Genoa (June 1, 1879):

> "Moreover you are well aware, my Venerable Brothers, that in order to justify acts of interference on the part of

> the civil power with Christian legislation concerning marriage, recourse is made . . . to the notion that the contract is separate from the sacrament. . . . To be sure, the conscience of anyone who is sincerely Catholic cannot accept this doctrine as the basis of Christian legislation on marriage. It rests on a dogmatic error condemned several times by the Church, an error which reduces the sacrament to an external ceremony, and to the level of a mere ritual. This doctrine disrupts the essential notion of Christian marriage according to which the conjugal bond, sanctified by a religious act, is identified with the sacrament and constitutes with it an indissoluble unity, an indivisible reality."[104]

An even more important intervention of the magisterium is contained, I believe, in the encyclical *Arcano divinae sapientiae* (February 10, 1880), no. 12 (DS 3145–46).

There the pope asserted the absolute inseparability of contract from sacrament in the marriage of baptized persons, so that "there can exist no true and legitimate marriage between baptized persons which is not at the same time a sacrament." The clearly stated reason is the very same as had been adduced by Pius VIII, and extensively developed during the previous century by the best theologians of marriage, such as Scheeben. This reason had already been suggested by Bellarmine: the conjugal reality itself is, precisely as such, the "symbol" of the union of Christ with the Church. This is why Leo XIII states that every legitimate marriage between Christians is a sacrament in itself and in its own right. Nothing could be more erroneous than to make of the sacrament a mere ennoblement of the contract or an attribute that is attached to the contract from outside, capable of being severed and separated from it at will.[105]

In his later teachings, Leo XIII always recalled this position without adding anything new: the marriage contract is inseparable from marriage as sacrament. The institution by Christ means that the contract "has become" *itself* a sacrament (apostolic letter *Il divisamento*; FIC, 3, § 2, 394), and can therefore no longer be separated from the sacrament. It will suffice to list these interventions: letter *Il divisamento*, February 8, 1893; allocution *In litteris Nostris*, March 18, 1895 (FIC 3, 469): "Marriage, which was a natural transaction and a natural contract, was raised from that level to the state of a sacrament"; letter *Quam religiose*, August 16, 1898 (FIC 3, 532); allocution

Afferre iucundiora, December 16, 1901 (FIC 3, 577); letter *Dum multa,* December 24, 1902 (FIC 3, 598).

The Code of Canon Law sanctioned this doctrine in canon 1012, § 1–2, and the papal teaching ceased to make any mention of it. In his encyclical *Casti connubii* of December 31, 1930, Pius XI himself was content simply to recall the doctrine previously taught by quoting the code (DS 3713), and did not deem it necessary to dwell any further on it.

4. FOURTH HISTORICAL CONTEXT: CONTEMPORARY CONTROVERSIES

The fourth context within which our problem comes to the fore is constituted by the problematic of our time. It is difficult to be precise when delimiting this context or even when defining the terms in which our problem is actually being raised nowadays. This difficulty arises from the nature of the sources, which sometimes lack clarity and precision, and from the fact that we are dealing here with a debate still fully in progress.

Assuming this indispensable qualification, our view is that the problem emerges because of an observed state of affairs and because of the pastoral concern occasioned by this state of affairs.

The state of affairs in question is this: ecclesial celebration of marriage is being requested by baptized persons who reject the faith entirely, or exhibit a religiosity devoid of any reference to Christ, or are engaged in a quest of the God and Jesus Christ.[106] The pastoral concern seeks to avoid taking a course of action that might sever any link which these persons may have with the Church.[107]

This pastoral concern leads in turn to a pastoral decision: to welcome these people not only as baptized persons in need of evangelization and catechizing, but also as people who want to marry. In other words, the Church ought to recognize in them the will to marry. Since in the three hypothetical situations mentioned above the celebration of the sacrament is out of the question, this decision implies a consequence which some regard as inevitable: the church would agree to regard nonsacramental marriages as true and proper marriages. In technical post-Tridentine language, we would say that these marriages are *legitima sed non rata,* or that they are valid yet nonsacramental contracts.

Thus far, this pastoral decision has become concrete in three forms:

– A religious nonsacramental celebration of the marriage of baptized persons who find themselves in the conditions described above. To the two baptized persons who have already contracted a civil marriage or are engaged to be married, the option is offered of taking part in a religious ceremony during which it is clearly stated that no sacrament is being celebrated. People would pray together, and perhaps words of blessing are even recited.

– The celebration of marriage in successive stages,[108] according to the model followed in the catechumenate.[109]

– The recognition of civil marriage as a true and proper marriage, albeit nonsacramental, for baptized nonbelieving persons.[110]

The crux of the problem becomes clear when this pastoral practice is examined in connection with the question of the separability of marriage as a contract and marriage as a sacrament.[111] The problem is precisely this: can the Church recognize a conjugal state to exist between two baptized persons who supposedly have been married nonsacramentally, or are we to say that, as far as the church is concerned, there exists between baptized persons no marriage except a marriage which is also a sacrament? Clearly enough, the pastoral practice described above opts for the former alternative: the Church can and should recognize as legitimately married two baptized persons who have contracted a nonsacramental union under the circumstances cited. This applies even if the church should ask them to try making their way toward the faith and consequently toward a sacramental celebration and should offer them the opportunity to make progress in this direction. What arguments are being set forth in favor of this position? Unless we are mistaken, the main arguments are these:

(1) Until Leo XIII the position which advocates the separability of contract from sacrament was freely debated among theologians. That this is the case appears from the following arguments: the Council of Trent had no intention of defining anything at all concerning this point; Benedict XIV did not take a position in this matter; even during the preparatory phase for Vatican I the inseparability position failed to win the day within the theological commission.

(2) The intervention of Pius VI, Pius IX, and Leo XIII took place within the context of the jurisdictional conflict between Church and state. Their utterances were worded so as to affirm the exclusive com-

petence of the Church in the matter of marriage between baptized persons. Today's problematic is entirely different. It follows that to appeal to these teachings of the magisterium entails an interpretation of them which unduly stretches their import.[112]

(3) Present canonical legislation does not take into account the case here under consideration. It speaks only of baptized persons "who do not practice" and "are not instructed," and assumes that baptized persons are also believers. "We are, therefore, entitled to say that the experiment in progress is not *contra legem* but *praeter legem* . . . no matter what theological perspective should underlie the canonical prescriptions."[113]

(4) The position which advocates the separability of contract from sacrament is even more solidly grounded now that Vatican II has proclaimed that the realities of this world are autonomous and has declared that religious freedom is for everyone, not only for non-Christians. Moreover, the Church may renounce rights of her own, even when legitimately acquired, whenever such renunciation is necessary for the sake of the gospel.[114]

(5) Many post-Tridentine theologians have asserted that a baptized person can choose between marriage as contract and marriage as sacrament. (Bellarmine is especially cited.)[115]

(6) Even if we grant that the Church has sanctioned the inseparability of contract from sacrament, "she is not absolutely bound to abide by this judgment, since there is no precept of divine law that would make it binding upon baptized persons to receive a sacramental marriage." We are dealing here with an obligation established "by a measure traceable to positive law."[116]

This last argument rests on the following observations. The Church had to take responsibility for the celebration of marriages between baptized persons to steer these people away from pagan celebrations. According to the conviction prevailing at that time, the validity of marriage was linked to this celebration. It also happened that the Church recognized as valid only those marriages celebrated with its own intervention.

The gifts of God are not sources of alienation. If God bestows upon marriage the riches of his grace, he does not take away from human beings the natural power to contract marriage.[117] Baptism does not deprive Christians of the freedom to dispose of themselves.[118] Inasmuch as marriage is an *officium naturae*, it retains its autonomy.

There is a difference between the nature of natural marriage and the nature of sacrament, a difference which applies even in the case of baptized persons.[119]

The specific character of the sacrament has the effect of rendering the contracting parties subject to an ecclesial mission, a subjection which cannot be imposed on anyone.[120] Consequently, marriage becomes a sacrament only through a faith which is actual and active, that is, through the will to accept a ministry from the Church.[121]

7) Lack of faith renders marriage as a sacrament absolutely nonexistent. "After all, we must agree that, in some way or other, faith is a constitutive element of the sacrament."[122]

This particular reason is presented from different points of view:

Is the distinction between validity, liciety, and fruit meaningless in the case of marriage?[123] The reception of baptism cannot be regarded as "an accident of fate"[124] which automatically produces the sacrament of marriage apart from any mediation from faith.

Just as the marriage of new converts becomes a sacrament by virtue of baptism, so too it can be argued that the civil marriage of two baptized persons automatically becomes a sacrament as they become believers.

In conclusion, the inseparability of contract from sacrament is not a given that cannot and should not be subjected to theological critique. It is imperative to change the canonical discipline to which the Church position on inseparability has given rise, and to pursue all the necessary consequences of this change at the level of pastoral practice.

Part Two

DOCTRINAL SKETCH

1. FORMULATION OF THE QUESTION AND AN ATTEMPT AT SOLUTION

a. Theological approach

The historical review has clearly shown that the problem before us is this: is there such a thing as nonsacramental marriage between baptized persons?

But the same review has abundantly demonstrated, I believe, that the problem can be approached from two complementary yet distinct vantage points.

Considered from an objective point of view, the problem concerns the relationship between marriage as a reality of the order of creation and marriage as a sacrament, insofar as this relationship has been established by God himself. Here the problem is approached *ex parte Dei* in keeping with a conception of theology according to which theology is *quaedam impressio divinae scientiae*, as St. Thomas maintains (ST, Ia, q.1, a.3, ad2): that is, a trace of divine knowledge left behind by what God has in fact done and revealed. God reveals what he accomplishes, and accomplishes what he reveals.

Considered from a subjective point of view, the problem concerns the possibility or impossibility of separating, as far as any baptized person is concerned, marriage as a reality of the order of creation from marriage as a sacrament. The problem consists, if you will, in discerning the subjective conditions by which this separation does or does not come about. This approach prevailed in Vasquez and Rebello as well as among other post-Tridentine theologians, and still prevailed in the fourth historical context.

My personal view is that in this whole problematic the first approach is the one that ought to dominate. Should theological reflection take a different course, it would lead to mistaken results. The choice of the first approach commends itself adequately on merely formal and methodological grounds, since theology is intended to ascertain what God has revealed in Christ. The problems that emerge when the second approach is adopted ought to be resolved by way of consequence. The question, then, is to discern the relationship which God in Christ has established between marriage as a reality of the order of creation and marriage as a sacrament.

Obviously, our reflections here presuppose the theology of the sacramentality of marriage both as a theological justification of this sacramentality and as an understanding of sacramentality and of the relation which sacramentality bears to baptism.

b. The validity of this approach

The solution must be sought, I believe, in the context of the relationship that exists between creation and Christ. Our problem refers to but one aspect, one particular instance, of this relationship, so the solution of the problem of marriage as a reality of the order of creation and as a sacrament depends entirely on how this relationship is conceived.

There are several reasons for proceeding in this way. It will help to recall these in capsule form. All the great New Testament texts on marriage refer more or less explicity to the relationship between marriage as it is in Genesis and as it is in the new covenant.

The most important interventions of the magisterium concerning marriage espouse the same approach. One of these, the encyclical of Pius VIII entitled *Traditi humilitati*, even refers explicitly to this relationship and finds there the key to the solution of the problem.

Our historical sketch shows a coincidence which can hardly be accidental, and provides much food for thought: our problem emerges at a time when the problem of the relationship between nature and grace is at the center of a new theological debate.

Having opted for this working hypothesis, we can identify the two essential phases that ought to mark our inquiry. In the first phase, we need to review very briefly and only to the extent necessary, the relationship that exists between creation and Christ. In the second, we need focus attention on the decisive importance of this relationship for the solution of our problem.

2. THE RELATIONSHIP BETWEEN CREATION AND CHRIST

a. An intrinsic link positively willed by God's love

The first theological given concerning creation, I believe, is this: Jesus Christ is the disclosure of the meaning of creation. That is, he reveals that creation is the deed which actualizes God's intention to mediate the trinitarian existence *ad extra*, or more precisely, to mediate *ad extra* the condition of the Word in the bosom of the Trinity in order to engender children for God in Jesus through the gift of the Spirit.

This assertion necessarily implies another, namely, that creation by God is a free act. The contention that God created out of necessity is contradicted not only by explicit affirmations in the data of revelation, but also by the truth that the being of God can only be absolute freedom.

b. Another hypothesis: creation without grace

On the basis of revealed data, we must also maintain the possibility of a creation which would be not the actualization of God's will to mediate his own trinitarian life *ad extra* in Christ (which, in fact, takes place in the history of salvation), but only the actualization of an essentially lower kind of mediation. There is no way to prove conclusively that a sharing other than the one which in fact exists is contradictory. To say it differently, we cannot demonstrate a necessary connection between the created spirit on the one hand and grace as revealed and realized in Christ on the other. We are faced with two essentially different possibilities: a creation performed in view of the covenant in Jesus Christ, and a creation in which this orientation to the covenant is absent.

It is extremely difficult to establish by positive proof that a creation different from the one actually realized is possible. The only experience of created reality at our disposal relates to the only order there is, namely, the order of trinitarian life being shared *ad extra* in Christ. It follows that any attempt at establishing by positive proof that a different creation is possible can only be an exercise in logical abstraction, a laborious act of prescinding from created reality as it actually is. In connection with this laborious effort two problems arise. Was it possible for the incarnation not to occur? The second problem is connected with the first: was it possible for human beings not to be raised to the order of the covenant?

These two problems are and remain within a correct theological context only inasmuch as we abstain from indulging in a reversal such as this: considering as real what has remained a mere possibility (that is, a creation which would not entail a sharing *ad extra* of the divine life in Christ, and yet be internally coherent) and considering as merely a possibility what is, in fact, the only reality there is (that is, creation as communication of trinitarian life). Within a correct theological context, correct in the sense just explained, the question of a creation without grace makes valid theological sense. It is the direct way of showing that grace is transcendent and absolutely unmerited, and the indirect and inferential way of achieving a deeper knowledge of human reality.

Creation, then, is in fact the communication of trinitarian life *ad extra.*

Creation exists by virtue of an absolutely gratuitous decision by which God willed the covenant with himself in Christ through the gift of the Spirit. This assertion constitutes the *core* of what is given in revelation concerning creation.

From this core assertion two other assertions follow by way of development and explication: creation is the revelation of the power and goodness of God which encounter no obstacles of any kind; and the whole world, matter included, owes its origin to God.

c. The danger entailed in substituting the methodological supposition for the reality of God's plan for the history of salvation

The three preceding assertions are not to be construed as if they were external to one another. They are three ways of saying in descending order – from the more comprehensive to the more particular – that creation is the communication of trinitarian life *ad extra.* Nevertheless, Christian thought historically has been compelled to pause longer and reflect more on the last of these assertions. This is because Christian thought has developed under a nonnegotiable and internal demand: Christians must speak out and defend themselves against outsiders.

The recurrent denial of the fact that all reality takes its origin from God the creator (e.g. Manichaeism) forced the Fathers to emphasize this idea, yet their insistence did not constitute a distortion within their thought. The introduction of Aristotelian thought into the Christian world exerted, I believe, a similar influence. The interventions of the magisterium (Lateran IV and Vatican I) stressed once more the fundamental position: all reality, matter included, owes its origin to God, and is as a consequence derived from nonbeing as Vatican I says; the council thus underlined the principle of metaphysical transcendence, whose denial is, to a large extent, the pivot of modern and contemporary culture. This principle of transcendence constitutes, in my view, the profoundest and most decisive condition that must be met if the kerygma is to be spared a curtailment that would render it subject to humanity and make it radically immanent.

The Arian controversy also exerted an influence in this area by causing people to forget Christ's mediation in creation, a mediation which was exposed to an unorthodox interpretation.

People forgot that this deeper understanding of the assertion that the whole world, matter included, owes its origin to God is only a partial element within the totality of the Church's reflection concerning creation – a reflection whose central axis is the affirmation that creation is for the sake of the covenant with God in Christ through the gift of the Spirit. As a result, there emerged a theology of creation, and consequently of all reality, in which the link to the center was lost, a self-sufficient theology of creation to which was later appended from outside a reflection on creation in view of the covenant. Once adopted, this approach favored the tendency to juxtapose the theology of the covenant to the theology of creation while granting to the latter an existence and a consistency independent of the former. In this arrangement, the theology of creation reflects on creation in its essential structures, and the theology of the covenant reflects on it in terms of the adventitious modification added to it.

These two efforts of reflective thought can correctly be joined in the manner already alluded to: we need to maintain that the revealed datum which posits creation in and through Christ constitutes the whole of which consequent propositions are but particular aspects. These are open to reflection and understanding only to the extent that they can be situated in the whole and linked to the datum which in that whole constitutes the center.

The framework of the present inquiry does not require us to develop this methodological point. For our purpose, it will be enough to submit three fundamental propositions, and to show how they affect our problem:

1) Human beings (and, therefore, marriage insofar as it is a human reality) are created in fact in view of the covenant with God in Christ through the gift of the Spirit.

2) Human beings (hence, marriage as well) are open to this same finality.

3) Human beings (hence, marriage as well) attain to their true realization in this covenant with God.

3. MARRIAGE AS A REALITY OF CREATION AND MARRIAGE AS SACRAMENT

a. Sacramental marriage is the only marriage willed by God as a means of sharing his love

The fundamental theological datum can be put in these terms: the covenant with God in Christ through the gift of the Spirit is the revelation of the meaning of marriage. This means that marriage is one of the possible places in which there occurs God's communication *ad extra* of his trinitarian life which is love. I say, "one of the places," for obviously it is not the only place. To affirm that marriage is an institution of the order of creation can have, theologically, but one real meaning: marriage is instituted for the sake of participation, in Christ, in the covenant with God.

This primary theological datum necessarily implies the affirmation that marriage is as described, and that no other kind of marriage exists. The sharing of trinitarian love is the only form of conjugal love between a man and a woman who, through baptism, have come to share the grace of Christ.

b. Two hypotheses of another type of marriage

However, this necessary implication raises the question of whether a marriage different from the one just mentioned is a possibility.

This problem may take on different meanings. It may coincide with the question that asks whether God was free to institute a different marriage (this question is analogous to the one that inquires about a creation not oriented toward the covenant). In this case, the question is appropriate to the extent that it reflects a conviction that it is impossible to prove that a creation not oriented toward the covenant is internally contradictory, and to show conclusively that the same internal contradiction marks any marriage which would not be a participation in the covenant. Consequently, the elevation that makes marriage an actualization of God's will to give man and wife access to the intimacy of his own love by putting his own self at their disposal in his holy godhead is a decision that, in relation to the *act of creation* by which marriage was instituted, constitutes an absolutely new beginning. Nevertheless, the question is inappropriate and fraught with errors to the extent that one forgets the center. One would then regard as real something which God's free decision has left within the realm of possibilities, marriage unrelated to the covenant, and as merely possible that which actually exists, marriage within the covenant, and whose existence is due to a divine decision which the creature had no right whatever to demand.

In the first case – appropriate approach to the question – the answer will be worked out by showing the supereminent transcendence, the absolute transcendence that pertains to marriage as a sacrament (the *elevatio* spoken of in the documents of the magisterium, or the *perficere* in the texts of Trent and Vatican II). It goes without saying that this supereminent transcendence of marriage as a sacrament is not to be restricted (as it perhaps was in one approach to moral theology) to the simple fact, merely juridically interpreted, of the absolute or even extrinsic indissolubility of marriage, the indissolubility that differentiates sacramental from nonsacramental marriage.

In the *second case* – the inappropriate approach to the question – the answer will be worked out by attempting to show that sacramentality is of no import for the reality of marriage as conceived in rational terms. Because this demonstration is cast within a mistaken context, it moves forward in a twofold direction. In the first direction, marriage as a reality of the order of creation is so constituted as to exhibit no intrinsic difference relative to marriage as a sacrament – *manet omnino eodem modo*. In the second place, and by reason of an unavoidable consequence, the argument moves in direction of portraying the relationship of marriage to the sacrament as something adventitious and extrinsic to it – "*quid supervagans*." The most coherent expression of this approach is, I believe, the theology of Vasquez, one of the least correct theologies of marriage. It maintains that everything found in marriage as a contract is in marriage as a sacrament – no more, no less. Both are equally indissoluble, and equally signs of the covenant. Sacramentality only helps in living out the marriage contract well.

c. *Reaction of the magisterium to the extrinsicist approach*

It is precisely against this approach that the magisterium issued its pronouncements, beginning with Pius VI. It rejects extrinsicism in all its forms, and thus safeguards the key datum of revelation by asserting both the absolute and unmerited transcendence of sacramentality (concept of *elevatio*) and its immanence (repudiation of all extrinsicism – *in se et per se*, as Leo XIII puts it). Thus, those who maintain that historically the magisterium issued pronouncements within the context of a jurisdictional conflict, and that therefore these pronouncements have no meaning in our day, are indulging in superficial theological thinking. This, at least, is my humble opinion. Note that, in the basic works devoted to this debate, the royalists and the adherents of Josephinism base their positions on arguments of the theologians such as de Launoy who work from a false *status quaestionis*. The difficulty these theologians could raise against this use of their own arguments was that the Church had reserved the mooted competency to itself *de jure* and *de facto*, or that Christ willed it thus. This is obviously a purely positivistic line of reasoning.

With this background, we can see from the texts which set forth the teaching that the magisterium intervened because the competency issue was linked with an erroneous and heretical understanding of marriage. It is quite easy to understand that the jurisdictional conflict should prompt the magisterium to intervene if we remember that this precise conflict had made obvious how grievously theology had wounded the faith and practice of the Christian community. In this context, the institution of civil marriage was another unambiguous result of the affirmation that the realities of this world are autonomous; this affirmation was untenable from the standpoint of the Church.

Two consequences follow. First, the teaching of the magisterium retains its enduring value. Second, we should refrain from interpreting unequivocally pieces of historical documents which share a common terminology, but have entirely different meanings, according to whether they are set within one or the other line of thought. For example, the term *perficere* may be used in two opposing senses. It may denote the fact that the elevation is unmerited and yet that marriage as sacrament is continuous with marriage as a reality within the order of creation, or it can imply that sacramentality is adventitious and extrinsic. In both cases, the term is used in an effort at resolving the same problem.

Only when we take the second (incorrect) approach and inquire as to the possibility of a marriage different from the one which does exist in fact does this question take on a second meaning. It can then coincide with the question whether a baptized person may marry in a manner different from the one shown by revealed data, that is, nonsacramentally. This problem is very deliberately placed at center stage by Vasquez and Rebello.

To the extent that the question emerges in this way, it is already devoid of meaning precisely as a question. It is a pseudoproblem. For to inquire whether a baptized person is given the choice between two ways of contracting marriage is to assume that two ways exist (marriage within and without the covenant) and that the second way is a real possibility which the baptized are free to choose. (Here the problem of the liceity of such a choice is secondary.) But to assume this is tantamount to turning upside down the biblical perspective on creation in general, and on marriage in particular, and to put a pseudo-theological perspective in its place. Marriage as a reality within the simple order of creation is a merely abstract possibility for baptized persons.

In reality, the only real way of contracting marriage is to "marry in the Lord," since marriage as a reality within the covenant is not located above or alongside marriage as a reality within creation or added to it; it is this marriage itself. This is also the reason why we cannot accept the answer which Vasquez, Billuart, and many others give to this question. The decision not to marry sacramentally does not produce a marriage which is real yet nonsacramental and true. It produces absolutely nothing. Since creation is in and through Christ, the only real marriage is marriage raised to the level of a sacrament.

d. A mistaken understanding of freedom before God

There is yet another reason, closely linked to the one just mentioned, why we must exclude the possibility of a nonsacramental marriage for baptized persons. This is the erroneous notion of freedom assumed in the Vasquez–Rebello position. There the *libertas indifferentiae*, as it is called, is regarded as the ultimate definition of human freedom. Human beings do not possess the same kind of freedom with regard to God that they possess in relation to their fellow creatures. Freedom *coram Deo* and freedom *coram mundo* are analogical, not equivalent, concepts. The former is set within the context of similarity to God, the latter within the context of dissimilarity. By virtue of the creative act of God, human beings are radically oriented toward God and constituted in their very being by this orientation itself. Freedom with regard to God is not an ontologically prior attribute of the human condition. It is a subsequent attribute, since human beings are not cast in a neutral situation from which they can exit by an act of free decision. The free decision not to welcome God's call is not ontologically identical with, even though it is opposite to, the decision to welcome that call. The result of the decision to reject God's call is not a different mode of existence; it is nonexistence. God performs his creative act for the sake of the covenant in Jesus Christ. Thus, human beings emerge from the hands of the creator not only as creatures oriented toward God but as destined to share the life of God through complete conformity with the Son. The free decision not to welcome this call to being in Christ cannot bring to existence a human reality possessed with the same ontological status as the opposite decision. What it brings about is nothing. Likewise, the decision to contract marriage out of conformity with its Christian purpose (a nonsacramental marriage) can by no means be equated in its efficacy with the opposite decision. Strictly speaking it effects nothing!

The notion of freedom as neutrality (*libertas indifferentiae*) and of human beings standing neutrally before God (a neutrality from which they can exit through a free act) is fairly common in later scholasticism. It has afflicted one of the most pernicious infections on Christian thought. The case under discussion proves this.

e. The current state of the problem

The teaching of the magisterium which excludes a choice between marriage as a sacrament and marriage as a contract has but called to mind the key revealed data concerning marriage. Unless we are mistaken, the fact that the problem of the separability of sacrament from contract for baptized persons has been reopened in the last few years deserves the same theological evaluation. It emerges in effect from the same presuppositions. Reduced to its essence, the question is this: are we to say that, when a baptized person fails to profess the faith, that person has access to a purely natural (that is, nonsacramental) conjugal bond? Deliberately staying within the framework of our reflections,[125] we believe that our answer must be as follows if we are to be consistent.

If the lack of faith involved refers to the condition of people who have refused, or do refuse, to ratify the baptism they have received, and to the extent that this is so, these people put themselves outside the economy of salvation. Therefore, their decision to marry cannot be recognized by the Church. This does not mean that, given their refusal to ratify their baptism, they are entitled to revert to a natural order alien to the economy of the covenant or that, since they exist outside of this economy, they may contract a marriage that has meaning within the context of the natural order. This cannot be, since that order does not exist. Such a return to a natural order is precluded by the fact that God has created human beings with the covenant in Christ in mind. Marriage as such has thus been enhanced so as to become a reality within the order of the covenant. To say it differently, it is not natural marriage that ought to be regarded as the reality and sacramental marriage as the accidental possibility left to the decision of the person (as though it were the content of an obligation). On the contrary, it is marriage as a sacrament that is the reality, whereas marriage as natural contract is only sheer supposition.

Persons who exclude the sacramentality of marriage or feel incapable of celebrating marriage as a sacrament place themselves outside the economy of God's grace in Jesus Christ and yet are not in a position to create, by way of an alternative, a natural law marriage with a meaning valid for their lives. Natural marriage, just like the whole economy of creation, can only subsist either in a state of alienation within worldly history or as a reality liberated and enhanced within the economy of the covenant. It seems to me that to take the opposite view amounts to maintaining that human beings are neutral, fundamentally and modally, that they are free in the presence of the two economies, and that they are capable of impressing on creation a liberating and sanctifying thrust apart from Christ. Unless I am mistaken, this is a substantially Pelagian position.

In the eyes of the Church, the decision to marry only *naturaliter* and not *sacramentaliter* can mean but one thing: a decision to marry outside the order of salvation, which is the only order in which the Church can and ought to recognize marriage.

If so, the problem is not, as some seem to believe, purely juridical and restricted to the canonical form of marriage. The problem is one of faith. The question is whether the Church is or is not in a position to recognize in some way a marriage realized outside the economy of salvation in Jesus Christ. To say the same thing differently, can the Church recognize in some fashion an economy of salvation which is not that of the covenant with God in Christ?

In the situations described above, the real problem is of a different sort. The whole Christian community must shoulder the obligation of fostering in baptized persons an ever more intelligent, mature, and conscious realization of what was bestowed upon them when they were baptized.

f. Christian marriage compared to what "we find outside"

The question concerning the possibility of a nonsacramental marriage can also take on a third and very important meaning.

Since Christian reflection on marriage aims at defending it against "outsiders," such reflection should show all the goodness and authentic meaning marriage possesses in itself. This effort can be made in two ways.

To the extent that the defense of marriage *vis-à-vis* outsiders is forced to take on a strictly apologetic tone, it develops into a reflection calculated to show that marriage ought to be regarded as a positive value in its own right. From this apologetic perspective, reflection is brought to bear mainly on the assertion that marriage as such does not pertain to the order of sin but derives its origin from God the creator. God himself instituted it in the midst of creation. This apologetic speaks, then, of marriage as a reality pertaining to the order of God's original creation. Its favorite text is Genesis 1:31 (in the New Testament, 1 Tim 4:3–4). In this connection, the Augustinian theology of the *bona coniugalia* directed against the Neoplatonists (Porphyry, for example) and against Manichaeism may serve as a point of reference.

It would be a serious historical mistake to reduce patristic theology to this particular apologetic component, since it is only one part of that theology. A confirmation of this is the fact that, in any case, the Genesis text is always construed with equal emphasis in a christological and ecclesial sense.

One of the most substantive benefits that resulted from this reflection was an understanding of marriage in terms of its essential structures, its constitutive elements. Medieval theology lent permanence and finality to this achievement, and even contributed further refinements such as the definition of the conjugal state (*in facto esse*), the role played by the consent of the spouses, the essential attributes of marriage as such.

Just as the Fathers before them, scholastic theologians were induced to strive for this deeper understanding of marriage by an apologetic need, since almost all the heresies of the twelfth and thirteenth centuries included a denial of the holiness of marriage. Their defense of marriage, too, appealed to the creative act of God.[126] But the scholastics achieved at this level a deeper understanding of considerable importance.

The dialogue with Greek (Aristotelian) ethics led theological reflection to elucidate what kind of reality marriage is as an institution in the order of creation by recourse to concepts borrowed from a natural right, or natural law, theory. As a consequence, the notion of marriage as created by God was to develop into the thesis that marriage is a natural-law institution. The rediscovery of Roman law contributed something to this development.

In this connection, St. Thomas's prologue to the question devoted to this matter in the *Commentary on the Sentences* is, I believe, very significant.[127] The Angelic Doctor announces that he will deal with two questions. The first concerns marriage as *officium naturae*; the second deals with the sacramental aspects of marriage.

Having thus formulated the problem, he offers a definition of natural marriage (*ratio naturalis ad ipsum inclinat*; *ibid.*, art. 1 c.) according to which the "goods of marriage" elaborated in the Augustinian tradition "pertain to the very nature of marriage. Therefore, there is no need to engage in extrinsic considerations to render marriage honorable."[128] This definition is formulated on the basis of the very nature of marriage rationally understood. From this nature the attributes of marriage are inferred. Both the nature and the attributes are grounded on natural law.

Note, however, that seeing marriage as a natural law institution (and more precisely, as a conjugal contract) did not prevent the great scholastic masters from integrating their reflection into the context of the economy and history of salvation. In fact, this type of reflection allows one not only to designate marriage – already determined in its proper and specific being – as the point of reference of the grace-event, but also to stress how inappropriate it is to determine the nature of marriage with no reference to its history in the economy of salvation.[129]

Yet, if I am right, scholastic theology did not succeed in integrating this new development into a complete vision of marriage as a reality of the created order elevated to the height of sacramentality. Perhaps this failure was in part due to the fact that, in the vision of the great scholastics, some elements in the natural structure of marriage, such as the exercise of sexuality, resisted integration into the work of creation and redemption.

It was thus inevitable that, once a less symphonic vision came into being, this positive development on the part of scholasticism should spawn elaborations and results of very dubious value. Scotus was the first to admit that marriage as a sacrament is separable from marriage as a reality of the order of creation. Durandus maintained that the concept of sacrament does not apply unequivocally to marriage precisely because marriage pertains "to the domain of natural reason" (*In IV Sent.*, dist. XXVI, q. 3, nos. 8–13).

This reflection, together with the most substantive beneficial results it produced, became a valid and useful instrument for a type of reflection similar to the one just described when the Church, by reason of her new missionary enthusiasm, was called upon to clarify her position with the regard to the marriage of the nonbelievers who were joining the Church. On the one hand, the Church recognized these marriages as true marriages, marriages in the proper sense of the word (*matrimonia legitima*), and on the other she regarded them as realities integrated, by virtue of baptism, into the economy of salvation.

Very significant in this connection was the theology of Vasquez and many others. For them, the key question was: is a new conjugal consent necessary for these marriages to become sacraments? This kind of question is only possible given two assumptions: the existence of two kinds of marriage and the juxtaposition of sacramentality to the human contract. The ecclesial practice which won the day in the end, to the exclusion of any other appeals to the central datum is that marriage as a reality of creation is oriented toward the covenant with God in the Christ. Hence, when people enter the covenant through baptism, their marriage becomes *eo ipso* sacramental.

Forever returning to its center, the reflection on marriage as a reality of creation played yet another role in this context. It helped to discern with precision what it is that is raised to the status of sacramental marriage. We could say, then, that theological reflection was making its way toward the center of the Christian truth on marriage in the company of those who were outside the christological circle. Marriage itself, as a reality of creation, correctly understood, is the sacrament of God's covenant with humanity (the Church) in Christ.

The clearest expression of this type of reflection is to be found, I believe, in the encyclical *Arcanum illud* of Leo XIII and in GS 48, 1–2.

g. Summary and conclusion

In the context of what has been said thus far, we may now by way of conclusion and summary indicate the meaning and import of the assertion of the absolute inseparability, for baptized persons, of marriage as reality of the created order and marriage as sacrament. We will do this in three statements:

1) In its negative aspect, the inseparability position means that, for baptized persons, there exists in reality no form of conjugal bond apart from the one according to which a man and a woman who agree to be husband and wife radically surrender their own selves in order to be taken up into God's absolute love in Christ for humanity (the Church). This is why, should the Church extend even minimal recognition to a conjugal bond other than this, she would betray the witness she must bear to Christ, and this is ecclesially impossible.

2) On the positive side, the inseparability position means this: marriage belongs to the economy of the covenant with God in Christ through the gift of the Spirit, that is, to the economy of the incarnation. It partakes of the incarnation's absolute gratuitousness (the concept of *elevation*). The fact that marriage belongs to the covenant becomes part of its human and created reality. It permeates that reality to the point that its constitutive and essential structure, already capable of being oriented toward becoming a sign of God's self-communication in Jesus Christ, does in fact receive this orientation to be this sign. In consequence, any right marriage between Christians is itself and in its own right a sacrament (concept of *perficere*; see Council of Trent and Vatican II; immanence of grace).

3) Should baptized persons decide to marry nonsacramentally, this decision would not effect in reality a different marriage; it would produce nothing real. This applies regardless of the grounds on which this decision rests.

4. REFLECTIONS ON RECENT PASTORAL PROPOSALS

In the light of these reflections, we may be allowed to submit a few remarks concerning the most recent pastoral proposals.

a. *Should the civil marriage of nonbelieving baptized persons be recognized in the name of the Church*

As mentioned earlier, the question here is not whether the Church should grant a canonical dispensation. We are dealing with a doctrinal question. In fact, the sacramentality problem would persist in its entirety even if a dispensation from the canonical form were allowed.

It is not within the scope of this inquiry to devote a theological reflection to the canonical form. It is enough to stress that the recognition under consideration here would inevitably obscure in the minds of Christian people the sacramental character of marriage and therefore its ecclesial value.

b. Should there be a religious nonsacramental celebration of marriage for nonbelieving baptized persons?

Just like the case just mentioned, this practice implies that marriage, as a reality of creation, is separable from marriage as sacrament. Consequently, it commits the Church to recognize between baptized persons a true and proper marriage that is not sacramental. For these reasons, this practice is unacceptable. It is worth repeating that the question is not merely to discern whether it is *contra* or *praeter legem.* We must ask ourselves whether such ecclesial recognition is possible on the part of the Church, the witness to God's grace in Jesus Christ. To this decisive argument other more particular considerations can be added.

By what criteria could we arrive at this discrimination within the Church between baptized persons? Motivations and internal factors almost inevitably have repercussions at the external level of ecclesial discipline and practice. In addition, if the celebration of a religious yet nonsacramental marriage were to become an accepted practice, one would have to be consistent and see in it the exercise of what is known as "the Petrine Privilege." These marriages could, therefore, be dissolved, and that dissolution could create the possibility of celebrating "religiously and nonsacramentally" a second marriage, which could be recognized by the Church, and so on. Thus we would have the dissolution of marriages contracted by baptized persons, even if they had been consummated. This practice is alien to ecclesial discipline and tradition. Moreover, what kind of witness would the Church bear in this case to the definitive character of the covenant, which entitles God in Christ to exercise sovereignty over a person?

Sooner or later, this practice would at the very least engender in the minds of Christians the notion that marrying sacramentally is a free choice for baptized persons, since the Church recognizes a nonsacramental marriage. Under these conditions, the only way of precluding this mistaken notion would be to insist on the obligation to contract a sacramental marriage, and therefore on the duty to achieve such progress in faith as is deemed necessary if the sacrament is to be truly celebrated. A pastoral arrangement of this kind is disconcertingly ill-advised. It forgets, and causes the faithful to forget, that here we are not dealing with a human obligation but with God's economy of salvation.

c. Should marriage be celebrated in stages, in a manner similar to the catechumenate?

A practice of this sort would often turn out to be indistinguishable from the one just mentioned, since the religious and nonsacramental celebration would be looked upon and presented as an initial phase, as the beginning of a journey which the two nonbelieving baptized persons are required to undertake, and which is to lead to a true sacramental celebration. But this proposal can also differ from the preceding one since, according to certain authors, this journey need not end in the "canonical celebration." Once the impediment (*obex*) is removed – that is, the absence of faith – the marriage becomes sacramental automatically.

Note first that, the analogy with the catechumenate does not hold here for the simple reason that we are dealing with already baptized Christians. This is something of a platitude, yet it points to a serious flaw which, I believe, mars these proposals: the soteriological importance of baptism received in infancy is being minimized in the extreme.

If we now inspect the language used to present this proposal more closely, the following observations suggest themselves:

1) The journey of the engaged couple toward faith

The catechumenal journey of the two baptized persons toward marriage may consist in effect in an evangelization and catechesis of the couple. In this case, the proposal appears very valid. Or this journey may consist in the evangelization of baptized persons who are already being recognized as husband and wife and are being guided toward the sacrament of marriage. In this case, the proposal comes up against the same difficulties as the preceding ones.

2) Trial marriage

The introduction of such an ecclesial practice can strengthen the conviction that trial marriage is valid and encourage the formation of such unions. This would in turn obscure in the minds of Christians the value of fidelity. On the one hand, marriage as a sacrament would be presented as the definitive fulfillment of the conjugal bond; and on the other the catechumenal journey would be presented as not necessarily leading to that marriage, since the persons involved would all along be regarded as husband and wife. What ought to be the attitude of these two spouses toward each other? Should they relate as two persons who have made a final and unconditional gift to each other or as persons who have made a conditional loan?

3) Forgetfulness of sacramental grace

Finally, the introduction of this ecclesial practice risks obscuring in the minds of Christians an essential dimension of sacramental grace: its healing (*sanans*) aspect, the aspect of liberation, assistance, support. According to the proposal in question, the sacrament is conferred on people mature in faith or on people who have surmounted the severest trials belonging to life in common. But under what rubric is the sacrament being conferred? Is it a reward for good behavior, or a seal of approval, or perhaps a frame put around a painting already finished?

d. The arguments advanced in favor of these pastoral solutions prove inconclusive

1) The teaching of Leo XIII

In the Church after Trent, some took the position that contract is separable from sacrament. As we have seen, this is an indisputable historical fact but one which does not constitute a decisive argument. Considerations of two kinds may be urged in this connection.

First of all, there are reasons to believe that the position has lost its probability because of the interventions of the magisterium which we have recalled in the historical section of this presentation. This was the opinion of a theologian like Sheeben, even though his writings antedate Leo XIII. In my humble opinion, it does not help to argue that the interventions of the magisterium were made in a context entirely different from ours. As noted above, the declarations of the magisterium were indeed prompted by the jurisdictional struggle then in progress, but the intention of the magisterium was to recall that the separability position could not be reconciled with the primary datum of revelation concerning marriage and that for this reason the juridical consequences derived from that position were equally unacceptable. The conflict about competency was not the primary object of concern. What was at stake was a point of Catholic doctrine as the popes from Pius VI to Leo XIII explicitly declared. The import and value of this teaching possesses a definitive importance for the Church.

In addition, we have already noted how this theological position fits into the context of a certain theology of marriage, a very debatable context to say the least. It emerged from a theology of the relationship between creation and Christ which is not above all suspicion. In particular, it is rather an ill-advised move, I must say, to appeal to Cano's position, since the orientation and intention of that position are in the opposite direction. Cano aims to assert that mediation of the Church is indispensable for the marriage of baptized persons.

2. Misinterpretation with regard to Vatican II

It seems to me downright unthinkable that anyone should appeal to Vatican II and its teachings on the autonomy of the realities of this world (GS 36). This interpretation is disavowed by the second paragraph of this same section. Most of all, one must read LG 49–51, and GS 45. We are told, in essence, that autonomy does not preclude worldly realities from being directed toward Christ as toward their final end, nor is this orientation purely extrinsic. This is certainly what we are dealing with.

Nor can we understand how a quote from *Dignitatis Humanae* could possibly have anything to do with our question. This declaration excludes civil coercion in matters of religion; it does not render the teaching of Christ and the magisterium optional.

3) Pastoral practice cannot do away with doctrine

There is an ambiguity in the ecclesiological argument which says: 'Between access to the sanctuary and a shut door, is there no middle ground where we can welcome seekers after truth?' (Msgr. Le Bourgeois in *Foi et Sacrement*, 179) That the Church should take an interest in those baptized persons who have not personally ratified their baptism and endeavor to evangelize and catechize them is beyond question. This effort is rightly regarded today as one of the Church's fundamental duties and tasks. But it seems wrong to say that this task necessarily requires the Church to recognize nonsacramental marriage. Not shutting the door to the sanctuary means that one assumes the task of initiating a true and profound evangelization. Here, I believe, we reach an essential point of the debate: we must be aware of the obligation of the Church to evangelize much sooner than when baptized persons come in to request marriage. Otherwise, we put ourselves in the position of having to redress the fact that the Christian community has failed to discharge its basic obligation with another error.

4) The church's intervention is part of its mission; it has nothing to do with being a temporary replacement

It has been argued that the Church functioned for a long time as a temporary replacement. Others have maintained that the Church in effect usurped a power it did not possess over the institution of marriage. This problem will be dealt with elsewhere in another chapter.

Finally, there are those who dissociate marriage from the body of the seven sacraments to the point of reducing it to the mere function of enabling Christians to render an ecclesial service. They locate its sacramentality in this enabling. This view can hardly be reconciled either with the teaching of the Council of Trent (Session 24, canon 1; DS 1801) or with that of Vatican II (LG, 11, 2; 41; GS, 48–49).

In conclusion, these pastoral proposals strike us as a mistaken response based on erroneous arguments to a *real* problem, namely, evangelization in general, and the evangelization of marriage in particular.

CHAPTER 5

The Indissolubility of Completed Marriage:

Theological, Historical, and Pastoral Reflections

by E. Hamel

1. INDISSOLUBILITY IN THE FATHERS OF THE CHURCH

It has been recently maintained in various places that in the early centuries many Fathers of the Church and ecclesiastical authorities permitted remarriage or at least the remarriage of husbands betrayed by their wives. This statement is obviously heavy with serious implications. It calls for a new inquiry into the discipline of the Church and its historical development.[1]

We offer here a few reflections which touch upon the following questions: Did the ancient Church permit a separation that did not include remarriage? What conception of marriage did the Fathers advocate? How should we interpret instances of tolerance in their pastoral practice?

Was Simple Separation Unknown?

It has been said that separation without remarriage was unknown in Roman and Jewish law and was therefore unthinkable for converts to Christianity or for the Church Fathers. But is it historically certain that people would not think of this option or that they were not interested in thinking of it? Is this so novel and modern a notion that no generation prior to the Middle Ages could conceive it, at least as an hypothesis? After new converts heard Christ's and Paul's declarations on marriage, could they not think of this possibility, and would they not have to think of it, even if it seemed harsh to them? New exigencies call for new solutions. A reality which, historically, had never been thought of, but was thinkable as hypothesis, could begin to be envisaged *de facto* because something new had happened, namely, the commandment of Christ, a commandment which amounted to a radical novelty.

Paul's First Letter to the Corinthians was written in the spring of the year 57 A.D. It mirrors the oldest tradition of the Church and shows that Paul did not reject all separation. He alludes to the fact that it is possible for a wife to live apart from her husband: "If she does separate, she must either remain single or become reconciled with her husband again" (1 Cor 7:11). Are we dealing here with a permission which Paul gives or with a concession made to a *fait accompli*? The reason for the separation is not mentioned. The context suggests that the reason was not adultery or lewd conduct (Dt 24) but a disagreement spiritual in nature. To be sure, we cannot maintain on the basis of this text that Paul devised a final solution for the problem of the juridical status of separation. He does exclude remarriage in the name of Christian demands and values. He does lay the incontestable foundations of the institution which church law will later formalize, especially since he speaks in the name of the Lord.[2]

The question has been asked whether the Church Fathers did not make the fatal mistake of falling in line with civil law in this area, allowing for a repudiation followed by remarriage. To begin with, note that postclassical Roman law (that is, after Constantine) was already beginning to recognize the notion of a separation without remarriage. Remarriage was henceforth forbidden and punished by law whenever the repudiation was not motivated. Should a citizen choose to ignore this prohibition and contract another marriage, was the bond of the first marriage rescinded? Opinions differ, but in any case, a penalty was inflicted for remarriage, so that a divorced person who wanted to escape punishment had either to return to his first wife or live alone.

Besides, the notion of separation without remarriage had already appeared in the *Shepherd* of Hermas (100-150 A.D.). In his *Moralia*, St. Basil made a clear distinction between separation and remarriage. He first deals with separation and with the reasons why it may be permitted or must be imposed. In a second chapter, he speaks of the possibility of remarriage for spouses who have separated.

It is difficult, therefore, to take for granted that because remarriage was accepted by Roman law the Fathers of the Church meant more than the termination of conjugal life when they spoke of dissolution in relation to marriage. Unless the opposite is explicitly asserted–a given Father of the Church explicitly stating that separated spouses are free to remarry, or using words to that effect–we may conclude that, when the Fathers speak of repudiation or broken marriage, they are implicitly referring to the termination of conjugal life, not to the right to remarry. The notion of separation without remarriage was known, even though there was no technical vocabulary by which to refer to it. The creation of a specific language, institutionalization, and the legal-technical modalities of institutionalization came later. As we are frequently told nowadays, praxis often precedes legislation.

Thus the repudiation of which the Fathers speak would be a moral, not yet a juridical, institution. It effected separation but did not give the spouses the freedom to remarry. Since theologico-juridical reflection was still embryonic at this time, the prohibition to remarry retained no doubt the quality of a moral prohibition.[3]

Mandatory Separation in Case of Adultery

Many Fathers believed that adultery by itself brought about the termination of marriage (Origen, Chrysostom, Theodoret), at least in the sense that the innocent spouse was obliged to separate from the adulterous spouse in order not to be an accomplice in his or her sin. To maintain association with an adulterous spouse was looked upon as equivalent to condoning adultery, and so ignoring the precept of the Old Testament.

From the theological perspective that sees marriage as a holy institution and salvation as an important concern, separation without remarriage makes sense. The writers who require the innocent spouse to refrain from cohabitation in case of adultery do so in the name of the holiness of marriage. The adulterous spouse must be dismissed, lest the innocent one should share in his or her guilt. Origen: "Thus, a man who has only one eye shall be saved, namely the man who has gouged out the eye of his own household, the adulterous wife, lest having kept her he should march with two eyes into the eternal fire." Basil says that a husband has not only the right but the duty to dismiss his unfaithful wife. His reason is not so much that Roman law demands this separation, but rather a conflation of Matthew 19:9, Jeremiah 3:1 and Proverbs 12:22a: "The man who keeps an adulterous wife under his roof is a godless fool."

The position that separation is required to safeguard the holiness of marriage in case of adultery was advocated by the ante-Nicene and the post-Nicene Fathers. This explains the very strong language which, if taken in a strictly juridical sense, could lead to the conclusion that the innocent spouse is entitled to remarry. The adulterous spouse is no longer a spouse, and the husband is no longer a husband. The couple is a small community. If one of the spouses lapses into adultery, he separates himself from Christ. For the Fathers, adultery was truly the offense against the holiness of the conjugal bond. What we have here is a strictly moral conception of adultery. Adultery was in their eyes the only legitimate ground for separation. The dismissal of a spouse without sufficient reason goes counter the law of the Lord. It was forbidden because it leads to adultery (Mt 5:32).[4]

Conversion and Return of the Guilty Spouse

There is another consideration which justifies separation without remarriage. The Fathers had a moral, not a juridical, conception of adultery. Adultery is thus an obstacle to conjugal life, but one that can be removed by conversion, forgiveness, baptism, penance. The innocent spouse has grounds for hoping that the guilty spouse will repent and return, in which case charity and patience are required. Tertullian: "Patience does not make an adulterer out of the innocent spouse; it rather favors amendment." If the repentant wife returns home, may the husband receive her? Hermas answers categorically: the husband is under serious obligation to receive her.

Why? Because this is an opportunity for conversion offered to God's servants. Remarriage is forbidden for the same reason. Marry again, and there is no longer any possibility for going back. For the sake of the repentance of the adulterous wife the husband should not remarry. In conclusion, persistent adultery is the only valid reason for separation. As noted, according to the mentality of the time and the way the scriptures were being read, this exception was meant to preserve the holiness of life together.

Ambiguity of the Term "Divorce"

How did the Fathers understand the term *divorce*? For them, this word did not have the strict and precise sense it has in contemporary usage. It could refer both to divorce as we understand it and to mere physical separation. When the Fathers used this word, they did not supply the necessary qualifications. Likewise, they used the synonymous expressions *to loose* and *to separate* (*solvere, dissolvere*) with no precise distinctions.

In Roman law, these expressions did indeed presuppose the possibility of remarriage. But are we to conclude that the Fathers used them in the sense which Roman law assigned to them? As a rule, the Fathers used the vocabulary current in their time with considerable freedom. They did not feel obligated to use words in keeping with their technical meaning. Therefore, one must consult the context to ascertain what they meant. Augustine, for example, had no doubt that remarriage is forbidden in case of adultery, and yet he spoke of the dissolution (*solutio*) of conjugal unions. If we are going to maintain that a particular Father of the Church permitted remarriage in case of adultery, it is not enough to point out that he says that the spouses can or should separate through divorce. He would have to say in addition that a divorced spouse may legitimately and in accordance with the Christian faith contract a new marriage while the other spouse lives. It turns out that Ambrosiaster is the only one who says this explicitly.

In this controversy, it has been too often overlooked that with the passing of time, the Church acquires a surer knowledge of the scriptures, and her awareness of what they mean grows more distinct. We should not be surprised, therefore, if we come upon ambiguous texts which seem to favor divorce and remarriage and which, taken in isolation, could be read to favor remarriage or the possibility of it. The ambiguity, if there be ambiguity, concerns only the way in which we should assess the consequences of adultery. Does adultery make another marriage possible, or only separation?

But let us suppose for a moment that what some people assert is true: namely, that some church fathers and councils did grant that marriage can be totally dissolved and that therefore remarriage after divorce is possible. Note, however, that the case with which they were dealing was very specific, that the ground was precise – adultery – and that they stressed an interpretation of the Matthean clause, *nisi fornicationis causa*, which has never gained currency because it is opposed to the texts of Mark, Luke, and Paul. We would have to conclude that we are dealing with a practice which, compared to what was permitted by civil law, was very limited.[5]

Moral, Nonjuridical Conception of Marriage

The Church has concerned herself with marriage since the beginning, at least by way of prohibiting remarriage. In spite of the absence of legal texts and precise canonical norms, a certain praxis existed. Athenagoras speaks of people who get married "in keeping with the laws current among us."[6]

However, there was as yet no in-depth reflection concerning the indissolubility of marriage. When the Fathers assert that separation dissolves, breaks, or loosens the bond of marriage, when they speak of a transgression that breaks the bond, we should not interpret these texts as meaning that they favored a juridical automatism and necessarily advocated a total severance with the right to remarry. When, on the basis of their interpretation of the clause *nisi fornicationis causa* (Mt 19:9), the Fathers allowed separation from an unfaithful spouse, the innocent spouse was indeed entitled to make use of the repudiation (*repudium*) allowed by civil law, but it did not necessarily follow that remarriage was permitted. Adultery did indeed rescind the obligation to live under the same roof, but solid proof would be needed before we could go on to say that, according to the Church Fathers, adultery made a total end of the conjugal bond and gave access to remarriage.

Remarriages Morally Null and Void

The early Church never issued pronouncements about marriage in terms of juridical validity or juridical nullity. Besides, if the ecclesiastical authorities had decreed the juridical nullity of a marriage which was not regarded as invalid by Roman law, they would have placed the faithful in a difficult predicament. However, granted that such terms as *nullity, validity, invalidity*, and the like, were never used, a certain notion of moral, nonjuridical nullity was already present in the thinking of the Church Fathers. When they speak of remarriage following repudiation, they never use the word *marriage* (*coniugium*, γάμος). Origen speaks of a liaison and says that the man does not really marry. Basil speaks of cohabitation. The Synod of Elvira uses the word *incest* for a union of a man with his daughter-in-law. The Fathers did, therefore, have some expressions by which to refer to a marriage that was null and void. Thanks to this notion of moral nullity, they were able to deny to certain unions the quality of a real marriage. Could we not perhaps speak here of an embryonic Christian legislation? When the Church decrees penalties against remarriages, should not this be taken to mean that she did not purely and simply canonize all the civil regulations relative to marriage?[7]

Toleration of Remarriages

The practice of divorce in case of adultery, sanctioned by civil law, was so deeply anchored in the ethos of the day that the Church Fathers felt constrained at times to tolerate the *fait accompli* in order to preclude even greater mischief. Origen says that those who, contrary to the teaching of the gospel, have allowed people to remarry have not done this entirely without reason or excuse. Basil speaks of remarriage as a custom which is contrary to scripture and for which a justification is difficult to find, but he also says that the spouse who has been deserted and has remarried is "forgivable."

The large measure of tolerance exhibited toward men can be explained at least in part by pointing out that men and women did not enjoy equal rights at this time and that inequality was accepted even by ecclesiastical custom. The tolerance toward the wife is traceable to the fact that a deserted wife would find it almost impossible, both materially and morally, to live alone. The law would afford her no protection, and she had no means of subsistence.

Pastoral Silences

In the early Church, the pastors were often at a loss in dealing with divorced persons who had remarried. That was a time when the wedding was celebrated in the family, and the marriage contract was kept in the family archives, although very early a liturgical celebration was added to the wedding ceremony itself. The bishops were often unable to recognize the remarried divorced people as they mingled with the other faithful. In principle, of course, the culprits were supposed to request the penance prescribed by canon law. But if they failed to do so, was the bishop in a position to impose such a penance? In short, in many cases the bishops did not know which way to turn. This is why they elected at times to remain silent with regard to a union which had been contracted before the civil authority and which could not be dissolved because of the consequences that would ensue.

Unable to Christianize in one stroke an institution so alien to the faith of the gospel, the Church hesitated to impose a burden too heavy to carry. It patiently tolerated what it knew was an abuse. The law of the Church, too revolutionary for the people of that time, was difficult for them to accept. This explains the tolerance of a Church that chose not to alienate peoples whose social structures were not yet Christianized. Without explicitly conceding the legitimacy of a marriage contracted by innocent spouses, the Church merely passed over their situation in silence, which is an act of tolerance, not of approval. Is this not the classic doctrine of profitless admonition (*monitio non profutura*)? People were simply allowed to go on in good faith.

Pastoral Silence Today?

These scattered cases of practical tolerance on the part of the ancient Church may be interpreted as an example of how an unflawed strictness in matters of doctrine can be combined with a measure of pastoral flexibility. For we should not overlook the fact that, in the early centuries of Church history, an impressive consensus existed as to the fundamental principle of the indissolubility of Christian marriage.

Against this historical background, some pastors ask today whether one cannot still follow this example and somehow reconcile fidelity to the gospel with mercy, punctiliousness with 'economy.'

The answer is surely yes, if what is involved is a pastoral practice that emphasized benevolent attentiveness rather than rejection. But can we go even further? Specifically, can we allow divorced Catholics to participate in the Eucharist, as they so loudly demand? We think not.

Besides noting the doctrinal reasons developed by Martelet, we must realize that, in spite of surface similarities between situations, the life and tradition of the Church cannot be a cyclic duplication of the past.

It is one thing to bide one's time, to shut an eye in the presence of abuses in an effort to restructure moral conduct in accordance with the severity of the gospel, and another thing to abandon this severity theoretically and practically once it has been established. Would we be willing to accept regression in matters of social justice and social progress on the grounds that it took a long time for people to perceive the rightness of social demands?

In the ancient Church, tolerance was equivalent to a preparation for the gospel (*preparatio evangelica*); it was part of the task of getting people to understand still obscure requirements. But after theological research has reached clear positions and the teaching of the popes has driven the obscurity away, after an ecumenical council has defined its position in the matter, can we still revert to a practice which, casuistic subtleties apart, legitimizes remarrriage after divorce, whether or not we have the courage to say so?

2. INDISSOLUBILITY IN THE TEACHING OF THE POPES 5TH TO 12TH CENTURY

In the early centuries, Christians lived in an environment in which divorce was admitted, and were exposed to the influence of that environment. Since the beginning of the fifth century, the popes have been consulted by bishops concerning cases in which the indissolubility of marriage was threatened. At times, the cases calling for resolution were unprecedented and difficult. Faced with the questions, the hesitations, and the excessively liberal interpretations of local churches, the popes, whose authority was unchallenged in the West, reasserted the principle of indissolubility and endeavored to contain and counteract abuses. Although the Church often adopted secular views when deciding which element was constitutive of the conjugal bond, she parted company with such views when it came to asserting the solidity of that bond. The demanding originality of the gospel in the matter of indissolubility was proclaimed and upheld.

INNOCENT I (401–17)

Letter to Exuperius, Bishop of Toulouse (PL 20, 500–501)

Was a husband entitled to remarry after divorcing his wife? Exuperius, Bishop of Toulouse, was uncertain on what course of action to take. In 405 he contacted Pope Innocent I in order to have the benefit of his opinion. This is how the Bishop of Rome replied: men who remarry while their spouses are still among the living, even if their marriage appears to be broken (*dissociari videatur*), cannot but be regarded as adulterers (*neque possunt adulteri non videri*). As for the women with whom they are now living, they too must be looked upon (*videantur*) as guilty of adultery. This accords with what we read in the gospel: ". . . whoever divorces his wife and marries another commits adultery, and the man who marries a divorced woman commits adultery." Note that the pope omits the clause *nisi fornicationis causa* in quoting Matthew 19:9. Why? Is it because he thinks the clause does not entail an exception and that it fails to accord exactly with Mark 10:12 and Luke 16:18? Or does he state here only a general principle, without considering the specific case of the deserted husband? The former hypothesis seems more plausible, since the gist of the answer is that the repudiation (*repudium*) to which the husband is entitled does not give him the right to a second marriage, and that because of Matthew 19:9.

In a letter to Victricius, Bishop of Rouen, written a year earlier, Innocent I had already declared that any woman who remarries during the lifetime of her husband must be looked upon as an adulteress (*adultera habeatur*). She will not be allowed to do penance (*nec si agendae poenitentiae licentia conceditur*). He declares that this is a common and unchallenged doctrine (*in omnibus haec ratio custoditur*; PL 20, 478–79).

Letter to the Magistrate Probus (PL 20, 602)

During the barbarian invasions, many were taken prisoner. The absence of a spouse was bound to exacerbate the indissolubility problem. Fortinius remarried because his wife Ursa, taken captive when Rome was besieged by Alaric in 409, had long been absent. But Ursa returned, went to Pope Innocent and announced that she was Fortinius's lawful wife.

Note first that according to Roman law, even under Constantine, captivity entails the immediate dissolution of the conjugal bond, both because life in common is no longer possible and because the spouse in captivity can no longer be juridically regarded as possessing the will required for the maintenance of the conjugal bond. Therefore, when Fortinius remarried, he did not violate any civil law. The pope, fully conscious of his authority and with the support of the Catholic faith (*fide catholica suffragante*), decided that the marriage which Fortinius has contracted with Ursa was the true one. A long absence is not sufficient grounds for dissolution and therefore, the second union was not legitimate (*nullo pacto posse esse legitimum*). The pope, then, did not admit the solution advocated by imperial law. Why? Because Ursa was alive, and she had not been dismissed by divorce (*nec divortio ejecta*). The first reason is clear; the second creates a problem. What is the point of the reasoning: Ursa has not been dismissed by divorce? At that time, captivity did cancel out marriage *ipso facto* but was not yet grounds for divorce. It became grounds only in the year 542, under Justinian. Therefore, Fortinius had no need to divorce Ursa, his captive wife. Did the pope suppose that Fortinius could have divorced Ursa on other grounds, but had not done so? Does the pope's reasoning imply that, had Ursa been dismissed through divorce, Fortinius's second marriage would have been valid? It does not seem so. The solution of a specific case is one thing; the argument supporting that solution is another. A specific response is not a doctrinal premise from which inferences not pertinent to the case may be drawn.

But why did the pope address his answer to the magistrate in the first place? In the year 399, Emperor Honorius had restricted the authority of bishops to religious matter. A bishop who rendered a decision on marital matters was not bound to apply the civil law, only the religious law. In accordance with this decree, Innocent declared: "Because of the captivities which had occurred, the marriage validly contracted by Fortinius and Ursa would have been dealt a demeaning blow had the holy decisions of religion not intervened." In the year 408, Honorius enjoined public officials to execute episcopal decrees whenever the parties involved agreed to submit their case to the bishop. This is why the Pope addressed his decision to the magistrate: he was responsible for executing it.

LEO THE GREAT (440–61)

Letter to Nicetas, Bishop of Aquileia (DS 311–14)

During his expedition against Rome, Attila too took a large number of captives. The spouses of some of these captives remarried. But some captives were subsequently released and returned home. Nicetas wrote to the Pope and submitted the case of husbands reunited with their families.

In his response, the pope spoke especially of the wives who had remarried and exhibited great severity with respect to them. He decreed that they were to return to their first husbands in keeping with the precept of the gospel: "Let no man separate what God has joined" (Mt 19:6). By way of corroboration, the pope uses a comparison which is none too complimentary to the wife. He compares her to goods abandoned in time of war (*bona tempore belli derelicta*) which must be returned to their rightful owner at war's end (*Omnique studio procurandum est, ut recipiat unusquisque quod proprium est*; DS 311).

It seems rather clear that the wives' obligation to return to their former husbands is made contingent on one condition: husbands must want to resume life in common with them. But what if the husband does not want this? The pope's answer seems to indicate that the husband is entitled to renounce his rights if he so wishes. Does this mean that he is entitled to remarry? It certainly seems so. It follows that, in extreme cases, the pope did not deem it appropriate to insist all the way on the indissolubility principle. However, as we have said above, we should not exclude *a priori* the notion that some husbands might have preferred to live alone.

Letter to Rusticus, Bishop of Narbonne (Written in 458–59; PL 54, 1204–05)

In Roman law, concubinage refers to a simple liaison between two persons who do not want to marry or to appear in public as husband and wife. It differs from marriage because conjugal love (*affectio maritalis*) and life in common (*communio vitae*) are not part of it. Concubinage could exist simultaneously with marriage, but was always distinct from it: a husband was entitled to have a slave concubine in addition to his lawful wife. As a juridical institution, concubinage began with postclassical Roman law, that is, at the time of the Christian emperors. Before that time, it existed in fact but was not subject to penalties. In 542, Justinian decreed that a married man was not to live in concubinage and that a single man was not to have more than one concubine.

About the year 458, Leo authorized the marriage of a man who had previously lived with a concubine. The pope did not regard concubinage as an indissoluble marriage. Therefore, he did not see it as an obstacle to a subsequent marriage. The pope's decision accorded with Roman law and had an additional advantage: it encouraged people to regularize a situation of which the Church disapproved. The pope made a clear distinction between the wife and the concubine and announced at the same time the conditions to be fulfilled if the marriage is to be valid. A woman is a wife (*uxor*) only if the marriage has been contracted between persons who are free, if it has been publicly celebrated, and if the dowry has been surrendered.

In order to justify his decision, the pope called on the authority of the Bible rather than Roman law: "The Lord himself has decreed this long before Roman law came into existence." (*Multo prius hoc ipsum Domino constituente quam initium romani juris existeret.*) A free man would be entitled to marry a slave only if the slave had been freed. This meant that everything depended on the good will of the master.

GREGORY THE GREAT (590–604)

The Case of Those Who Enter Monastic Life

The letters of Gregory the Great (over 850 of them) are the largest contribution any pope made to Church law during the sixth and seventh centuries. Two of these letters pertain to the matter at hand. They state that marriage is not dissolved even by entry into monastic life.

The first of these was written in the year 601 to a patrician lady by the name of Teotista. In it, the pope lamented the fact that, on the strength of civil law, entry into monastic life on the part of one spouse is regarded by the other as a legitimate ground for dissolving the marriage and remarrying. The pope did not hesitate to brand this second marriage illicit and unclean. When one spouse enters monastic life, the other is obligated to practice continence, since the marriage is indissoluble. Of course, a serious temptation is there in the making. Speaking to the spouse who has entered monastic life, the pope asks: "What kind of conversion is this, where one and the same flesh moves partly into continence, while the other part persists in impurity?" (PL 77, 1161).

The second letter was written the same year to a notary of Palermo. It concerns the complaint of a woman by the name of Agathosa. She had written to the pope to complain that her husband had become a monk against her will. In the year 542, Justinian had decreed that entry into religious life must count *bona gratia*, that is, by way of benevolent concession, as grounds for divorce. Despite this law, the pope states that God's law must prevail: "Except in case of lewd conduct, a husband is not entitled to dismiss his wife since, once they have consummated their union, the spouses become one flesh. One part of that flesh cannot turn to monastic life, while the other remains in the world." Note that the pope was attempting to protect the rights of both parties against a unilateral decision imposed by one party upon the other. If life in common is to be interrupted, the spouses must freely agree to the interruption. Entry into monastic life should not serve as an excuse for dissolving marriage. Once the marriage has been consummated, a spouse is not permitted to enter monastic life, thus creating for the spouse who remains in the world an occasion of sin (PL 77, 1169).

GREGORY II (715–31)

A Case of Impotency

In his letter *Desiderabilem mihi*, written in 726, St. Gregory II answered several queries of St. Boniface, Bishop of Mainz. The Bishop had raised the problem of a wife who was ill (*infirmitate correpta*) and could not fulfill the conjugal obligation. What was her husband to do?

The pope's reply is in two parts. He first mentions the solution he prefers: "It would be good if the husband would remain as he is and cultivate continence." (*Bonum esset, si sic permaneret ut abstinentiae vacaret.*) However, this solution is beset with difficulties. Perhaps the husband is not strong enough to live in continence. Continence is for strong people. (*Hoc magnorum est.*) Eventually, remarriage may be the solution: if he cannot restrain himself, let him marry. (*Qui si non potuit continere, nubat magis.*) However, he should not forget his obligations toward the woman who is deprived of conjugal life only because of illness, and has not lost her rights because of a detestable fault (PL 89, 525).

Gregory, then, showed tolerance toward human weakness, but tolerance did not abridge his sense of justice. All the same, we cannot help noticing that, as pope, he advised a husband to divorce his wife and remarry, which contradicts the constant teaching of the Western Church. It is imperative that we try to assess the precise import of this particular letter.

The text of this letter is often called the crux of canon lawyers; it has caused much ink to flow. The severest difficulty in the interpretation of the text, the one difficulty that cannot be removed on the basis of the available documents, has to do with the malady in question. Since we do not have the letter in which Boniface gives the particulars of the case, we do not know about the nature of the malady that occasioned the query. But no matter what malady was involved and what its consequences were, the important question is whether it was equivalent to what is known technically as impotency. Did it begin before the marriage or was it contracted after the marriage? Did it prevent consummation? Was it curable or incurable? None of these questions can be answered on the basis of either the text or the context. The text merely says: "afflicted by illness" (*infirmitate correpta*). In the absence of this information, how can we trust ourselves to make a judgment as to the pope's response? Was the marriage valid? Has it been consummated? The wording is so vague and the particulars so scanty that we are in no position to decide on the sense of the passage and make an interpretation which is proof against challenge.

The passage has generally been interpreted as referring to a case of impotency arising after the celebration of the marriage. The pope, then, would have been tolerating a custom contrary to the law of the gospel but current in Germany at that time. According to some commentators, the letter represents a concession to the Thuringians. Pope Gregory's position is that a man who discovers that his wife cannot have intercourse must resign himself to a life of continence. However, this solution could hardly have been applied to the Thuringians, for they had only recently converted to Christianity and were still unaccustomed to living an integral Christian life. The solution was simply too harsh for them. And so a concession seems to be in order, else they might have lost heart and turned away from Christianity. There is, however, no way of determining on what grounds the concession rested. Was it antecedent impotency, or nonconsummation because of consequent impotency? This text will always be a problem.

We cannot state, then, that the pope dissolved a marriage contracted and consummated (*ratum et consummatum*), even though we cannot exclude the possibility that he did so.[8]

STEPHEN II (752–57)

Pope Stephen II was consulted by English monks concerning the possibility of remarriage after separation. He replied by referring to the decisions of Pope Innocent I and Leo the Great. With regard to another question, his answer was as follows: "If a person contracts marriage and one of the spouses should happen to be unable to render the conjugal duty, separation is not permitted. Nor is any other malady a valid ground for separation, with the exception of the devil's malady and leprosy . . ." (PL 89, 1024).

Here we are dealing at least with a form of impotency or an illness that sets in after the celebration of the marriage, but perhaps also with an impotency that antecedes the celebration. According to the pope, neither is a valid ground even for separation. This text bears a great resemblance to that of Pope Gregory II, and yet the answer it contains is diametrically opposed to the answer given in that text. Either the two popes assessed the same situation differently, or the situations look the same but are different.

NICHOLAS THE GREAT (856–67)

The popes of the second half of the ninth century, beginning with Nicholas I, endeavored to combat abuses and to reassert firmly the indissolubility principle, thus reinforcing the foundation of the institution of marriage. The popes were prompted to do so by some sensational marital cases. Also to be taken into account is the fact that

Church discipline had already deteriorated in the churches of the Franks, and certain ecclesiastical judges had exhibited precious little firmness.

The Divorce of Boson and Engeltrude

The Count of Boson had dismissed his adulterous wife. Pope Nicholas I wrote a letter to Hincmar, Archbishop of Reims, invoked his apostolic authority (*praecipimus vobis apostolica auctoritate fulti*), and ordered him to have Engletrude return to her husband. Should she refuse, Hincmar should not hesitate to excommunicate her (MGH: *Epistolarum* 6, 267). On March 7, 867, Pope Nicholas stated that Boson could not take another wife, even if he was not responsible for the fact that the efforts at reconciliation failed (MGH: *Epistolarum* 6, 333). In the end, the pope excommunicated the fugitive wife, but the Council of Metz (869) went over his head and removed the excommunication.

The Divorce of Lothair II

Lothair had divorced his barren wife and married Walrad, who had been his mistress. The divorce had been approved by the Council of Metz, but Pope Nicholas had the Lateran Council rescind this decision in the year 863. Walrad was excommunicated and so was the offending bishop. In the end, Lothair severed relations with the mistress and was reconciled with the pope.

Divorce and Remarriage

At the end of the year 861, Adon, Bishop of Vienne, consulted the pope to ascertain whether a husband might, without the approval of a general council, divorce a wife who has been charged with a crime, and remarry or take a mistress.

The wording of the query strongly implies that, in the matter of second marriages, some ecclesiastical judges tended to be rather accomodating. The pope's answer was firm, to say the least: "In the name of our apostolic authority and in accord with the mandate of the gospel, we resist them. We do not permit those who do things of this sort to enjoy sexual intercourse with another wife, nor do we give them permission to have a mistress." (MGH: *Epistolarum* 6, 618–19.)

It is clear that Nicholas is asserting here the primacy of jurisdiction of the see of Rome, which is competent to ratify or rescind decisions taken by local councils.

ALEXANDER III (1159–81)

In response to a query by the Archbishop of Canterbury, Pope Alexander III explicitly asserted the indissolubility of marriage in case of leprosy. This disease is not adequate grounds for the separation of the spouses, even if custom often forces them to separate: "Since husband and wife are one flesh, the one may not be without the other for long." If they should separate, "you are to order them to practice continence, as long as the other partner lives. Should they refuse to obey, excommunicate them." (CJC: *Decretales Gregorii IX*; ed. Ae. Friedberg, col. 690–91).

In another passage, the pope declared that, should a wife leave her husband because of unfaithfulness on his part, she may not remarry, "because, even though they have separated, they still remain husband and wife." The pope asserted that the spouses are equal. He explicitly added: "This sentence applies in the same form even to men." (CJC: *Decretales Gregorii IX*; ed. Ae. Friedberg, col. 720).

Modern canonists quote far less frequently than their predecessors the interesting letter of Alexander III written in the year 1170 to a bishop named Vicentinus. The pope had been told that a certain bishop had issued a decree of divorce within the ecclesiastical assembly, then granted permission to remarry to a woman whose husband had been in foreign lands for over a decade. Taken to task, this bishop had refused to change his decision. In his letter, Alexander III first asked Vicentinus to conduct an investigation. If the investigation proves that the facts are as reported, the pope says, Vicentinus should simply legitimize the children, since the woman had remarried "on the authority of the aforementioned bishop, without resistance on the part of the Church." (*auctoritate praedicti episcopi, sine quaestione et contradictione Ecclesiae*). Considering that the ecclesiastical superiors had been themselves at fault and that the woman had obviously been in good faith, could the pope have gone further and insisted on indissolubility and its consequences? The pope obviously could not, and so he kept silent and merely requested that the situation of the children born of this union be regularized. (CJC: *Decretales Gregorii IX*; ed. Ae. Friedberg, col. 712).

CELESTINE III (1191–98) AND INNOCENT III (1198–1216)

Celestine III extended the Pauline Privilege to cover cases of apostasy. An archdeacon had authorized a Christian woman to remarry after she had been forsaken by her husband who had apostatized. The pope was asked whether this had been a wise decision. He replied: "It seems to us that should the first husband return to the Church, the wife would not be bound to desert her second husband and go back to the first, since it is he who, in the eyes of the Church, has deserted his wife." According to Gregory, the contempt of the creator dissolves marriage for the spouse who has been deserted out of hatred for the Christian faith (. . . *teste Gregorio contumelia creatoris solvat jus matrimonii circa eum qui relinquitur odio fidei Christianae*; CJC: *Decretales Gregorii IX*; ed. Ae. Friedberg, col. 587–88).

In May 1199, Innocent III, Celestine's successor, repudiated this solution in his answer to a query from the Bishop of Ferrara. The bishop had inquired whether, if one spouse lapsed into heresy, the other could be permitted to allow the heretical spouse to remarry. The Pope replied that the Pauline Privilege did not apply to heresy or apostasy, "although a certain predecessor of ours seems to have entertained a different opinion." (. . . *licet quidam praedecessor noster sensisse aliter videtur*; *CJC: Decretales Gregorii IX*; ed. Ae. Friedberg, col. 722).

Pope Innocent III likewise resisted the demands of Philip Augustus, King of France (1180–1223), who wanted to divorce Ingeburg of Denmark.

3. ROME AND GREEK OR EASTERN CUSTOMS 13TH CENTURY TO THE COUNCIL OF TRENT

The only pope who made pronouncements on the customs of the Greeks before the Council of Florence is Honorius III (1216–27). He was asked by John, the papal legate, what should be done about Greeks who divorced their wives and remarried. The pope answered on August 10, 1218: "The question of divorce cannot be settled, or a dispensation granted, since the bond is indissoluble both for the faithful, be they Greek or Latin, and for infidels." (*Regesta Pontificum Romanorum*, n. 5834).

A letter of Innocent IV, dated March 6, 1254, and addressed to the Greeks of Cyprus, recommends the adoption of Latin rites. It does not mention indissolubility (DS 830). A constitution *Ad Graecos et alios*, issued by Alexander IV (1254–61), does not mention divorce. (See *Constitutio instruens Graecos et alios*, 14, in *Pontificia Com-*

missio ad redigendum Codicem Iuris Canonici orientalis; *Fontes*, Series III, Vol. IV, Tomus 2, 111.

In the year 1279, Gregory IX held the Council of Lyon in which Michael Palaeologus established full communion with the Church of Rome. However, the divergent discipline of the Eastern Churches, and particularly of the Byzantine Church, was practically ignored. We do find an implicit repudiation of the practice of divorce and remarriage when we are told about second marriages that death alone frees the spouses from the conjugal bond (DS 860).

The fathers of the Council of Sis in the year 1342 were invited by Pope Benedict XII (1334–42) to disavow a list of errors and abuses. They declared that abuses concerning divorce were still practiced in Armenia (which was not united with Rome), whereas in Cilicia bishops who granted divorces were deposed. The acts of this Council were brought to Pope Clement V (1342–52); he asked for further clarifications, but not precisely with regard to divorce.

At the Council of Florence, the Eastern custom of remarrying after separation due to adultery was mentioned in passing. However, by a sort of gentlemen's agreement, the question was not discussed. The union was established without any change being made in the discipline of either party; see the bull *Laetentur caeli*, July 6, 1439 (DS 1300–1308). The question was raised at the very last minute by Eugene IV (1431–47), but by that time the decree of reunion had already been signed. The Greeks replied that if they did at times permit divorce there was valid reason for doing so (*non sine iustis causis*; recognize here Origen's formula). The Latins did not press the point. (See Perrone, *De Matrimonio*, III, 364.)

On the contrary, when the Armenians signed the act of union a few months later, they were not allowed to retain the Eastern custom. The decree *Ad Armenos* explicitly declared that betrayed spouses may not remarry. In case of adultery, physical separation is in order, but divine right does not authorize a second marriage, "since the bond of marriage legitimately contracted is forever" (*cum matrimonii vinculum legitime contracti perpetuum sit*; see the bull *Exultate Deo*, November 22, 1439, DS 1327). This decree was imposed on the Syrian Jacobites united with Rome in 1442 (DS 1351).

If we except the interventions of Honorius III and Clement VI and the discussions at the Council of Florence, there are no other decisions of the Holy See prior to the Council of Trent concerning the practice of divorce among the Greeks and Easterners, both those united with

Rome and those separated. We must conclude that, in spite of the rigidity of its doctrinal position, the Apostolic See thought it opportune to procrastinate. Undoubtedly it reserved the right to take action later, but the opportunity to do so did not arise.

4. INDISSOLUBILITY AT THE COUNCIL OF TRENT

At the Council of Trent the situation with regard to the indissolubility of the conjugal bond was as follows. Catholic theologians were agreed that marriage is indissoluble even in cases of adultery. The only controversy concerned the theological note to be assigned to this assertion and what censure ought to be inflicted on those maintaining the opposite position. Parallel to this doctrine the three "great doubts" of Cajetan, Erasmus, and Catharinus had surfaced. The least we can say about their novel views is that they had not been well received by theologians. On the other side, Luther was accusing the Catholic Church of having lapsed into error. The Church, he contended, was a tyrant. She had usurped power. The pope has no authority to dissolve marriages or to interdict the dissolution of marriages any more than to erect impediments to marriage. All this belonged to the state. Finally, there was the tradition of the Eastern Churches, which permitted divorce at least in cases of adultery.

After many discussions, in the 24th session the council voted canon 7, which is the charter to which theologians and canonists refer when dealing with indissolubility: "Should anyone say that the Church commits error when she taught and teaches, in accordance with the doctrine of the gospel and of the apostles, that the bond of marriage cannot be dissolved because of the adultery of one of the spouses, and that neither spouse, including the innocent one who has not provoked the adultery, may contract another marriage while the other spouse is living, and that a man commits adultery who, after dismissing his adulterous wife, marries another woman, and that a woman commits adultery who, after dismissing her adulterous husband, marries another man, let him be anathema."[9]

This canon should not be considered in isolation, but in connection with canon 5, which disawows other grounds of divorce allowed by the Protestants: heresy, incompatibility of temperament, estrangement. Canon 7 should also be read in connection with canon 8, which defends the right of the Church to grant separation *quoad torum*. Finally, it should be interpreted in the light of the council's basic assertions on marriage (DS 1787–99).

Canon 7 came to the defense of Catholic teaching, even if it did not declare that this teaching is unchangeable in all its nuances. It simply said that the Church "has taught and teaches" (*docuit et docet*); it did not add "always" (*semper*). Therefore, the council did not deny the existence of practices and doctrines in the present and especially in the past that diverged from its own doctrine. All the same, the past was referred to in the verb *docuit*.

The teaching of canon 7 was not purely disciplinary in nature, that is, meant only to uphold canonical legislation. Neither was it purely doctrinal and theoretical, for it alluded to the Church's practice as presented and articulated in the documents of the teaching office.

As far as its content is concerned, canon 7 denied the possibility of dissolving the conjugal bond in case of adultery and the liceity and validity of remarriage. It made no distinction between intrinsic and extrinsic indissolubility. The context favors the view that intrinsic indissolubility was meant, but this was not explicitly stated. Nor did canon 7 make a distinction between consummated and nonconsummated marriages. It did not decide the question of whether the Church has any power over sacramental and consummated marriage.[10]

All the same, it is difficult to see how, both from a logical and a doctrinal point of view, anyone could object to the interpretation of Pius XI, who went beyond the limited opportunities of the sixteenth century and interpreted the teaching of the council by saying: "If the Church has not been, and is not mistaken, when she offered and offers this teaching, it is absolutely certain that marriage may not be dissolved, even on grounds of adultery. It is just as evident that the other and much weaker grounds of divorce that could be adduced are worth even less, and cannot be accorded any consideration at all" (see CC, December 31, 1930, AAS 22 (1930) 574; Latin text also in DS 1807, note 1).

Theological Note

We should not infer from this text more than hermeneutics allows. It is wiser to seek out the didactic intention of the council, that is, what it intended to say and teach. It affirmed that the Church has not lapsed into error. This means that the council impressed upon its own statement the quality of a doctrine. However, when indissolubility is at stake, the council's assertion must be filtered through the indefectibility of the Catholic Church. We shall briefly say why this is so.

A council is under no obligation to say all that can be said about a given question. Obviously, it may not say more than it is entitled to say, but it also may say less for doctrinal and pastoral reasons. When an anathema is involved, is not a council obligated to restrict itself to the minimum? The consent of canon 7 does not exhaust what can be considered as theologically established in the doctrine and practice of the Church in the matter of indissolubility. It is only proper to situate the canon within the framework of the doctrine of the teaching office as such, considered in its totality.

What note should we assign to the general assertion that marriage is indissoluble? It is a Catholic doctrine (*doctrina catholica*), a firm assertion of the teaching office, even if it is not presented as a doctrine of defined faith.[11]

The Council of Trent and the Greek and Eastern Practices

The council chose to reaffirm Catholic doctrine and to formally condemn the error of the Protestants. However, it did not want to create yet another obstacle to the reunion of the Christian churches by explicitly and formally condemning the doctrine and practice of the Eastern Churches. Nor did it want to risk severing from Rome the Greek ecclesial communities which remained united with it by a bond which, all things considered, was not very sturdy. At the council the Venetians defended the practice of the Easterners, for at that time Venice occupied the islands of Crete, Cyprus, Corfu, Zante, and Cephalonia. For the sake of public peace, it was quite important that the Byzantine subjects of Venice not fall into formal heresy and be exposed to repression when they made use of the 'economy' of remarriage allowed by their Church. If they wanted to escape repression, they needed only to refrain from contending that Rome was mistaken and to practice pluralism and tolerance.

For reasons which anticipate somewhat the spirit of ecumenism, the Council of Trent preferred not to push the doctrine of indissolubility to its ultimate consequences and to stay on this side of what it could and perhaps wished to say.

To be sure, the council did not advocate a double evangelical and apostolic tradition, one element favoring indissolubility, the other favoring divorce in case of adultery. The doctrine of indissolubility which the council proclaimed is declared to be "in accordance with the doctrine of the gospel and the apostles" (*juxta evangelicam et apostolicam doctrinam*). And yet the council chose not to formally condemn the practice of the Eastern Churches and their faithful. Practically, then, the council faced what we call today a conflict of values. The value represented by an explicit definition of indissolubility, as distinct from an indirect proclamation, was less important in the mind of the council than values related to religious and public tranquillity. The council decided that it could take this course of action – that is, making an indirect proclamation – without betraying the gospel.

By deciding not to condemn the Easterners, Trent did tolerate a practice which, taken as it is, cannot be justified. Although it was prevented by its own interpretation of the gospel from adopting that practice, the council did countenance it.[12]

The Eastern practice remained contrary to the Scriptures. Even if it was not formally condemned, it was not justified as such. The only thing in its favor is that it was not entirely groundless – it could appeal for support to some patristic and medieval authorities. Trent looked upon it as something that can be conceded for the sake of avoiding greater mischief (*ad vitanda peiora*). To strike at the Greeks in the name of orthodoxy would have had an unpleasant result. They would have been deeply offended, and union with them would have become all the more difficult to achieve. For the sake of union, Trent chose to limit the obstacles as much as possible.[13]

We have here an official conciliar definition which resolved a value conflict. Is this the only conclusion we can draw? We cannot be sure *a priori*. Some will no doubt think that we have in the council's decision an indication of how to proceed, a pastoral attitude which could give us guidance even today. Can we further apply this indication? Could the Church, in order to safeguard more important values, refrain from always drawing the ultimate consequences from those doctrines which, according to Vatican II, do not occupy the first rank in the hierarchy of truths? It is not our responsibility to make this determination. But here one must also bear in mind that there is a difference between quiet tolerance and affirmation of principles, between closing an eye to existing situations on the one hand and letting abuses have their way on the other. Rome's long struggle against tolerating the remarriage of divorced persons in the uniate Churches is a theological argument which also deserves consideration.

CHAPTER 6

Pastoral Care of the Divorced and Civilly Remarried Catholic

by Archbishop E. Gagnon

I. The Situation of the Divorced and Remarried in the Church

For the last several years, problems concerning divorced and civilly remarried Catholics have been the object of studies by various episcopal conferences, especially in Europe and the United States. The subject has also been addressed by the Sacred Congregation for the Doctrine of the Faith in two important letters: April 11 and May 29, 1973.

1. DOCUMENTATION

Among the episcopal interventions, we would like to note the ones that have been particularly significant before 1978:

A note in the document *Matrimonio e Famiglia oggi in Italia* from Italian Episcopal Conference, 74.[1]

A pastoral letter of the bishops of the Ivory Coast published in *L'Osservatore Romano,* French edition, April 21, 1972, and in DC, 1972, 739–740.

The intervention of Cardinal Joseph Höffner, Archbishop of Cologne, *Sexualmoral im Lichte des Glaubens–zehn Fragen and zehn Antworten,* French translation in DC, March 18, 1973, specifically 265 *et seq.*

The pamphlet *Communautés chrétiennes et Divorcés remariés* of the Commission for the Family of the French Episcopal Conference. This document is the fruit of an extensive study undertaken by the National Secretariat for the Pastoral Care of Families.

In the United States there is one document of particular importance: a letter (Prot. No. 3333) of March 21, 1975, from the Sacred Congregation for the Doctrine of the Faith to the President of the National Conference of Catholic Bishops and a statement issued by Most Reverend Cletus O'Donnell after the general meeting of May 1977 and published in *Origins*, 6, 1977, 765.

Interesting in themselves as well as by reason of the response given them by the secular press are the Pastoral Directives of the Bishop of Strasbourg (see OR, August 24, 1977).

A declaration of the Permanent Council of Chilean Bishops, September 1977, forbidding the extra-sacramental blessing of non-sacramental unions (DC, 1977, 898).

An address by Most Reverend Le Bourgeois, Bishop of Autun, "*Quelques précisions*," (DC, 1977, 645–46).

The problem has been discussed to an equal degree by synods held by Catholic bishops in the Federal Republic of Germany and in Switzerland. It has also been the topic of five general meetings of the bishops of German-speaking countries and the Scandinavian Episcopal Conference (See *Avvenire*, July 12, 1975, 5). Finally, the document *Evangelizzazione e sacramento del Matrimonio*, prepared for the National Meeting of the Church of Italy, in a section entitled *Evangelizzazione e Promozione Umana*, gave much attention to efforts by the Church on behalf of spouses in difficult situations (see *Avvenire*, August 20, 1975, 6 for a commentary by D. Tettamanzi).[2]

2. GENERAL PRINCIPLES

a. An Environment of Justice

The interventions of the bishops are inspired by two different motivations: (1) a desire to demonstrate the interest and solicitude of the church for people who find themselves in irregular situations and to make some effort toward reconciling them; and (2) a desire to defend and uphold the Church's traditional doctrine of the indissolubility of marriage.

The problem has become urgent because the number of divorced and remarried Catholics has increased notably and because these people have a sincere desire for greater participation in the life of the Church.

Above all, the bishops emphasize the necessity of considering the problems of the divorced and remarried in a rather broad pastoral context. Too often the problem is discussed only in terms of admission or nonadmission to the sacraments. Moreover, the problem is often considered only from the point of view of the divorced and remarried themselves.

It is also necessary to consider other categories of persons who are hurt by decisions made. One cannot forget the courage of Catholics who respect and faithfully transmit the Church's teaching on marriage, the forceful example of Catholics who make a decision not to remarry in order to witness to the law of God. Also at issue are the spouse and children left behind by the divorced and remarried. One must not forget the young and weak Christians who would be scandalized and confused if the divorce and remarried were admitted to a wide range of participation in the life of the Church. Finally, one must not forget the pastors of the Church who have the responsibility of watching over the integral transmission of the law of God.[3]

b. The Irregular Character of the Situation of the Divorced and Remarried

Research conducted with a view to solving the problems of the divorced and remarried has given rise, in the episcopal statements, to certain important and fundamental principles for the formulation of pastoral directives.

The divorced and remarried must recognize the irregular character of their situation. Pastors must help them understand their situation in view of the whole Church. The pastoral care of the divorced and remarried has as its end not resignation to their situation but a true reconciliation with the Church and the law of God. It is useless and unjust for the divorced and remarried to ignore the irregularity of their situation and for priests to allow them to hope for unrealistic solutions.

c. Repentence is a Lengthy Process Toward God

Current theological reflection on repentance and religious psychology shows that sin is often not an isolated act that abruptly breaks the relationship between man and God but rather a choice that develops out of many little actions, decisions, and attitudes, which together lead to a gradual but definite rupture with God. In some cases this culminates in a definitive and symbolic decision.

The case of the divorced and remarried reflects such a process. The failure of the first marriage results, very often, from a psychological separation which gradually develops between the spouses and which culminates in a definitive act, divorce. This act acknowledges and manifests *de facto* the rupture that has already occurred.

The return to a regular situation in the Church calls for a progressive change in mentality, a process of repentance which should take into consideration a person's lifestyle. Such was the normal process of repentance in the early Church.

Another parallel can be found in the case of converts to Christianity. Before baptizing them, the Church requires a period of catechumenate, during the course of which they are all instructed in faith and Christian morals and formed through prayer. The Church demands a change in attitude and in the values by which they live. Admission to baptism reflects a true change in one's inner person.

For the divorced and remarried also, repentance will be a long road. Admission to the sacraments is never purely mechanical; it always presupposes a reform of life, full acceptance of the law of God, and fidelity to full ecclesial communion.

On the other hand, the divorced and remarried are not alone as they walk this road. The entire Church supports them in their effort to achieve full communion. Furthermore, all the members of the Church are sinners, and all Christians must see in the witness of the divorced and remarried a rebuke of every form of egoism and self-satisfaction.

d. *Ecclesial Life Does Not Consist in the Sacraments Alone*

At a time when theologians are calling the Church to a heightened commitment to the world and the social order as well as to a greater insistence on the witness of faith and life, it seems contradictory to view the admission of the divorced and remarried to the sacraments as the only solution to their problems. The life of the Church comprises more than just the sacramental life.

The sacraments, especially the Eucharist, are the summit of participation in the life of grace. But the sacrament loses its significance the moment it is separated from the current of Christian life.

The life of charity, the life of prayer, family life, work, and social life are all accessible to the divorced and remarried. They must live these aspects of existence in a Christian spirit. They are enabled to live thus by virtue of a certain sacramentality, that of baptism received and of absolution hoped for on the day when the process of conversion is complete.

e. The Pastoral Care of the Divorced and Remarried is a Special Apostolate

As members of the Church, the divorced and remarried have the right to spiritual assistance with their problems. However, not every priest is suited to this particular apostolate. To wait patiently, to support and counsel, and yet to hold fast to the teaching of the Church and to never encourage delusory hope for impossible solutions calls for a combination of prudence, understanding, and empathy.

Priests and married people who devote themselves to this apostolate need special training. It seems best that this apostolate be exercised as a service that each local church provides, under the direction of a responsible priest.

Normally, because the divorced and remarried justifiably fear publicity, this apostolate is addressed individually to the couples involved. If groups of divorced and remarried persons are established, an effort must be made to avoid the formation of enclaves or pressure groups.

II. Types of Pastoral Care for the Divorced and Remarried

1. WHAT DOES ONE DO WHEN DIVORCED PERSONS REMARRY?

It is necessary, first of all, to determine whether there is any possibility of pursuing a declaration of nullity or a papal dispensation. Every Catholic has the right to benefit from all the opportunities that the law allows him/her and to receive assistance from competent authorities.

Some writers recommend the internal forum solution. In cases where juridical proof is too difficult but where one has moral certitude of the nullity of the first marriage, recourse to the internal forum would seem to be indicated, in order to appease the consciences of the interested parties and to bring them closer to reception of the sacraments, according to the decisions of the Sacred Penitentiary. One recalls, however, how difficult it is to be one's own judge.

What should the attitude of the priest be toward persons who intend to contract a second civil union? He is never permitted to deny the essence of the official teaching of the Church. He is never permitted to mislead the interested parties by giving them unconditional permission to receive the sacraments.

The priest should first examine the particulars of the case and explore every possible approach to resolve the first marriage; then he must thoroughly explain the position of the Church in such a manner that will foster understanding of the reasons why the Church forbids admission of the divorced and remarried to the sacraments.

Although the Church cannot admit the divorced and remarried to the sacraments because an unbreakable matrimonial bond exists, that does not mean that the Church cannot understand their plight. To the extent possible, the Church gives them a fraternal reception; it receives them as its members and children.

For the past few years, some pastors have envisaged the possibility of commending to God, through private prayer, the lives that the divorced and remarried are leading, whatever their situation might be. From the start, the relevant directives attempted to avoid confusion between such paraliturgies and the sacrament. They were to retain a private character, should be held in a particular house and not on the same day as the civil ceremony. One was to omit, especially, the blessing of the rings and celebration of the Eucharist.

Despite all these precautions, this effort proves negative. Whether one wishes or not, those who attend such ceremonies and those who hear about them get the idea that a second Christian marriage is possible. The impression is that the Church is progressively renouncing its principles and norms on the indissolubility of marriage. One cannot avoid interpreting the indulgence and merciful benevolence shown to persons when they discard the law of Christ as a concession, a resignation, an abandonment of the fidelity owed to Christ.

2. THE PASTORAL CARE OF THOSE CIVILLY REMARRIED

Pastoral practice concerning reception by the Church: the divorced and remarried need a fraternal and evangelical welcome by the Christian community. The priest or the couples who are involved with this apostolate extend this welcome in the name of the Church. The purpose of this apostolate is to help and sustain the divorced and remarried so that they can find their place in the life of the Church, while working toward full reconciliation.

Groups of divorced and remarried: at the moment of entry into the community, in places where divorced and remarried are few in number, it would be useful to foster the formation of groups of divorced and remarried in which they can share and discuss mutual problems. Recall what we said above about these groups and on the importance of their having a qualified director.

The divorced and remarried who have broken contact with the Church: by reason of their irregular situation, many divorced and remarried have broken this contact. Perhaps this is due to a misunderstanding on their part concerning their case (they believe themselves to be excommunicated); perhaps it comes about because they were not treated charitably when they approached the Church on a previous occasion.

It is necessary to develop among Catholics a better understanding of the situation and problems of the divorced and remarried. It is interesting to note that each time that the Church makes a statement on this topic in a particular place, priests and diocesan offices receive many letters and phone calls from persons who want to regularize their situation.

Normally this reestablishing of contact will take place on the individual level between a priest and the interested parties. The priest should persuade the divorced and remarried that no person should ever feel excluded from the love of God in his Church.

3. INCORPORATION OF THE DIVORCED AND REMARRIED INTO THE LIFE OF THE CHURCH LITURGICAL LIFE AND PRAYER LIFE

The divorced and remarried are able to participate in the Church's prayer life in several ways: privately (with their families), communally (with prayer groups), and liturgically. In the liturgical realm, it is necessary to stress the importance of Sunday Mass. The divorced and remarried should seek a way of participating fully in the liturgy through scriptural meditation and eucharistic devotion. Their participation can be deepened by a study of the liturgical year and in particular by special periods of penance.

The divorced and remarried can take part in nonsacramental penitential liturgies: the penitential act of the Mass, the signing with ashes, Lenten celebrations, and penitential liturgies where one does not give general absolution.

The presence of the divorced and remarried at a penitential liturgy where general absolution is given is the cause of much confusion. The priest who presides at such liturgies must tactfully explain that Catholics who find themselves in irregular situations must, before being eligible to obtain sacramental absolution, attempt to remove the obstacles that prevent their full communion with the Church.

The divorced and remarried can not be godmothers or godfathers. One should avoid, to the extent possible, choosing them for this role, remembering that they themselves have need of special spiritual help. One should substitute more qualified persons instead. Depending upon the individual case, one can permit them to exercise other liturgical functions (serving at Mass, reading scripture), if such a function is suited to the good of the community.

APOSTOLIC LIFE

a. Possibilities

The divorced and remarried are able to participate in different apostolic activities of the Church. Catholic organizations and societies should offer divorced and remarried a share in their work. In particular, groups and movements centered around the family ought to welcome them to their activities.

The divorced and remarried can take part in the apostolate of active charity and in the apostolate to workers and professional groups.

They are equally able to take part in movements whose purpose is the deepening and defense of Catholic faith and morality; for example, pro-life movements.

b. Apostolates Which Are Not Open to the Divorced and Remarried

Normally, in their participation in the apostolic life of the Church, the divorced and remarried cannot serve in leadership capacities or as official representatives of the Church. They must understand that their involvement in certain activities, however justifiable it may be, would have an unfavorable effect on the Church's work. This is why they are often given only subordinate roles.

FAMILY LIFE

Although not married in the eyes of the Church, the divorced and remarried must, in their particular circumstances, lead a Christian family life. In particular, as parents, they are obliged to raise their children in the faith and in a Christian life of prayer. This experience will be both happy and sorrowful. The impossibility of participating fully in the sacramental life of their children (especially at first communion) will be perhaps the heaviest cross in the life of the divorced and remarried who are trying to live good Christian lives.

In this context, the divorced and remarried should be welcome in groups that prepare children for the sacraments, when this preparation is provided in common by the families.

FUNERAL LITURGIES

Apart from the case of scandal, the divorced and remarried may have Church funerals if they have shown at least general regret for their sins (see the letter of the SCDF). The priest ought to be aware of every opportunity that is offered him for contact with the family of a dying divorced and remarried, so that he can bring Christian values to bear on the education of the children on the occasion of their baptisms and at the funerals of their parents.

The divorced and remarried often try to hide their situation by attending church in a different parish. The priest should use much tact in trying to remove these barriers which the interested parties set up.

The problem of the divorced and remarried is one that exists at the very heart of the Church's existence. It is a problem for the whole Church. It is necessary to assure the divorced and remarried of the possibility of exercising the rights of all Christians as sinners.

The pastoral care of the divorced and remarried must be related to other pastoral practices in the Church. It is important to recall, for example, the necessity of adequate preparation for the sacrament of marriage. The real problem of many of the divorced and remarried arises from the fact that they entered into their first marriage without serious reflection and preparation. Assistance should be offered to couples who encounter marital difficulties in order to forestall an eventual rupture. One should also provide pastoral care for divorced Catholics who continue living alone. The problems of loneliness or the education of the children often bear heavily on such persons, if the entire community does not support them in the good example of fidelity they give to the radical demands of the Gospel.

Conclusions

TEACHINGS OF PAUL VI

These pastoral directives summarizing recent episcopal teachings and instructions perhaps reflect the tension between fidelity to Christ and mercy toward weak and unhappy human beings. The temptation of some episcopal statements is to deal with the issue of minimizing Christian marriage. Others believe they must protect marriage by avoiding any indulgence toward individuals.

On the level of fidelity to Christ and the greater good, Paul VI addressed on November 4, 1977, to the Council on the Laity and the Council *Cor Unum* a call for vigilance:[4]

> Vigilance, for you know the gravity of the threats which press upon this sacred institution of marriage, whether by reason of conditions of life that are unfavorable to its stability, or by reason of moral decay, or even, unfortunately, by reason of a growing permissiveness regarding certain laws. It is the responsibility of the Church to protect what God has written most deeply in men's hearts: the love, in its most noble acceptance, upon which two beings base a covenant which is called to reflect, in its indissolubility, the fidelity of God's covenant with humanity.

The Christian viewpoint suppresses neither mercy toward individuals nor confidence in the action of grace. This is indeed why the pope added:

> Do not let indifference or even opposition to the Christian ideal of marriage discourage you in your effort to educate people's consciences and hearts. The action of the Lord accompanies you in your apostolic service. This action of God is at work, let us not doubt, in the very hearts of those who lack preparation, or where human weakness or the deleterious influence of a permissive ambience has led to the failure of a love that they would have without doubt wished to be more stable. Those persons whose illegitimate situations do not permit them to live in full communion with the Church must not be excluded from your reflection and your attention.

Part III

AUXILIARY STUDIES

CHAPTER 7

The New Testament Doctrine on Marriage

by A. L. Descamps

The gospel passages on indissolubility are Mark 10:1–12; Matthew 19:3–9; Matthew 5:31–32; and Luke 16:18. To these texts must be added 1 Corinthians 7:10–11, especially since Paul there refers directly to the teaching of Jesus. Some conclusions of the exegetical and historical studies[1] of these passages are quite certain; others are controverted. However, scholarship has reached two almost unanimous decisions: (1) the apostolic Church represented in this case by Mark, Luke, and Paul taught clearly the indissolubility of marriage, and (2) this teaching goes back to Jesus himself.

The first conclusion is affected by the discussion of the two celebrated Matthean clauses "except for fornication," and the great agreement within the apostolic Church is weakened or reinforced by the interpretations given them. A few questions have arisen recently concerning the second conclusion, as we shall see below, on the basis not of definitive interpretation but of very tentative grounds. Beyond these two rather sure conclusions, a number of particular points are debated. Thus can be seen the framework in which our own conclusions are written.

This very rapid overview does not take into consideration hermeneutical analyses that today prolong exegetical and historical research. In this domain, however, we desire to take a position. We shall try to say, at the end of the chapter, how we see the scope of similar research in view of an eventual hermeneutical process.

One can surmise the essential outline of our approach. First we shall try to understand each of the texts *prout iacet*, that is, as the testimony of a redactor. From there we will go backwards, to draw out a fixed oral or written tradition. Finally, we will attempt to discover the teaching of Jesus himself. To the extent possible, this schema will appear also in the subdivisions of the article. In all this, we proceed in a manner which may appear tutioristic and almost scrupulous. Indeed, the redactional character of the passages of Matthew excepted, the wording of our texts will allow their antecedents in the teaching of Jesus to show through: from the point of view of the history of the pregospel tradition, the collection of passages on indissolubility constitutes a privileged case. Our way of proceeding is justified, however, in principle, and also because it permits us at the same time to show throughout certain characteristics of the redactional work.

In this material it is important to distinguish three things: separation *de facto*, repudiation, and remarriage. We believe, with others, that an ambiguity in the vocabulary here was the source of much confusion.

1. *Separatio de facto* refers to a simple situation with no juridical force. This is probably not involved in Mark 10:2–12. Generally speaking, separation is not taken into consideration in our texts, because Jewish law was interested only in repudiation in due form. But, in fact, the practice of separation is likely. Certainly the normal course of events was for the husband to give the decree of divorce to his spouse and then to send her away (Dt 24:1–4). But is it credible that sending her away never preceded the giving of the decree or the juridical act of repudiation? Is it even likely that there was never a *de facto* separation although the husband refused to draw up the decree? Moreover, some texts of the New Testament – rare, indeed – seem to refer to simple separation.[2]

2. Repudiation as understood by Deuteronomy 24:1 and the entire Jewish tradition concerns a dismissal which the husband alone can initiate, and it has precise juridical implications: his act – which calls for delivery of a decree of repudiation – annuls the marriage and gives both him and his spouse the right to remarry.[3]

Jewish *repudiation* then equals what we call *divorce*, on the condition that the latter term is understood as the separation by annulment of the first marriage and the right to remarriage, nothing more nor less. Unfortunately, the terms *divorce* and *to divorce* are not always rigorously employed. *To divorce* is sometimes improperly used for *to separate.* And the words *divorce* and *divorced* are equally ambiguous inasmuch as they can refer either to separation with annulment of the marriage and simple right to remarriage, or to separation and annulment effectively followed by a remarriage. In exegesis it would be clearer to use only the terms *repudiate* and *repudiation* and to avoid the term *divorce*, which, in any case, is not biblical. We will do this. It is better because our term *divorce* makes no important distinction between husband and wife, while *repudiation* at least among the Jews, is almost always an act of the husband.

3. Remarriage was the normal result of repudiation because the latter would give the right to remarriage and because it was without doubt motivated by the desire for a new marriage. It can nevertheless be held that remarriage, especially of the wife, would not always follow. Remarriage is called adultery by both the evangelists and by Jesus. One must ask if repudiation itself was not already tacitly considered adultery, since it gives the right to as well as the concrete occasion for remarriage, which is adultery.

I. Mark 10:2–12

1. THE REDACTION OF MARK[4]

a. The controversy (Mk 10:2–9) as understood by Mark.

Mark 10:1 shows Jesus leaving Galilee for good and going to Judea on the other side of the Jordan, a stage on his way to Jerusalem; thus, this verse is one of the principal hinges of Mark's structure. Matthew 19:1–2 is an exact parallel, even stressing the departure. ("When Jesus had finished these sayings, he went away from Galilee.") Luke notes in other ways the inauguration and progress of this long journey toward Jerusalem (Lk 9:51; 13:22; 17:11; *etc.*).

Although it is a simple formula of transition, and not really a part of our pericope, Mark 10:1 is quite significant for the shift in perspective which was begun after the first announcement of the passion (Mk 8:31): from now on the activity of Jesus unfolds most clearly in view of his impending death. Now, if this death is necessary for the coming of the kingdom, it is without doubt normal in Mark's eyes that the progress of Jesus toward his death be accompanied by other divine requirements. In fact, in the broader context of our passage, the master makes some harsh statements (Mk 9:42–50 on scandal; Mk 10:23–27 on the difficulty of entering the kingdom;); among the actions of Jesus, he is seen cursing the fig tree and driving the money changers from the temple (Mk 11:12–25). In brief, there is here without doubt a body of statements akin to the exacting teachings of the master on indissolubility.

Mark 10:2 reads: "Pharisees came up [to Jesus], and in order to test him [in this] asked, 'Is it lawful for a man to divorce his wife?' "

As the words that we have supplied in brackets suggest, the sentence does not flow from the source, as is frequent in Mark. (Thus Jesus is no longer named after 9:39, that is, much before this.)[5] Certain manuscripts omit mention of the Pharisees and have simply *they* (that is, the crowds mentioned in 1) *asked,* a reading that is not likely to be primitive. The verb ἀπολθειν (*to dismiss*) has a precise meaning because it implies a juridical concept familiar to the Jews: it signifies repudiation with all that this means in the body of Jewish legislation and custom.[6]

Put in these terms, the question of the Pharisees is somewhat unnatural. For them, it is very evident that a man can divorce his wife, at least in certain cases. Since they are questioning Jesus to embarrass him, they would like to formulate their question in a manner that would lead him into a scandalous response through his nonconformism. For example, "Is it true that a man can never divorce his spouse?" The wording of Mark, "Is it permitted a man to divorce his wife?" would sound better coming from the lips of Jesus or from an argumentative Christian rather than from the mouths of the Pharisees. The wording is slightly awkward because Mark is not making an eyewitness report but is writing a literary composition developed at a spatial and temporal distance; this makes it difficult to preserve the nature of the original dialogue.

The redactor knows only that he is dealing with repudiation in the context of a controversy; in Mark 10:2, a somewhat Christian manner of interrogating Jesus may have seemed to Mark a valid way to begin the dialogue.

Mark 10:3: "He answered them, 'What did Moses command you?' " The way that Jesus appeals at once to Deuteronomy 24:1 is again somewhat unnatural. The master seems to call upon Moses as his best guarantee against the Pharisees when the latter held to the Mosaic text of which Jesus was to dispute the validity.[7] The verb ἐντέλλομαι (*to command*) is also somewhat unnatural. Though Moses permitted repudiation, he did not really command it.[8]

Mark 10:4: "They said, 'Moses allowed a man to write a decree of divorce and to put her away.' " This time the verb επιτρέπω (*to permit*) is appropriate. The Greek text of the quotation is elliptical but conforms to Dt 24:1.

Mark 10:5–8: "Then Jesus said to them, 'For your hardness of heart he wrote you this commandment. But from the beginning of creation[9] [God] made [human beings] male and female; for this reason a man shall leave his father and mother and be joined to his wife and the two shall be one. So they are no longer two but one.'" Two subjects – God and Moses – must be supplied as well as the direct object, "human beings." In verse 8[b] the redundance is a little awkward and indicates again an unpolished redaction.

Σκληροκαρδία is not a concept borrowed from secular psychology, as would be expressed for example by the translation *intractable character*.[10] By virtue of its biblical antecedents, the term must be given a precise religious meaning: it specifically refers to the incapacity of the Israelites to submit to the divine will, their spirit of rebellion against God.[11] The Jesus of Mark thus touches an essential and constant point of salvation history, and his denunciation holds even in the present day (our hardness of heart).

Despite its brevity, this condemnation of the Pharisees by Jesus cannot be treated by the exegete as an *obiter dictum*. In the writing of Mark, it has perhaps lost its force in relation to the teaching of Jesus as it was perceived by his hearers. The evangelist was not in Palestinian territory, and criticism of Moses had been current for some time in a Church that henceforth was largely Helleno-Christian. But this was no obstacle. Mark was writing at a time when the rupture of Christianity with Judaism was far advanced but not complete. Yet the condemnation of Mosaism still has a dramatic character and the contemporary reader of Mark could not have been insensitive to it.[12] In order to perceive the audacity of this condemnation, it is necessary to place this text in its original *sitz-im-leben*, in the ministry of Jesus himself. This we will do below.[13]

Verses 6b–8a juxtapose two different quotations, Gn 1:27 and 2:24 – more evidence of a developed gospel text, the work of a Christian scribe rather than the report of a witness. These quotations conform very literally to the LXX, which excludes the possibility of an Aramaic source[14] but not, however, the possibility that the texts from Genesis were used by Jesus in the context of this controversy on the indissolubility of marriage. Another revealing detail: in v. 7 the words *for this reason* (ἕνεκεν τούτου) come as the sequence of Gn 2:24 but they receive another a different application. In Gn 2:24 the narrator of Genesis uses τούτο to refer to the words Adam spoke concerning the unity of husband and wife (Gn 2:23). Mark 10:7 has Jesus referring to Genesis 2:24, but the τούτο of Mark 10:7 can only refer to what he has just written (Mk 10:6), a citation of in another text of Genesis (1:27). Nevertheless, this τούτο sounds right; for what Adam proclaimed in Genesis 2:23 about the unity of the human couple, Jesus in Mark 10:6 says in entirely equivalent terms when he announces – following Genesis 1:27 – that God has made human beings male and female.

Mark 10:9: "Thus what God has joined, let no man put asunder." It is a particularly striking logion which, though presented here as a conclusion, lends itself to an autonomous use in the controversy between Christians and Jews.[15] This aphorism does not have the legal style of the following logia (Mk 10:11–12) and their parallels; thus the laws do not mention God himself directly. It is rather a matter of an exegetical conclusion phrased as a maxim in which one can hear either a sapiential tone or a prophetic accent. In any case, its scope is quite clear.

The active verb χωρίζειν means simply *to separate, to hold apart.* It would be possible to apply it to every form of physical separation.[16] One wonders whether Mark 10:9 does not condemn separation in itself; strickly speaking separation would in itself violate the union promulgated by the creator. However, this conclusion would be uncertain, for the controversy that is concluded in verse 9 pertains specifically to repudiation and so to a separation comprising annulment of the first marriage and the possibility of remarriage.[17]

On the whole, through his rather laborious redaction of verses 2–9, Mark intends to show clearly the opposition of Jesus to the divorce of a woman by her husband, in such a way that two lines of reasoning are found in the material: the teaching of Moses on divorce was a provisional concession to the Israelites' hardness of heart; this concession conflicted with the initial order of things willed by God, which the Jesus of the Gospel of Mark intends to restore.

b. The rules of conduct (Mk 10:11–12) as understood by Mark.

Mark 10:10: "And in the house, the disciples asked him again about the matter." This verse marks a change of scene (the house) and of questioners (the disciples). Contrary to certain real houses in Galilee, notably that of Peter (Mk 1:29; 2:1), the dwelling of 10:10 – we are in Transjordania – is a literary device. The evangelist creates here a formula that reveals a different audience[18] (cf. Mk 4:10; 7:17; 9:18). In addition to the sketch of a dispute with the Jews, Mark's source material contained statements on marriage cast in legal language, namely, Mark 10:11–12. These statements could perhaps be traced back to the Q source, as claimed by some solutions of the synoptic problem which are otherwise hardly plausible.[19] It is more probable, however, that they existed alongside Q, which includes them, as we shall see. For Mark, such rules as these, proclaimed as they are within the Church, are directly meant for Christians rather than for Jews. He regards it, therefore, as more consistent to have Jesus formulate them for the benefit of his disciples rather than to have them being addressed to the Pharisees.

Mk 10:11–12: "If anyone divorces his wife and marries another woman, he commits adultery[20] against the first; and if a woman, having divorced her husband, marries another man, she commits adultery."

The form in which these verses are cast is obviously entirely different from the form of the exchange that goes before. Instead of a dispute related to the Old Testament (Mk 10:2–9), we have here assertions in typically legal style. Note the two opening formulae: Ὃσ ἄν (*if anyone*) and καὶ ἐάν ("and if [on the contrary] a woman . . . "). More precisely, we are dealing here with one kind of phraseology proper to the legal style – the conditional style, referred to at times as *casuistic* by contradistinction to the style which is apodictic and constitutional.[21]

The content of these logia, which for the moment is to be interpreted from within Mark's own text, raises a number of problems.

The first of these is this: Does each of the verses 11–12 condemn two distinct things, or just one? Do they, first, tacitly stigmatize divorce and adultery, then go on to condemn also remarriage by branding it explicitly as adultery? Or does each of the two verses limit itself to condemning remarriage as adultery, divorce being mentioned only incidentally?

One is inclined toward the first alternative if one considers that, among the Jews, divorce includes the right to remarry, a right which Mark rejects unconditionally. The conclusion will then be that, for Mark, divorce contains the seed of adultery. Thus, we could paraphrase the text as follows: "Anyone who divorces his wife virtually already commits adultery. Should he marry another woman, adultery becomes evident." This is how many authors implicitly understand the text. Some do so explicitly. They go as far as to understand the text thus: "Anyone who divorces his wife commits adultery; anyone who marries another woman commits adultery."[22]

Dupont disagrees with this reading. "Nothing entitles us to maintain that, in the absence of a second marriage, divorce as such is being branded as adultery." Then he goes on to give his interpretation of Mark 10:11–12 as follows: "Although the charge of adultery relates grammatically to both of two distinct transactions, namely divorce and remarriage, in reality it affects only remarriage. The sin of adultery is located strictly and precisely in the second marriage, not in the divorce as such." In short, Dupont opts for the second alternative. He takes the view that verses 11–12 limit themselves to condemning as adultery, with, however, the additional stipulation that, if divorce does not fall under this condemnation, it is understood to exclude the right to remarry.

The argument on which Dupont leans most heavily is the Semitic syntax which, in his view, underlies verses 11–12. In Hebrew and Aramaic, two sentences may appear in coordination to each other, and yet the first sentence may express no more than a circumstance relative to the second. As example: "Why . . . do we fast and your disciples do not?" (Mt 9:14), or, "How many times will my brother do wrong, *and* I will forgive him?" (Mt 18:21). These two sentences mean respectively: "*since we fast*, why don't your disciples fast?" and "*Suppose that my brother should do wrong*, how many times am I to forgive him?" Dupont believes that Mark 10:11 may likewise be read as follows: 'Suppose that a man divorces his wife, he commits adultery if he marries another."

There is another point to consider. If we suppose that, for Mark, divorce does not deserve to be branded specifically as adultery, is not divorce at least condemned (in 10:11–12) as being very much against the will of God which Jesus has promulgated? Here an even larger number of authors answer in the affirmative. Often they do not even bother to say so, for they regard the point as self-evident. Yet Dupont dissents: "Nowhere does Jesus say: 'Divorce is forbidden'. . . . He speaks with the assumption that divorce does take place ('Anyone who divorces . . .'). The repudiation process is part of his presuppositions. . . . Jesus passes no value judgment upon the act of divorce itself; he takes a position only on its practical consequences. If the husband who has dismissed his wife, or the wife who has been dismissed, decide to remarry, they lapse into adultery."

Yet is it not true that the divorce which Mark supposedly does not condemn is in effect divorce as practiced by the Jews, that is, the kind of divorce which entitles one to remarriage and which Jesus, therefore, obviously forbids? Not so, says Dupont. Jesus retains the term *divorce* but empties it of its meaning, or gives it a whole new meaning. "The divorce of which Jesus speaks is no longer a divorce properly so called. The word is retained, but it is emptied of its substance." "Jesus may give the impression of contradicting himself, but he does not. He merely gives the verb *to divorce* a new meaning." Dupont refers here to what he regards as "one of the most characteristic traits of Jesus' teaching method." He cites several instances, especially the debate on purification (Mk 7:1–23; Mt 15:1–20), where Jesus retains the word *unclean* but only to give it the entirely new meaning of moral rather than ritual uncleanness.

All this is tantamount to saying that Jesus has in mind not Jewish divorce but what we call simple separation, a separation which does not entail the dissolution of the conjugal bond. Of course, Jesus "does not intend to issue a juridical decision as to what simple separation is as a legal concept, nor does he formally authorize such separation," yet the concept of separation "derives directly from the teaching of Jesus himself."[23]

A detailed discussion of Dupont's argument would take us too far afield. Yet the choice before us is momentous, for, as we shall see, simple separation is precisely the notion on which an entire exegetical tradition relies to resolve the difficult problem occasioned by the Matthean clauses. According to this exegesis, it is precisely simple separation (which does not include the right to remarry) that would be allowed by way of an exception (that is, in case of fornication), and this in spite of the fact that the texts retain the phrase *to divorce* whose normal meaning is entirely different.

Which is the "good choice" as far as Mark 10:11–12 is concerned? When we earlier attempted to clarify the concepts involved here, we readily admitted that simple separation must have existed at the time of Jesus and even that it surfaces in a few New Testament texts. We may thus seem to have conceded Dupont an argument in support of his position. Yet, all things considered, we are most reluctant to go along with him, mainly for the following reason.

Even if we suppose that one could interpret the text of Mark 10:11–12 taken in isolation as Dupont interprets it, the context in

Mark and in Matthew seems to call for a different reading. In Mark 10:2–9, it is obviously Jewish divorce with all its consequences that is being categorically condemned, if not as adultery, at least as a grievous fault. Since verses 11–12 follow from verses 2–9, how could they suddenly speak of divorce as if it were but a circumstantial detail? Could Mark really intend verses 11–12 to extend only to remarriage, without including the divorce that they explicitly mention? We would have a hiatus of a sort that is hardly plausible. The argument can also be turned around: if, for Mark, verses 11–12 condemn remarriage, not divorce, are we not to extend this interpretation to verses 2–9? But how can verses 2–9 be understood to refer only to a condemnation of remarriage, if remarriage is not directly at issue there? It is especially difficult to read in verse 9 in this sense because χωρίζειν, as we have shown, means *to separate* in a very broad sense, that is, to separate in any way at all.[24]

Note again that we are still reasoning here from within Mark's own text, and that we must, in consequence, pay careful attention to the context. Dupont always speaks globally of Jesus. In fact, if the logia were restored to the status of isolated units (being still regarded, however, as sayings uttered by Jesus), it would be easier to interpret them as he does. The paradox is that it is precisely Dupont who ought to be particularly sensitive to the context, since he favors Daube's view who maintains that the logia and the debate had not existed in isolation from each other but had constituted a single unit from the start.[25] We, on the contrary, see this passage as redactional and trace it back to two originally distinct situations, but both plausibly pertaining to the ministry of Jesus himself.

Be that as it may, it is by first staying rigorously within Mark's own viewpoint that we perceive a fundamental reason for dissenting from Dupont's reading of Mark, 10:11–12.[26] We thus take the position that it has not been proved that Mark 10:11–12 implies the notion of a simple separation which may be looked upon as morally indifferent as long as it does not lead to remarriage.

A few minor problems arise if we again read Mark 10:11–12 for the purpose of discerning to whom the saying recorded there is addressed.

Verse 11 addresses the man, to whom Jewish law and custom grants the right to take the initiative in a divorce. Let us agree for the sake of convenience to call this man M1.[27] The moment M1 divorces his wife, he already transgresses the creator's will. Tentatively, we may also say that he perhaps dooms his wife (W1) to adultery. At any rate, if he takes another woman (W2) in marriage, he does commit adultery against his former wife (W1).

The last words in the preceding sentence are not verbatim in the text, which reads instead ἐπ' αὐτήν (*toward her*). This is an ambiguous expression which could even more easily be read to refer to what comes directly before it, namely, to the other or second woman (W2). This is, by the way, how N. Turner interprets the expression.[28] However, the authors generally agree that the adultery spoken of here is committed against the first woman, and their consensus is good enough for us.

If, according to Jewish custom, divorce restores to a man the freedom to remarry, it restores the same freedom to the woman as well. Jesus does, of course, condemn the woman's remarriage as well, and so we are prepared for the parallel legal saying which interdicts remarriage for the woman. However, the word απολυσασα in this second interdiction (v.12) creates a problem. Taken strictly, this word assumes that the wife is entitled to divorce her husband, which seems to contradict Mosaic and Jewish custom that reserves the right to divorce exclusively to the husband. In a Jewish context, we would expect something like this: The woman who has been dismissed (or repudiated, or driven out) commits adultery, if she remarries.

But here we have a prior question of textual criticism. Codex D and others speak of "the woman who has left the house of her husband."[29] J. Wellhausen adopts this reading and remarks: "This is the only wording Mark could possibly have used." Others entertain the same view, V. Taylor for example.[30] But this choice of reading conflicts head on with the well-known principle: the more difficult reading is the preferable reading (*lectio difficilior potior*). A copyist is inclined to correct texts that make for difficult reading, and so the easier reading is suspect. In textual criticism, the need to clarify always arouses suspicion. H. Zimmermann agrees with this reasoning, yet he allows for a more radical solution, which he borrows from Beyer: the entire verse 12 is unauthentic, and this for reasons internal to the text (of a linguistic kind).[31] These reasons do not, however, seem decisive; so it seems wise to retain the accustomed text, which is supported by the main uncial manuscripts, and adopted by most editors of critical editions, K. Aland included.[31]

Even so, we still need to decide what Mark intends to say as he speaks of a woman who divorces her husband. This question has been answered in several ways.

Most exegetes take the view that Mark deliberately elected to mention specifically the woman's case because of the Greco-Roman context which grants the right to divorce to a wife as much as to a husband.[33] But very few authors, who depend mainly on Josephus and the Elephantine papyri, believe that the Jews were acquainted with the right of a wife to divorce her husband.[34] Besides, could we not suppose that the word ἀπολύσασα only exemplifies a slight misuse of language of no real consequence? The very contention that man and woman are equal before the gospel precept which enjoins indissolubility was for Mark reason enough to mention the woman's situation next to that of the man in exactly symmetrical terms. We need not suppose that Mark intended to go on record as asserting that the woman has the right to divorce her husband.

In all the possible interpretations just mentioned, it is plain that Mark has taken pains to have Jesus legislate not only with regard to the husband but also to the wife. This is a fact that deserves a mention, for in the debate just concluded (Mk 10:2–9) the husband is the sole focus of attention, which is what we would expect within the context of Jewish tradition. We will say, then, that in the present case the woman is treated symmetrically with respect to the man only in order to warn her in the same way as the man. Paradoxically, this reading discloses all the same that Jesus is determined to resist all discrimination between man and woman. His attitude is one of principle. Applied to other matters, it will afford greater protection to the woman's rights.

To bring out the content of Mark 10:11–12 we may put it this way: By divorcing W1 and marrying W2, M1 commits adultery with respect to W1. Likewise, by divorcing M1 and marrying M2, W1 commits adultery (with regard to M1). Or: no matter which spouse takes the initiative, divorce violates God's will. This initiative does not dissolve marriage, for marriage is itself proof against dissolution. In any case, any subsequent remarriage is adultery. In terms of Jewish sensitivity, and to the extent to which Mark and his readers are at home within that sensitivity, we discern in Jesus' saying a twofold revolution against accepted custom: first, the Jews permitted divorce, hence remarriage; second, the Jews would never think of equating remarriage by the man with adultery.

In sum, Mark 10:2–12 appears to be composed of two different elements: first, a remnant of a debate about scripture between Jesus and the Jews which gave him the opportunity to issue an unconditional condemnation of divorce; second, a saying which expresses this condemnation in the language of law and make it more precise. In the scriptural debate, divorce is utterly condemned–taken in isolation, the text as word could even apply to the mere fact of separation. The saying sustains this condemnation, but moves from the statement of principle to the consideration of various cases. We thus have the conclusion that divorce–objectionable in itself–normally results in remarriage, which then earns a more precise condemnation: it is called adultery.

2. THE TEACHING OF JESUS

To what extent can we trace back to Jesus himself the various pieces of which Mark 10:2–12 is composed?

We have already suggested a stylistic analysis that clearly distinguishes between the controversy and the teaching; this distinction will prove very useful here because our effort to explore the current of transmission will follow two different lines of reasoning.

a. Mark 10:2–9 and the Teaching of Jesus

The redactional imperfections do not hinder us from postulating the kinds of material that Mark draws upon for the controversy with the Pharisees: they were biblical quotations, memorable sayings of Jesus such as Mark 10:9, or even a fragment of dialogue which originally contained these words or into which the quotations in question were inserted. The imperfections themselves surely reveal redactional work, but it would be difficult to picture Mark as writing 10:2–9 on a blank page.

It is not foolhardy to conclude in favor of the historical reality of one of the materials suggested above: one or several confrontations on divorce between Jesus and the Jews. Whether it involved the Pharisees or another distinct group of the Jews, such controversy was a constant element in the development of the teaching of Jesus.[35] Moreover, the historicity of this particular passage can be deduced from the very audacity of the teaching.

In the time of Jesus there was no dispute over the custom or the doctrine that gave the husband the right to divorce; consequently, each spouse had the freedom to remarry. Discussion centered only on the grounds for divorce, a subject which is not treated here but will be discussed partially by Matthew, as we shall see. What Jesus challenges, then, is the steadfast conviction of the Jews on the very legitimacy of divorce. The attitude which Mark attributes to him is one of great audacity; and this, in our eyes, is one of the best guarantees of its historical authenticity.

This authenticity is confirmed by 1 Corinthians 7:10–11: "To the married I give the charge, not I but the Lord, that the wife should not separate from her husband, (but if she does, let her remain single or else be reconciled to him) and that the husband should not divorce his wife." Without going into a detailed exegesis here, it will suffice for us to note that this text, at least twenty years older than *The Gospel According to Mark*, agrees perfectly with Mark in attributing the condemnation of divorce to the historical Jesus.[36]

This attitude of Jesus is best expressed by Mark 10:9, "What God has joined let no man put asunder." And there are valid reasons for thinking that the very formulation of Mark 10:9 reflects as Aramaic substratum going back to Jesus himself.

The Greek term συζεύγνυειν, "to place under the same yoke," is practically a *hapax Novi Testamenti*, since Matthew 19:6 is little more than a copy of Mark 10:9. Indeed, it is almost absent from the LXX, where it appears only twice.[37] One may ask, therefore, whether the corresponding Aramaic term *zawwegh*, found in the *Targums*, was not in use in the time of Jesus.[38] The entire logion would seem to have been preserved, a supposition supported both by its striking conciseness, and by its vigorous antithesis between God and man: these two traits agree well with the style of Jesus and would facilitate memorization. In contrast to the rather synthetic dialogue which precedes it, here we would seem to have a logion of Jesus already present as such in the source of Mark, either as a conclusion to this dialogue (which itself would undoubtedly have been quite informal in the supposed source) or as an isolated logion that Mark himself very smoothly joined to an extant debate between Jesus and the Pharisees.

Is it possible to go even further and attribute the essential biblical argument developed in Mark 10:2–9 to Jesus? We have sufficiently indicated that this passage is not a word-for-word account of a controversy. But perhaps some evidence hidden beneath the rather unpolished redaction of Mark lets us trace back to Jesus the two arguments advanced, that the Mosaic law was only a provisional concession to the hardness of heart of the Hebrews, and that the followers of Jesus must return to the original will of God. Because these two considerations imply the nullity of the law, they are blasphemous in the eyes of the Jews. Since the historian has already traced the condemnation of divorce back to Jesus, he can seek to attribute the supporting arguments to him.

It is unlikely that the Judeo-Christian Church of Palestine or the diaspora, which would surely have been predisposed to accommodate Judaism in some ways,[39] could have invented a teaching so radical – in both thesis and argumentation – and gratuitously attributed it to Jesus in Mark's redaction. Nor would the gentile Christian Church have done so, for such a severe message would only hinder its efforts at evangelization, as 1 Corinthians 7:10–16 discreetly attests.[40] But if it is relatively easy to dispose of an anonymous milieu of the Church as *sitz-im-leben*, cannot one argue that Paul himself must be considered as a possible source here?

At first glance, one can see Paul as the true creator of an argument as anti-Mosaic as it is anti-Semitic. It suffices to recall that the Pauline system of justification (Romans and Galatians) is specifically predicated on the condemnation of the law; with its collection of weaknesses and sins, the law has been put to death on the cross, in order that grace may rule. It seems possible to explain Mark's idea of the nullity of Deuteronomy 24:1 in this approach, to focus fully on the creative genius of Paul, and to avoid the necessity of going back to Jesus. For other passages, Mark's Paulinism was and still is a theme of contemporary exegesis of the second gospel.[41] Finally, present-day exegetes of the gospels, sometimes influenced in their task by the more recent Jewish historians of Jesus, state that Jesus differed much less with his Jewish contemporaries than Christian tradition considers.[42]

But these are general considerations, and for our present purpose we must come to a precise comparison. Compare Mark's theme, that Moses watered down the original will of God on marriage to accommodate the religious indifference of his people, with the Pauline theme that Jesus Christ abrogated the Mosaic law through the reign of faith and grace. While these two themes share a common ground, namely the definitive condemnation of the teaching of Moses, the two arguments are very clearly different.

First of all, in the Gospel the nullity of the law is announced by the word of Jesus (supposed to be the very Word of God), while, for Paul, the law is conquered only by the death and resurrection of Jesus.

We should not, however, insist on this difference, because it can be explained by the obvious difference in the situations (teaching of the historical Jesus, faith in the heavenly existence of Christ).

More clear is the fact that while the Jesus of Mark finds the divine will in the account of creation, Paul for his part discovers it in an event more immediately "pre-Mosaic," namely in the testament made in favor of Abraham's faith and inaugurating the rule of faith.[43]

There is another important consideration. We are fortunate enough to possess the exact teaching of Paul on indissolubility (1 Cor 7:10). Now the apostle tells us, in summary, that he conforms his teaching here to that of the historical Jesus.[44] Such a reference by Paul to Jesus contrasts with his usual development of the theme of the general nullity of the law (Romans and Galatians). To refer to rules laid down by the historical Jesus is quite another thing than to argue as a theologian the superiority of Abraham the believer to Moses the legislator. But while this argument causes Paul to exalt faith, it does not permit him to decide a question as concrete as divorce; for this question, as for others, Paul characteristically consults the exact traditions which go back to the pre-Easter Jesus (1 Cor 7). On the contrary, in his great orchestration of the antithesis law–faith (Romans and Galatians), Paul does not appeal to logia of Jesus nor to Mark's themes of the Mosaic compromise and of the necessary return to the initial order of creation.[45] We have, therefore, no reason to consider these as Pauline themes that Mark would have uncritically ascribed to Jesus.

Finally, the idea that the opposition between the law and creation (Mk 10:2–9) originates with Jesus would seem to be supported by other gospel texts. Certainly the question of the attitude Jesus took towards Moses and the law is particularly difficult, and we cannot treat it here.[46] It is probable that his attitude was complex, paradoxical, and very nuanced. It is certain in any case that Jesus distinguished the true Moses from the Moses altered by the traditions of the doctors,[47] and it may be that the master went so far as to oppose Moses to God. This is perhaps what happens, for example, when Jesus, interpreting God, proposes new rules in place of the Mosaic commandments. This is the object of the "antitheses" of the Sermon on the Mount (Mt 5:20–48), which is precisely where we find the passages condemning divorce.[48] There is possible support here for the authenticity of Mark's "reasoning" (10:2–9) on creation and the law.

In commenting on Mark 10:2–9 as understood by Mark, we have raised the question of the exact focus of the critique of the Mosaic text evoked by verses 5 and 6 on hardness of heart or, if you prefer, on the antithesis of creation–law.[49] It would be especially important to resolve this question here, that is to say, at the moment when we ask ourselves about the thought of Jesus himself. For Jesus, did Moses compromise with the hardness of heart of his people by permitting divorce? Or did he excuse Moses,[50] and reprobate the contemporaries of Moses, and even more their descendants, in this case the Pharisees? It is difficult to say. Let us say only that this second hypothesis is brilliantly defended by Dupont in a lengthy article.[51]

After having attributed to Jesus himself the use of the texts from Genesis on creation juxtaposed with the ones from Deuteronomy on divorce, can one determine their originality? It can be admitted that such conflation and precisely of marriage is attested to in a few biblical texts (Mal 2:3–16; Tob 8:6–8) and also in some Essene documents: the Documents of Damas and the Temple Scroll.[52] In one sense this observation confirms the probability of the argument *in ore Jesu*, and in another sense it does not detract from its originality: facing his surroundings and above all the Pharisees who were questioning him, Jesus employed here a nonconformist exegesis. This latter has been called "nonrabbinic" by Bundy,[53] and this is cause for reflection even if the remarks of this author are only "partially exact."[54]

b. Mark 10:11–12 in the Message of Jesus

With almost all authors we admit that these verses existed before Mark in an isolated state.

It is true that a serious attempt has been made by Daube to demonstrate that the sequence of disputed sentences, far from being redactional, is on the contrary pre-Marcan and even original.[55] This exegete appeals to the rabbinic writings, which bring two elements closely together: the teaching to the people on the outside, then in-depth explanation to the disciples. Without contesting the interest of these remarks from various points of view, we do not think that they can prevail here against an attentive examination of Mark's redaction. From the point of view of historicity, which concerns us here, the subject of this discussion is limited, inasmuch as the literary doubling Mark 10:2–9 and Mark 10:10–12 does not hinder us from recognizing for each of the two sections a *sitz-im-leben Jesu.* This solution has the advantage of suggesting that Jesus treated indissolubility on a number of separate occasions, which can only emphasize the importance that he attached to this teaching.

When attempts are made to recover the teaching of Jesus himself on marriage, present-day exegetes have a tendency to give a privileged place to the isolated logia, especially those of Mark 10:11–12. It is clear that, compared to the short sentences, the pericope on the controversy reveals very important redactional work.[56] But the verses of the genre of Mark 10:11–12 are sometimes also regarded suspiciously, especially when, as here, they take the form of legislative rules. These latter are understood better in the context of the primitive Church;[57] the historian wonders to what extent Jesus was preoccupied during his life with legislating, in the proper sense of the word, for the messianic community. But as certain writers have noted, Jesus adopted on many occasions the sapiential language of the proverb, that is to say, a style which is not far from that of rules for a way of life. Moreover and above all, in the present case evidence in favor of these logia is exceptional, since they are present (with a few differences it is true) both in Matthew and Luke, and before that in Q, Mark, and 1 Corinthians 7:10–11. This is a decisive argument in favor of their authenticity as the teaching of Jesus.

One can add that in all the forms attested to except one (Mt 19:9),[58] there are two logia; moreover, the respective subjects are different. This doubling is a sign of primitive data,[59] although the question of the identity of the two subjects remains temporarily open.

Beyond this general remark on the authenticity of the doubling, there is a body of research on the precise formulation which is equally important. In the eyes of some exegetes who have written recently, each of the gospels (Mark, Matthew, Luke) has claims to authentic value.[60] We shall examine much later the problems of the Matthean and Lukan versions. Let us content ourselves here with a few remarks on the formulation of Mark 10:11–12.

In Mark 10:11 only the words ἐπ' αὐτήν ("against her") seem to be a redactional addition.[61] Without this ending, verse 11 (which is found in Mt 19:9, but with an insertion) appears to be practically identical to Luke 16:18a and even fundamentally similar to Matthew 5:32 (without the insertion). We say "fundamentally similar" because the Matthean expression "makes her an adultress" is probably – as we shall see – a revision of the original verb: *commits adultery* (Mark and Luke).

This verb merits our attention for a moment. Although absent from 1 Corinthians 7:10–11, it has every chance of being primitive, by reason of evidence found throughout the gospels. Jesus no doubt employed it in referring directly to the decalogue (Ex 20:14). By means of this very expressive term, he will stigmatize here all remarriage during the life of the first spouse, and he will do this in a body of teaching on divorce, as the beginning of the logion indicates. It is a teaching which already condemned divorce itself, notably because it implies the possibility of remarriage and thus contains the seed of adultery. We have no reason to interpret this logion differently, as does Dupont, who holds that Jesus spoke on divorce without forbidding it as such, stating precisely throughout that it does not authorize a new marriage. In order for this exegesis to be valid, it would be necessary to suppose, that in the ministry of Jesus situations arose when the teacher considered only remarriage, and then mentioned divorce as a simple circumstance of fact; however, we have no evidence that this happened. Up to this point, in every case, the context has been a discussion of divorce: the controversy in Mark 10:2–9 and also the very formulation of Mark 10:11–12. Let us note for now that Matthew 5:31–32 also calls to mind the same context (divorce), but this time under the form of a "teaching by antitheses." We will return later to discuss the primitive context of Luke 16:18.

On the other hand, let us stress with Dupont how revolutionary[62] is the attitude of Jesus. What we have noted on this subject in the interpretation of Mark acquires its value here. It is in Jesus' own milieu rather than communities already emancipated from Judaism that the teaching of Jesus made its impact. It is in this way especially that one can speak of a true revolution in ideas. Divorce and remarriage are denounced by Jesus as contrary to the divine will. His is a unique way of going aginst law and custom, since the Jews admitted divorce in many cases, and thereby accepted a new marriage. Moreover, the generic idea of offense or of sin is specified by the accusation of adultery, which is applied at least to remarriage. This was a new manner of upsetting Jewish sensitivities: for a Jew, a man can never be said to be adulterous in relation to his own wife.[63]

On the whole, there can be seen behind various versions of the first logion this original form: "Every man who divorces his wife and marries another, commits adultery."

As to the second logion, let us recall the version of it given in Mark 10:12: "Every woman who, after divorcing her husband, marries another, commits adultery." The formulation alludes to Greco-Roman law (or to some particular Jewish customs), unless it is a mere carelessness of style; in any case, as it stands, the formula does not reflect the language of Jesus well.

Among the versions of Mark 10:12, that of Paul approaches that of Mark in the sense that the apostle, too, addresses himself to the man and to the woman (M1, W1), although in an order opposite to that of Mark, while Luke 16:18b and Matthew 5:32b address the new husband (M2) after having questioned the first (M1). The choice is difficult between, on the one hand, Mark–Paul and, on the other hand, Luke–Matthew (that is to say Q as well). We will leave open, then, the question of knowing if the second sentence of Jesus was addressed to the first wife (W1) or to the second husband (M2). In any case the teaching implied is the same: in each hypothesis it is a matter of denouncing remarriage as adultery as long as the spouse lives.

If our preceding analyses are correct, this last formulation summarizes the tenor of Mark 10:11–12 as these verses reflect the teaching of Jesus.

Up to this point, we have discovered nothing which confirms certain other recent hypotheses. It seems arbitrary to reduce the original passage to the single verse Mark 10:11 and to read there, either the sole prohibition of divorcing one's wife in order to espouse another (J.H.A. van Tilborg) or Jesus' exclusive preoccupation with defending the divorced woman (B.M.F. van Iersel). For this last author, Jesus would not be speaking on indissolubility but would be defending the weaker party as he did with regard to the adulterous woman, the publicans, and the sinners. What we have said about the origin of the statements of Jesus directs us toward the classical discussions among the Jews of divorce and perhaps also of the extension of the right to divorce. We have found nothing to recommend the thesis of A. Isaksson. According to this author, Jesus, in reestablishing the indissolubility of marriage, only intended to say that the Old Testament was supposed to be addressed to the members of the priestly families serving in the temple of Jerusalem: "They shall not marry a woman who has been a prostitute or who has lost her honor, nor a woman who has been divorced by her husband, for the priest is consecrated to his God" (Lev 21:7).

Even further from our conclusions about Mark 10:2–12 seem to be the ideas of B.K. Diderichsen, who simply discards Mark as a witness to the thought of Jesus, not only because he prefers Luke 16:18 but also that he may speculate, on the basis of this verse, that Jesus intends to forbid a new marriage to the one who has left or divorced his wife for the cause of the kingdom. The study of the texts of Matthew and of Luke will allow us to return to some of these hypotheses.

Only after we examine the complete collection will we attempt to state precisely the motivations and the meanings of the teaching of Jesus on indissolubility.

II. Matthew 19:3–8

The Controversy

After having commented in Part One on the texts in the oldest gospel (Mk 10:2–9 and 10–12), we present here the other elements of the record, beginning with Matthew.

We will first read Matthew 19:3–9 in comparison with Mark 10:2–12, which has already been explained.[64] Mark 10:2–12 is divided into two parts: a controversy (vv. 2–9) and rules of conduct (vv. 10–12). It is otherwise in Matthew 19:3–9. We find integrated in the account of the controversy, by virtue of the conclusion (Mt 19:9), the legislative statement which in Mark 10:10–12 was the object of a distinct pericope. However, since Matthew 19:9 requires a rather long explanation on account of the difficult exception clause inserted there, for the sake of clarity we are led to distinguish it from verse 3–8, and thus to comment on Matthew 19:3–9 in two sections, Parts 2 and 3.

We are going to comment on the Matthean form of controversy which we already met with in Mark 10:2–9 between Jesus and the Pharisees. Again, the problem of marriage is approached through divorce. This circumstance, however, cannot narrow our horizon or make us ignore the complete doctrine of marriage among the Jews.

In the time of Jesus people had an exalted notion of marriage, and there is no indication that practice varied greatly from theory. On the contrary, it is striking to note that none of the many reproaches that Jesus addressed to the Pharisees concerned marriage.[65] For the Jews of the time of Jesus, marriage was for the most part monogamous and indissoluble.[66] This is shown in two ways: the gravity of adultery is, in a sense, a subtle tribute to marriage;[67] and the regulation of the right to divorce granted the husband reveals also a care to preserve the conjugal union.

On this second point, certainly jurisprudence varied and with it the destiny of monogamous marriage. However, we have no evidence that divorce was very common. In any case, the Pharisees were rather of the rigorist school of Shammai. The gospels are silent about what in that milieu[68] would constitute noteworthy laxity in the matter. Nowhere does Jesus reproach the Pharisees or any other persons for divorcing their wives for trifling reasons.[69]

There is one more negative point for this brief summary – the very masculine approach to conjugal union. For a long time marriage has been for us a synallagmatic contract; the spouses are on an equal footing in regard to conjugal morality. Such a view was unknown to the Jews of the first century, the result of a long oriental atavism; to reproach them for it would be to commit an anachronism. For them, it was especially the woman who was guilty in cases of infidelity; moreover, only the husband[70] had the right to divorce. For them, there was no complete social equality between a man and a woman. If Jesus himself addressed the husband particularly in promulgating required conjugal morality, he doubtless did not explicitly do so in order to grant social equality to the woman. But in refusing the husband the right to divorce, he *de facto* took the defense of humiliated wives. Did Jesus express himself thus with this precise aim? The texts do not say so. We can, however, reasonably suppose that this consideration played some part in the master's thought when we bear in mind that an analogous solicitude animated him in regard to women sinners and the woman taken in adultery.[71]

In approaching Matthew's text let us limit ourselves to an understanding of the account, that is to say, the thought of Matthew himself.[72] Matthew 19:3: "Some Pharisees came up to him and said to test him, 'May a man divorce his wife for any reason whatever?' " The verse is very similar to Mark 10:2, but Matthew has placed πειράζοντες (*to test him*) in a better place. He has put the question in direct discourse (as in 12:2), perhaps to place it in higher relief. Above all, he has modified the meaning of the question in adding the words "for any reason whatever." But this addition can be understood in two different ways.

It is often interpreted as follows: the Pharisees in Matthew were interested in the various motives for divorce and not, like those in Mark, in its very possibility. More precisely, they alluded to a well-known controversy that, in the time of Jesus, divided the respective partisans of the two great Jewish doctors, Hillel and Shammai.[73] According to Shammai, divorce and remarriage were authorized only for grave reasons, most notably for the wife's lapse from fidelity and honor. On the contrary, according to Hillel, the husband could be authorized for numerous motives to divorce his wife and remarry. Hillel's position could almost be expressed in the following terms that we borrow freely from Matthew 19:3: "divorce effectively permitted *for any cause*." Jesus would then be called upon to say whether he approved such laxity, the Pharisees being implicitly on the side of Shammai.

This exegesis offers a first difficulty, at least if we leave aside for an instant the explanation of the account in order to place ourselves in the broad context of the life of Jesus. The Pharisees could hardly be ignorant of the fact that Jesus was very far from accepting the doctrine of Hillel. In inviting him to pronounce against this doctrine, they would only draw him nearer to themselves, and would not be testing him; consequently the word πειράζοντες would become unintelligible. Nevertheless, one could object that this logic is valid in regard to oral dialogue; it is less impressive where writing is concerned. In other words, in writing on his own "for any cause whatever," Matthew could have thought of Hillel and Shammai, even if the interlocutors of Jesus could not have done so without being illogical. To this, one can retort that the writer could not have been so forgetful of historical probabilities.

The exegesis in question is open to another objection. It leads us to suppose that Matthew 19:3–9, while following Mark 10:2–12 rather closely, would have completely altered the meaning since, as we have seen, Mark 10:2–12 in no way states the motives for divorce but denies its very possibility. To conjecture that in adding "for any cause" Matthew willed to make an allusion to the laxity of Hillel is to admit that for him, Jesus is going to discuss the reasons for divorce. In fact, like Mark, Matthew is about to deny the possibility of this separation even if the exception clause justifies divorce in a unique case.[74]

We can prefer, therefore, another interpretation of the last words of Matthew 19:3, one that remains faithful to Mark in his refusal to permit divorce. Matthew prepared his readers to anticipate that there would be one exception, that of the clause (Matthew 19:9).[75] While repeating the words of Mark 10:2: "Is a man permitted to divorce his wife?" Matthew may have hesitated to stop there so as not to lead the reader to expect the absolutely negative answer that Mark gives.

Matthew 19:4–8. We refer the reader to a synopsis of the gospels or at least of the Matthean pericope. If, as we think, Matthew depends upon Mark, his essential intervention consists in reversing the latter's order of exposition. Instead of going back from Moses to the creation, the Matthean dialogue proceeds from the creation to Moses.[76] In doing this, Matthew undoubtedly thought it more natural. In reading Mark 10:3, Matthew seems to have been aware of the weakness noted above. In Mark, by alluding to Deuteronomy 24:1, Jesus appeals to Moses when the latter contradicts him.[77] The true argument of the master is found in Genesis, and that is why Jesus begins with that argument in Matthew. The Mosaic text appears in Matthew 19:7 in its true light: not as an argument in favor of Jesus, but rather as an objection to him, an objection introduced very naturally by the Pharisees in the name of scripture itself and then refuted by Jesus. Moreover, the procedure seems in conformity with rabbinical practice.[78] Let us say then with Crouzel[79] that Matthew's composition appears much better; this is a typical result when Matthew reworks Mark's text.

Having thus noted the essentials, let us add that Matthew improved Mark's account in numerous details. We will limit ourselves to a few remarks.[80] In verse 4, Matthew named a subject (God the creator ὁ κτίσας, avoiding the anacoluthon of Mark 10:6, where the subject was not named when it was apparently God, while verse 5 had Moses as the subject. Besides, in writing καὶ εἶπεν (v. 5), Matthew has at least sought to distinguish two quotations which, in Genesis, are effectively separated one from the other.[81] Moreover, Matthew 19:5 reproduces Genesis 2:24 in its entirety. Beginning with Matthew 19:7, there are other small changes, in part necessitated by the inversion in the order of exposition. The most remarkable is the addition of 8c, "from the beginning it was not so," which opposes the initial order willed by God to the Mosaic tolerance. The formula is concise and reads almost like a general principle.

On the whole, Matthew 19:3–8 is a reworking of Mark 10:2–9, and its most important change is the addition of the words "for any cause whatever" as a discreet foreshadowing of the inserted clause in verse 9.

We need not seek a way to go back from Matthew 19:3–8 to Jesus: this link can be assured only through Mark. In our understanding of the synoptic problem, Matthew gives no evidence here of any other contact with Jesus a distinct from the one we have discerned Mark.[82]

III. Matthew 19:9

The Rule of Conduct with the Exception Clause[83]

For the moment we shall limit ourselves to examining the text from the viewpoint of its composition. After 19:8, Matthew omits Mark 10:10. This perhaps is intentional, for the difficulty created in Mark by the word *house* is a real one.[84] However, in suppressing the mention of the house, the place of the disciples' questioning, Matthew was led to two small changes that in their turn raise some questions. In verse 9, Jesus directs to the Pharisees the rule that Mark 10:11 proposes to the disciples themselves. In verse 10, Matthew puts the disciples on the scene abruptly without the transition found in Mark 10:10, a transition certainly artificial in the sense that the house is "literary," but plausible in the sense that the precise laws on indissolubility are addressed to the disciples more than to the Pharisees.

Matthew 19:9 reproduces Mark 10:11 and introduces there the famous clause. Before tackling this, let us notice two minor points. After 19:9, Matthew omits Mark 10:12, perhaps because he is aware of the singularity of this verse that, by alluding to the divorce of a husband by his wife, sounds strange to all readers who know the Jewish milieu.[85] In relation to Mark 10:11, Matthew 19:9 shows, besides the insertion of the exception clause, the omission of the last two words ἐπ' αὐτήν (*against her*). The simplest explanation is that Matthew judged them superfluous, and by the single word μοιχᾶται (*he commits adultery*), he means to stigmatize divorce followed by remarriage as the adultery of the husband *vis-à-vis* the divorced wife, which we have judged to be the probable intent of Mark.[86]

Seeing the importance of Matthew 19:9, on account of the exception clause,[87] we think it advisable to consult first of all the specialists in textual criticism.

1. LECTIO GENUINA OF MATTHEW 19:9

Let us begin with the form of 19:9, which is quite long if we take into account all the principal manuscripts; and for the sake of clarity, subdivide it into 9a: "I now say to you, whoever divorces his wife (lewd conduct is a separate case) and marries another commits adultery"; and 9b: "and the man who marries a divorced woman commits adultery."

At the end of a recent and thorough study, Duplacy, approved by Dupont, formulated his conclusion as follows: verse 9a is to be retained just as it is habitually presented by the editors and just as we have translated it a moment ago. The clause ought to be read μὴ ἐπὶ πορνείᾳ. The manuscripts having παρεκτὸς λόγου πορνείας, a reading equivalent in meaning, could not prevail here, the less so as they are suspected of harmonization with Matthew 5:32. The two exception clauses, those of Matthew 19:9 and 5:32 have the same significance, and the testimony is firm in the manuscript tradition of the two passages. Only the absence of the exception clause in the patristic quotation could have led Crouzel to decide in favor of the omission; but it would be very difficult to follow the eminent patrologist on this point. For the rest of 9a, the variant ποιεῖ αὐτὴν μοιχευθῆναι, which is rejected in the critical apparatus of the editions, is also rejected by Duplacy; it is also suspected of harmonization with Matthew 5:32.

9b or a variant is found in B, C, W, O, P, among others, but is generally not retained by the classical editors, including the most recent, K. Aland. Duplacy is not categorical, but does not exclude its authenticity. He bases his verdict on internal evidence, and he is supported by Dupont. We can only ratify this judgment, and add a remark to it. If 9b is authentic, it presents this peculiarity: it applies the condemnation of divorce to the partner M2. We do not find this in Mark, but we do find it in Matthew 5:32b and Luke 16:18b.

Having thus admitted the textual authenticity of the clause, we must now try to understand it as Matthew understood it.

2. THE CLAUSE IN ITSELF

a. The Negation μὴ ἐπὶ

In translating Matthew 19:9 as we have done above with the majority of translators ("*except* for lewd conduct"), we have supposed that μὴ ἐπὶ very clearly marks an exception. A rather large number of authors reject this meaning of *except*. Some speak of a "preteritive" meaning and read "the case of lewd conduct not being considered," a case which would then be reserved, subject to a special solution that the evangelist does not indicate elsewhere.[88] Others defend an inclusive interpretation (the one who divorces his wife, a thing forbidden *even* in the case of lewd conduct, . . .).[89]

What should we think of these two explanations? They are suspect, first from the fact that they are somewhat subtle, second because they eliminate as if by magic a difficulty that has been prominent for a long time. This leads us to think that they have been invented just in order to escape this difficulty. In favor of the idea of a true exception, we could thus apply an analogue of the principle of textual criticism, *lectio difficilior potior.*

But the decisive argument lies in the grammatical analysis of the entire verse 9. The most penetrating analysis is that of Dupont; and we conclude with him that it is necessary to read: "Whoever divorces his wife, *unless* for lewd conduct, and marries another commits adultery."[90]

In order to strengthen this interpretation, let us observe that it is already suggested, so to speak, by the expression in Matthew 19:3: "for any reason whatever." This formula would be difficult to understand if in the mind of the author there did not exist good and bad reasons for divorce. It already requires, so to speak, an answer of this kind: "No, one cannot divorce for any reason whatever, but for such or such exceptional reason."

b. The word πορνεία

In profane Greek, the normal meaning of the word, likewise attested to in the New Testament, is lewd conduct, fornication, carnal relations outside of marriage. In itself, the word πορνεία like the English equivalent just mentioned, has a generic meaning, for it is applied to all relations outside of marriage.[91] Here, however, the verse as a whole shows that the matter under discussion is the lewd conduct of the wife, hence an adultery, one kind of fornication, or something of the sort.[92]

However, some exegetes understand the word πορνεία in Matthew 19:9 quite otherwise; that is, in the sense of a marriage forbidden by the Jewish law, yet contracted *de facto,* such as, for example, marriage between close relatives. As a result, the verse would be understood thus: "if someone divorces his wife, unless it was a question of an invalid marriage . . . " The exception then would not apply to true marriages, and the absolute indissolubility of the latter would be saved.

Bonsirven, an authority on Judaism, stated this hypothesis some thirty years ago;[93] it gained a rather wide acceptance, perhaps because the exegetes were happy to resolve the difficulty the clause presents by eliminating it.[94] Bonsirven bases his theory on the fact that in the New Testament πορνεία often shows its Semitic substratum to be the word *zenuth* that in post-Biblical Hebrew designates a false marriage, a union forbidden by the Law.[95] More recently, certain Essenic texts have given to *zenuth*, in the sense of a marriage between close relatives, testimony contemporary to the New Testament, and therefore more ancient than the citations referred to by Bonsirven.[96]

What must we think of this exegesis? Let us remark at once that an evangelical word does not necessarily have the same meaning as its Semitic substratum, supposing that the latter has been correctly identified. Even then one would still have to prove that the evangelist understood the Greek term in conformity with the Hebrew term and with a meaning contrary to the Greek lexicon itself. The process is delicate. What we are trying to interpret at the moment is the text such as it came from the pen of an author who was writing in Greek.

The major difficulty with Bonsirven's hypothesis is, the following. If it is probable that in Acts 15:20, 29; 21:25 the word πορνεία effectively covers the word *zenuth*, we must, above all, note that these texts have a different bearing in regard to Deuteronomy 24:1 and to the problem of divorce treated in Matthew 19:9 as an echo of Deuteronomy 24:1. The apostolic decree (Acts 15) is a warning; and it is, therefore, logical that the future spouses be exhorted beforehand to avoid what could be a forbidden union. In the problematic connection with Deuteronomy, on the contrary, it is a question of a defect after marriage. As Dupont notes very justly, regarding the expression of Deuteronomy, " 'if he (the husband) has found some indecency in her' (his wife), it can hardly be a question of 'discovery' of an invalid marriage or one forbidden by the Law. In short, Bonsirven's explanation also risks being only a 'loophole.' "[97]

In order to resume the reading of the clause in itself, we can translate it thus: "lewd conduct (of the wife) being a separate case."

3. THE CLAUSE IN THE SENTENCE

The real difficulty lies in the way the clause is linked to the sentence as a whole. Even if the clause is correctly translated, it remains true that the verse, read in its entirety, is not so transparent as it appears at first sight. Let us reread Matthew 19:9: "If any one divorces his wife (lewd conduct is a separate case) and marries another, he commits adultery." The thorny question is this: is the exception allowed for the act of divorce only, the prohibition of remarriage remaining the same, or is the exception allowed for both the divorce and remarriage? It is only after settling this point that we can grasp the significance of the clause.

In the first case, the verse must be paraphrased thus: if someone divorces his wife–(something forbidden) unless for lewd conduct–and marries another, he commits adultery (this in all cases, whether the divorce was legitimate or not). In the second case, the judgment comes to this, which is entirely different: if anyone divorces his wife and marries another, he commits adultery, unless it was a question of lewd conduct (on the part of the wife). In this last case, divorce and remarriage are permitted.

The problem thus caused is really difficult and its resolution is perhaps impossible. The difficulty has divided interpreters from the most ancient times. The two paraphrases above reflect the two principal types of interpretation, and we shall examine them in turn.

To begin with, let us observe with Dupont that the Council of Trent, in affirming the Church's right to reject *every* dissolution of the matrimonial bond, voluntarily abstained from condemning Catholic authors, among them illustrious Fathers of the Church, who admitted this dissolution in the case of adultery, either justifying this by the incidental clause or, more often perhaps, by other gospel texts.[98] From an exegetical point of view, therefore, the question remains open.[99]

a. In the case of lewd conduct (on the part of the wife): separation is permitted, remarriage forbidden

The reader has probably already recognized the familiar concept of *separatio tori et mensae*, a separation permitted in certain cases, the conjugal bond remaining firm and remarriage being excluded. Saint Jerome, who was no innovator in this matter, understood the text in this way and his interpretation has prevailed for a long time among Catholics, where it was classic and, moreover, has remained so in large measure. This exegesis has been brilliantly defended by Dupont.[100]

Grammatically this reading is altogether possible, as the first of the two paraphrases just given suggests. Such an interpretation has in its favor the fact that the clause immediately follows the mention of divorce and precedes that of remarriage, which could imply that the latter does not benefit from the exception, which would then be admitted only for a "simple" separation. On the other hand, the interpretation has something labored about it, for it supplies two words just before the clause: "(something forbidden) unless it be for lewd conduct . . . ", which is plausible but nothing more. Dupont has explained at length the support that the grammatical order can give to this reading.[101] A detailed discussion of the subject is not necessary here, since the other interpretation is also grammatically possible; Dupont himself, as we shall see, expressly recognizes this. We cannot settle the dispute on the basis of grammar alone. Let us see then the other arguments that plead in favor of the separation of body and goods.

A major argument is that this exegesis allows Matthew's text to be harmonized with those of Mark and Luke, who without exception have condemned remarriage. This remains true for Matthew even if he is interpreted as we have just seen, since simple separation never gave the right to remarriage. Granted that Matthew thus interpreted differs from Mark and Luke in specifying that divorce not followed by a remarriage is permitted in case of lewd conduct. This had not been said by Mark 10:10–12 and, as we shall see, it will not be said by Luke. But this double silence does not contradict Matthew in any way, and a sufficient harmony is found assured among the three evangelists.

But this argument has value only insofar as it goes back to Jesus. As an echo of the master's word, the totally negative response suggested by Mark and Luke seems to prevail over the testimony of Matthew, who imputes this exception to Jesus. But this is not our point of view at the moment. We are trying here to reconstitute the Matthean writer's thought, and this person, who did not know Luke, could have added something of his own to Mark.

Another argument is that, as Jerome interpreted Matthew's text, it harmonizes well with 1 Corinthians 7:10–16; Paul, we shall see, alludes there to several forms of simple separation. In response to authors such as A. Vaccari, who object to Jerome's theory by saying that simple separation was unknown to the Jews, Dupont calls attention to the fact that it was sufficient to have simple separation known to the Christians, and this was the case in 1 Corinthians 7:10–16.[102] In relation to Matthew, the Pauline text is clearly older by about some twenty years; the practice of simple separation, tolerated by Paul, could have existed at the time of the evangelist. To admit this point it would suffice to suppose that Matthew 19:9 reflects an environment more Helleno-Christian than Judeo-Christian, which is far from being impossible. In such a milieu one can imagine for the first time separation in fact, while noting that this separation does not give the right to remarriage. The case would be strange for a Jew, but for Christians it is called to mind in 1 Corinthians 7:10–16. This is the solution preached by *The Shepherd* of Hermas.[103]

b. In the case of lewd conduct (of the wife) divorce and *remarriage permitted*

This interpretation "is very generally admitted by Protestant exegetes; it is found also, with slight differences, among some Catholics;"[104] we ourselves have adhered to it *per transennam.*[105] Since Dupont's statement on the literature of the subject (1959), this exegesis has received new adherents.[106]

Let us repeat: the first exegesis, that made the text refer to simple separation, is grammatically possible. From the same grammatical point of view, the present opinion can be defended even better. Let us reread Matthew 19:9: "If anyone divorces his wife (lewd conduct is a separate case), and marries another, he commits adultery." Instead of supplying the words "a thing forbidden," we can change slightly the place of the inserted clause and read the verse this way: "If anyone divorces his wife and marries another, he commits adultery, unless the reason for the divorce is lewd conduct." Dupont himself recognizes that "from the point of view of Greek grammar there is no decisive objection against this interpretation."[107] We would add that the latter is even more obvious than the other and it would have the votes of uninformed readers.[108] But it remains true that we cannot decide here between the exegetes only on the basis of grammar. Let us, therefore, see the other arguments of those who hold this second opinion.

There is, first of all, the apparently adventitious character of the clause.[109] Deprived of it, the verse Matthew 19:9 would read more smoothly; this is confirmed by its parallels, Mark 10:11–12; Luke 16:18; 1 Cor. 7:10–11. This clause appears stylistically as a parenthesis that one can easily represent as an addition. Nothing is easier for an editor than to insert some words in a sentence. It is a step made attractive by its very simplicity; it does not oblige the writer to recast his sentence entirely. A rather striking fact is that in both cases (Mt 19:9 and 5:32) the clause apears to be the result of an insertion, a kind of interruption in the sentence. Besides, we know that throughout his whole Gospel, Matthew worked into Mark's text or his other sources additions of various kinds – details, commentaries, *etc.* In short, this kind of editing is known in rabbinical literature; and R. Le Deaut has spoken on the subject of insertion of a halakist type.

The reasoning could be pursued in this way; if the clause is secondary, that is to say, specifically Matthean, let us try to understand it as a function of the care of the editor or of his ecclesial milieu.

What was this milieu? This is the historical aspect of the problem, already considered by the partisans of the first opinion when they supposed that certain Helleno-Christians had admitted, even created, the concept of simple separation in case of adultery. But another hypothesis is presented: the existence of Judeo-Christian communities pushing tolerance as far as to admit, in case of adultery, separation and remarriage. We perceive at least the possibility of such a *sitz-im-leben,* where the converts from Judaism did not give up the right to remarriage inscribed in the Mosaic law. Certainly, strict Judeo-Christianity must have been active before the time of Matthew's Greek. But paradoxical as this appears, it happens more than once that this Judeo-hellenistic Gospel had echoes in more ancient communities whose tendencies were not those of Matthew as a whole. In these cases, the evangelist did not try to alter the conservative texts in order to reconcile them with a new interpretation; he preferred to leave them as they were, content to place the innovating sentences beside them.

To this recourse to Judeo-Christianity, one can object, it is true, the explanation is simply a hypothesis.[110] However, the hypothesis does not seem to us gratuitous. Before the year 70 A.D., the date of the fall of Jerusalem, conservative Judeo-Christianity was an unquestionable reality; let us think of St. Paul's combats. Again the first gospel, while not a narrowly Judeo-Christian work, contains at least some material reflecting such a tendency. It is sufficient to turn to texts such as Matthew 5:17–19 or 10:6–23; 15:24–26, and in a more general way, Matthew's presentation of Christ as the new Moses.

One will object that if Jesus condemned divorce and remarriage without reserve, it is not easy for a historian to imagine that some Christians still envisaged real exceptions. To this we can answer, at the risk of appearing subtle, that the condemnation of Jesus could have been interpreted as a general rule which left room for exceptions. Moreover, it is a unique exception; if the πορνεία is limited to the adultery mentioned, this makes the clause at least as restrictive as the judgment of Shammai, the most severe of the Jewish doctors in this matter. Such a limited mitigation of the words of Jesus doubtless did not appear to the Jewish converts as a betrayal of his message or as a return to the hardness of heart stigmatized by the master (Mt 19:8).

The matter can be explained in still another way. For strict Judeo-Christians, Jesus, in spite of his radicalism, could not have questioned what to them was obvious, namely, that an adulteress was like one dead and consequently her marriage was dissolved. We cannot forget that in Judaism, an adulteress was normally condemned to be stoned. Certainly there is every reason to think that this practice, perhaps already attenuated in the Jewish milieu surrounding Jesus, did not persist in the Judeo-Christian communities; the memory that Jesus preached mercy above all else (Jn 8:3–11, *etc.*) would have turned them away from a rule that was perhaps out-of-date. But even though spared, that is, not stoned, such a woman would remain the victim of an insurmountable taboo; no one could have anything to do with her, she was legally "dead." The husband who divorced her and remarried had not injured the conjugal bond that such a "death" had dissolved; in short, his remarriage was not perceived as a true exception to the rule of indissolubility.[111] In still other terms: we would have here the remnant of a Judeo-Christian practice on the margin of the Great Church; we cannot state precisely to what degree Matthew would ratify. Perhaps he merely tolerated its coexistence in a particular group with the more general and more severe standard, namely, the unconditional prohibition of remarriage.[112]

On the whole, each of the two opinions offers us a serious probability. For an exegete, the choice is presented concisely under this rubric: does Matthew's text reflect a Helleno-Christian community or, on the contrary, a Judeo-Christian milieu? Both hypotheses are plausible. Inasmuch as it was written in Greek during the eighties, the first gospel normally reflects relatively late usages, ones that are therefore Helleno-Christian, among which could be placed the simple separation evoked in 1 Corinthians 7. If the Judeo-Christian sources or customs are involved, on the contrary, Matthew may not have been familiar with simple separation, which was at best imperfectly known to the Jews, and he may therefore have retained a Mosaic tolerance regarding a standard which he otherwise interpreted strictly, holding that the adultery of the wife permitted her husband to separate from her and to remarry. Without denying that Jerome's exegesis has serious probability, we continue to incline toward this second interpretation.

IV. Matthew 19:10–12

The Word about the Eunuchs

To be complete, our commentary on Matthew 19:1–9 cannot ignore Matthew 19:10–12. Matthew 19:1–9 continues thus: "His disciples said to him: 'If that is the case between man and wife, it is better not to marry.' He said, 'Not everyone can accept this teaching, only those to whom it is given to do so. Some men are incapable of sexual activity from birth; some have been deliberately made so; and some there are who have freely renounced sex for the sake of God's reign. Let him accept this teaching who can.' "

We do not wish to explain this passage in itself, but only in the extent that it throws light on Matthew 19:1–9. Indeed, the link between the two pericopes is undoubtedly on the editorial level.

There is certainly a hiatus between verses 9 and 10. In verses 4–9, Jesus was addressing the Pharisees, while in verse 10 it is the disciples who are speaking and then receiving the explanations reserved for them.[113] This is obvious since it is a question of celibacy. Matthew, no doubt like Jesus before him, would not favor a dialogue with the Pharisees that consider indissolubility and celibacy at the same time, the more so since all husbands – the Pharisees included – are obliged to respect indissolubility. The disciples are invited to understand celibacy "if they can"; therefore, they are to be free in their choice. But in spite of this difference in audience and subject Matthew brings together marriage and celibacy; this only reveals better his intention of illuminating one by the other.

Verse 10 does not present any difficulty; "the case of a man" is that of the husbands, which Jesus has just defined with severity. Verse 10 thus confirms that the teaching of Matthew 19:4–9 clashes with the convictions and usages of the time, both in the first and the second of the two interpretations of the exception clause.

In regard to verse 11, the exegetes differ greatly on the meaning of "this teaching." For Matthew, does it refer to the sentence in verse 12 concerning the eunuchs, or to the word the disciples had just spoken in verse 10, or to the rule pronounced by Jesus himself in verse 9? Each option has its partisans. Even those who identify the "teaching" of verse 11 with the sentences on the eunuchs (v. 12) cannot deny the bond between them and verse 9 or 10, and it is this link that is important for Matthew.

Like Kittel,[114] we link verse 11 with verse 9. It seems to us that Matthew understood verse 11 this way: the prohibition to divorce and remarry can be accepted only by those to whom it is has been given.

According to this interpretation, verse 12 appears as the reason for what Jesus said in verse 11, not as the content of the teaching contained in verse 11; we give full value to the intitial γὰρ. For the rest, verse 12 offers no particular difficulty. The major reason that throws light on verse 11, and by that on verse 9, is that there is a third class of eunuchs, namely, those who have made themselves so for the sake of the kingdom of heaven. *In recto*, it refers to those who, in view of the kingdom, have renounced marriage. But if, as we think, Matthew links verse 11 to verse 9 in some way, he brings these voluntary eunuchs close to the married men who decided in advance to observe the strict precept of Jesus on indissolubility, and perhaps even to those husbands who have already experienced this hard observance, either in renouncing remarriage in spite of the infidelity of their wives or in not consenting to remary in a single case of grave infidelity.

These statements are important. Apparently Matthew here tries to interpret the precept on indissolubility as if it were an ideal proposed only to the members of the kingdom. We shall come back to this clear difference from what seemed to us as a return on the part of Jesus to the absolute will of the creator above the law.

The conclusion is forced upon us that Matthew seems to be committed to such an endeavor, not only because of the choice we have made in linking verse 11 to verse 9, but in any exegesis of the expression λόγος τούτος. In no case, we have said, can we escape the link between the teaching of Jesus on those eunuchs and his words on marriage; it is understood, however, that we limit ourselves for the moment to understanding Matthew himself. Now voluntary eunuchs are clearly said to have made themselves so for the kingdom. Husbands who accept an indissoluble marriage are, if we dare say so, drawn along the same path: they can understand and respect indissolubility only in the perspective of the kingdom. A question remains. Does this link between indissoluble marriage and the charter of the kingdom come only from the evangelist (and his community) or has he only reproduced a preredactional chain leading back to the very discourse of Jesus?

All that we have just said of the necessary connection between Matthew 19:10–12 and Matthew 19:4–9, that is, between celibacy and marriage, is of worth for the evangelist. Let us now add that it has worth *only* for him, that is, that the joining of the words on eunuchs to the dialogue on marriage is purely redactional. Indeed, if we suppose that Matthew read Mark, he found there, immediately after the pericope on indissolubility, those presenting the little children, then the rich young man (Mk 10:13–31). We see that Matthew has used the same pericopes in 19:13–30, just after the logion on eunuchs (Mt 19:12). This is to say that Matthew 19:10–12 is clearly a redactional insertion.[115]

In order to show that Matthew 19:10–12 is truly in place – that is, already connected thus in a former writing, even in a discourse of Jesus – those who refuse to admit the dependence of Matthew on Mark must suppose the existence of an ancient and historically privileged form of the first gospel that would have influenced Mark, since in any case we must account for the parallelism in the two gospels. We end then with a different aporia: why would Mark depend either on a proto-Matthean form of Matthew 19, presenting all the pericopes of our Matthew 19 except one (namely, vv. 10–12), or on a Matthean chapter identical with our chapter 19 but from which Mark would decide to take all the pericopes except a single one?

In short, Matthew 19:10–12 appears to be an insertion; it follows that it is the evangelist who illuminated the statement on marriage by a reference to celibacy and placed it in the perspective of the kingdom. We can even glimpse the reason why Matthew brought together marriage and celibacy. We have seen that the inserted clause probably reflected a desire to tone down the radicalism of the principal tradition. In bringing together marriage, indissoluble with a single exception, and voluntary celibacy, Matthew lessened the radicalism in another way: in a sense, marriage is indissoluble – rather, almost indissoluble – only for Christians.

V. *Matthew 5:31–32*

Another Rule on Indissolubility with an Exception Clause

"It was also said, 'Whenever a man divorces his wife, he must give her a decree of divorce.' What I say to you is: 'Whoever divorces his wife – lewd conduct is a separate case – forces her to commit adultery. The man who marries a divorced woman likewise commits adultery.' " (v. 32)

In textual criticism, it is doubtless necessary to read (v. 32) πᾶς ὁ ἀπολύων as we have translated it, rather than ὃσ ἂν ἀπολύοση (a variant perhaps inspired by Mt 19:9 or Mk 10:11). The meaning is identical, but on the purely formal plane there is another stereotype beginning ("every man who does this or that"). This variety shows that in legislating, the community returned to traditional biblical formulas, to which perhaps Jesus at times conformed his oral style. The Greek text raises no other difficulty worthy of mention. Verse 32, which is the most delicate, is read in the same way by Nestle, Merk, Huck, and Aland.

1. THE CONTEXT OF MATTHEW 5:31–32

Just as it is, the sermon on the mount (Mt 5:1–7:29) is evidently a redactional composition. Our two verses form part of a rather homogenous section (5:21–48), made up in its present state of six antitheses provided with a kind of introduction (5:17–20). In this section, as in the rest of the sermon, the writer's work was undoubtedly complex, since he had at his disposal various written sources that he abridged here, lengthened there – for example, by inserting parts that had already been written. Besides, the writer intervenes in a more personal way, either by constructing links or by inserting here and there a specific word or commentary on his own.

The last three of these operations will be considered here cumulatively. In introducing verses 31–32, Matthew lengthened a former series of antitheses;[116] to do this, he had to compose a formula of liaison (v. 31); finally, he inserted in the middle of a traditional logion (v. 32) the clause already examined in regard to Matthew 19:9: "lewd conduct is a separate case."

The antitheses are all formed on this pattern: "You have been given such a commandment, but I give you another." Moses is not named, but he is clearly the one aimed at. Thus we find here something of the opposition encountered above in Mark 10 and Matthew 19 between Jesus and Moses, the supreme authority for the Jews. But the grounds brought forth in Mark 10 and Matthew 19 do not appear. In Matthew 5, Jesus does not say that he means to return to the origins, beyond the laws that Moses had simply conceded to human weakness; he is rather the one who affirms with power an authority by far superior to that of the law. But the result is similar. Here, as in Matthew 19, Jesus promulgates in place of a temporary disposition or of an imperfect commandment a more exacting commandment. This is the case not only in regard to indissolubility but also in all the antitheses.

2. THE MEANING OF MATTHEW 5:31–32 FOR THE EVANGELIST

Let us first read Matthew 5:31: "It was also said 'Whenever a man divorces his wife, he must give her a decree of divorce.' " This is an allusion to Deuteronomy 24, a text already we have seen, in Mark 10:4 and Matthew 19:7.

It is important to insist on this; for the first time the question of divorce is at the center of the debate. The crux is neither the problem of adultery nor that of remarriage; the latter is considered only because it results from the divorce and makes its malice more clearly seen. The divorce by itself causes scandal. In Mark 10 and Matthew 19, we saw that a controversy concerning only divorce preceded the judgment on remarriage. But Matthew 5:31 is concerned only with divorce, not remarriage. As to the adultery mentioned in verse 32, it is the explicit object of another antithesis, that in Matthew 5:27-28.

Let us consider Matthew 5:32a, removing the inserted clause: "What I say to you is: everyone who divorces his wife . . . forces her to commit adultery." In relation to Matthew 19:9, the difference is notable. While Matthew 19:9 refers to the remarriage of the husband in addition to divorce, Matthew 5 does not mention remarriage, but affirms the husband's responsibility towards the wife he divorces: "he forces her to commit adultery"; more exactly, "he makes her commit adultery."[117] This expression is explained by the customs of the time, which scarcely had a place for the celibacy of a woman (or, for that matter, of a man). In these conditions, a divorced woman would be led to accept another marriage by which she would become adulterous, that is to say, in a state of having broken the conjugal bond that united her to her first husband. But it is the first husband who is declared responsible for this adultery. In short according to Matthew 19:9, M1, in divorcing W1 and marrying W2, committed adultery toward W1; according to Matthew 5:32, M1 in divorcing W1 led her to become adulterous toward M1, because inevitably she would marry M2.

The disastrous results of divorce differ then in the two texts. In

Matthew 19:9, the consequence evoked is the remarriage of the husband who divorces, a remarriage that constitutes adultery or confirms the adultery contained in germ in the divorce. In Matthew 5:32a, the consequence to be feared is the remarriage of the wife, and it is the first husband who is responsible for it. The fundamental teaching is always identical, but its expression lends itself to variations, according as one considers a particular one of the persons concerned, of whom there are at least four.

From the Jewish point of view, Matthew 5:32a is as revolutionary as Matthew 19:9, but in a different way. In 19:9, the challenge consists in declaring a man an adulterer toward his own wife, which is contradictory. In 5:32a, the paradox consists in saying that a woman can become adulterous towards her first husband in remarrying, which is equally without precedent. One can even wonder whether in divorcing W1, M1 does not lead her to commit, in spite of herself, both adultery in regard to him and injustice in regard to him, the two aspects being linked in the eyes of the Jews. The paradox would then be at its height.

Let us go to Matthew 5:32b: "the man who marries a divorced woman likewise commits adultery." Exactly the same assertion appears in Matthew 19:9b, but we saw that the text is critically dubious there; here it is received by all editors. The assertion comes to this: if M2 marries W1, he commits adultery. This is an additional consequence of the repudiation, which is not envisaged either in Mark 10:11–12 or in Matthew 19:9a. For the first time the case of a man marrying a divorced woman is brought up; in so doing he commits adultery, that is to say, he violates the conjugal bond which joined W1 to M1, and which is supposed to remain firm.[118] We see that if the evangelist presents a new personage, it is always to teach the same message on indissolubility; one could speak of the moralist's reflex, applying the doctrine to various cases.

3. THE EXCEPTION CLAUSE IN MATTHEW 5:32

a. *The clause in itself*

The particle παρεκτός usually translated *except*, suggests to some the same problem as the words μὴ ἐπὶ of Matthew 19:9; it too would then be susceptible of receiving the preteritive or inclusive meaning of which we spoke above. It is clear that for ἐκτός and (by analogy) for παρεκτός, better than for μὴ ἐπὶ, one can quote texts which at first sight suggest the inclusive or additive sense.[119] All things considered, however, for παρεκτός as for μὴ ἐπὶ one must stay with the idea of exception. As for the sense of πορνεία we refer to the conclusions given above.[120]

One more remark: the fact that the clause is presented in Matthew 19:9 and Matthew 5:32 (its only two attestations in the whole New Testament) under two different lexicographical forms, but with an identical meaning, proves the importance of the idea of exception conveyed by the two incidental clauses. If Matthew was simply dependent on a ready-made formula, one could treat this one as an *obiter dictum*; the fact that he wrote two different formulas tends to prove that the will to posit an exception was sufficiently strong to give place to various expressions.

b. The clause in the verse

Having admitted that the incidental clause must indeed be translated "lewd conduct in a separate case" we again encounter the problem of Matthew 19:9: how to articulate the clause in the statement which contains it. On this painful point, the two principal opinions alredy set forth with regard to Matthew 19:9 are also the important ones here.

1) The exegesis of St. Jerome

The defenders of this explanation, already discussed in connection with Matthew 19:9, understand Matthew 5:32a as follows.

The man who divorces an innocent spouse is responsible for the adultery she will commit in remarrying; it must be implied that he cannot remarry. In the case of lewd conduct of the wife, the husband can leave her and he is not responsible for the adultery that she will commit in remarrying; but here again, it must be inferred that he cannot remarry.

2) The exegesis of numerous modern scholars

The partisans of this second exegesis, likewise presented above with regard to Matthew 19:9, understand Matthew 5:32a in the following manner.[121]

He who divorces his wife when she is innocent is responsible for the adultery she will commit in remarrying. Here also these exegetes infer that the aforesaid husband may not remarry. In the case of lewd conduct of his wife, the husband may leave her, and he is not responsible for the adultery she will commit by remarrying.[122] Moreover, the aforesaid husband may remarry.

Comparing these two paraphrases with each other, we notice again that both are probable. As in Matthew 19:9, we lean towards the second, chiefly because, in the ideas of the time, a legitimate divorce necessarily brought the right of the husband to remarry.

c. Does the clause apply to Matthew 5:32b?

The incidental clause of Matthew 5:32a does not reappear in 32b, and it would therefore be better not to conjecture whether it is implied there. But 32b is so complementary to 32a that the hypothesis is inevitable.

The clause of 32a, about the wife who is unfaithful to her husband, speaks of divorce under two headings: the exceptional case of the woman of lewd conduct and the ordinary case of the faithful wife. In spite of the use of the singular (his wife, W1), there are implied in 32a two categories of spouses. When one notices this, one must wonder whether, in spite of the singular ("a divorced woman"), verse 32b does not tacitly refer us back in turn to two types of the divorced woman, the innocent and the guilty.

On the whole, various indications make one think that the clause must not be 32b. First of all, a slight grammatical indication: without the article in 32b before ἀπολελυμένην, it is translated *a divorced woman* rather than *the divorced woman*, that is to say, the one just mentioned in 32a. In other words 32b seems to refer to any woman, without the evangelist's thinking of the woman of 32a, or rather, the two types of women referred to implicitly in 32a. Although complementary with regard to 32a, 32b seems to be a new sentence relatively independent of the other.

Another indication is that 32b is practically identical with Luke 16:18b and that in the Lucan text the clause could not be implied since it is ignored in Luke 16:18a and indeed appears nowhere in Luke. The presumption then is that Matthew 5:32b and Luke 16:18b come from Q, the source of words common to Matthew and Luke. Q, furthermore, is also the source of Matthew 5:32a and Luke 16:18a. It is understood, however, that Matthew 5:32a contains two important Matthean alterations, the clause and the formula proper to Matthew: "render adulterous".[123]

VI. Luke 16:18

Rules on Indissolubility

"Everyone who divorces his wife and marries another commits adultery. The man who marries a woman divorced from her husband likewise commits adultery" (Lk 16:18).

This logion is preceded immediately by two others which are summarized thus: not a minute part of a letter of the law will pass away (v. 17); and, the law and the prophets were in force until John (v. 16). Not only are the three logia rather dissimilar from each other, but they form an eccentric little block in the midst of a vast context on the use of terrestrial goods: Luke 16:1–15 (the parable of the shrewd manager, with corollaries which fit together well) and Luke 16:19–31 (the parable of the rich man and Lazarus, on an analogous theme).

Placed as a clear interruption of a homogeneous text, the three logia reveal the redactor's hand. Why such an insertion? Were an answer available, it would not enlighten us on the meaning of Luke 16:18. Let us suppose only that the three sentences were already joined in Luke's source – which could be Judeo-Christian. Indeed, if we must find at all costs an element common to the three logia, it is the problem of the value of the law in the Christian economy. Perhaps the source is quite simply Q, the classic collection of sayings of the Lord reconstructed from Matthew and Luke, since we have already encountered the approximate equivalent of Luke 16:18 in Matthew 19:9.[124]

The content of Luke 16:18 amount to two schemata already encountered: if M1 divorces W1, he commits adultery; if M2 marries W1, he commits adultery.[125]

Apart from minor details of vocabulary and syntax which do not affect its content, the first of these two sentences appeared in Mark 10:11 and Matthew 19:9, although an exception clause complicates the version in Matthew 19:9. Even in Matthew 5:32a, the protasis is partially the same. In Mark 10:11, Matthew 19:9, and Luke 16:18, the proasis formulates the case: a husband divorces his wife and marries another. This is the most common referent of the term *divorce*.

Now that we have finished examining the various evangelical logia on indissolubility, the time has come to ask whether they are authentic *in ore Iesu,* and to choose which of them most closely approach *ipsa vox Iesu.*[126]

Together with Matthew 19:9, Luke 16:18a confirms the presence of such a saying in an earlier source, probably Q. The sentence is found elsewhere in Mark 10:11. If we admit with most exegetes[127] that Mark does not depend directly on Q, we can then posit that for this point they all depend on a small collection of logia older than Q. Moreover, the sentence is in harmony with the controversy whose intrinsic probability we have shown above; it is not far-fetched to suppose that Jesus and the Pharisees discussed indissolubility. If we add 1 Corinthians 7:10–11, we are justified in pleading for the historicity *in vita Jesu* of the message on indissolubility as formulated in Luke 16:18a, that is, its concrete phrasing in a precise and very well formulated principle and not merely in a more general sentence like Matthew 19:6a ("They are no longer two, but one flesh") or 6b ("Let no man separate what God has joined.") To specify the chances of Luke 16:18a being *ipsissimum verbum Iesu,* we must compare it more closely to its parallels. Compared with Matthew 19:9, Luke 16:18a is superior because it does not include the exception clause, which, as we have sufficiently shown, is redactional. For the rest, the two sentences agree perfectly. Mark 10:11 is identical to these two versions except for the additional two words ("against her") which only make the sense of the logion more explicit. Finally, compared to these three texts, Matthew 5:32a only partially agrees in its protasis, and has two secondary elements: the clause, which is equivalent in sense to Matthew 19:9, and the unique expression, "[by divorcing W1, M1] makes her adulterous."

It is difficult to claim literal historicity for this last unique expression; rather, it appears to be the result of Christian reflection on the responsibility incurred by the one who divorces. Such a reflection, moreover, develops what Jesus had said about divorce. In short, with its two redactional elements, clause and apodosis, Mt 5:32a is probably a revision of a logion of this type: if M1 divorces W1 (and remarries) he commits adultery. On the other hand, let us repeat, Luke 16:18a has the advantage of being both fundamentally identical with all the other witnesses, and free from the various expansions which the Matthean form chiefly exemplifies. It has the better chances of being authentic. One can attribute to Jesus an original statement like the following: the husband who divorces his wife and remarries commits adultery (towards her).

Let us proceed to Luke 16:18b: if M2 marries W1, he commits adultery. This sentence differs completely from the second rule of Mark (Mk 10:12), but it is found in Matthew 5:32b and perhaps, we have said, it lies behind Matthew 19:9b. On the basis of these statements, one may say that the assertion existed in a pre-Matthean document. Two other considerations favor its antiquity – even its presence in the discourse of Jesus.

a) In the four gospel versions, the sentences on indissolubility have a binary form. The only – dubious – exception is Matthew 19:9b, whose authenticity is barely plausible according to textual criticism. Certainly, in Mark 10:12, the second of the two elements has a strange form: if W1 divorces M1, she commits adultery. This anomaly can be explained in various ways, all of which consider it a redactional insertion.[128] Nevertheless, this insertion in its own way is informative; Mark involuntarily attests by his imperfect editing that he has his eyes on two sayings rather than one, and that the second one, which he discarded, has all the marks of having been of the kind solidly attested elsewhere: If M2 marries W1, he commits adultery.

b) The exegetes of the Old Testament often speak of the parallelism of structure which characterizes the psalms and proverbs. One will admit without difficulty that this binary rhythm may still have marked the spoken language of the Jewish teachers in the time of Jesus, when they formulated maxims with some solemnity. The presumption would be true for Jesus also. One may specify that the present case is an example of a parallelism of complementarity, a well known type of binary construction in the psalms and proverbs. Likewise, on the level of content, a statement of the type of Luke 16:18b is truly a natural complement of the preceding one.

Granting to Luke 16:18b the greatest fidelity, after having granted it to 18a, let us say that one may ascribe to Jesus these twin statements: "if a man divorces his wife and marries another, he commits adultery, and the one who marries the divorced woman commits adultery." Of our four parallel pericopes, Luke 16:18a and b best approach the *ipsa vox Jesu.*[129]

Jesus thus takes a view contrary to even the most severe Jewish doctrine, which only rarely granted the right to divorce and then to remarry. That Jesus absolutely condemned remarriage is the almost unanimous conviction of commentators. These agree also in general in thinking that Jesus at the same time condemned divorce itself.[130]

VII: 1 Corinthians 7:10–11 Rules on Indissolubility

In 1 Corinthians, after having treated on his own authority several subjects, especially current divisive factions in Corinth, Paul comes to the questions which were put to him by his correspondents (1 Cor 7:1). The first had reference to sexual morality. After various instructions (1 Cor 7:1–9) of which the last (v. 8–9) are addressed to celibates and widows, the apostle continues thus: "To those now married, however, I give this command (though it is not mine; it is the Lord's), a wife must not separate from her husband. If she does separate, she must either remain single or become reconciled to him again. Similarly, a husband must not divorce his wife" (1 Cor 7:10–11).

The spouses thus addressed are both Christians, since mixed marriages are treated separately immediately after (vv. 12–16). What the apostle prescribes to Christian spouses is done in the name of the Lord, that is, in conformity with the teaching of Jesus on earth, a teaching that Paul received in the Church as coming from Jesus (1 Cor 11:23)[131].

The apostle distinguishes clearly both the rules that he himself establishes (1 Cor 7:12–16) and the simple counsels that he gives (1 Cor 7:25–40) from the precepts coming from the Lord.

In 1 Cor 7:10, Paul addresses the woman first. To the extent–difficult to estimate–that this priority in attention is really intended, it breaks the tradition which took shape in the Gospels: the prescriptions there are addressed to men, not only primarily, but almost exclusively. The only exception is Mark 10:12; it forbids the woman to divorce her husband–but only after it first addressed a similar prohibition to the man. It is possible that the order Paul chooses is inspired by the same motive that, according to some, moves Mark to address the woman explicitly (after having called upon the husband): the apostle perhaps remembers that in the Greco-Roman world, contrary to Jewish usage, it is not rare that the woman takes the intitiative in the rupture.

In *commanding* (this is indeed the strong meaning of the Greek verb παραγγέλλειν) that the woman not leave her husband, the apostle surely intends to condemn the simple fact of separating, which confirms our exegesis of Mark 10:2–12 where, according to us, Jesus had already condemned the act of divorce and not only remarriage.[132]

However, the Apostle offers a hypothesis: let us suppose that a woman has, even so, left her husband (v. 11). We do not have to understand this to mean that Paul is thus attenuating the prohibition made to the wife about leaving her husband;[133] he is merely stating that she has broken the precept, no doubt because she remains under the influence of Greco-Roman customs. He sees in that, at least, a problem. We do not know whether he was the first to attempt to solve it, but the present verses are the first Christian text *ad rem.*

Pursuing our reading, let us note the importance of another precept: "if she left, she must not remarry." Although the verb is in the subjunctive, there is doubtless room here to read a prohibition pure and simple,[134] because the prohibition of remarriage was absolute in the message of Jesus: it is a point on which almost all the exegetes agree, even if some hesitate on the subject of simple separation. Certainly, with its two verbs in the subjunctive, the parenthesis which 1 Corinthians 7,11a constitutes no longer depends clearly on the expression "the Lord commands"; but one cannot suppose that Paul thinks differently from Jesus on the important question of remarriage. We must, however, recognize that for the apostle, the wife has no absolute obligation to rejoin her husband; in fact, by requiring "that she remain not married," Paul lets it be understood that in certain cases she may remain separated. So this time we are faced with what Catholic tradition will call the *separatio tori et mensae.*[135]

Moreover, Paul does ask the wife to become reconciled. But he leaves her the choice: the wife must either be reconciled or abstain from remarriage while remaining separated. The reconciliation is no doubt the ideal: and in proposing it, Paul expresses in a new way something of the message of Jesus, centered on the indissoluble union of the spouses.

To end his instructions to Christian spouses, Paul orders the husband not to divorce his wife (1 Cor 7:11b). Grammatically, these words are again governed by παραγγέλλω, like the parentheses containing the two subjunctives. They clearly convey an imperative precept of the Lord. Effectively, 1 1 Corinthians 7:11b partially restates an essential formula of the gospels, which we have noted goes back to Jesus: "the husband who divorces his wife and marries another, commits adultery". We say "partially" because Paul speaks of divorce without speaking of remarriage (as also does Mt 5:32a).[136] Paul uses here the mode of expression ("send away") which corresponds to the language of the Jews, without forgetting Greco-Roman manners, which also recognized, *ad sensum*, the case of the man sending away his spouse.[137]

To sum up, the two precepts formulated as coming from Jesus are: the wife must not leave her husband, the husband must not divorce his wife. These essential formulas are conformable to those of Jesus and recall once more the specific framework in which the master had spoken of the custom of divorce. Somewhat similarly, Paul addresses the woman first, which would be unexpected in the Jewish milieu. For the rest, the apostle approaches a case necessarily new at the time of Jesus: that of a wife who had left her husband, the two being supposedly Christian. The sole fact of having left the partner is contrary to the teaching of Jesus (1 Cor 7:10) but the apostle does not brandish thunderbolts; the main thing, it seems, is that the wife who has deserted the home not remarry; one would say that, on this point, the words of Jesus seem too clear to admit of violation. Besides, Paul also recommends reconciliation, which, in his eyes, would best safeguard the marriage as desired by Jesus.

Conclusions

In our analyses of the gospel texts, we have proceeded backwards, as today's method of exegesis recommends. We started from the texts as they present themselves, that is, as words of authors reflecting at the same time Church situations, and from there we went to the historical Jesus. The Pauline text made its contribution to clarity as much on Jesus as on the apostolic Church. For the sake of clarity, it is now expedient to present the conclusions in reverse order, that is, chronologically.

1. MARRIAGE IN THE MESSAGE OF JESUS

a. Teaching of Jesus himself

1) Jesus understood marriage as a monogamous and indissoluble union. He therefore condemned unconditionally all remarriage in the lifetime of the partner.[138] On this subject, the consensus among the exegetes is almost unanimous.[139]

2) It is very probable that Jesus also condemned in the same

manner the simple separation in itself. However, one cannot totally exclude the possibility of a tolerance by Jesus on this precise point, this notably by reason of the authority of the exegetes who are of this opinion.[140] But it remains understood, as these very exegetes agree, that separation gives no right to remarriage.

3) It is probable, in spite of the small number of texts, that Jesus spoke several times on the subject of marriage and notably on the occasion of the controversies with the Pharisees.[141]

4) The center of Jesus' argument was probably the recourse to the text of Genesis against that of Deuteronomy, that is, the appeal to the perfect will of the creator against the weaknesses of Moses; or again, the appeal to the Lord of the universe against the legislator of a particular people, even the people of the covenant.[142]

5) It is probable that Jesus concluded his responses to the Pharisees by an aphorism: "that man not separate what God has united," and that he was also led to formulate the teaching he directed to his disciples into certain practical rules. On this subject we have retained as probable *ipsissima verba* a double rule obviously addressed to the disciples, a kind of *mashal* which may have been a "canonical" rule before it was put down: "whoever divorces his wife and marries another, commits adultery; and he who marries the divorced woman commits adultery."

b. The importance of the teaching of Jesus in his own eyes

To state the essential assertions of Jesus is one thing; to establish the importance in his own eyes is another, more delicate, task. However, this brings up again the question of the competence of the historian;[143] and in addition, it sheds more direct light on hermeneutics.

1) On the basis of the text – a controversy and some statements – one cannot assume that the words of Jesus on marriage occupy an absolutely central place in the totality of his message. In any case, as always in the Gospel controversies, Jesus does not initiate the dispute; this contrasts with the proclamation *motu proprio* of the coming of the kingdom and its "constitutional laws." At the extreme, one might imagine that the result of the controversy is the simple dodging[144] in conjunction with the referral of the Pharisees by Jesus to a text of Genesis which embarrasses them.

However, if the Pharisees wish to put Jesus to the test, it is no doubt because they know that the Master has greatly criticized elsewhere and *motu proprio* the Jewish practice of divorce. One can then understand that Jesus was not content to leave the Pharisees nonplussed, but rather pronounced clearly the principle of non-remarriage and even of non-separation and made the application of it in several statements directed to the disciples.

2) The Jewish milieu, which Jesus shared, had a high regard for monogamous marriage;[145] practice largely conformed to this ideal, and it contrasts, in the eyes of today's historian, with the laxity of Greco-Roman customs. By expressing himself as he did on marriage, Jesus was not led, (at least there is no indication of it) by a desire to extirpate grave abuses. Thus, one cannot invoke these as circumstantial explanations of his message. In short, nothing tells us that Jesus would have been constrained to severity in order to dam up flagrant excesses. On the contrary, the master seems to be inspired only by a concern for perfection. The Pharisees whom Jesus opposes here were, among the Jews and in comparison with other religious groups, rather severe in the matter of conjugal morality. The fact that Jesus openly confronted them is a quite striking confirmation of his radicalism.

3) It is possible that Jesus was moved to oppose divorce in part by his solicitude to defend the divorced woman. What permits us to suppose this is that Jesus often came to the defense of humiliated women.

4) To clarify this radicalism, in spite of the scantiness of our texts, we have at our disposal a vast gospel context whose historicity is not in doubt; it is clear that Jesus required of his disciples, in all domains of the moral life, a new rigor and a will for "perfection." It is in this framework of a uniformly demanding ethic that we must situate our texts.[146]

5) However, there is quite a problem here. Taking the gospels as a whole, the ethic of Jesus is polarized by two different goals, each of which would suffice to establish the ethic. On the one hand, the disciple must be capable of all renunciations because the kingdom which is to come has no price. On the other hand, if they place themselves in God's view, the disciples – and even, one would say, all men – can perceive the loftiness of the divine will, even the existence in God of a "perfection" which requires imitation. The motivation is more eschatological on one side, more theological on the other.[147]

A clear example of renunciation for the cause of the kingdom is voluntary celibacy (Mt 19:12). One would say, as we noted, that Matthew has drawn the exacting word of Jesus on marriage into the same path. But for Jesus himself, indissoluble marriage responds to the perfect will of God, promulgated from the very beginning, prior to what is properly called the economy of salvation; thus the will of God is directed to the disciples and to all men. In other words, the demand in the matter of marriage is not of the same nature as the call to voluntary celibacy or to selling one's goods; on the one hand, there is voluntary choice and an attitude of exception for the sake of kingdom; on the other, there is pure and simple submission to the absolute will of God.

Another way of expressing the same thing is to say that here Jesus presents himself as a moralist rather than as founder of the kingdom. The distinction certainly is somewhat subtle. But it seems that for Jesus, the perfect will of the creator is imposed on every upright man and not only on those who, in addition, await the coming of the kingdom and are ready to sacrifice all for it.

The "timeless" God is here the norm of morality. To walk in righteousness is to understand the height of the divine will or to live under the glance of God. The analysis, we see, is of a theological and moral type; it is centered on the sense of God and the idea of interiority. It is a question only *in obliquo* of the charter of the kingdom of God.

2. HERMENEUTIC SCOPE OF THE TEACHINGS OF JESUS

Let us define hermeneutics summarily as the actualization of the Word of God, the totally final manner of understanding and applying it; it is the last proceeding of the theologian and the believer.

Until recently, the assured result of exegesis, such as it is, was accepted as the norm of faith and of conduct. Thus people thought that if indissolubility is taught by Jesus it is willed by God. Even while appealing to the Jesus of history, theologians and believers knew, however, that on other issues the teaching of Jesus was sometimes only a point of departure; it remained for them to make it more precise through tradition, a tradition already attested to in the New Testament.[148]

In its evaluation of the gospel as norm, present day hermeneutics seems pulled in opposite directions.

a) On the one hand, it seems drawn by "the purity of origins" and from there is disposed to make a great case of the teaching of Jesus reconstituted with all the historical rigor desirable. Consequently, this hermeneutic sometimes treats development after Jesus as a superstructure to be criticized; it takes pleasure also in opposing Jesus to the Church.

On this subject, may we not judge that the return to the historical Jesus[149] could not give us an iron rule? The relationship between the Church and Jesus is complex. For example, from apostolic times the Church's stance has differed when it faces those teachings of Jesus which demand a hearing through their power and clarity, and when it reflects on those *dicta Jesu* which have a prophetic or apocalyptic tone. In these cases, it must be remembered that "the period of the creation of a religion can only be considered as finished when it possesses a tradition by which it is expressed and justified and when it is endowed with the necessary organs for the exercise of the functions by which its life and stability can be assured."[150]

However, the words of Jesus on marriage are dependent on cases of the first type: they were imposed on the apostolic Church as a normative fact because they appeared clear and "historically" established. Hence, a hermeneutic operating in the logic of a "return to Jesus" seems to be able to welcome the exegetical conclusions exposed above in part 1.

b) Another tendency of present day hermeneutics literally takes a point of departure from what the Jesus of history thought and willed. We allude to some markedly different types of reading – structuralist, psychoanalytical, materialistic, and so forth – which yet share a desire to make the texts speak rather than the person, or, if you prefer, to distill from the four gospels a fifth gospel,[151] which is shaped by the existential needs of modern man (in fact, of one of the many types of modern man: linguist, psychologist, economist, and so forth). This fifth gospel then functions as criteria. If it is in harmony with the rigorous exegesis of the four gospels, no problem arises; otherwise, the hermeneutic will consider that even the historically established teaching of Jesus was culture-bound and therefore is no longer valid.

Paradoxically, these attempts are an involuntary homage to the idea of tradition. The intuition of all times was also that the gospel is not a relic but a living text; however, the "fifth Gospel" is then the Church.

In the case occupying us, what was taken to be the will of the earthly Jesus was ratified for nineteen centuries by a dominant tradition, already existing and attested to in the New Testament. Can it still be so for the man of today, confronted with new situations, in some ways without precedent? Such is the question posed by some. We would say that on the plane of principles, we cannot contest the legitimacy of research; it is right indeed to be sensitive to the signs of the times, even if they reflect quite new ways of thinking and of expression. The apostle said in a somewhat analagous manner: "Do not stifle the Spirit; do not despise prophecies." (1 Thes 5:19–20) However, he added immediately: "Test everything; retain what is good" (1 Thes 5:21). It belongs to the Church to decide in the last instance.[152]

3) Marriage in the eyes of the apostolic Church

The gospels, we know, witness *also* to the ecclesial theology of the first century; and even more so does St. Paul.

a. Paul

The apostle is the most ancient witness of the memory that the Christians keep of the teaching of Jesus of Nazareth (1 Cor 7:10–11). In the present case, as in others, he has faithfully preserved the tenor of the message of Jesus: Christian spouses may not separate and in no case remarry, even if there has been a separation *de facto*. This last hypothesis appears clearly through Paul whereas we would not dare to say it with certitude for Jesus.

In the time of Paul, it evidently happened that in the pagan (or Jewish) home, one of the partners was converted.[153] In this case, if the other wished to co-inhabit peacefully, that is, without preventing the convert from practicing his (her) faith, things could remain as before (1 Cor 7:12–16); the apostle tacitly supposes that marriage between pagans (or Jews) is a true marriage. This presupposition is enlightening in that it confirms that marriage is, first of all and in itself, a natural institution; in this sense, the idea of Paul is in line with the teaching of Jesus on marriage as an element of the charter of the created world, anterior to any idea of a chosen people.

If the unconverted spouse prevents the Christian partner from practicing his (her) faith, or takes the initiative of departure, the converted party may separate (1 Cor 7:12–16). May he (she) also remarry? In exegesis, two opposite answers are possible. If one answers No, one quite confirms the remark formulated just now: the marriage which had been concluded between pagans (or Jews) is already so sacred that it is absolutely indissoluble.[154] If one answers yes,[155] one does not for all that ascribe to the apostle a vague idea of a natural (or Jewish) marriage, but rather admits that Paul, without renouncing the principle of the validity of such marriages, here creates a true exception, making allowance for the interests of faith which are sovereign. One will then speak very exactly of a *privilege* granted by Paul to the Christian party, and it is thus that the Church understands 1 Corinthians 7:15, at least since the Middle Ages.

After this almost letter-by-letter analysis, we must investigate the scope of these declarations in the eyes of Paul himself; and this is properly an exegetical question. That question is posed in the following terms: did the apostle simply adjudicate a few particular cases, or did he intend to really legislate? We need not raise the question for 1 Corinthians 7:10–11, where Paul recalls a precept of the Lord, a precept which in his eyes is assuredly imposed without reservation, but for 1 Corinthians 7:12–17, where the Apostle speaks in his own name.

The response can be found by examining the context. It would certainly be an anachronism to represent Paul as having full consciousness of promulgating a law for the universal Church and especially a law valid "forever and ever."[156] But one would fall into the opposite excess by believing that Paul aimed only at such and such a particular case. It is clear that in this chapter 7, the apostle is still thinking of *categories* of Christians, differently from chapters 5 and 6, where he treats of two problems, each time after having learned the fault of a definite individual.[157] Besides, the matrimonial morality is very important for the apostle.[158] One may then conclude that for him even *his own* instructions on this subject are imposed on all Christians concerned. This does not deny that the Pauline privilege has acquired its full force only by its ulterior ratification in the Church, as we will repeat when we speak of hermeneutics.

b. Mark and Luke

The analysis of Mark and Luke has shown that the redactional elements are not really important. There is then no need for us to stop here on what would be a very new apostolic interpretation. For what is controversial (Mk 10:2–9), we have insisted on its chances of authenticity rather than on its character of being specifically of Mark.[159] As for the statement of Mark 10:10–12, its most redactional element is the unusual Mark 10:12, addressed to a woman who is divorcing; but only the statement of the case is new, not the doctrine expressed. 1 Corinthians 7 has already made us notice this tendency to consider various possible cases: one understands from this how rules diffused with variants, which however have no effect on the content of the message of Jesus. It is probable that the Church of the first century had still other formulations, but which circumstances did not preserve for us.

Luke, let us recall, did not report the controversy, perhaps because it seemed too anchored in a Pharisaic framework which was no longer current in his day. As for his version of the statements (Lk 16:18), it is as traditional as possible, and so it reveals no intention of personal interpretation.

c. *Matthew*

Matthew's case is different. We are not going to recall all his redactional interventions but only the two most important ones, those which allow one to speak of an eventual "apostolic" interpretation of the teaching of Jesus.

There is first of all the exception clause, which already affects the presentation of the controversy (Mt 9:3) and still more the very formulation of the traditional rule (Mt 19:9; 5:32). If, as we have judged most probable, the exception clause permits remarriage in case of adultery, the moment has come to question ourselves on the scope of this innovation in the eyes of the Matthean editor.

Unfortunately, a certain answer is impossible. First of all the very form of the moot text–a brief parenthesis–prevents it from taking on a "coefficient of importance." Did Matthew presume that Jesus, while condemning divorce and remarriage, had to consent, in the face of his contemporaries, to grant them an exception (*Historisierung*), when for the evangelist himself, the Church had opted legitimately against all exception, thus remaining faithful to the basic teaching of Jesus? Did Matthew, on the contrary, make himself the interpreter of past or contemporary Judeo-Christian groups, admitting the aforesaid exception without, however, contesting the more strict discipline of the great Church? Such questions will remain forever without a firm answer.

In addition to the exception clause, there is another properly Matthean intervention: the linking of the teaching of Jesus on marriage with his call to voluntary celibacy. By so doing, Matthew seems to suggest that if the master has shown himself so strict concerning marriage, it is because he has made of it a law of exception, an ideal proposed "to those who can understand." For, let us repeat, even furnished with an exception, the sentence of Jesus on marriage remains severe in the eyes of Matthew.

Again, it is practically impossible for us to determine the exact scope of the link between celibacy and marriage in the eyes of the writer himself. Did he truly wish to bring the "matrimonial right" into this ethic of exception which is also expressed in texts such as 1 Cor 7:29–31: "time is short; let those who have a wife live as if they did not . . . ; because the figure of this world passes"? In our analysis, we have been led to speak of suggestion or insinuation: these terms mark the limits of our certitudes. The stage will have to be taken here again by hermeneutics and, first of all, by Christian tradition.

4) Hermeneutic scope of the apostolic teachings

Where Paul and the evangelists merely reproduce the teachings of Jesus, their texts call for the same hermeneutic as these teachings.[160] But there is also a hermeneutic of those teachings that are properly apostolic. If the New Testament *preserves* the gospel which Jesus had preached, it also comments on it with a certain liberty. The question then arises to what extent is the specific contribution of the witnesses to Jesus normative for the theologian and the believer today?

The ancient response remains truly valid: the teaching given in their own name by the authors of the New Testament is covered by an authority analagous to that of the words of Jesus. This authority is defined by the double quality of word of God and inspired Scripture, which the Christians of today still recognize in the New Testament.[161]

Another criterion of hermeneutics applies with greater clarity to the assertions properly apostolic than to the major declarations of Jesus himself: it is the manner in which these assertions have been received in the post-apostolic Church until our day. Thus, if the Pauline privilege has indeed survived, it is because the Church has recognized in it, at least since the Middle Ages, a principle which appeared to it apt for regulating the case of mixed marriage. On the other hand, the two Mattheisms spoken of above have not benefited by such a clear reception.

The first is the exception to the rule of indissolubility in favor of the deceived spouse, at least according to the exegesis that we have considered most probable. Compared with the texts of Paul, Mark, and Luke, the Matthean interpretation has remained isolated in the New Testament and so in the Church of the first generations. Even if there were hesitations in the course of the following centuries, the Council of Trent set aside this interpretation. But in so doing, it did not wish to define the literal sense of the Gospel texts; it limited itself to claiming that the Church had the right to take a position on the points which were not absolutely clear. The prudent formulas of the council contain, then, a quite nuanced hermeneutic: total respect for the texts of the New Testament, fleshed out with the right of the Church to its own reading. What comes out of this, on the whole, is the nonconfirmation of the exception clause understood as the right to remarriage.

For its part, the insinuation of Matthew regarding indissoluble marriage, inasmuch as a voluntary choice has remained a pure Matthewism: nothing indicates that the tradition, even ancient, took this path.[162] The suggestion of Matthew cannot prevail against the manner in which Jesus, in accordance with the will of the creator promulgated in Genesis, understood the eternal attributes of marriage. In the West, a whole theological current seems to have retained this intuition of Jesus, in thinking that marriage can be regarded in itself or, if you will, in the sight of God: all marriage, and not only that of Christians, is of itself indissoluble.[163] To people tempted to prefer the interpretation suggested by Matthew, according to which indissoluble marriage is almost as specific of Christianity as celibacy for the kingdom, those who hold to a universal morality of indissolubility could answer exactly as did A. Loisy to the Greeks and Protestants concerning the exception clause. Their interpretation of the clause, said A. Loisy, "is indeed the natural meaning of the passage"–that is, its meaning for Matthew–"but it also has every chance of *not* being that of Jesus. . . ." "The Catholic Church, by refusing to admit any case for divorce, has maintained the principle established by Jesus, and it matters little that it could only do so by sacrificing the historical sense of the passages where Matthew treats the question."[164] Applying to our subject what Loisy thus wrote of the clause, we would say that to renounce the natural indissolubility of marriage would probably be to choose Matthew against Jesus.[165]

Finally, the last criterion of hermeneutics for the teachings of the apostles as for those of Jesus is awareness of the present situation of Christian marriage. Three points pose a question: the Pauline privilege, the exception clause of Matthew, and the apparently Matthean attenuation of indissolubility (even accompanied by an exception) as an attribute of every marriage. On this triple subject, modern commentaries must, at the very least, take into account the nuanced conclusions of critical historical exegesis and the weight placed on these three problems by ecclesiastical tradition. This being said, it is also legitimate to take into account the present situation, notably the manner in which failures occur today in many families, even though the victims sincerely want to live according to the gospel and in agreement with the Church.[166] However firm the framework of the principles may be, it does not seem that accommodation should be excluded *a priori;* but the decisions, strictly speaking, belong to the Church of today and tomorrow.[167]

Let us recall in two sentences the scope of our conclusions. First we sought to establish the teaching of Jesus on indissolubility by distinguishing its tenor and scope. We then applied a hermeneutic similar to that used in the New Testament itself and in tradition, and indeed is used even today. We covered the specifically apostolic teaching in two similar stages.

CHAPTER 8

Sixteen Christological Theses on the Sacrament of Marriage

by G. Martelet

1. THE SACRAMENTALITY OF MARRIAGE AND THE MYSTERY OF THE CHURCH

The sacramentality of Christian marriage is much more evident if one does not separate it from the mystery of the Church. "Sign and means of intimate union with God and of the unity of the whole human race," as the council said (LG, 1), the Church rests upon the unbreakable relationship that Christ established with her, making her his Body. The identity of the Church does not depend just on the power of men but on the love of Christ that apostolic preaching never ceases to proclaim and to which we adhere through the outpouring of the Spirit. As witness to this love that gives her life, the Church is then the sacrament of Christ in the world because it is his visible Body and the community that proclaims the presence of Christ in human history. The Church, the sacrament whose greatness Paul declared (Eph 5:32), is certainly inseparable from the mystery of the incarnation because it is the mystery of the Body. It is inseparable also from the economy of the covenant because it rests upon the personal promise that the risen Christ made to remain "with" her "all days, even to the end of the world" (Mt 28:20b). But the Church as sacrament depends further on a mystery that one can describe as conjugal. Christ is bound to her by virtue of a love that makes the Church the spouse of Christ in the power of the one Spirit and the unity of one Body.

2. UNION OF CHRIST AND THE CHURCH

The marital union of Christ and the Church does not destroy, but rather fulfills what the conjugal love of man and woman in its own way announces, implies, or already realizes in the realm of communion and fidelity. The Christ of the cross accomplishes the perfect oblation of himself that spouses desire to accomplish in the flesh but can never realize perfectly. He accomplishes for the Church, which he loves as his own body, what St. Paul said husbands should do for their wives. The resurrection of Jesus in the power of the Spirit reveals that the Church, so loved by Christ that he would die for it, can initiate the world into communion between God and men from which the Church itself benefits as the spouse of Jesus Christ.

3. CONJUGAL SYMBOLISM IN SCRIPTURE

The Old Testament rightly used a conjugal symbolism to express the inexhaustible love that God feels toward his people and which he intends, through his people, to reveal to all mankind. Especially in the prophet Hosea, it presents God to us as the husband whose unlimited tenderness and fidelity will finally win over Israel, which from its earliest days is unfaithful to the boundless love that has been freely given to it. In this way, the Old Testament opens to us a clear understanding of the New Testament in which Jesus is many times called the perfect bridegroom. He is named the bridegroom by the Baptist in John 3:29; Jesus calls himself this in Matthew 9:15; Paul refers to him in the same way in two places (2 Cor 11:2 and Eph 5); Revelation makes a similar reference in chapter 22:17–20; finally, there are many explicit allusions to Jesus as bridegroom in the eschatological parables of the kingdom in Matthew 22:1–10 and 25:1–12.

4. JESUS THE PERFECT BRIDEGROOM

We can find fresh meaning in this title, ordinarily neglected by Christology. Just as Jesus is the way, the truth, the life, the gate, the shepherd, the lamb, the vine, and the man himself because he received from the Father "the primacy in everything" (Col 1:18), Jesus is also truly and rightfully the perfect bridegroom, that is to say, the "master and lord" who loves another as he loves his own flesh. This title of bridegroom, then, and the mystery to which it refers should be the starting point of a Christology of marriage. In this and every realm, "no one can lay any foundation except the one that has been laid, namely Jesus Christ" (1 Cor 3:10). However, the fact that Christ is also the perfect bridegroom should not be separated from the fact that he is "the second" (1 Cor 15:47) and "the last Adam" (1 Cor 15:45).

5. ADAM, IMAGE OF HIM WHO IS TO COME

Jesus refers to Adam in Matthew 19 when he treats the question of divorce; the first Adam, inseparable from Eve, is not fully identified unless one sees in him "the image of him who is to come" (Rom 5:14). The person of Adam as the primary symbol of all humanity is not an isolated individual; like Eve, he is a type.

Adam is related to Christ, to whom he owes his final meaning, and to us. Adam cannot be thought of without Christ, but Christ in his turn cannot be thought of without Adam, that is to say, without all humanity, whose appearance Genesis sees as willed by God in a very special way. This is why marriage, which makes Adam truly human, comes to life again in Christ, through whom it is fulfilled by being restored. The inherent truth of this union, which was ruined by a failure of love that even Moses had to acknowledge, is recovered in Christ. Jesus appears in the world as the perfect bridegroom who can, as "the second" and "last Adam," save and reestablish the true marriage that God has not ceased to will for the good of "the first Adam."

6. JESUS, RENEWER OF THE ORIGINAL TRUTH OF THE MARITAL UNION

Jesus considers the Mosaic law on divorce the historical result of "their hardness of heart," and dares to present himself as the renewer resolved to restore the original reality of the marital union. In the power that he has to love without limit, and to realize an unparalleled union with all mankind by his life, death, and resurrection, Jesus reestablishes the true meaning of the passage of Genesis, saying, "man should not separate what God has joined together." In the vision of Jesus, man and woman can love each other from now on as God has always desired, for in Jesus is manifested the source of love which establishes the kingdom. Also, Christ leads all married couples to the original purity of their promised love. Christ abolished the prescriptions which he considered to be an acceptance of the people's shortcomings by Moses, who could not eliminate the causes of their misery. Jesus reveals what the original couple were always meant to be in the eyes of God: the archetypal couple in whom God reveals the conjugal love to which mankind aspires, for which mankind is made, but which can become real only in Christ, who teaches men what it is to love. From then on, faithful, everlasting love, the conjugal love that hardness of heart transformed into insubstantial dreams, again finds the place in reality that Christ alone, as the last Adam and perfect bridegroom, could give it.

7. THE SACRAMENTALITY OF CHRISTIAN MARRIAGE, SEEN BY FAITH

The sacramentality of Christian marriage can clearly be seen by faith. Since the baptized are visibly incorporated into the Body of Christ, which is the Church, Christ draws into his sphere of influence the conjugal love of the baptized in order to communicate to it the human authenticity that love would lack without him. He does this in the Spirit, through his power as second and last Adam to appropriate and make successful the conjugal love of the first. He does this in accord with the visible nature of the Church, in which conjugal love, consecrated to the Lord, becomes a sacrament. The spouses attest within the Church that they are committed to conjugal life and that they await the power from Christ to realize this form of love that would perish without him. For this reason, the mystery proper to Christ as the bridegroom of the Church shines forth and can shed light upon the couples that are consecrated to him. Their conjugal love is not disfigured but deepened because it refers back to the love of Christ who supports and sustains them. The special outpouring of the Spirit, as the grace proper to the sacrament, makes it possible for the love of the couples to become the image of the love of Christ for the Church. Yet this constant outpouring of the Spirit never eliminates the problems of fidelity from the Christian couple caught in the human condition, because the mystery of the second Adam has never supplanted or suppressed in anyone the reality of the first Adam.

8. CIVIL MARRIAGE

As a result, the recognition of a purely "natural" right to marriage, whatever may be the religious value that one ascribes to this right or that it actually possesses, cannot alone justify the couple's entering into Christian marriage. In effect, no natural right by itself can ever define the content of a Christian sacrament. If, in the case of marriage, one claims such a right, one would falsify the meaning of the sacrament, which has as its goal the consecration of the love of the baptized spouses to Christ so that Christ may accomplish in them the transforming effects of his mystery.

Consequently, in contrast to the secular states who see in civil marriage an adequate act for establishing, from society's point of view, a conjugal community, the Church, which does not fail to recognize the value for the non-baptized of such marriages, wonders whether civil marriage can ever constitute a marriage for the baptized. The sacrament of marriage alone applies to them, assuming that the future spouses wish to consecrate to Christ a love whose human value ultimately springs from the love that Christ has and shares with us. Consequently, the identification of the sacrament with the "contract," on which the papal magisterium formally pronounced in the nineteenth century, must be understood in a way that does justice to the mystery of Christ and Christian life.

9. CONTRACT AND SACRAMENT

The act of creating a conjugal convenant, which is usually called a contract but is in reality a sacrament in the case of baptized spouses, does not happen simply by virtue of the juridical effect of baptism. The exchange of vows of a Christian husband and wife is a true sacrament because it arises from their Christian identity, affirmed by them along with the love that they vow to each other in Christ. Their marital covenant, by their mutual free self-giving, also consecrates them to the perfect Bridegroom who will teach them to become perfect spouses. The personal mystery of Christ then penetrates to the heart of the natural human covenant or "contract." This contract becomes a sacrament only if the future spouses freely consent to enter into married life by passing through Christ into whom they were incorporated by baptism.

Their free incorporation into the mystery of Christ is so essential to the nature of the sacrament that the Church tries, through the ministry of the priest, to assure itself of the Christian authenticity of this commitment. The covenant of marriage does not become a sacrament simply by virtue of a canonical statute, as if this contained its own efficacy, independent of any adherence to a freely chosen baptism. It becomes a sacrament because of the publicly Christian character which affects their mutual commitment and which permits us to specify in what sense the spouses are themselves the ministers of the sacrament.

10. THE SPOUSES, MINISTERS OF THE SACRAMENT IN AND THROUGH THE CHURCH

Since the sacrament of marriage is the free consecration of a couple's conjugal love to Christ at its beginning, the spouses are the ministers of a sacrament that is of primary importance to them. However, they are ministers by virtue of a power which is not absolute and whose exercise the Church has every right to regulate.

They are ministers as living members of the Body of Christ, in which they exchange their vows, without their irreplaceable decision making the sacrament the mere offshoot of their love. The sacrament as such comes in fullness entirely from the mystery of the Church, in which their conjugal love makes them share in a privileged way. As a result, no couple can bestow the sacrament of marriage on themselves without the consent of the Church. Nor can they do this in a form different from that which the Church has established as most expressive of the mystery into which the sacrament introduces them.

It thus belongs to the Church to see if the dispositions of the future spouses really correspond to the baptism that they have received. It is her duty, moreover, to dissuade them, if need be, from performing an action which would be contradictory to him to whom it should witness. In their exchange of consent which constitutes the sacrament, the Church remains the sign and the guarantee of the gift of the Spirit that the spouses receive in committing themselves to each other as Christians. The baptized couple are never ministers of the sacrament of marriage without the Church, and still less, beyond the Church. They are ministers in the Church and by the Church and never leave in the background the Church whose mystery governs their love. A sound theology of the minister of the sacrament of marriage not only has great importance for the spiritual authenticity of the couple, but also has important ecumenical repercussions for our relationship with the Orthodox.

11. THE INDISSOLUBILITY OF MARRIAGE

In this context, the indissolubility of marriage also appears in a fresh light. Christian marriage cannot become and remain an authentic image of the love of Christ for the Church without displaying the fidelity that marks Christ as spouse of the Church. Whatever may be the suffering and the psychological difficulties which can result from this fidelity, it is impossible to consecrate to Christ–in order to make it a sign or sacrament of his own mystery–a conjugal love which involves the divorce of one or both of the parties whose first marriage was truly valid. (In some cases the validity of the first marriage is subject to doubt.) If divorce declares that a legitimate union is destroyed and, for that reason, permits a person to contract another marriage, how can we pretend that Christ would make of this other "marriage" a real image of his personal relationship with the Church? Even if the new marriage can claim some degree of justice, especially for a partner who is unjustly abandoned, it cannot be a sacrament and it creates an objective incapacity to receive the Eucharist.

12. DIVORCE AND THE EUCHARIST

While one must not ignore extenuating circumstances and even the quality a civil remarriage after divorce sometimes possesses, the reception of the Eucharist by divorced and remarried people is plainly incompatible with the mystery to which the Church is the servant and witness. By admitting divorced and remarried people to the Eucharist, the Church would allow them to believe that they can communicate with Christ in the sacraments, although they disavow his conjugal mystery in life. Moreover, for the Church to do this would be her declaration that she is in agreement with those who are baptized, at the very moment when they are entering into or remaining in a state which is in evident contradiction with the life, thinking, and very being of the Lord himself as spouse of the Church. If the Church could give the sacrament of unity to those who have broken with her on an essential point of the mystery of Christ, she would no longer be the sign of witness to Christ but rather a sign and a witness against him. Nevertheless, this right of refusal does not justify any action that injures an individual's reputation, and thus contravenes the mercy of Christ toward us sinners.

13. WHY THE CHURCH CANNOT DISSOLVE A MARRIAGE THAT IS *RATUM ET CONSUMMATUM*

This Christological vision of Christian marriage enables us to see why the Church does not recognize the right to dissolve a marriage that is *ratum et consummatum*, that is, a marriage that is sacramentally contracted in the Church and consummated by the spouses. In effect, the full communion of life, which humanly speaking defines marriage, recalls in its own way the realism of the incarnation in which the Son of God becomes one with mankind in the flesh. In committing themselves to each other by mutual and unreserved self-giving, the couple signifies by this act their effective transition to the conjugal life in which love becomes the most absolute sharing of each other possible. They thus enter into the human condition, whose irrevocable character was recalled by Christ, and which he made an image that reveals his own mystery. The Church cannot have any power over the reality of a conjugal union that has passed into the power of him whose mystery she must announce and never hinder.

14. THE PAULINE PRIVILEGE

What we call the Pauline privilege does not in any way contradict what we have just said. Basing herself on Paul's words in 1 Corinthians 7:12–17, the Church recognizes the right to annul a human marriage in which it is impossible for the baptized spouse to live as a Christian, on account of the opposition that the unbaptized party creates for him or her. In a case where the privilege truly applies, it plays a role in favor of the life in Christ, whose importance can legitimately prevail in the eyes of the Church over a conjugal life which cannot and could not be effectively consecrated to Christ.

15. CHRISTIAN MARRIAGE CANNOT BE UNDERSTOOD APART FROM THE MYSTERY OF CHRIST

Whether we treat of its scriptural, dogmatic, moral, human, or canonical aspects, Christian marriage can never be understood apart from the mystery of Christ. This is because the sacrament of marriage – to which the Church witnesses, for which she educates, and which she permits couples to receive – can be fully lived only in an ongoing conversion of the spouses to the person of Christ. This conversion to Christ is intrinsic to the nature of the sacrament and it directly governs the meaning and scope of the sacrament in the life of the couple.

16. A VISION WHICH IS NOT TOTALLY INACCESSIBLE TO NONBELIEVERS

This Christological vision is not totally inaccessible to nonbelievers. Not only does it have its own coherence, which points to Christ as the sole foundation of what we believe, it also possesses an excellence which can speak to human consciences, even to persons who are strangers to the mystery of Christ. Moreover, the human approach can be explicitly subsumed into the mystery of Christ by reference to the first Adam who cannot be separated from the second and last Adam. To show this fully in the case of marriage would open the present reflection to considerations that cannot be treated here. Our purpose has been to recall how Christ is the true foundation, often ignored by Christians themselves, of marriage insofar as it is a sacrament.

CHAPTER 9

Nature and Grace in the Theology of Vatican II:

A Note on Caffarra's "Marriage as a Reality in the Order of Creation and Marriage as a Sacrament"

by Monsignor Philippe Delhaye

During the discussions on the institution of marriage and its sacramentality, we noticed that the problem of the relation between nature and grace surfaced time and time again. Prof. C. Caffarra remarked that the issue of the separability of Christian marriage from the human covenant and contract "surfaces at a time when the problem of the relation between nature and grace is at the center of a new theological debate."[1]

Here, as during the debates within the International Theological Commission,[2] our purpose is to get a bearing on the contemporary discussion of the relation between nature and grace, which in turn is a way of retrieving, in modest fashion, an old project which the ITC has contemplated more than once.[3] This effort is all the more necessary in view of the fact that, in the last thirty years, theological thought has been drenched by a veritable cold shower. In the 1940s theological textbooks still allowed a generous amount of space to "pure nature" (*natura pura*), which the scholasticism of the sixteenth and seventeenth centuries had first suggested as a hypothesis, then treated in its own reasonings as if it were a reality. Accordingly, grace was made to look like something adventitious, which is the reason why the word *supernatural* was so much in vogue. After the Second World War, some theologians insisted that all human beings are summoned to divinization and friendship with God. In the ensuing debates theologians who were scholastically minded maintained that the unmerited character of the supernatural was being called in question and that the natural character of the human person was being negated, as had been done earlier by Baius and the Jansenists. This controversy never managed to be completely honest, and it never achieved decisive results. As a consequence, when Vatican II opened, the distinction between nature and grace was, like original sin, a topic about which people gladly kept silent. There are now people who think that the council shied away from this point of doctrine and merely dropped it.

Very briefly, we would like to situate the problem, recall the positions taken by the pure nature school, and see how Vatican II, both in explicit and in equivalent terms, used the nature–grace distinction, a distinction we cannot do without when discussing marriage. We do not intend to make a choice between Second Scholasticism and Neo-Augustinianism, but to follow the middle way which the council has suggested. That is to say, we aim to situate the relation between nature and grace within the framework of salvation history.

First, however, in order to preclude suspicion of equivocation, I will say quite frankly that I share the position which de Lubac has recently taken and about which I have just spoken.[4] "Not only are the two distinctions between nature and supernature and between nature (freedom) and grace not superseded (to say that a thing is superseded means nothing unless the reasons why it is superseded are disclosed), but they retain their basic importance. A reminder to this effect may be useful today." There is no question of abolishing one of the terms of this pair. If we supress nature we fall into Jansenism and eventually deny man's freedom. If, on the contrary, we call grace into question, we end in Pelagianism, in the "Christian Stoicism" of the seventeenth century, and in contemporary secularism. In this view, man achieves his own freedom apart from grace. Political liberation is mistaken for liberation from sin.

The problem consists rather in perceiving what is called nature and supernature and in deciding how these should relate each to the other. We will soon notice that a momentous choice is in the making here. We may choose to take nature, or man in himself (at the philosophical level) apart from any reference to God, or at least to the Christian God. Or we may choose to place nature[5] within the history of salvation, in which case we view nature as a benefaction which God bestows on man, but do not separate it[6] from a second benefaction, namely grace, supernature, and divinization.

1. NATURE AND THE SUPERNATURAL IN CLASSICAL THEOLOGY: (SEVENTEENTH AND EIGHTEENTH CENTURIES)

"Pure Nature"

1.1 A Supernatural Which Suppresses Nature

It is fashionable today to blame all the afflictions of modern Christian history on the counterreformation and its theology. This criticism is not entirely unfounded, as evidenced by the fact the Leo XIII attempted to revive the thirteenth century scholasticism instead of that of the sixteenth and seventeenth centuries, and by the determination of Vatican II to revert to scripture and the Fathers of the Church. All the same, people are entitled to be judged fairly. We have the duty to gauge with precision the tasks which confronted them. In the matter at hand, the theologians of the seventeenth and eighteenth centuries had to do battle on two fronts. On the one side there were those who maintained that man is not worth anything and that we must entrust ourselves exclusively to grace. On the other side, there were those who would reduce to a minimum the role of God and grace in order to promote the autonomy of man and of nature.

In the camp of the rights of God we find above all Luther. He credits salvation to Christ alone, who imprints faith on human beings who are bereft of freedom of choice. Remember all that Luther writes against humanism in his *De Servo Arbitrio*! Calvin broadens some Augustinian perspectives, and so restricts salvation to people whom God's favor predestines apart from his own foreknowledge of their merits or demerits (*ante praevisa merita et demerita*). Within Catholicism, Baius and Jansenius pay only lip service to human effort. They empty natural men of all worth and all genuine freedom.[7] In their view, man has been despoiled of the gifts of grace and wounded in his natural endowments (*spoliatus a gratuitis et vulneratus in naturalibus*). A human act has value before God only if actually informed by charity. Natural virtues, the virtues of the pagans, are vices.[8]

1.2 Exaltation of Nature

At the other extreme of this spectrum of ideas, we need locate the camp of those who are bent on an exclusive exaltation of man. True, these do posit a connection between man and a creator God, but, in spite of Pascal's expostulations, this God is and remains the "God of philosophers and scholars." He is not the God "of Abraham, Isaac, and Jacob." Still less is he the God of Jesus Christ, the head of the Church. Artists, litterateurs, philosophers, jurists, scientists, and experts in political science accept the view which Grotius adopted in his new conception of natural law. "Natural right is to be construed as if there were no God–*quasi Deus non daretur.*"Christian dogmas and sacraments are not necessarily disavowed. Yet the supernatural is looked upon as nothing more than the frame of a painting. The painting itself is natural man learning how to create himself by his own resources, how to change the world, how to erect a political order where the Christian viewpoint no longer plays a role. The discovery of new lands, once the initial illusions of easy evangelization fades, promotes the myth of the noble savage and of the return to pure nature. As modern man gains control over nature, he no longer takes into account what happens to be given in that nature. He is only interested in what he himself transforms and constructs.[9]

1.3 An Attempt at Solution: Hypothesis of a Pure Nature

It may have been a tactical move, it may have been contamination; the fact remains that a sizable number of theologians let themselves be taken by the hand into the camp of their own enemies–naturally in the hope of changing their minds. The importance of grace and salvation in Christ, original sin and its consequences, were now deemphasized in the extreme. Of course, man has been wounded in his nature, these theologians announced, but the wounds are only skin-deep. This means that man receives fewer graces, and yet he is capable all the same of great accomplishments. How did these theologians come to terms with the whole Catholic tradition? By erecting a hypothesis–and then promptly forgetting that what they have erected is a hypothesis.[10] God did, in fact, intend to summon all human beings to a union with Christ, to his trinitarian life. But we can hypothesize that God would have been content to create a natural man, the kind of man, for example, whom Aristotle describes. And there it is: the famous hypothesis of pure nature, the mere-man hypothesis. Theologians entertained at this time such an anachronistic view of Aristotle that they no longer realized that Aristotle's prime mover (whom they identified in the meantime with the Christian God) is neither creator nor conserver. This prime mover in Aristotle's system, even before the empiricist turn of the third period is only a final cause: he is that toward which all things strive. For Aristotle, as for Plato, things exist before the divine comes onto the scene and acts. As a consequence, man is not the image of God and the cosmos does not show forth his footprints.

Theologians of this persuasion go as far as to congratulate themselves for being able to say that the pure nature theory has a great merit: it proves the gratuity of the supernatural, for God could have decided not to add the supernatural to nature.[11] The result is that theological thinking now unfolds exclusively within the perspective of nature. This shows in many areas of theological reflection. In moral theology, for example, they construct the treatise *de virtutibus* so as to accommodate only the natural virtues. Virtues, we are told, are engendered by human effort; they conform to the law of the rightful environment. At the end of each chapter they then explain that these theories do not apply to the theological virtues, which are God's gifts and are subject to no limitations. From this an even more serious consequence follows: faith, hope, and charity are excluded from the exploration of the Christian life, to be annexed to systematics and investigated as if they were dogmas of faith. This is how we get an analysis of the act of faith, and discussions as to whether it can be right for man to love God out of concern for his own self.

1.4 Difficulties

Those who point a finger at the flaws within the philosophico-theological theory of pure nature are resisted on the basis of the proposition that grace is unmerited and superadded from without. They are told that, by objecting to pure nature, they deny the gratuity of the supernatural. Whatever they reply to this objection does not seem to make any difference. This is how the pure-nature theology comfortably manages not to face the task of responding to objections raised against it. Jacques Maritain shows that the result of one branch of natural law theory was to invent a natural end for man, whereas in truth God calls all human beings to his grace and to the beatific vision.[12] It is quite amazing how firmly negative was the reaction to Maritain's position on the part of some who would be the great defenders of a pure-nature morality.[13] When de Lubac[14] showed that the pure-nature hypothesis – in itself a justifiable hypothesis – transforms the supernatural into an adventitious supplement and an encumbrance, he was accused of lapsing into Baianism. Later he was accused of leading Vatican II into the same error.[15]

We shall return to this point shortly. But let us conclude this first section of our presentation with the remark that the pure-nature hypothesis has had the gravest of consequences for marriage. It induced theologians to take as their starting point the marriage of human beings situated at the merely hypothetical level of philosophical nature. Only subsequently would they ask themselves what the sacrament added to the natural contract, to the purely human covenant of love between a man and a woman. And the irony is that, after paving the way for royalists and secularistic theoreticians, these theologians ask why they were so misunderstood! However, it is only proper to recognize that some recent authors exhibit more coherence than that. For they themselves now take the lead, reciprocally as it were, and advocate a merely natural marriage (read: a civil marriage) and a denial of grace and redemption. In their writings radical secularization is affirmed throughout.

2. NATURE AND SUPERNATURE AS ELEMENTS IN THE HISTORY OF SALVATION

2.1 Vatican II on the Question of the Supernatural

What position did Vatican II take with regard to the problem of the supernatural? Is it correct to say that the council did not even use the word *supernatural*? This statement is quite baffling for anyone who cares enough to open a concordance.[16]

The term *supernatural* occurs in thirteen passages: *Lumen Gentium*, 12 and 61, with reference to the theological virtues; *Christus Dominus*, 17, on the supernatural goal of the apostolate; 20, on the activity of bishops; 28, on the bond of supernatural charity that ought to mark the relationship between bishops and priests; 35, on the supernatural attitude of minds and hearts; *Optatam Totius*, 11 and 21, on natural virtues and a supernatural spirit; *Apostolicam Actuositatem*, 6, in connection with the proposition that Christ unites to himself all things, both natural and supernatural; 8, in connection with the contention that, in the act of taking on man's nature, Christ united the whole human race to himself in a certain supernatural solidarity; 24, on temporal and supernatural deeds; 30, on the supernatural goal of certain works; *Presbyterorum Ordinis*, 16, in connection with the advice given to priests to make use of both the natural and supernatural helps available to them. This is not a bad harvest.

It is even more important to note that Vatican II refers to the natural and supernatural order by using the words *grace* (*gratia*: 151 instances) and *nature* (*natura*: 100 instances), *natural* (*naturalis*: 17 instances), *naturally* (*naturaliter*: two instances). We also notice that, in the terminology traced by Prof. Caffarra, Vatican II formulates its doctrine by speaking of the work of creation and redemption. Add to this the distinction between *human history* and the *history of salvation* and between the *earthly* and the *heavenly city*. We also have the expressions *heavenly goods* and *earthly goods, divinization* and *humanization*. I cannot quote all the texts. I will list only a few: GS 41, 2(Abbott, 240–41): "For though the same God is Savior and Creator, Lord of human history as well as of salvation history, in the divine arrangement itself the rightful autonomy of the creature, and particularly of man, is not withdrawn. Rather it is established in its own dignity and strengthened in it." GS 43, 1(Abbott 242–43): "The Council exhorts Christians, as citizens of two cities, to strive to discharge their earthly duties conscientiously and in response to the gospel spirit. They are mistaken who, knowing that we have here no abiding city but seek one which is to come, think that they may therefore shirk their earthly responsibilities." GS 21, 3: "For man was made an intelligent and free member of society by the God who created him. Even more importantly, man is called as a son to commune with God and to share in his happiness."

2.2 The Meaning of This Re-Balancing

What lies behind this effort at establishing the correct balance? Those who followed Vatican II in the making, and those who read the texts of its documents, will notice that an intention comes clearly to light. The council by no means intends to relinquish the distinction between man's natural side – namely, the fact that he is an intelligent and free member of society, as we have just read in GS 21 – and the work of divinizing grace – God has made man his adoptive son, and has called him to an intimate union with himself and finally to a share in his own happiness in the same passage. Yet the magisterium of Vatican II does not support the pure-nature hypothesis. It rather expresses the distinction and coordination of the two orders – creation and redemption – by placing both within the perspective of salvation history, as God willed it to be. May I try to condense this conciliar theology into a few succinct propositions? First, man's ultimate end is one: divinization. Second, paradoxical though it may seem, the humanization of man is better served in this perspective, and so is man's authentic autonomy. Finally, by linking nature to the various phases of salvation history, we more aptly account for the facts than by postulating a pure nature.

a. Only One Ultimate End

The council reverts to the biblical and patristic assertion that the deed of God is predicated on one purpose: God freely created humanity in order to divinize it. It is, therefore, a mistake to reason as if there were both a natural and a supernatural end, even if we add the remark that the hypothesis never came to fruition. This assertion that man's final end is one appears, for example, in the first lines of LG 2 (Abbott, 15): "By an utterly free[17] and mysterious decree of His own wisdom and goodness, the eternal Father created the whole world. His plan was to dignify men with a participation in His own divine life. He did not abandon men after they had fallen in Adam, but ceaselessly offered them helps to salvation, in anticipation of Christ the Redeemer, 'who is the image of the invisible God, the firstborn of every creature' (Col 1:15). All the elect, before time began, the Father 'foreknew and predestined to become conformed to the image of his Son, that he should be the firstborn among many bretheren' (Rom 8:29)."

GS 22, 5 (Abbott, 221), uses even more striking language: ". . . the ultimate vocation of man is in fact one, and divine. . . ." GS can of course restate the faith with greater assurance than the theologians of the seventeenth and eighteenth centuries, who did not know how to answer the thorny question of the salvation of pagans of good will.[18] In the same passage, GS 2 adds: "All this holds true not only for Christians but for all men of good will in whose hearts grace works in an unseen way." (Abbott, 221)

b. Humanization as Consequence of Divinization

Are we then to say that there are in man no values and no endowments except those which grace might bestow? Are we perhaps reverting to an extreme form of Augustinianism? We are not, for in the perspective of divinization there is room for humanization. Humanization is not only a means to an end (see AA 7. par. 2); but the result of the work of grace in man. Using a different terminology, we thus repeat what Thomas Aquinas said at the beginning of the Ia IIae: it is legitimate for man to seek an imperfect beatitude in the form of happiness and fulfillment, yet this quest is located within the quest for a perfect blessedness which is the vision of God. This theme surfaces a hundred times in the texts of the council. See, for instance, GS 37; 38; 40 (Abbott, 235–37; 239). In the last of these texts we read: "Pursuing the saving purpose which is proper to her, the Church not only communicates divine life to men, but in some way casts the reflected light of that life over the entire earth.

"This she does most of all by her healing and elevating impact on the dignity of the person, by the way in which she strengthens the seams of human society and imbues the everyday activity of men with a deeper meaning and importance. Thus, through her individual members and her whole community, the Church believes she can contribute greatly toward making the family of man and its history more human."

If we combine the text of GS 43 with AA 7), we uncover six reasons why the Christian who is called to heavenly blessedness ought to be interested also in the created world and in the task of making it human: (1) Created things are good, for they come from God. (2) Charity toward our brothers and toward God demands it of us. (3) Human values are lofty in themselves. (4) Christ willed to be part of our everyday life. (5) The resurrection has a cosmic import because of the encompassing power of its spiritual grace.

c. *The Autonomy of Earthly Realities*

Paradoxically, and yet logically enough, to affirm that divinization is the ultimate goal of salvation history and of human history is to insure that human realities will be authentically autonomous. The pure-nature hypothesis always retained to some extent the peculiar scent of Greek philosophy from which it originated. The cosmos, man, and nature were thought of as realities existing before the demiurge who presided over the world and drew it to himself, but was not its creator. The situation changes when human values come from God the creator who is also the God who redeems and divinizes. Human realities may then be welcomed for what they are in themselves, since they are not temptations for man, nor do they divert him from divinization. This is certainly what we read in GS 37 (Abbott, 235), where we are told that "all human activity" is "constantly imperiled by man's pride. . . ." This text does indeed stress the autonomy of human institutions and of the secular disciplines, as long as methodical investigation is carried out "in accord with moral norms" (GS 36: Abbott, 234) and we do not forget that "without the creator the creature would disappear" (GS 36; Abbott, 234).

This text has recently been applied to marriage in an attempt to promote a desacralization of it. This attempt must be declared abortive. No one denies that there are human and earthly aspects to marriage, nor do GS and AA pass this over in silence. And yet Vatican II folds these aspects into the sacrament, so that "married love is caught up into divine love" (GS 48; Abbott, 251). This text, as well as Mt 19 and Eph 5, emphasizes that marriage in the climate of grace corresponds to marriage as it was at the beginning (*ab initio*)–that is, at creation.

d. The Stages in the History of Salvation of Mankind

Does this mean that we are ignoring the history of mankind and particularly the imperfect forms of marriage which have surfaced in history in such plenty? Are we forgetting that the law of Moses provided for divorce? Does grace cancel out the historicity of nature?

Certainly not. Vatican II recalls the various stages of salvation history, noting the interplay of grace and nature, just as some Church fathers and the great scholastic theologians of the thirteenth century mentioned by Caffarra (note 129) did. Human nature has never existed in history apart form a determinate correlation to grace, and this because God freely willed it so. The correlation is not the same in the various phases of salvation history. We have, first, human nature at the moment of creation (*natura condita*), then nature after sin has been committed (*natura lapsa*), and finally redeemed nature (*natura redempta*). *Gaudium et Spes* states this notion in its first lines,[19] then returns to it throughout chapter one. The vocabulary is biblical and patristic. It is the vocabulary of man's godlikeness. Man was created by God in his image to know and love him (GS 12, 3;). God's image has been and is being defaced by sin (GS 13;). It is restored by the redemptive act of Christ (GS 22; Abbott, 221): "The Christian man, conformed to the likeness of that Son who is the firstborn of many brothers, receives the 'firstfruits of the Spirit' . . . by which he becomes capable of discharging the new law of love."

Should we inquire how this view accounts for the fact that the law of Moses makes provision for divorce? The scholastic theologians who subscribe to a historical view of nature will say, with Hugh of St. Victor: divorce is incompatible with the rule of grace, and with nature redeemed, but it is compatible with sinful nature. Unless divorce has been allowed, husbands who no longer found pleasure in their spouses might have been tempted to kill them. The law of nature after sin managed at least this much: it demanded the promulgation of the decree of divorce and so protected the life of a dismissed wife. The problem is far more intractable for theologians who are committed to the so-called pure-nature hypothesis. They find themselves in a predicament, just as when they discover that, in the Old Testament, God commands or allows things which are repugnant to the nature of man philosophically considered. We refer to texts which report, for example, how Abraham was ordered to sacrifice his son Isaac, how the departing Israelites robbed the Egyptians, and how Hosea was required to take a prostitute for a wife. Raïssa Maritain has discussed all this in her booklet, *Abraham and Natural Law*. With regard to divorce, we will have to take the position that either it does not contradict natural law philosophically understood or that God may allow a violation of natural law.

Conclusion

I have said too much, no doubt–and yet perhaps too little. My excuse is that I felt it necessary to review the problem of nature and grace in the light of the Council–a problem which, because it has taken perhaps too much room in the theological debates of the last forty years, makes us a bit afraid–and so gain a better understanding of the article of Caffarra, and of other problems as well. The fathers and the theologians who took part in the work of the council were not ashamed of what was being taught by the ordinary magisterium of the pope and the college of bishops. Thus they successfully defend the faith against secularization in disguise. They promote humility and foster attention to the action of grace, while acknowledging the legitimacy and the accomplishments of science and technology. Finally, they infuse a new pride into the moral theology of earthly realities and of human values. We see then that through Christ, in Christ, and for Christ (Rom 14) both our divinization and humanization are assured.

CHAPTER 10

The Contribution of Liturgical History to the Theology of Marriage

Aimé-Georges Martimort

The history of the liturgy of marriage is very complex. Since the seventeenth century, however, its object has been to inventory some of the sources and studies to facilitate our study of the meaning of this history. I will mention four of the more useful and accessible works for those who wish to study the documents:

1. *De antiquis ritibus*, by Dom Edmond Martine;[1]
2. *Ritus orientalium*, by H. Denzinger;[2]
3. "Marriage dans let églises chrétiennes du Ier au XIe siècle," by Don Dorbinian Ritzer;
4. "Le rituel du mariage en France du XIIe au XVIe siècle," by J. B. Molin and P. Mutembe.

Three questions on such a collection of diverse materials merit our attention:

1. What is the origin and meaning of the diverse rites with which local churches have surrounded the celebration of marriage?
2. What doctrinal message have these liturgies proclaimed to families and to the community?
3. What relationship have the rites had with the conjugal bond?

I. The Origin and Meaning of the Liturgical Rites of Marriage

The first impression one gets from even a summary study of the liturgical sources is the extraordinary diversity of the customs and rites of marriage, a diversity recognized and accepted even when the

Church has sought unity in other aspects of the Christian cult.[5] However, in the midst of this diversity, two basic tendencies manifest themselves: Christians ask for the priestly blessing of their marriage; and diverse ceremonies of the family or of the locale where the marriage is celebrated or announced are soon introduced into the liturgy itself.

1. THE PRIESTLY BLESSING OF MARRIAGE

It is difficult for the historian to prove the existence of a priestly marriage blessing before the second half of the fourth century. Here is the advice given by Saint Ignatius of Antioch:

> It is fitting that men and women who marry contract their union with the counsel of the bishop, so that their marriage will be made according to the Lord and not according to passion.[6]

This advice does not imply any liturgical rite and remains isolated; it cannot be found in the canonical literature of the third century.[7] We can include here the argument of Tertullian in *Ad Uxorem*:

> How is it possible not to rejoice at the happiness of this marriage? The Church binds it, prayer confirms it, the blessing seals it, the angels announce it, the Father ratifies it.[8]

The apparent clarity of the text does not render its interpretation very easy. The text praises marriage between Christians as opposed to mixed marriages. This union, conformed to the ideal proposed by the Church, is established by the participation of the two parties in the Eucharist; but what is the meaning of *obsignat benedictio* ("the blessing seals it")? The context leads Ritzer to doubt it, because Tertullian is speaking here of the second marriage of a widow; such marriages did not have the right to a blessing in the Western tradition.[9] Much later Tertullian, in *De Pudicitia* and *De Monogamia*, required the faithful who want to marry to fulfil certain prerequisites in order to obtain the permission of the community; but these are evidence of his Montanist rigor, not of common practice of the Church.[10]

Neither can one use as evidence the argument that Clement of Alexandria put forth against the feminine fashion of wigs, when he exclaimed:

> Indeed, on what head does the priest impose his hands? Whom will he bless? It is not the woman who is dressed up, but rather someone else's hair, and therefore someone else's head.[11]

It would be necessary first to prove that a marriage rite required the imposition of hands, and secondly that Clement referred to it rather than to the traditional impositions in the liturgies of initiation or reconciliation.[12]

Must we conclude from this absence of earlier reliable historic witnesses that the blessing of the spouses of which Pope Siricius or St. Ambrose[13] speaks is an innovation of the second half of the fourth century in the Church of Italy? That is not likely, because all the pagan peoples of Mediterranean antiquity accompanied marriage with religious gestures, and especially because the Bible furnished an example of prayer and benediction for the spouses[14] and Jewish custom fixed the tradition.[15] What is new, in relation to Jewish tradition, is that the blessing is prayed not by the father of one of the two spouses, but by the bishop or the priest. The reason for this evolution escapes our knowledge, as is the case for a good number of institutions of the Church in the first centuries.

The most ancient Christian formula for the blessing of spouses that we possess is suspect, since it appears in the *Acts of Thomas* and may not even be part of the original redaction. Yet, as it appears in the Greek recension,[16] the formula does not show any Encratite tendency, and it gives us "an idea of the way we can imagine, from the earliest period, the blessing of a couple by a bishop or a priest present among the guests" at a wedding.[17] In this apocryphal account the apostle himself says the prayer, and he says it in the nuptial chamber. This was destined to become the official and traditional liturgical action of several great churches of antiquity until the Middle Ages. The blessing *in thalamo* because one of the characteristics of the Gallican liturgy,[18] and of the Visigothic liturgy.[19] Through the latter it was introduced into Anglo-Norman custom.[20] Perhaps it was practiced by the Chaldeans[21] and became a Judeo-Chaldean custom.

Elsewhere this blessing of the spouses took place on the eve of the wedding, or during various formalities performed at the home of the parents.[22]

These various customs gradually gave way to a generalized practice, except among the Chaldeans, in which the blessing of spouses took place at the church during a liturgical celebration which included a Mass or a preconsecrated communion, or even – as among the Syrians – the Liturgy of the Word. The Roman custom, destined to become the common source of the Latin rituals, is the one that can be verified in the most ancient documents, dating back to the fifth century.[23] Its formula is a prayer, one of the great priestly prayers composed perhaps even before St. Leo the Great.[24] This prayer is pronounced by the celebrant of the Mass. The Gelasian Sacramentary (*Reginensis* 316) tells the precise moment: between the Pater Noster and the kiss of peace.[25] Moreover, it is inserted in a complete formulary of the Mass, including even an intercession in the middle of the eucharistic prayer;[26] the spouses receive communion at the Mass. The same sacramentary presents a second formula of blessing to be pronounced after the communion.[27]

2. THE ADOPTION OF FAMILY CUSTOMS BY THE LITURGY

The other great tendency which the liturgical history of marriage reveals is the transfer to the bishop or priest of the gestures or acts which were once performed by the family, according to the customs proper to each of the ancient cultures.

These gestures or actions corresponded either to the betrothal or to the wedding; the two stages were distinguished nearly everywhere among ancient peoples because the betrothal generally took place before the girl had reached the age of puberty. Due to the influence of Christianity on local customs, the betrothals drew closer and closer to marriage, to the point of immediately preceding it in the same liturgy. At the end of this development, the practices of the betrothal became a part of the marriage itself.

From the customs of betrothal among the Latins, according to Pliny the Elder, also derived the practice of the groom's giving a ring to the bride.[28] This ring at first was iron, and then of gold.[29] Later, there was an exchange of rings. This practice entered into the liturgies of most of the Christian rites and took on a new meaning as a sign of fidelity. The blessing of the ring by the priest became, in the Eastern churches, quite an elaborate ceremony; finally, it came about that the priest himself sometimes placed the ring on the finger of the betrothed.[30]

Within the custom of betrothal itself, the ring symbolized the material promise, the deposit required by the marriage contract. Besides the ring, a deposit of money was given in some countries. From the ring and the money, a blessing entitled *blessing of the ring* (arrhes) became characteristic of the Visigothic liturgy, and it spread throughout the various regions whose rituals borrowed from this liturgy.[31]

The engagement kiss, considered to be a ratification of the contract, is also taken into the liturgy. It is attested to in the *Liber ordinum* of the Visigoths[32] and, in the tenth century, in the Byzantine *Euchologion.*[33]

Concerning practices to be performed in the marriage ceremony itself, the ancient Church of Rome and of Italy knew only one, the *velatio*, but it is attested to from the fourth century onward. One would be tempted, at first glance, to think that here again is the acceptance into the liturgy of a familial ceremony in a Roman marriage: the father's giving his daughter a *flammeum*, a colorful veil which covers her head on her wedding day. However, we are dealing here with quite a different practice, whose exact origin has not yet been sufficiently explained, but which St. Paul of Nola already describes for us at the beginning of the fifth century[34] and which lasted until the end of the Middle Ages:[35] a veil was spread over the heads of the two spouses by the celebrant at the moment when he pronounced over them the prayer of benediction. This practice is significant, since, in the letters of Siricius and Ambrose, (and with the passage of time in the Roman sacramentaries), the liturgy of marriage came to be called *velamen* or *velatio* (the taking of the veil).

In the East, marriage took the name *coronation, stephanōma.* But this truly reflects a practice borrowed from family ceremony that became a liturgical rite. The custom of spouses wearing crowns at their wedding existed in the East, primarily among Jews and in the Roman Empire. This practice is attested by Gregory of Nazianzus in a letter in which he regrets not being able to attend the wedding of a friend and expresses his wishes for the betrothed:

> This is what I would have wished for you had I been present, and what I wish for you now. For the rest, think about the ceremony, and let the father [of the bride] impose the crowns (*stephanouto*), as he desires. It is this we have decided, when we have occasion to assist at these weddings: that to the fathers belongs the imposition of crowns and to us the prayers, and these, I know, are not limited by their places."[36]

From the end of the fourth century, priests progressively took the place of fathers in placing the crown on the heads of the spouses. It seems that this development was part of the Armenian culture newly converted to Christianity.[37] The reticence of Gregory of Nazianzus did not stop this development: the rite of coronation by the bishop or priest was adopted very rapidly by the Greek-speaking churches, the Syrians, the Copts, and the Chaldeans.[38]

In Spain, a ceremony formerly reserved for the father, the *traditio puellae*, the handing over of the bride to the groom, became a part of the liturgy. Again, from the Spanish church the custom spread widely and survived in medieval rituals.[39] It corresponded, moreover, in many respects, to the ancient Roman custom of the *dextrarum iunctio* (joining of hands) which the Greeks called *ekdōsis*. Gregory of Nazianzus, regretting not being able to assist at the marriage of the daughter of Vitalianos, a ceremony at which several bishops were present, wrote: "In desire, I am with you; I am joining in your celebration. I unite one to the other the hands of the young spouses, and I unite their joined hands to that of God."[70]

Can it be deduced that, had Gregory been present, he himself would have performed this action – he who refused the honor of crowning the couple? I do not know; at any rate, the *ekdōsis* figured in the subsequent Byzantine rite, at least until the time of the euchologion manuscripts.[41]

II. The Doctrinal Message Proclaimed by the Liturgical Rites

The ceremonies just described were familial and local customs which became liturgical; the bishop or priest took the place of the father or the other person traditionally charged with them. But this involved more than a simple transfer of responsibility. First of all, why did the Christians even assign this role to the priest? St. Gregory of Nazianzus showed us above: in uniting the hands of the young spouses, he united them, to God's. Thus a profound change is suggested here. For Christians, marriage surpasses the purely familial or social plant – it calls for the action of God.

At the same time, the customary gestures receive a new meaning from Christianity. For example, St. John Chrysostom explains the crowning thus:

> As a symbol of their victory, a crown is placed on the head of those spouses who have not been conquered by pleasure. If someone, a slave of pleasure, has given himself over to harlots, why should he also wear a crown on his head, since he has been conquered?[42]

Furthermore, when these ceremonies became liturgical actions, they received prayers which impart a spiritual meaning to them. From then on they lose their character as local customs and the Church can introduce them into countries or cultures where they were previously unknown.

New, specifically Christian, actions have also been created which assume a particular solemnity in the marriage ritual. There was the blessing and the presentation to the spouses of the common cup proper to the Byzantine liturgy; there was also eucharistic communion. One may wonder whether the common cup perhaps originated as a substitute for communion under the form of wine either because the communion of the spouses took place under the form of the presanctified or because the spouses were Christians who were not admitted to the Eucharist. The blessing calls to mind the wedding feast at Cana and the miraculous gift that Christ gave to the couple there.[43]

But eucharistic communion realizes what was announced by the wine at Cana. Eucharistic communion has always been considered in the liturgy and spirituality of the churches to have an important, perhaps even essential, place in the celebration of marriage. Some Egyptian canonists made it a condition of validity; for the Ethiopians, marriage was made indissoluble by the spouses' communing together.[44] The Eucharist, according to the testimony of Simeon of Thessalonica, "perfects and seals every sacrament and every divine mystery."[45]

We must not, however, seek the meaning of the rite of marriage in the commentators on the liturgy. Rather, we must turn to the liturgy itself, insofar as it has been celebrated in the language of the faithful, and examine the prayers that they heard pronounced by the priests, the biblical readings that were used, and the songs that accompanied the rites. These not only expressed hope and offered petitions for the couple's happiness but, more importantly, affirmed the place of marriage in the economy of salvation and stressed the demands of Christian marriage.

In the synthesis we are attempting to make here, we prefer to cite the oriental rites, not because liturgies of the Latin West have misunderstood or passed over in silence these perspectives but because their formulation seems brief and scanty alongside the lyrical luxurance of the prayers of the East.

1. MARRIAGE IN THE ECONOMY OF SALVATION

In order to present the doctrine of Christian marriage and to draw inspiration from the prayers and hymns, it is sufficient to focus on the New Testament texts that have always been part of the liturgies of marriage. The three principal ones are: Ephesians 5:20–33, which, with some variations in editing the pericope, we find in the Roman liturgy,[46] at Milan, among the Chaldeans, the Syrians, the Maronites, the Byzantines, the Armenians, the Coptics; Matthew 19:1–11, which, equally with some variations in omissions, is proclaimed in the Roman liturgy, at Milan, among the Chaldeans, the Syrians, the Maronites, the Armenians, the Coptics; finally, John 2:1–11, which is characteristic of the Byzantine liturgy and the Visigothic liturgy.[47] But even where one or another of these pericopes is not found among the readings, it has evidently been present in the minds of those who have composed the prayers and the hymns.

The message of Matthew 19 does not limit the teaching of Jesus to the indissolubility of marriage; rather, it grounds indissolubility in the plan of God revealed by the narrative of Genesis 1:27–2:24. God himself is the "creator of marriage" according to the expression of a Syrian prayer:[48] it is he who willed that they should be man and woman; it is he who united them and who still unites them today. From the beginning, then, marriage is not a purely human work; the Lord has given it a blessing that survives in spite of sin. Therefore the law which governs it cannot be a human law, but one from God: "What God has joined, let no man separate." This recollection of Genesis along with the new clarification of it by Jesus in the gospel returns as a constant refrain in all the rites.[49]

Another constant feature in the rites, in both the East and the West, is the attention given to pointing out in the books of the Old Testament models of conjugal union and, above all, signs of the goodness of God with regard to certain couples: Abraham and Sara, Isaac and Rebecca, Jacob and Rachel, Joseph and Asseneth, Moses and Sephora, Elcana and Anne.[50] It was through these couples, by their virtue and fecundity, that the promises were transmitted.

A new dignity is given marriage by the prophets. It becomes the image of the covenant between God and his people, and conjugal love appears as the reflection of the love of God for his chosen spouse, the virgin daughter of Zion. Not only is marriage the beginning of a revelation that will be fulfilled in the New Testament, in the new covenant established in the blood of the Son of God; but everything said in the psalms, the Song of Solomon, and the prophets about the espousal of God and his people applies to the Church. All the Old Testament texts (Ps 8, 18, 20, 44, 127; Is 61–62)[51] are read or sung as expressing the mystery of the Church and the love of Christ in light of the Epistle to the Ephesians, the parables which compare the kingdom of God to a wedding, and, above all, the Johannine texts. The Old Testament images, illumined by the New Testament, accompany all the parts of the nuptial liturgy and they have a profoundly spiritual quality:

> How beautiful you are, daughter of the nations, how beautiful you are! You are like the sun that shines over the whole world; on your brow the sign of the cross is traced, your pure mouth sings glory; your lips are impregnated with the blood of the Son of God and your children sing praise night and day . . . King Solomon sang of you, holy Church. The perfume you distill is like that of the rose in April, your lips distill honey. You are all beautiful, O Church, and there is not a spot in you. Christ the King keeps you so that you may adore his cross.[52]
>
> Sing the praise, O Queen Church, daughter of the King, of the one who espoused you and brought you into the nuptial chamber. For dowry he gave you the blood that flowed from his side; he clothed you in a resplendent and imperishable robe; he crowned your head with a magnificent crown of glory [at this moment the priest places the crowns on the spouses] and in the view of all he has made your perfume sweet as the pure smoke of incense; he has made your beauty flourish like that of the rose, the bud and the flower in April; on Golgotha he freed you from the slavery of idols. Adore then the cross on which he suffered for you and exalted your lowliness.[53]

These hymns and many similar ones[54] which punctuate the liturgy almost seem to forget the spouses standing before the priest and to see only Christ espousing the Church; in reality, they invite one to transpose the earthly ceremony into the heavenly mystery. The man and woman who are here crowned or married are the sign of Christ and the Church, so that the liturgy, especially in the East, illustrates concretely the teaching of the Epistle to the Ephesians.

Even in the churches that do not read John 2:1–11 during the ceremony, the wedding at Cana is fully commemorated, the joy afforded by the miraculous wine of Christ is recalled. But what is most strongly emphasized is that here today, as at one time in Cana, Christ is present, and consecrates the wedding. It is not enough to say that Christ has effected the union of the couple; as the following prayers affirm, Christ himself is the very substance of their union:

> You yourself are the link of love and the norm which regulates their union.[55]

> Lord, who in uniting them, makes a couple with different and distinct beings, and who ties them together in indissoluble fashion. . . .[56]

> Unite them, Lord, in their union of love as you have united the just who have always pleased you; you are, indeed, the beloved of the all-beautiful beloved, resplendent with spiritual beauty.[57]

One must not, then, be surprised at the overwhelming optimism which springs from the nuptial liturgies. It would be interesting to show how far they are from giving any pretext for misogyny! It is important to add, however, that the nuptial liturgies also call for a going beyond marriage, not only because "by engendering children for the earth," the Christian spouses prepare "sons for the Church,"[58] but also because earthly weddings are a prefiguration of the heavenly wedding:

> Make us worthy, Lord God, to participate in the joy of your feast which has no end, in the happiness of your nuptial chamber which knows no decline, in the felicity of your banquet which is not limited by time; may we share in the joy of the invited ones and in the happiness of the guests who exult there. . . . And we shall sing hymns of glory and thanksgiving.[59]

Marriage is the sign of the heavenly wedding, but virginity is already an anticipation of it. Christian marriage cannot be understood without virginity as its complement: "The heavenly crown for the holy virgins; the earthly, for those who are united in marriage here below."[60] The praise of virginity is thus proclaimed to those assembled for a nuptial liturgy; likewise, the liturgy of the consecration of virgins is modeled on the rite of marriage and is centered above all on prayer to Mary as spouse, mother, and virgin, "the pure nuptial chamber of the pure betrothed."[61]

2. THE EXACTING DEMANDS OF CHRISTIAN MARRIAGE

It is not necessary to describe in detail the model and requirements of the conjugal and familial virtues which the nuptial liturgies propose; the texts of the Old Testament furnish beautiful examples in the lives of the patriarchs. The Book of Tobit will be considered the ideal program of marital spirituality. The epistles of Paul and Peter also contain numerous exhortations to spouses, parents, and children. They are sometimes read; more often they are alluded to in prayer.

The exacting requirements of Christian marriage lie in its transcending of pleasure – it is stressed in the prayer of Tobias – and especially in its indissolubility. Remarkably, the reading from Matthew 19 has been proclaimed in all marriages in the churches of the West that use the Roman lectionary, in Milan, and throughout the non-Byzantine East. Very often, the pericope is read in its entirety along with the reflection of the disciples: "If such is the situation of a husband in reflection to his wife, it does not profit him to marry," for "what is impossible for a man is possible for God," and it is he upon whom the prayer for the spouses is grounded, he who "placed his fidelity above his inheritance," according to a Byzantine formula.[62] This is the fidelity, vowed in disregard of the day-to-day struggle and the vicissitudes of life, that the medieval Norman custom of the exchange of vows expressed in striking terms:

> N., do you wish to take N. as your wife and spouse, and to protect her in health and in sickness, to share with her fairly your body and your possessions; neither in sickness nor in health departing from her, all the days of your life?[63]

III. The Liturgical Rites of Marriage and the Conjugal Bond

A reader unfamiliar with the history of the liturgy of marriage will be surprised that we waited so long to mention the exchange of vows. It is a relatively recent development in the celebration of Christian marriage, both in the East and in the West. This is not always remembered. Furthermore, canonists and theologians have found it somewhat difficult to determine the precise point at which the spouses find themselves irrevocably committed in marriages celebrated both in the customs of the peoples and in the liturgy; these ceremonies involve a series of steps that sometimes follow one another over considerable intervals of time. One must especially recall that it was not until the end of the ninth century in the East and until the promulgation of the decree *Tametsi* by the Council of Trent in the West that the intervention of a priest was required for the validity of marriage.

1. *NUPTIAS FACIT CONSENSUS*: CONSENT MAKES THE MARRIAGE

The Church adopted this principle of Roman law, but gave it a wider application, a deeper meaning, and a different expression in practice. Secular society affirmed that consent alone made the marriage, not consummation: *nuptias consensus, non concubitus facit*; the Church, rather, affirmed the equal rights of the man and woman in marriage, an equality often forgotten in human institutions. In the customs of the barbarian tribes and in Roman law, the exterior acts surrounding marriage were important insofar as they revealed the consent of the spouses. This is the meaning of the response that Nicholas I gave to the Bulgarians in 866.[64] That is why, until the end of the ninth century in the East and the Council of Trent in the West, none of the rituals discussed in this article entered into the conditions for the validity of marriage; they are only public proof of consent. In Roman law it was the privilege of free individuals of equal social status (*pares honestate*) to view their marriages as civilly recognized solely on the basis of mutual consent of the spouses, without any public celebration. The Church recognized the value of what were called clandestine marriages until she expressly forbade them. Clandestine marriages were forbidden because they were open to very grave abuses. However, *Tametsi* did affirm the validity of such marriages contracted before its promulgation:

> Tametsi dubitandum non est, clandestina matrimonia, libero contrahentium consensu facta, rata et vera esse matrimonia, quandiu Ecclesia ea irrita non fecit, et proinde iure damnandi sunt illi, ut eos sancta Synodus anathemate damnat, qui ea vera ac rata esse negant . . . [65]

Furthermore, the ancient Church generally refused its blessing and sometimes even the presence of a priest at the second marriages of widows and widowers, but it nonetheless recognized their validity.[66]

There is some merit in enunciating the principle so strongly, since practice indeed demonstrated the very grave abuse that it permitted. Therefore, the council immediately added: "However, the holy Church of God, for very just reasons, has always hated and forbidden [these weddings]." "Always" is perhaps historically inexact; but for a long time in all regions of the Christian world, the Church tried to suppress marriage by simple mutual consent and to require publicity. But the approach in the East was different from that in the West.

2. IN THE EAST: THE BLESSING OF THE PRIEST IS REQUIRED

A paradox of the liturgical history of marriage is that the Byzantine emperors, the heirs of the tradition of Roman law, rendered the public celebration of marriage obligatory. Their effort was an attempt to respond to two problems: the principle of *consensus solus* and the difficulty of distinguishing, in the series of public acts by which a marriage came into being, the ones that corresponded to a clear manifestation or proof of matrimonial consent. The clearest of these steps, often marked by a contract and the blessing of the priest, was the betrothal: an engagement which originally obligated only for the future, not for the present, and which was revocable.

This is not the place to describe the various edicts by which, from Leo III the Isaurian (717–740), to Leo the Wise (886–912) and Alexis Comnenus (1084), the Byzantine discipline was formed. This discipline made betrothal the first stage of marriage, suppressed the interval which separated the two acts, and refused to recognize a marriage which did not receive the blessing of a priest. The liturgy of marriage was henceforth celebrated following the liturgy of betrothal, in the same ceremony. This rule was also followed by the Eastern churches, at least in the essential principle; some still kept the usage of celebrating by stages. Modern jurisprudence has tried to determine which of these involved consent and validity.[67]

3. IN THE LATIN CHURCH: THE EXCHANGE OF VOWS *IN FACIE ECCLESIAE*

Another paradox of the liturgical history of marriage is that consent, alone considered essential, did not enter into the rituals of the Latin Church before the twelfth century. Moreover, its expression as a response to a question of the priest did not take place within the Mass or even in the place of worship but in a vestibule or doorway where the celebrant welcomed the future spouses. From the evidence, this seems to have been a kind of preliminary inquiry to verify the free consent of the parties. It is described in rituals of Anglo-Norman origin and in two books coming from the Moissac-Albi region, that is, in the liturgies that retained Visigothic echoes.[68] Around this dialogue gathered a number of rituals which constituted betrothal: a present pledge (*de praesenti*) took the place of promises concerning the future (*sponsalia de futuro*). From the inquiry the dialogue developed into an expression of the mutual giving of the spouses, often with very beautiful formulas such as those cited above.[69]

In the East, the expression of consent was introduced into the liturgy in a precarious form, mainly due to the influence of Latin theology and disciplines, for example, in the rite of Peter Moghila.[70]

The formation and development in the West of a rite of matrimony at the door of the Church had the effect of conferring on the priest the function of a witness. There was the temptation, in speculative theology, of seeing the priest as the minister of marriage, but this was kept in check by three things:

1. by the fact that the exchange of vows by reason of the very place where it occurred was not a priestly function like the nuptial blessing, at least originally;
2. by the fact that some other solemn forms of contract were admitted and even considered valid by *Tametsi* (71); and above all,
3. by the fact that, until *Tametsi*, marriage by simple consent without priestly intervention was considered valid.

To repeat, clandestine marriages gave rise to abuses which the Church wanted to eradicate and with which it struggled for several centuries prior to attaining a solution in *Tametsi*. But Trent's solution came five centuries after the Byzantine world had already remedied the problem of these marriages by requiring the presence of a priest. A movement also existed in the Latin Church, especially after the Pseudo-Isidorian collections of the 9th century, to make it obligatory to have recourse to the priest. Even in the middle of the 8th century, synods were tending in this direction, and the effort increased throughout the Middle Ages. However, Western churchmen did not envisage refusal of validity to marriages that were of simple consent, and they limited themselves to requiring publicity and to threatening with censure those who did not submit. It must be admitted that the decrees of the local synods and councils did not find complete acceptance among the faithful. Some bishops bitterly protested the inefficacy of the ecclesiastical censures, seeing the number of their people who had incurred excommunication as a result of them.

In addition to the dangers that accompany clandestine marriages with regard to the unity and the indissolubility of the bond, there is another which does not seem to have preoccupied men in the medieval Church but which would have been very grave in modern times. In medieval Christian society, even those who did not request the blessing of a priest or benefit from the proclamation of the faith that the rites called for from the spouses and their families were more or less impregnated with Christian doctrine by virtue of the social milieu and general liturgical practice of the age. On the contrary, in a world that does not have a vision of marriage derived from revelation and does not look favorably upon its requirements, the rites take on an irreplaceable importance. Created, as it were, spontaneously in antiquity, they provided this education which the exigency of changing one's life had reinforced among the catechumens. At a time when society seemed naturally Christian, there were other dangers which stirred pastors.

Conclusion

Responses to certain medieval and current questions have been omitted from this essay. The prayer of the Church has transmitted, in this area as in others, the *lex credendi*, but its message must not be interpreted with anachronistic presuppositions. Therefore we must guard ourselves against the temptation of using solutions of an earlier age to respond to today's pastoral problems.

Thus, for example, one would be greatly mistaken if one imagined that the medieval Latin Church, in organizing the exchange of consent, was usurping a role which belonged to the family or to civil society. A formal and public exchange had never been imposed for marriage; it was only for the betrothal. The marriage rituals have simply transformed the promises for the future (*sponsalia de futuro*) into promises for the present (*sponsalia de praesenti*) to obtain the expression of a consent which did not yet have juridical formulation.

Nor should conclusions be drawn from the statements made here about the custom in some churches of having a succession of several stages in the celebration of marriage. It is true that the ancients were not greatly preoccupied with determining the precise moment when an engagement was contracted and when a sacrament was realized, but they sought more or less quickly to dispel the confusion which might reign in the minds of the faithful between the solemnity of the betrothal – a formal but revocable engagement – and the silent but definitive commitment to marry. At no point in pastoral practice has it been imagined that one can have a marriage in two stages, the first being a true marriage but nonsacramental, and the second being a sacrament added on through the intervention of a priest. But have the theories of a few writers who have made the priest the minister of the sacrament ever gone beyond the "walls of the school" as have many other theological speculations?[72]

The dangers caused by clandestine marriages in the Middle Ages are perhaps less than those that the doctrine and spirituality of marriage encounter today in the secular world. It is there that the lesson of the liturgical history of marriage can without doubt be most valuable. The active, practical, and popular catechesis constituted by the rituals, when these rituals represent the fullness of the teaching in the actions and words man uses in his culture and life, is one of the surest means of bringing about the triumph of the Christian ideal.

ABBREVIATIONS

AA: *Apostolicam Actuositatem* Vatican II, "Decree on the Apostolate of the Laity"

AAS: *Acta Apostolicae Sedis*

Abbott: *Documents of Vatican II.* W. Abbott, S.J., ed. N.Y., 1966

AC: *L'Annee Canonique*

BJ: *Bible de Jerusalem* (43 vols. Paris: 1948–54; 1 vol ed. Paris 1956 rev. 1957–) in fasicles

BL: *Bibel Und Leben*

BT: *The Bible Translator*

BTB: *Biblical Theology Bulletin*

CC: *Casti connubii.* Dec 31, 1930

CIC: *Codex iuris canonici* Rome 1918

CICF: *Codicis iuris canonici fontes* 9 vols. P. Gasparri et al, ed. Rome, 1923–39

CICOF: Sacra Congregazione Orientale, *Codificazione orientale, fonti* (Rome, 1930–) in 3rd series, *Pontificia Commissio ad redigendum Codicem iuris canonici orientalis; Fontes*

Conc: *Concilium*

CorIC: *Corpus iuris canonica,* ed. E. Friedberg (Leipzig 1879–81)

CSEL: *Corpus Scriptorum Ecclesiae Latinae*

CT: *Concilium Tridentinum. Diariorum, actorum, epistularum tractatuum nova collectio,* ed. Görres-Gesellschaft, 13 v. (Freidburg i. Br, 1901–38).

DBS: *Dictionnaire de la Bible, Supplément* e. L. Pirot et al. (Paris 1928–)

DC: *La Documentation Catholique*

DS: H. Denzinger, *Enchiridion Symbolorum,* ed. A. Schönmetzer (32nd ed. Freiburg 1963).

DSp: *Dictionnaire de spiritualitè ascetique et mystique. Doctrine et histoire,* ed. M. Viller et al. (Paris 1932–)

DTC: *Dictionnaire de théologie catholique,* ed. A Vacant et al. (Paris, 1903–50)

EE: F. Heinrich and V. Eid, ed. *Ehe und Ehescheidung* (Munich, 1972)

Ehe: K. Reinhardt and H. Jedin (eds.) *Ehe, Sakrament der Kirche des Herrn* Berlin, 1971

ETL: *Ephemerides theologicae Lovanienses*

EV: *Esprit et Vie*

FIC: *Fontes Juris Canonici*

GS: *Gaudium et Spes*, Vatican II "Pastoral Constitution on The Church in the Modern World"

IJC: M. Conte a Coronata, *Institutiones Juris Canonici: De Sacramentis tractatus canonicus* (2nd ed. Turin, 1951)

IKZ: *Internationale Katholische Zeitschrift* (1972)

ITC: International Theological Commission

ITZ: *Internationale Theologische Zeitschrift*

JB: *Jerusalem Bible*

LG: *Lumen Gentium* Vatican II, "Dogmatic Constitution on the Church"

LTK: *Lexikon für Theologie und Kirche*, ed. J. Hofer and K. Rahner, 10 v.(2nd. new ed. Freiburg 1957–65)

LV: *Lumière et Vie* (Bruges, Belgium 1951–)

MD: *La Maison–Dieu*

MGH: *Monumenta Germaniae Historica* (Berlin, 1826–)

MGHE: *Monumenta Germaniae Historica Epistolae*

NRT: *Nouvelle Revue Théologique*

NT: *Novum Testamentum*

NTS: *New Testament Studies*

O: *Origins*

OCM: *Ordo Celebrandi Matrimonium*

OCMP: *Ordo Celebrandi Matrimonium, Praenotanda*

OCP: *Orientalia Christiana periodica*

OR: *L'Osservatore Romano*

PG: *Patrilogia Graeca* ed. J. P. Migne 161 v. (Paris, 1857–66).

PL: *Patrologia Latina* ed. J. P. Migne 217 v. (Paris, 1878–90).

PMCL: *Periodica de re morali, canonica liturgica*

RDC: *Revue de droit canonique*

RSR: *Recherches de science religieuse*

RTL: *Revue théologique de Louvain*

SC: *Sacrosanctum Concilium* Vatican II, "Constitution on the Sacred Liturgy"

SCDF: Sacred Congregation for the Defense of the Faith

SE: *Sciences ecclésiastiques*

SM: *Sacramentum Mundi* (1969)

ST: *Summa Theologiae*, St. Thomas Aquinas

TE: H. Greven, ed. *Theologie der Ehe* (Augsburg, 1972)

TS: *Theological Studies*
TTZ: *Trierer Theologische Zeitschrift*
TWNT: Kittel et al. *Theologisches Wörterbuch zum Neuen Testament*
TZ: *Theologische Zeitschrift*
VC: *Verbum Caro*
VOCTH: *Vera Oecumenici Concilii Tridentini historia*
ZNW: *Zeitschrift für neutestamentliche Wissenschaft*

NOTES

1. INTRODUCTION AND COMMENTARY

1. For the translation of the Propositions into French, we are indebted to the collaboration between Fr. Renard, S. J., and the Secretary of the ITC. The Latin text appeared in *Gregorianum* for 1978, fascicle 3. The subtitles for each of the propositions have been supplied by the General Secretariat.

2. We need to distinguish carefully three texts for which we are indebted to the zeal and expertise of Prof. W. Ernst. In March 1977 he produced a long working paper, a French translation of which appears in EV 88 (1978): 2–10; 17–28; 69–79, and which has been republished separately by the *Cahiers du Livre* under the original title, "Le mariage comme institution et sa mise en cause actuelle." Ernst then produced a text entitled "Institution et mariage," which was presented to the ITC as a "report" and was intended as an introduction to the discussion to be held in December 1977. This much shorter piece presupposes the working paper, but goes further when it comes to examining contemporary objections. Finally, in a third document, Ernst gives an extensive commentary on the first set of propositions (1.1–1.10). The second and third of these texts are to be published soon in a volume being prepared by the ITC under the title, *Problèmes doctrinaux du mariage chrétien.*

3. Three studies turned out to be particularly valuable in terms of this inquiry, especially with regard to the history of institutions: A.G. Martimort, "Contribution de l'histoire liturgique à la théologie du mariage," EV 88 (1978), 129–37 [see c.10 below – Trans.]; H. Schürmann, "Neutestamentliche Marginalien zur Frage nach der Institutionalität, Unauflösbarkeit und Sakramentalität der Ehe," *Studia Moralia* (October 1978); V. Mulago, "Mariage traditionnel Africain et mariage chrétien," soon to appear in *Revue de Théologie Africaine*, published by the Theological Faculty of Kinshasa (Zaïre).

4. Fr. H. de Lubac, who for years has been studying the question of nature and grace, has recently published a synthesis and a clarification under the title, "Petite catechèse sur la 'nature' et la 'grâce,' " in *Communio* [French edition] 2 (1977), 11–23. De Lubac shows, among other things, that the distinction between nature and grace is by no means superseded. It is essential to Christianity (p. 11). Cf. also, Ph. Delhaye, "Note conjointe sur la nature et la grâce à propos du texte du Professeur Caffarra," EV 27 (1978); 412–16 [See below, c.9. – Trans.]

5. To save time, we may refer to the bibliography in the latest theological encyclopedia, *Dizionario teologico interdisciplinare*, 2:517 ff.

6. J. Feiner and L. Vischer, *Nouveau livre de la foi: La foi commune des chrétiens* (Paris, 1976), 564; German original: *Neues Glaubensbuch* (13th ed.; Freiburg, 1973), 590; ET: *The Common Cathechism* (New York, 1975), 601.

7. J. Feiner and L. Vischer, *Nouveau livre*, 565; ET, 591. The learned study by J. Paquier in DTC 9:1274–83, has lost none of its value.

8. The paper by K. Lehmann is entitled, "La sacramentalité du mariage chrétien. Le lien entre le baptême et le mariage." A French translation will appear in the volume mentioned in note 2 above [See c.3 below–Trans.]

9. The very precise category of efficient causality as Aristotle understood it was first applied to sacrament between the years 1140 and 1150. See D. Van den Eyende, *Les définitions des sacrements pendant la première période de la théologie scholastique* (Rome, 1950). Earlier, the terminology was less precise, but the word *virtus* was used instead of *causa*. In the *Sentences*, Book 4, Distinction 1, No. 2, Peter Lombard (died 1159) offers the following definition: "We speak properly of sacrament when we mean something which is such a sign of God's grace and such an invisible form of grace that it carries the image of that grace and is the cause of it. Hence, sacraments are instituted not only to signify sanctification, but also for the sake of bringing it about."

10. St. Isidore of Seville writes in his *Etymologiae*, 6, 19, nos. 40–42 (PL 82, 255): "They are called sacraments because, under the cover of things temporal, God's power (*virtus*) more secretly works the salvation of those same sacraments (*eorundem sacramentorum*). Hence they are called sacraments both because of the secret power operative in them, and because they are sacred. This is why in Greek a sacrament is called a mystery. It has a secret and hidden power."

11. The notion "power of the sacrament" (*virtus sacramenti*) occurs in many of the Church Fathers. St. Cyril of Jerusalem says that while in baptism the water washes the body, the power of the Holy Spirit purifies the soul independently of the worthiness of the one who administers the sacrament. See *Catechesis*, 3, 4. Augustine insists against the Donatists that the sacred sign is an objective means of grace, independent of the worthiness of the minister. Against the Pelagians he maintains that, at times, the efficacy of the sacrament is not even dependent on the personal consent of the recipient, as when infants are baptized. See *Letter* 98, 9; *In Johannem*, 26, 11; *Enarrationes in Ps.* 77, 2; *In Epistolam Johannis*, 6, 10.

12. When Hugh of St. Victor, for example, deals with the question of the "marriage of unbelievers" in *De Sacramentis*, 2, 11, 13, he only thinks of infidels, Jews, and pagans. When we use the term *unbeliever* in connection with marriage, we think rather of baptized persons who have no faith, or have it no longer.

13. The complete report of Prof. Caffarra will appear in the volume already mentioned in note 2 above. Large excerpts are to found in "Le lien entre mariage-realité de la création et mariage-sacrement," EV 88 (1978), pp. 353-64; 369-84. [See c.4 below–Trans.]

14. See ITC "Seize thèses de christologie sur le sacrement de mariage,"DC (1978) 571–75. This text, prepared by Fr. Martelet, has been approved in general by the absolute majority of the members of the ITC. [See c.8 below–Trans.]

15. See Ph. Delhaye, "Note conjointe sur la nature et la grâce à propos du texte du Professeur Caffarra," EV 88 (1978) 412–16. [See c.9 below–Trans.]
16. In the past few months we have all heard, specifically in relation to marriage, remarks such as, "Marriage is a worldly affair," or, "GS 36, has proclaimed that earthly realities are autonomous." Anyone who would take the trouble to read this text in its entirety will notice that the reference there is to scientific disciplines and political institutions. Twice, "moral norms" are explicitly excluded. Not a word there about marriage, which is later examined from a Christian and personalist perspective (see GS, 47–52). Are we going to say that, a few pages apart, the Council has contradicted itself?
17. The pure nature theory amounts to saying that God could have created intelligent and free persons without summoning them to friendship with himself, to filial adoption, to divinization. In the eyes of its advocates, this working hypothesis has merits because it allows them to better explain the absolute gratuitousness of adoption. God would have not contradicted himself by not extending his love for human beings to the point of divinizing them. In addition, these theologians entertain the illusion that, as we explore this human being in the state of pure nature, we discover man as described by philosophers and jurists who allow for no original sin and for no redemption, two elements which are of the essence in the history of salvation. Worst of all, after have posited pure nature as an hypothesis, these theologians reason as if it actually existed and as if not all persons were called to supernatural divinization. In their opinion, the pagans, the savages, both good and bad, who still are to found in the colonies, exist in the state of pure nature, and not in the state of sinful nature, or of nature summoned to divinization.
18. The ITC is very grateful to Msgr. Denis, Honorary Dean of the Faculty of Canon Law in Paris, for his help in this connection. Msgr. Denis has also presented his views in *Etudes de droit et d'histoire*: Mélanges Msgr. H. Wagnon (Lovain-la-Neuve, 1976), 479-96.
19. Sociologically, a Catholic church wedding commands such prestige that pagans (unbaptized Japanese, for example) try to take advantage of it during their honeymoons abroad. Msgr. M. Coppenrath, Archbishop of Papeete, "L'Eglise, témoin du mariage de non-chrétiens," in *Année canonique* 22 (1978): Homage to His Excellency Msgr. Ch. Lefebvre 25–32.
20. Fr. Hamel will soon publish a complete and precise commentary on these propositions, as well as the "report," in the volume mentioned in note 2 above. [See c.5 below–Trans.]
21. I am alluding to a procedure once used in many textbooks, a procedure whose legitimacy I do not intend to endorse. When writing the history of a doctrine, one would run into an empty period. At this point it was customary to say that this doctrine was so well known and accepted that people would not speak of it. Of this argument from silence I keep only this fact: when a doctrine is resisted and controverted, the arguments for it grow more plentiful than they are during times when the doctrine is taken for granted and admitted by everyone.

22. See the learned and serious study of Fr. Wenger in *Vatican II: chronique de la quatrième session*, 6, 200–246. The Patriarchal Vicar for Egypt and Sudan took the position that the economy as practiced in the Oriental Churches not in communion with Rome should be extended. The spouse who has been deserted should be allowed to contract a second marriage which would not be sacramental yet would be recognized by the ecclesiastical authority.

23. The expressions *catholic truth* and *catholic doctrines* are used interchangeable, as noted by J. Beumer, in "Katholische Wahrheiten," LTK 6 (1961): 88. The exegesis of this technical term is to be found in A. Michel, "Verité," DTC 15 (1950), 2681. See the valuable observations of L. Ott, *Fundamentals of Catholic Dogma* (6th ed.; St. Louis, MO, 1964), 8: "Corresponding to the purpose of the teaching authority of the Church of preserving unfalsified and of infallibly interpreting the truths of revelation (D 1800) the primary object (*obiectum primarium*) of the teaching office of the Church is the body of immediately revealed truths and facts. The infallible doctrinal power of the Church extends, however, secondarily to all those truths and facts which are a consequence of the teaching of revelation or a presupposition of it (*objectum secundarium*). Those doctrines and truths defined by the Church not as immediately revealed but as intrinsically connected with the truths of revelation so that their denial would undermine the revealed truths are called *catholic truths* (*veritates catholicae*) or ecclesiastical teachings (*doctrinae ecclesiasticae*) to distinguish them from the *divine truths* or divine doctrines of revelation (*veritates vel doctrinae divinae*). These are proposed for belief in virtue of the infallibility of the Church in teaching doctrines of faith or morals (*fides ecclesiastica*)."

24. His Excellency Mgr. Ch. Lefebvre, Dean of the Rota, has been kind enough to assist the ITC in the exploration of this question. He has prepared a very valuable document which will soon be published in a canonical journal. We want to express here our respectful gratitude.

25. God's love is never "self-seeking" (1 Cor 13:5). There also comes to mind this scholastic description of love: [to love is] to take pleasure in the good of the other (*delectari in bono alterius*).

26. This is certainly the import of note 1 in GS.

27. E. Gagnon, "Problems pastoraux relatifs aux catholiques divorcés et civilement remariés," EV 88 (1978): 241–45. [See below c.6 – Trans.]

28. Specific directives to be found in the Pope's allocution and in the article of Bishop Gagnon. Experience of another sort has evoked a rectification by Msgr. Le Bourgeois which some seem to ignore. See DC n.1723 (July 3, 1977): 645–47.

2. MARRIAGE AS INSTITUTION

1. GS 47–52, and the whole body of literature pertinent to this text and relative to marriage.

2. The definition of G. Hasenhüttl: "An institution is the result of a social functioning of roles aimed at the attainment of an objective. It is durable, conventional, and open to change. It is binding upon the individual person, and connotes a formal authority and juridical sanctions." This definition is quoted by J. H. Fichter, *Grundbegriffe der Soziologie* (Vienna 1970), p. 115.

3. "Hence, no society agrees to regard sexuality and eros as an exclusively private affair, entirely subject to the discretion of individual persons. By their very nature, sexuality and eros are subject to social regulation." Thus Cardinal Ratzinger, in H. Greven (ed.) TE (Augsburg, 1972), p. 106.

4. Cf. H. Schelsky, *Soziologie der Sexualität* (Hamburg, 1955), p. 27: " The sexual instinct is certainly not capable of insuring anything beyond occasional encounters of the sexes. Therefore, it cannot be regarded as the decisive factor *par excellence* in the constitution of marriage, which has been the case only too often. This is all the more so in view of the fact that the sexual instinct does not provide for the permanency of the social bond which is the essence of marriage."

5. W. Molinski, "Marriage," SM 3 (1969), 390: "The factors which determine the concrete structures of marriage can never be sought merely in terms of sex-life and sexual hygiene, or merely in terms of the relationship between man and woman. They are above all the needs of the family and society, that is, the demands of education, economics, property, social security, public morals and the like; because in the long run general social conditions are decisively affected by married life and family life."

6. This definition comes from F. X. Kaufmann, as quoted by F. Böckle, *Das Naturrecht im Disput* (1966), 41. By no means does the definition imply the evolutionistic position, which the author has already refuted, and which postulates an evolution from promiscuity to monogamic marriage through such intermediate stages as group unions and polygamy. The definition merely aims at establishing the fundamental elements of marriage. Cf. C. Duquoc: "In fact, marriage is a constitutive element of society, insofar as it is a rigorously defined and stable institution, regulated by laws, and one which cannot have been invented either by man or by woman." See J. David and F. Schmalz, *Wie unauflöslich ist die Ehe*? (1969), 2.

7. P. Adnès, *Le mariage* (Tournai, 1963), 115: " The community, or the stable union of man and woman referred to as marriage, is a natural institution." Adnès adds that this definition emerges from a "purely natural reflection" according to which "an institution is called natural when it is necessary for the good of human nature, and we incline to it because of the spontaneous drive of our nature."

8. There is no need to present here the interpretations of contemporary exegetes. We need rather describe the way in which marriage has in fact

evolved in history. But cf. at least P. Grelot, *Le couple humain dans l'Ecriture* ("Foi Vivante," 118; Paris, 1969), ET: *Man and Wife in Scripture* (New York: Herder and Herder, 1964 [translation of the first edition]); "The Institution of Marriage: Its Evolution in the Old Testament," *Concilium* 55 (1970), 39–50.

9. Adnès, *Le mariage*, 117, note 1.

10. R. Pesch, "Die neutestamentliche Weisung für die Ehe," in N. Weil, *et al.*, *Zum Thema Ehescheidung* (Stuttgart, 1970), 28: "The Genesis narratives are easily subjected to a naturalistic interpretation, as we notice even today, and yet they are not at all so constructed as to allow such interpretation."

11. In this connection, we may note that exegetes entertained different views concerning the interpretation of this complex. However, there seems to be a consensus that, when godlikeness is affirmed, this affirmation is functional in nature. This is to say, the intention is to show to what extent godlikeness is bestowed upon humans.

12. Cf. H. Riesling, *Ethik des Leibes* (Hamburg, 1965) 12: " . . . procreation itself is not endowed with any sacrality. It pertains to what is given to human beings together with the power to rule the earth. In order that they may be able to exercise this dominion, God grants them fecundity." The same in P. Grelot: "All mythic and cultic sacralization is excluded. It is the creative word of God that grounds the value of sexual love" (323; cf. ET, 28–39).

13. Cardinal J. Ratzinger, TE 84.

14. J. Gnilka, *Der EphEserbrief* (Freiburg i. Br., 1971), 288: "In a theology systematically oriented it is customary and right to appeal to our text to lend a systematic structure to the notion of marriage, and to enhance its sacramentality. In the eyes of history and theology, the discussion which has unfolded around Eph 5:32 is burdened by the fact that, in most cases, the discussion hinged on the text of the Vulgate, and on the concept of *sacramentum* which that text suggests . . . However, the mystery in question in the text is not marriage, but . . . the union between Christ and the Church. In consequence, from a purely exegetical point of view, the evidential value of that text is inadequate."

15. R. Schnackenburg writes: "This is why it is not arbitrary to characterize his moral message as a *prophetic summons*. In the eyes of the post-resurrection community, and of all those who beleived in Christ, his word was endowed with a new and definitive authority. The expression *ethical model* says much too little. *Precept aimed at the achievement of a goal* is a problematic expression, since the prohibition of divorce is not simply irrealizable . . ." "But his answers transcend particular cases, and cases bound up with particular situations. They take on the quality of solutions based on principle, and of a directive." Cf. R. Schnackenburg, "Die Ehe nach der Weisung Jesu," in F. Heinrich and V. Eid (eds.), EE (Munich, 1972), 22.

16. R. Schnackenburg writes: "When it comes to problems of historical-philological exegesis, we tend to agree more and more. But when we move to the theological implications and, therefore, to the application of texts to our present situation, we tend to diverge from one another, even as exegetes." Cf. R. Schnackenburg, "Die Ehe nach dem Neuen Testement," in H. Greven (ed.), TE (Augsburg, 1972), 10.

17. P. Hoffmann holds the view that this addition does not in the least detract from the original assertion, for "to the Jews divorce and remarriage go together." See "Jesus' Saying about Divorce and Its Interpretation in the New Testament Tradition," *Concilium* 55 (1970), 51–66; quotation, 52, note 3.

18. According to P. Hoffmann, Luke teaches that the will of God is already disregarded in the separation, even before the official divorce and remarriage. According to F. J. Schierse, Christians separated and remarried were probably excluded from the community.

19. P. Hoffmann writes: "But the principle of the revocation of marital obligations is so strongly formulated that the Christian partner may well in fact be free to enter a second marriage if he wants to." See *Concilium* 55 (1970), 63.

20. R. Schnackenburg holds the view (TE p. 30) that the primitive Church "cannot impose on her members the indissolubility and monogamy of marriage without allowing concessions. Under the pressure of circumstances and situations, the Church was induced to adopt an interpretation which seems to have allowed certain deviations from the absolute interdiction of divorce." F. Böckle admits that in Paul we find a "differentiated juridical expression" of Jesus' ethical demand, and that the synoptics transferred this demand "into the domain of law." He adds: "It is certain that Jesus' demand, so unambiguously grounded, and so unconditional, occasioned very early discussions in the community concerning its practical consequences. For this very reason an effort was made to formulate juridical and casuistic rules. As a result, Jesus' demand soon came to be interpreted as a law, and yet it was still obviously possible to distinguish the rejection of divorce on the basis of the demand which faith makes from the juridical and pastoral application. . . . See *Das Naturrecht im Disput*, p. 61.

21. Cardinal Ratzinger, TE 94–97, notes that in St. Augustine sexuality is endowed with a moral quality "on the strength of a personal-social context," and that marriage is assigned a theological significance, as a remedy for concupiscence.

22. Cf. Cardinal Ratzinger TE 98. However, we must grant that theologians regarded certain presuppositions as clearly established, as for example the presupposition that sexual intercourse is exclusively oriented toward marriage. This is why the sexual act in itself was not what they were concerned about, but the moral liceity of the act within marriage. From an anthropological point of view, the naturalistic outlook of this ethics of the

sexual act would be unacceptable if man's nature were to be reduced there to only one dimension, and were for this very reason misconstrued.

23. Cf. Pope Leo XIII, *Arcanum divinae,* ASS 12 (1879) 392: "Since marriage is a divine institution, and, in a certain sense, was since the beginning a prefiguration of the Incarnation of Christ, a religious quality is ingredient in it, a quality which is not adventitious, but inborn, not bestowed upon it by human beings, but built-in." See also K. Lehman, "Zur Sakramentalität der Ehe," in F. Heinrich and V. Eid, (eds.), EE, 65.

24. On this point, see L. Otto, *Fundamentals of Catholic Dogma,* or like works.

25. Cardinal Ratzinger, TE 82.

26. However, let us mention: the reticence in the presence of mixed marriages until the matter was first discussed in the 4th century; the refusal to allow for divorce which is the case in civil legislation; the legislation relative to consecrated celibacy.

27. Cf. A. Dordett, "Grundsätze einer Reform des kirchlichen Eherechts," in 78: "It is only during the period between the tenth and the twelfth centuries that there occurs a development in the excercise of the Church's authority with regard to marriage, while the laws of the state and canonical laws exist side by side. Within this context, the juridical competence of the Church took shape, a competence whose beginnings can be noted as early as the ninth century."

28. DS 1803; 1804; 1812; and Pius VI, DS 2659.

29. DS 2968; 2969; 2970; 2974; CIC, 1960.

30. DS 2598; CIC, 1960.

31. It is important to perceive the precise import of this last argument. To invoke the practice of the Church can hardly be enough to prove the Church's exclusive competence, since at the beginning there was, in fact, no juridical legislation on marriage proper to the Church and since during the first millenium the Church did not claim exclusive competence. This competence did expand in the course of the centuries, and yet, as shown above, not even the Council of Trent taught the exclusiveness of that competence. The claim to exclusive competence took shape rather during the modern era, in connection with the disputes between Church and State.

32. See the evolution of the Pauline Privilege (1 Cor 7). It was extended by Paul III (1537), Pius V (1571), and Gregory XIII (1585) and issued in the legislation of 1924. According to this legislation, a marriage is dissolved by pontifical dispensation if at the time in which it was contracted one of the spouses was a Christian and the other was not. After 1945 this norm was extended in practice to cover marriages contracted with the dispensation from the impediment of "disparity of cult."

33. The revision of the code allows for a first new stipulation. We cannot mention here the particulars of this change.

34. Cf. CIC canon 1081, par. 2.

35. CIC, canon 1086, par. 2.

36. Cf. in this connection an opinion of the Apostolic Signature recently published under the title, "Conjugal love and matrimonial consent," *L'Osservatore Romano*, June 28, 1977, p. 9.

37. Canonists tend to prefer the term *contract* which made its way into the schools in the twelfth century, even though Roman law, which was then adopted, had not used the term in relation to marriage. Vatican II has not taken up this term. In GS, 47-48, we find the terms *partnership, community* and *institution* applied to marriage already contracted and the terms *covenant* and *consent* applied to marriage being contracted.

38. N. van der Wal, "Secular Law and the Eastern Church's Concept of Marriage," *Concilium* 55 (1970), 76.

39. According to the historical information now available, Hincmar of Reims was the first to dissolve a marriage contracted but not consummated.

40. The Council of Trent recognizes the validity of clandestine marriages contracted until that time, but makes the validity of clandestine marriages to be contracted contingent on a new condition: the canonical form and the exchange of consent in the presence of the local pastor. The extraordinary form allows for marriage to be contracted in the presence of two witnesses if a competent priest is not to be found within a month's time.

41. Cf., for example, canon 1014, according to which, in cases in doubt, the presumption of the law favors the validity of the marriage. From this various kinds of difficulties arise.

42. DS 1816.

43. CIC, canons 1094–1109.

44. P. Gradauer, *Das Kirchenrecht im Dienste der Seelsorge*, p. 63.

45. A controversy has developed in Germany between Professors Kasper and Schmaus. The problem involved is reducible to the following questions: Does the essence of sacramental marriage necessarily require an ecclesial form? Could the Church regard herself as adequately represented by the spouses themselves in virtue of the priesthood in which they share at the moment when they contract a civil marriage?

46. Here we can present only in global and abridged fashion various particular factors. Note also that, under different cultural circumstances and conditions, a different development would occur.

47. Cf. G. Scherer, TE p. 223: "Terms such as *personal love, sexual partnership, unity between sexuality and love* manifest an understanding which differs from the understanding embodied in the old theory of marriage, which had a dualistic basis, and insisted mainly on right and institution, and was grounded more on the biological ends of marriage than on love."

48. The criticism expressed with regard to the traditional understanding of marriage, namely, that it absolutizes the institution, appears in almost all the writings concerned with today's understanding of marriage. Cf. Ch. Duquoc, G. Scherer, J. Ratzinger, J. R. Hertlet, J. David-F. Schmalz. And yet none of these authors excludes the institution in principle, and this is decisive. They all attempt to work out a correct balance between personal and institutional factors.

49. This is certainly the reason why Mounier does not speak only of a "personalist revolution" but also of a revolution which is "personalist"and "effects community." The person does not exist apart from the community.

50. K. Lehmann correctly emphasizes the following: "It would likewise be a mistake to take into account the personal factors in a merely dynamic fashion, that is, only at the moment in which they actually operate. In order to realize itself, a fully developed personality needs factors which are properly institutional and even juridical in nature." "This law, grounded as it is on a personal foundation, which supplies an institutional element as guarantee of personal freedom . . . is perhaps law in the purest of forms." See "Zur Sakramentalität der Ehe," 53.

51. Ratzinger, EE 108, expresses a similar view: "Personal love cannot by itself provide the foundation of marriage, nor the required regulations. It can do this only if it be accountable to the community, and insofar as it is regulated by law. Now law is law only when it appears as a positive reality, in keeping with the very notion of law, which entails transcendence."

52. Lehmann, *op.cit.*, 63.

53. GS 48.

54. GS 48.

55. GS 48.

56. GS 50.

57. See, among others, K. Rahner, "Marriage as Sacrament," *Theological Investigations* 10 (1977) 199–221; W. Kasper, "Die Verwirklichung der Kirche in Ehe und Familie," *op. cit.*, 81–115; K. Reinhardt and H. Jedin, *Ehe: Sakrament in der Kirche des Herrn* (Berlin, 1971), 7–59: K. Lehmann, "Zur Sakramentalität der Ehe," *op. cit.*, 51–71.

58. L. Scheffczyk, "Eucharistie und Ehesakrament," *Münchener Theologische Zeitschrift* 27 (1976) 351–375, refers both to the declaration of the Synod of German Bishops and to this notion of sacrament when he submits the following critical remarks on p. 361: "When it comes to establishing the sacramentality of marriage, it is not enough to say that 'it is rooted in the fundamental sacrament which the Church is' by reason of which 'God's indefectible fidelity is promised' to the spouses. Nor is it enough, when it comes to establishing the sacramental character of marriage, to point out the fact that in the sacrament of marriage the life and action of the Church converge."

59. Lehmann, *op. cit.*, 57–59, takes as point of departure the "consent" which involves "the unconditioned acceptance of the other," an acceptance which is subscribed to for its own sake, and to which fidelity lends the capacity to endure. "But as acceptance perseveres through time in permanent fashion, it lends to the person whose fidelity sustains the acceptance the feeling of being sheltered by something which is not vulnerable to the passing of time. This does not mean, as a widely spread misunderstanding has it, that this acceptance is something stationary, something dead and static."

60. Kasper, *op. cit.*, 344.

61. GS, 48.

62. Kasper, *op. cit.*, 344.

63. Lehman, *op. cit.*, 65, stresses that marriage as sacrament is not the only form of marriage within which the requirement of unconditional fidelity, which comes to the fore in the Christian conception of marriage, can be met. For, "there is no validity to the simplistic distinction which opposes sacramental marriage to an entirely profane form . . . . Christian marriage is not an event of grace only when it becomes a sacrament. A pagan who lives a nonsacramental marriage can experience grace . . ."

64. Obviously, the question always remains whether this grace is or is not accepted. But that this grace *is offered* by God is not doubted here. This explains the distinction between valid reception and fruitful reception of the sacrament.

65. Kasper, *op. cit.*, 348.

66. Lehmann, *op. cit.*, 64.

67. Thus Kasper (249): "We are dealing here with positive ecclesiastical norms, which must be assessed in terms of their particular character, and not in terms of theological inevitability. The promise of fidelity which the spouses make to each other is a reality which has meaning in itself, and not only by virtue of a positive stipulation on the part of the Church. When this sign is posited within the faith in Christ, the Church may not arbitrarily refuse to grant to it a sacramental character." According to Lehmann, when it comes to public commitment, "it is not of primary importance whether the public character of it be non-religious or ecclesiastical in nature" (64).

68. Ratzinger, *op. cit.*, 106.

69. *Ibid.*, 107.

70. Cf. G. Klaus and M. Buhr, *Philosophisches Wörterbuch* (10th ed.; Leipzig, 1974), 403.

71. *Kultur-politiches Wörterbuch* (Berlin, 1970), 142.

72. *Philosophisches Wörterbuch*, 403.

73. Here the point of departure is the notion that ethics and law must be

subservient to economic and social interests in various interplays of circumstances. They must, in consequence, be susceptible to change.

74. G. Schmabl, *Mann und Frau intim* (Berlin, 1971), 320.

75. The advocates of this conception form the so-called "Frankfurt School." Their theories are grounded on research in the fields of ethnology, ethology, sociology, and depth-psychology. These inquiries are not worthless, and yet behind them lies, in the background as it were, the Marxist-Leninist theory of sexuality, with various nuances and qualifications. Judged by the standards of orthodox Marxism-Leninism, these variations would be branded as revisionist.

76. G. N. Groeger, "Vorformen der Ehe," *Ehe* 7 (1970), 24, maintains that in places where the sexual act is excluded in principle "we meet with the domination of a morality bereft of anthropological sophistication." Groeger remarks that in modern sex education, including that given within the Church, we always hear about the need for structuring sexual energies. "But can young people effect a structuring of these energies and achieve a responsible behavior if, after acknowledging that need, we forbid them to try and practice anything, or to experiment with anything in this whole area of premarital sex? We cannot have it both ways: we cannot, on the one hand, advocate the structuring of sexuality, and, on the other, interdict sex altogether."

77. This conception is advocated not only by the young. More and more frequently we see it advocated by psychologists and educators, even among Christians. Cf., for example, E. Ell, *Dynamisches sexual Moral* (Zürich, 1972), 134: "But the young are able to live *that* form of sexuality which matches their degree of development, namely, masturbation, necking and petting, contraceptive sex. If they behave like this, it means that we should regard them as 'morally mature' that is, as mature as the degree of their development calls them to be." Same view in G. N. Groeger, *op. cit.*, 28.

78. GS 48 ff.

79. Gerhartz, *op. cit.*, pp. 89–91.

80. Lehmann, *op. cit.*, p. 71, notes, with regard to personal and sacramental elements in marriage, that " the matter of fact adoption of the notion that a marriage is shipwrecked–and even irreparably shipwrecked–amounts to positing a problematic category. From a Christian viewpoint, this category of the shipwrecked marriage implies that the capacity for forgiveness is lost." Lehmann cautions, however, against having recourse indiscriminately to the capacity to forgive, and warns against the danger of "solidifying situations which, humanly speaking, have become hopeless."

81. According to Scheffczyk, *op. cit.*, 364, a theory which maintains that personal love can die out ignores the specific character of conjugal love,

which possesses an ontological quality and dignity different from those proper to sensual inclination and psychological affinity.

82. Cf. Schüller: "It seems to me, in the end, that theology does not command the resources needed to explain why the institutional consequence of a marriage which has failed differs according as the marriage is a consummated sacramental marriage or not. Theology can only say that God has not extended the privilege of dissolubility to a sacramental and consummated marriage as such."

83. Concerning the historical development, cf. the first section of this paper. For the whole, see P. Huizing, who shortly before the Council pointed out that opposing the community of love to the community of law, as is so often done, involves a misunderstanding. Nor should we forget the learned and lucid article "Mariage" in the DTC.

84. However, the revision of the Code of Canon Law does not seem to have made changes in this direction. See Gerhartz, *op. cit.*, 95: "Since the mission of the Church with regard to marriage consists in the proclamation of what is truly Christian, the ecclesial regulation of marriage could in the future limit itself to what is typically Christian."

85. See SCDF, *Declaration on Certain Questions Concerning Sexual Ethics*, December 29, 1975 (Washington, D. C.: United States Catholic Conference, 1976), No. 7, 7–8.

86. Thus, H. Crouzel, *L'Eglise primitive face au divorce: Du premier au cinquième siècle* (Paris, 1971) 382 ff. By the same, "Divorce et remariage dans l'Eglise primitive: Quelques réflexions de méthodologie historique," NRT 98 (1976), 891–917.

87. Charles E. Curran, *Ongoing Revision: Studies in Moral Theology* (Notre Dame, IN, 1975) 75: "I argue that a change in the pastoral practice really involves and should lead to a change in the teaching on the absolute indissolubility of marriage."

88. R. Gall, *Fragwürdige Unaflöslichkeit*, (Zürich & Würzburg, 1970) p. 222.

89. Curran notes in this connection with a touch of sarcasm: "The Church has so interpreted the teaching of Jesus throughout the years that now less than twenty percent of the marriages in the world are absolutely indissoluble" (*op. cit.*, 89).

3. SACRAMENTALITY

1. See the bibliography in "Christliche Ehe und getrennte Kirchen," *Okumenische Beihefte zur Freiburger Zeitschrift für Philosophie und Theologie* 1 (Fribourg [Switzerland], 1969), 95–124; E. Christen, "Ehe als Sakrament: Nuen Gesichtspunkte aus Exegese und Dogmatik," *Theologische Berichte* 1 (Zürich, 1972), 11–58.

2. See the recent commentaries of J. Ernst, J. Gnilka, and H. Schlier.

3. See J. Gnilka, *Der Epheserbrief,* Herders theologischer Kommentar zum Neuen Testament, 10/2 (Freiburg i. Br., 1971), 286 ff.

4. G. Bornkamm, "Μυστήριον, " TWNT 4 (1942) 825 ff.; 829 ff.; ET: *Theological Dictionary of the New Testament* 4 (1967) 819 ff.; 822 ff.

5. J. Gnilka, *Der Epheserbrief,* 289.

6. *Schriften zur Theologie,* 8 (Einsiedeln, 1967), 539; ET: *Theological Investigations,* 10 (New York, 1977), 220. See also, *Grundkurs des Glaubens* (Freiburg, 1976) 404 ff.

7. *Die Mysterien des Christentums* (Freiburg i. Br., 1941), 497; ET: *The Mysteries of Christianity* (St. Louis, 1946), 561.

8. On this point, see K. Rahner, *Schriften zur Theologie,* 8: 539; ET: *Theological Investigations,* 10: 220.

9. K. Reinhardt, "Sakramentalität und Unauflöslichkeit der Ehe in dogmatischer Sicht," in K. Reinhardt and H. Jedin (eds.), *Ehe, Sakrament der Kirche des Herrn* (Berlin, 1971) 7–59; quotation, 25.

10. LTK 3 (2nd ed.; 1959) 680–84; quotation, 681. For more details see H. Vold, *Das Sakrament der Ehe* (2nd ed.; Münster, 1956).

11. See also W. Kasper, *Zur Theologie der christlichen Ehe* (Mainz, 1977), 44 ff.

12. See M. J. Scheeben, *Die Mysterien des Christentums,* 496; ET: *The Mysteries of Christianity,* 560.

13. LTK 3 (2nd ed.; 1959) 683.

14. For further development, see K. Lehmann, "Zur Sakramentalität der Ehe," in F. Heinrich and V. Eid (eds.), EE (Munich, 1972) 57–72; esp. 57–65; *Gemeinsame Synode der Bistümer Bundesrepublik Deutschland: Offizielle Gesamtausgabe* I: *Synodenbeschlüsse* (Freiburg, 1976) 425–30.

15. *Der Brief an die Epheser* (4th ed.; Düsseldorf, 1963) 234.

16. Rahner, *Schriften zur Theologie,* 8: 535; ET: *Theological Investigations,* 10: 215. See also, *Kirche und Sakramente* (Freiburg, 1961); and the well-known publications of O. Semmelroth, E. Schillebeeckx, L. Boff, and others.

17. Rahner, *Schriften zur Theologie,* 8: 531; ET: *Theological Investigations,* 19: 211.

18. It is strange how this point has been sadly neglected in traditional theology; see P. Adnès, *Le mariage* (Tournai, 1963).

19. In the same sense, see K. Reinhardt, *loc. cit.,* 36 ff.

20. In this same volume, see the study of C. Caffarra. Also, E. Corecco, "Die Lehre der Untrennbarket des Ehevertrags vom Sakrament im Lichte des scholastischen Prinzips 'Gratia perficit naturam.' " *Archiv für katholischen Kirchenrechts* 143 (1974): 379–442.

21. See for example, J. M. Aubert, "Foi et sacrememt dans le mariage: A propos du mariage de 'baptizés incroyants'," MD 104 (1970) 116–43.

22. See for example, L. Boff, "Das Sakrament der Ehe," *Concilium* 9 (1973): 459–65; ET: "The Sacrament of Marriage," *Concilium* 87 (1973): 22–33.

23. Concerning this reasoning, see R. Gall, *Fragwürdig Unauflöslichkeit der Ehe?* (Zürich, 1970), 91–94; P. Huizing, "Um eine neue Kirchenordnung," in A. Müller, *et al,*, *Vom Kirchenrecht zur Kirchenordnung?* (Einsiedeln, 1968), 55–83, esp. 74 ff. J. David and F. Schmalz (eds.), *Wie unauflöslich ist die Ehe?* (Aschaffenburg, 1969), 238–48.

24. On this point, see *Foi et sacrement* (Lyon, 1974) with additional bibliography.

25. *Ibid.*

26. Saint Robert Bellarmine is especially responsible for establishing this point; see E. Corecco, "Die Lehre der Untrennbarkeit des Ehevertrags," 338–93.

27. O. H. Pesch, *Theologie der Rechtfertigung bei Martin Luther und Thomas von Aquin* (Mainz, 1967), 805; E. Schillebeeckx, *De sakramentele Heilseconomie* (Antwerp, 1952), 641–46; K. Rahner, *Kirche und Sakramente* (Freiburg, 1961), 22–30.

28. O. H. Pesch, *op. cit.*, p. 805.

29. F. Cappello, *Tractatus canonico-moralis de Sacramentis*, 1 (7th ed.; Rome, 1962), 49, n. 74.

30. See M. Conte a Coronata, *Institutiones Juris Canonici: De Sacramentis tractatus canonicus*, 1 (2nd ed.; Turin, 1951) 64, n. 94.

31. On this point, see U. Mosiek, *Kirchliches Eherect* (3rd ed.; Frieburg, 1976), 206 ff.; 219 ff.

32. By way of example, compare J. Neumann, "Die Möglichkeiten des gelteden katholischen Eherects," in, *Interkonfessioneller Arbeitskreis für Ehe und Familienfragen: Christliche Einheit der Ehe* (Mainz/Munich, 1969) 44: "Thus the juridical act (that is, the contract of marriage) is presented as an element constitutive of the sacrament, and detached from the faith of the contracting parties. Thus, the event that is significant in terms of salvation is thought of as radically independent both of the will and the faith of the parties, since their will brings itself to bear only on the contract as contract."

33. On this point, see Thomas Aquinas, ST III, q. 68, a. 8, ad 3m; q. 64, a. 9, ad 1n, and a. 10, ad 1n. L. Villette, *Foi et sacrement*, II: *De Saint Thomas à Karl Barth*, Travaux de l'Institut Catholique de Paris 6 (Paris, 1964), 38.

34. On this point, cf. H. Volk, *Glaube und Glaubwürdigkeit* (Mainz, 1963), 19; 46.

35. These views refer both to the intention of the minister and the recipient of the sacrament; see *Concilium* 4 (1968) 54–61; ET: "Sacramental Questions: The Intentions of Minister and Recipient," *Concilium* 31 (1968) 117–33; quotation, 130.

36. On this topic, see E. Schillebeeckx, *Christus, Sakrament der Gottbegegnung* (Mainz, 1965), 112–14; ET: *Christ, the Sacrament of the Encounter with God* (New York, 1963), 108 ff. J. Tomko, "Il matrimonio dei battezzati non credenti," in *Matrimonio, Famiglia et Divorzio* (Napoli, Ed. *Dehoniane*, 1971), 347–67, esp. 353–60. Unfortunately disappointing is the dissertation of L. V. Vanyo, *Requisites of Intention in the Reception of the Sacraments* The Catholic University of America Canon Law Studies, 391 (Washington, D. C. 1965); see also, U. Navarrete, "Matrimonio cristiano e sacramenti," in P. Adnès, *et al.*, *Amore e stabilità nel matrimonio* (Rome, *Gregorian University*, 1976) 75, esp. 71 ff; E. Schillebeeckx, "Die christliche Ehe und die menschliche Realität volliger Ehezurrüttung," in P. J. M. Huizing, (e.d.), *Für eine neue kirchliche Eheordnung* (Düsseldorf, 1975), 41–73, esp. 54–57.

37. On this matter, see P. Beguerie and R. Beraudy, "Problèmes actuels dans la pastorale du mariage," MD 127 (1976): 7–33.

38. Editio typica; Typis Polyglottis Vaticanis, 1972; Praenotanda, No. 7, p. 8.

39. The text refers to SC 59: "They [the sacraments] not only presuppose faith, but by words and objects they also nourish, strengthen, and express it; that is why they are called 'sacraments of faith.' " (Abbott, 158)

40. On this point, see *Document pastoral de la Conférence Episcopale Italienne*, "Evangelizzasione e Sacramento del Matrimonio" (Milan, 1975); D. Tettamanzi, *Matrimonio cristiano oggi: Per una lettura teologico-pastorale del documento "Evangelizzasione e Sacramento del Matrimonio"* (Milan, 1975); A. M. Triacca, and G. Pianazzi, "Realtà e valori del Sacramento del Matrimonio," *Biblioteca di Scienza Religiosa* 15 (Rome, 1976).

41. *Ibid.*, No. 5, p. 8.

42. See the documents offered in the collaborative work, *Foi et sacrement de mariage*, 182–87.

43. See also R. Didier, "Sacrement de mariage, baptême et foi," MD 127 (1976) 106–38.

44. On this point, see the important article of J. Ratzinger, "Taůfe, Glaube und Zugehörigkeit zur Kirche," ITZ 5 (1976): 219–34; also by the same, "Taufe und Formulierung des Glaubens," ETL 49 (1973) 76–86.

45. Additional details in K. Lehmann, *Gegenwart des Glaubens* (Mainz, 1966), 131–43.

46. ST III, 73, 3.

47. On this point see G. Baldanza, "Il matrimonio come sacramento per-

manente," in *Realtà e valori del Sacramento del Matrimonio* (see above, note 40), 81–102.

48. See LG 8; 14; more precision in M. Kaiser, "Zugehörigkeit zur Kirche," IKZ 5 (1976): 196–206.

49. M. Kasier, *loc. cit.*, 206.

50. "Religiös ohne Kirche? Eine Herausforderung für Glaube und Kirche," in K. Foster (ed.), *Auftrag des Zentralkomitees der deutschen Katholiken* (Mainz, 1977), 53. As far as our question is concerned, the consequences have not yet been worked out.

51. *Schriften zur Theologie*, 8: 534; ET: *Theological Investigations*, 10: 214–15.

52. *Ibid.*, with additional indications in n. 30; ET: 214.

53. M. Kasier, *loc. cit.*, 205 ff.

54. "Die Sakramentalität christlicher Ehe in ekklesiologischkanonistischer Sicht. Thesenhalfte Erwägungen zu einer Neubesinnung," TTZ 83 (1974) 321–38.

55. See also E. Corecco, "Die Lehre der Untrennbarkeit des Ehevertrags," 441–42.

56. For more details see K. Reinhardt, *loc. cit.*, 32.

57. On this point see E. Corecco, "Der Priester als Spender des Ehesakramentes im Lichte der Lehre über die Untrennbarkeit von Ehevertrag und Ehesakrament," in A. Scheuermann and G. May (eds.), *Ius Sacrum:* Festschrift für K. Mösdorf (Munich, 1969) 521–57.

58. See also G. Martelet, "Mariage, amour et sacrement," NRT 85 (1963): 577–97.

59. When we speak of God or Christ as lawgivers, considerable care is in order.

60. Also on this point, see K. Reinhardt, *loc. cit.*, 44–51; M. Kuppens, "Les époux vrais ministres du sacrement de mariage," *Revue Ecclésiastique de Liège* 44 (1957): 44–56.

61. See the article of G. Martelet quoted above, note 58.

62. On this point, see also H. Volk, "Von der sakramentalen Gnade der Ehe," in H. Volk, *Christus alles in allem* (Mainz, 1975), 70–95; esp. 76 ff.; also, *Ihr sollt meine Zeugen sein* (Mainz, 1977), 101–18.

63. See P. Adnès, *Le mariage* (Tournai, 1963), 153; 155. U. Mosiek, *Kirchliches Eherecht*, 41.

64. On this point see especially J. Dauvillier, *Le mariage dans le droit classique de l'Eglise depuis le dècret de Gratien (1140) jusqu'à la mort de Clément V (1314)* (Paris, 1953), 76.

65. On this point see the patristic studies of O. Casel on the "nuptial night."

Bibliographical information in A. Mayer, J. Quasten, B. Neuheuser, *Vom christlichen Mysterium* (Düsseldorf, 1951).

66. On this subject see U. Navarrete, "De notione et effectu consummationis matrimonii," PMCL 59 (1970): 619–60.
67. GS 48.
68. LG 11: "The family is, so to speak, the domestic church."
69. See the few and merely formal remarks of P. Adnès, *Le mariage,* 146; there are only thirteen lines in a text two hundred pages long.
70. See for example, E. Schillebeeckx, 1 *Le mariage,* (Paris, 1966), 141; ET: *Marriage: Human Reality and Saving Mystery,* 1 (New York: Sheed and Ward, 1965), 155.
71. See P. Adnès, *Le mariage,* 161.
72. Concerning this discussion and for an account of the state of the question, see U. Navarrete, "Indissolubilitas matrimonii rati et consummati. Opiniones recentiores et observationes," PMCL 58 (1969): 415–89.
73. See for example, R. Charland, "Le pouvoir de l'Eglise sur les liens du mariage," RDC 16 (1966): 44–57; 17 (1967): 31–46; also L. C. de Léry, "La dissolution du mariage et le pouvoir des cléfs," SE (1958): 335–39. For the other positions, se U. Navarrete, *loc. cit.*, 422–45.
74. See J. G. Gerhartz, "Unauflösigkeit der Ehe und kirchliche Ehescheidung in heutiger Problematik," in R. Metz and J. Schlick (eds.), *Die Ehe – Band oder Bund?* in *Kirche für Morgen,* 1 (Aschaffenburg, 1971), 142–77; same in French, RDC 21 (1971): 198–234.
75. See the brief sketch of U. Navarrete, *loc. cit.*, 475 ff.
76. See still and always A. Bride, "Le pouvoir du Souverain Pontife sur les mariages des infidèles," RDC 10–11 (1960–61) Mélanges en l'honneur du Cardinal A. Jullien;" 52–101 J. Tomko, "De dissolutione matrimonii in favorem fidei eiusque fundamento theologico," PMCL 64 (1975) 99–139.
77. See especially L. de Naurois, "Le problème de la dissolution du mariage par l'Eglise," NRT 93 (1971): 50–77, esp. 63 ff.
78. See de Naurois, NRT 93 (1971): 69, n. 19.
79. K. Reinhardt, *loc. cit.*, 55: also J. Ratzinger, *Zur Theologie der Ehe,* 112 ff.

4. MARRIAGE IN ORDER OF CREATION/MARRIAGE AS SACRAMENT

1. Duns Scotus, *Opus oxoniense; In IV Sent.*, dist. 26, quaestio unica, ed. Vivès (Paris, 1894) vol. 19, 167 ff.
2. Duns Scotus, *Reportata parisiensia; In IV Sent.*, dist. 28, quaestio unica, ed. Vivès (Paris, 1894) vol. 19, 384; see also 387.

3. G. Le Bras, "Mariage," DTC 9, col. 2204.
4. Thomas de Vio, *De sacramento matrimonii triplex quaesitum;* quaes. primum, II, in S. Thomae Aquinatis *Opera Omnia* (Rome: Leonine edition, 1906), vol. 12, 370.
5. G. Vasquez, *De matrimonii sacramento,* disp. 1, c. 2, no. 10, in *Commentariorum ac disputationum in Tertiam Partem S. Thomae tomus quartus* (Lyons, 1620), 275.
6. G. Vasquez, *op. cit.*, disp. 2, c. 5, no. 53; 307; see also no. 57 and 62; 308.
7. G. Vasquez, *op. cit.*, disp. 2, c. 7, no. 77; 311.
8. G. Vasquez, *op. cit.*, disp. 1, c. 2, no. 10; 275; disp. 2, c. 10, no. 135; 320.
9. G. Vasquez, *op. cit.*, disp. 138, c. 5, nos. 63–64; t. 6, 265–66.
10. G. Vasquez, *op. cit.*, disp. 2, c. 10, nos. 116–38; 317–20.
11. G. Vasquez, *op. cit.*, disp. 3, c. 5, no. 67; 331.
12. F. Rebello, *De contractu matrimonii*, p. 2, lib. 1, quaest. 1, no. 38.
13. That is, between a Christian spouse and an unbaptized spouse.
14. F. Rebello, *op. cit.*, p. 3, lib. 2, quaest. 5, no. 6.
15. Salmanticenses, *Cursus theologiae moralis*, tractatus IX, *De sacramento matrimonii*, c. 3, db. nos. 3, 76–77 (Venice, 1724), vol. 2, 75.
16. P. Sporer, *Theologia moralis*, p. 4, c. 1, sec. 4, no. 356 (Venice, 1735), t. 3, 300.
17. R. Billuart, *Cursus theologiae; Tractatus de matrimonio*, diss. 1, a. 5 (Brescia, 1883), vol. 3, 672.
18. R. Billuart, *op. cit.*, diss. 6, a. 2; 716.
19. F. Schmalzgrüber, *Jus ecclesiasticum universum*, ps. 1, tit. 1, nos. 301–320 (Naples, 1728), vol. 4, 42–43.
20. St. Alphonsus de Liguori, *Theologia Moralis*, ed. Gaudé (Rome, 1905–1912), 4, 75.
21. St. Robert Bellarmine, *De sacramento matrimonii, liber unicus*, controversia prima, c. 7, in *De controversiis christianae fidei* (Venice, 1721), vol. 3, 630.
22. Bellarmine, *op. cit.*, 626.
23. Bellarmine, *op. cit.*, c. 4; 621.
24. Bellarmine, *op. cit.*, controversia 2, c. 6; 629.
25. With regard to the minister, the position of Melchior Cano is strongly opposed by Bellarmine.
26. On this, read the whole chapter 6 of controversy 2; 628 ff.
27. Bellarmine, *op. cit.*, 626–27; 632.
28. Bellarmine, *op. cit.*, controversy 1, c. 5; 626: ". . . no less than the other

sacraments, Christian marriage is a sign not at anyone's discretion, but because of divine institution."

29. Bellarmine, *op. cit.*, 628.
30. F. Suarez, *Commentarii ac disputationes in Tertiam Partem D. Thomae*, disp. 13, sec. 2 (Lyons, 1614), t. 3, 159.
31. Suarez, *op. cit.*, disp. 1, sec. 1; 5: "A sacred sign which confers or signifies a sanctification to man."
32. Suarez, *op. cit.*, disp. 2, sec. 2; 21; sec 3; 25; disp. 16, sec. 1; 191.
33. Suarez, *op. cit.*, disp. 2, sec. 6; 32.
34. T. Sanchez, *Disputationum de sancto matrimonii sacramento libri decem*, lib. 2, disp. 9, no. 5 (Venice, 1607), t. 1, 138.
35. Sanchez, *op. cit.*, 6.
36. Sanchez, *op. cit.*, disp. 10, no. 6; 139.
37. Sanchez, *op. cit.*, 6.
38. M. Cano, *De locis theologicis libri duodecim*, lib. 8, c. 5 (Rome, 1890), t. 2.
39. Cano, *loc. cit.*, par. 10; 102–103.
40. Cano, *loc. cit.*, esp. par. 14; 105–108.
41. St. Robert Bellarmine regards it as heretical.
42. G. Estius, *In IV Sent.* (Venice, 1778), t. 6, 109–113.
43. P. Lambertini, *De synodo diocesana*, lib. 8, c. 13, IV (Patro, 1844), 281. He concludes: "As the contracting parties make a valid contract with each other, they do not necessarily perform a sacrament."
44. Benedict XIV, *Redditae sunt,* in P. Gasparri (ed.). CICF 2 (Rome, 1924), 42.
45. Benedict XIV, CICF 2, 42: "With regard to those who attempt to contract marriage apart from the form required of them, the Council of Trent explicitly states that not only the sacrament is invalid, but the contract itself."
46. Benedict XIV, CICF 2, 92.
47. Sacred Congregation of the Council, *Thesaurus resolutionum S. Congregationis Concilii* (Rome, 1752), 20, 92.
48. St. Alphonsus de Liguori, *Theologia moralis*, ed. Gaudé (Rome, 1905–1912), 4, 75. In the year 1852, Antonio Rosmini still defended the position that the priest is the "ordinary" minister of the sacrament of marriage, and that the contracting parties are the "extraordinary" ministers. See *Sul matrimonio*, in *Opere* (Rome/Stresa, 1977), vol. 30, 197–202. But he also maintained that the inseparability of the sacrament from the contract is "a dogma of faith" (22), from which it appears that Cano's position does not entail the affirmation that contract and sacrament are separable. Rosmini is not the only one who proves this to be so.

49. *Concilium Tridentinum*, ed. EHSES (Freiburg i. Br., 1924), vol. 9, 372–470.

50. *Ibid.*, 380, 3–4.

51. *Ibid.*, 382–408. For the list of the theologians who took part in these discussions, see 381.

52. *Ibid.*, for example, 386, 7–35; 387, 37; 388, 1–4; 395, 19–21; 396, 32–34.

53. *Ibid.*, 639, 21–22.

54. "that [marriage] is in the proper sense one of the seven sacraments of the New Dispensation."

55. "that [marriage] is a sacrament instituted by Christ, and that it confers grace."

56. "the marriage of Christians."

57. "Canon 1 should read: 'in the proper sense one of the seven sacraments of the new dispensation.' This makes reference to the opinion of Durand [of St.-Pourçain], who said that marriage is a true sacrament, but not in the same univocal sense as the others. To the word 'sacrament' add also, 'instituted by Christ' and that ' it confers grace.' "

58. The reason behind this rejection is explained by the Master General of the Dominicans, V. Giustiniani (618, 32–36): "Canon 1 should not include the words, 'of Christians' (*Christianorum*) because there are theologians who maintain that not every marriage contracted by Christians is a sacrament. A marriage by proxy, for example, is a true marriage, but it is not a sacrament. Likewise, in the Council of Cologne, Gropper maintains that a clandestine marriage is not a sacrament as long as it is clandestine." The reference is to the Council of Cologne held in 1536, which represents one of the most important moments in the Catholic reform in Germany prior to Trent. The promulgation of the Council's decisions coincided with the publication of an important "handbook" of moral and pastoral theology by J. Gropper, Vicar General of Cologne, and one of the chief promoters of and active participants in the council itself. This *Enchiridion christianae institutionis* was disseminated in Italy by M. Giberti, bishop of Verona, a great promoter of reform, and exerted a large influence. It was quoted at the Council of Trent. This book clearly takes the position that marriages contracted without the blessing of the priest are to be regarded as nonsacramental, even though, they are valid insofar as they are natural contracts.

59. The second article submitted to the "minor theologians" of the "first group" was worded as follows: "Parents can invalidate clandestine marriages. Marriages so contracted are not true marriages. It is proper that in the future the Church should invalidate them" (880, 5–6).

60. "The Church . . . has the power to invalidate sacraments which happen to be clandestine. That is, she has the power to invalidate the way of con-

tracting marriage and the contract itself. For, once the contract is invalidated, the marriage is invalidated as well, since marriage is not a sacrament unless it be a contract." Thus Diego of Pavia (401, 21–26). Cf. also 402, 35–36; 405, 9–10; 408, 36–37.

61. The discussion stretched between July 24 and July 31 (642–80). The text under discussion was worded as follows: "Should anyone say that clandestine marriages contracted through consent freely given by the contracting parties are not true marriages, and that they are not ratified, and that, as a consequence, the parents have the right to ratify or invalidate them, let him be anathema" (640, 3–5; what is involved in this first draft is the third of the eleven canons submitted for discussion).

"[The Council] decides and decrees that the marriages which shall be secretly contracted in the future in the absence of three witnesses will be null and void, as by the present decree it invalidates and annuls them" (640, 37–39).

Some of the fathers continued to defend clandestine marriages: the bishops of Terni (656, 25), Yprès (669, 35–37), Milapotamos (652, 21–24), Lucera (660, 41–47). With these exceptions, the fathers unanimously condemned clandestine marriages, but they too asked themselves the question which had plagued the theologians: how should this authority on the part of the Church be grounded? Some fathers remarked that the suggested change would offer the heretics the opportunity to object that the Church plays fast and loose with the sacraments. See the intervention of the bishop of Rossano, who spoke very forcibly on this issue (647, 36–648, 7): "Look what kind of sacraments the papists have! A sacrament which has been a sacrament for 1563 years is all of a sudden a sacrament no longer."

Besides, the heretics themselves "condemn clandestine marriages. We should not go along with them." Thus the archbishop of Venice (643, 37–38). It was also noted that canon 3 and the decree stand to some extent opposed to each other. On the other hand, the fathers could point to a well-established ecclesial practice: the Church erecting impediments to marriage. The problem was, then, how the decree could be justified on the basis of the Church's authority to invalidate marriages. This was very clearly perceived by the archbishop of Granada (644, 17–29).

62. Cf. 645, 15–16; 650, 30: ". . . for we are not affecting the sacrament, but the contract"; 651, 41–43; 654, 28–33: ". . . in this way, the sacrament is not being affected, but the contract is invalidated"; p. 665, 18–19: ". . . the Church does not invalidate the sacrament, but the contract." Also 666, 5–7; 667, 34–40.

This justification was harshly taken to task: it is impossible to "touch" the contract without touching the sacrament. This position was taken by the bishops of Tortosa (671, 12–13), Calvi (671, 26–30), Alès (677, 30–33).

63. This proposal was linked to the suggestion of the cardinal of Lorraine according to whom the pastor must be one of the three witnesses (642, 40–41). It was advanced by the bishops of Evreux (653, 10–13), Segovia (657, 10–14), Orléans (660, 10–12), Lerida (666, 29–31). Some went as far as to request that the priest should be declared the minister of the sacrament. Thus, for instance, the bishop of Alife (674, 40–675, 1).

64. The proposal was made by the patriarch of Aquileia (64, 32–34) and seconded by the bishops of Braga (650, 22–23), Taranto (651, 7–9), Volturara (660, 26–27), Hierapetra (654, 5–6), Pesaro (673, 41–42) and the abbott of Eutichio (678, 6–9).

65. *Ibid.*, 779–95.

66. Sforza Pallavicino, *Vera Oecumenici Concillii Tridentini historia*, lib. 22, c. 9, 5–9 (Milan, 1844), 6, 88–91.

67. CT, 781, 8–10; cf. Pallavicino, *op. cit.*, lib. 22, c. 8, 19; 83.

68. This fact is overlooked by E. Duval, "Contrat et sacrement du mariage au Concile de Trente," MD 127 (1976) 34–63. It takes on an even clearer significance if we analyze very briefly the debate on canon 12 in session 24 (DS 1812).

    The "minor theologians" of the "fourth group" had been presented with the following text: "The inability to have intercourse, and ignorance about the contract, do of themselves alone invalidate the marriage contract. Matrimonial causes fall under the competency of secular rulers" (CT 380, 18–19). Unfortunately, this text was only scantily debated, for the theologians involved in the debate were forced to come together before the appointed time to make it possible for the cardinal of Lorraine to attend the debates of the "third group" of theologians. Massarelli gives us a summary of only one intervention, which is indeed interesting: on the strength of the distinction between contract and sacrament "which many have adduced," many theologians draw the conclusion that "the Church is competent only to deal with sacramental cases in which a divine law is violated." The fathers were presented with the following canon: "Should anyone say that matrimonial cases do not fall under the competency of ecclesiastical judges, let him be anathema." The assertion of this competency met with opposition. Some of the fathers requested that the canon be dropped (660, 1–10; 661, 29; 663, 21; 664, 16). Others wanted a more specific text that would name the cases in question (672, 13–14). In this context, the distinction between contract and sacrament resurfaced: ". . . it should be specifically stated: matrimonial cases relative to the contract" (662, 19–20); "it should be specifically stated: matrimonial cases relative to the sacrament of marriage" (717, 5). Once more, the council refused to adopt this distinction for it tends to separate contract from sacrament.

    The words of Cardinal Morone quoted in CT, 406, n. 3, should also be taken into account: "There are as yet no truly important controversies, with two exceptions . . . The first is whether all marriages contracted by Christians are sacramental. The opinion of William of Paris according to whom only marriages blessed by the priest are sacramental has been defended by two bishops, and with as much fervor as it has been resisted by all others." Cf. also Pallavicino, VOCTH, 5, lib. 20, c. 4; 290.

69. *De sacramento matrimonii*, controversia VI, c. 32 (Venice 1721) 687: "Catholics make distinctions with regard to matrimonial cases. Some of these are entirely civil in nature: they have to do with dowries, successions, inheritance, *etc.* Others are entirely spiritual: they concern the elements of the sacrament, the blessing by the priest, *etc.* Others still are civil in part and in part they are spiritual: they concern degrees of affin-

ity, divorce, impediments, and other things relative to the marriage contract itself. To the extent to which that natural contract is the foundation of the sacrament, and a matter of conscience, it is spiritual in nature. We do not refuse to admit that the cases of the first kind do purely and simply fall under the competency of the magistrate of the state . . . As to the cases of the second kind, no one may deny that the Church alone is competent to deal with them. The question which stands out most prominently concerns the cases of the third kind. Our position is that these cases can pertain to the civil magistrate, but subordinately to the authority of the ecclesiastical magistrate. Purely and simply, however, they pertain to the ecclesiastical ruler. This has been defined by the Council of Trent, session 24, canon 12."

70. A. de Dominis, *De matrimonio*, t. 2, p. 3, c. 11.

71. We shall quote according to the following edition: J. Launoii, *Opera omnia* (Cologne, 1731), t. 1/2. The work is lengthy and repetitious. It is divided in three parts, the first of which is doctrinal, the second and the third of which are historical.

72. Launoy quotes – more or less to the point – some sixty theologians grouped, first, according to universities: Paris (631–35), Bordeaux (635–36), Reims (636–37), Louvain (637–39), Douai (639), Salamanca and Alcala (640–43), Italy (643–45), then according to the religious orders to which they belong (645–50).

73. The demonstration proper consists of eleven arguments (art. 1, cc. 10 and 11; 650–52; 653–56). Seven of these merely summarize the contents of the preceding pages, four claim to be original. There is no need to analyze these arguments here, since, as the author himself states, they all rest on the following affirmation: ". . . we must take the position which is necessarily demanded by the truth of the thing itself, namely, that in marriage two aspects are present. The first is the civil contract, the nature of which has remained unchanged in both the Old and the New Testaments. The second is the sacramental aspect, which has been superadded to the civil contract, without effecting any change whatever in it. Opponents who concur with this widely and absolutely indispensible distinction are caught, for any arguments for the opposite view come totally to grief against the rock of this distinction" (651).

74. For Launoy, the whole problematic boils down to this point: marriage is a civil reality and always remains such, and the sacrament is an accidental addition to it. All his arguments rest on this point. Because marriage is a civil reality, "it follows that it is subject to the ordinance and disposition of civil laws." The fact that marriage is a sacrament "makes no difference . . . since the sacramental aspect that comes to be added to marriage does not change the human contract" (651).

75. Launoy, *op. cit.*, 758: ". . . per Reges alteramve Ecclesiae personam [impedimenta matrimonium dirimentia] potuit constituere et constituit."

76. Z. B. van Espen, *Jus ecclesiasticum universum* (Louvain, 1700). We quote here according to the edition published in Venice in 1781.

77. With regard to impediments that only prevent marriage, van Espen has no misgivings: "There is no doubt whatever that, even with regard to

their Catholic subjects, Catholic secular rulers have the power to establish impediments that prevent marriage, so that a marriage contracted in spite of such impediments is illicitly contracted, although the offending parties may not be punished, or deprived of the civil effects which are attached to marriage on other grounds . . ." Cf. p. 2, tit. 2, sec. 1; tit. 13, c. 1, no. 10; 138.

As regards diriment impediments to marriage, van Espen adopts the position of Sanchez: "As Sanchez correctly notes, . . . secular rulers by the very nature of their power are certainly entitled to decree for just cause diriment impediments which affect their Christian subjects. . . . As Sanchez also says, the fact that marriage is a sacrament does not curtail the power of the secular ruler, since by its nature marriage is a civil contract. On this ground, the ruler may, therefore, invalidate marriage, as if it were not a sacrament" (*ibid.*, no. 11; 138).

78. See *Revue des questions historiques* 55 (1894) 488.

79. J. le Plat, *Dissertatio de sponsalibus et matrimonii impedimentis* (Freiburg i. Br., 1782); J. A. Petzck, *De potestate Ecclesiae in statuendis matrimonii impedimentis* (Freiburg i. Br., 1783); J. N. Pehem, *Praelectiones in jus ecclesiasticum* (Vienna, 1784); L. Litta, *Del diritto di stabilire impedimenti dirimenti il matrimonio* (Cremona, 1784); P. Tamburini, *Praelectiones de justitia christiana et de sacramentis* (Pavia, 1784); G. Silvestri, *Additamenta ad van Espen* (Venice, 1784).

80. See *Atti e decreti del Concilio diocesano di Pistoia dell'anno 1786* (2nd ed.; Florence, 1788).

81. This text was republished in ASS 25 (1892–93) 701–02. The Latin original of the two passages translated here is as follows: *Haeresis igitur est Sacramentum Matrimonii a matrimonii contractu* per modum regulae, *et absolute seiungere, perinde ac si contractus essentiam atque substantiam Sacramenti minime divinae institutionis vi ingrediatur, neque aliud Matrimonii Sacramentum esse reperiatur, nisi qualitas contractui supernatans, aut corona pictam tabulam, cui extranea est, circum ornans.* A little further: *Matrimonium . . . ideo Sacramentum est, quia contractus ipse Sacramentum est, seu quia contratus et ad substantiam pertinet, et definitionem ingreditur Sacramenti: atque hoc dogma catholicum est. Quamvis autem quispiam ponere velit, aliquod inter fideles matrimonium Sacramentum non esse posse, semper tamen erit de fide, minime inter fideles Matrimonii Sacramentum reperiri, quod semper contractu essentialiter haud aedificetur; neque in lege evangelica matrimonii contractum esse posse, quod non sit Sacramentum; matrimonii tamen Sacramentum esse non posse in quo contractus ipse non sit Sacramentum. Atque hoc dogma est, in citato Tridentini contentum canone . . . Haeresis igitur . . . est, asserere in lege evangilica contractum matrimonii regulariter et essentialiter e Matrimonii Sacramento secerni, et Sacramentum non aliud esse, nisi contractus ornatum, qui ad valorem ipsius atque consistentiam indifferens sit, seu extraneus.*

82. *Bullarium romanum* (Prato, 1856), 9, 26–27: *Ac pro temporum quae nacti sumus ratione id insuper quam maxime vestro de animarum salute studio commendandum duximus ut nimirum de matrimonii sanctitate solliciti eam erga ipsum gregi vestro injiciatis religionem ut nihil plane*

quod magni huius Sacramenti detrahat . . . patrari unquam contingat; id porro fiet unice si non humana tantum ex lege sed ex divina regi ipsum debere ac non terrenis sed sacris rebus ipsum accensendum esse ideoque Ecclesiae omnino subjici, christianus populus accurate edoceatur. Quae enim paritalis coniunctio antea non alio spectabat quam ut stirpen ex se gigneret . . . ea nunc a Christo Domino sacramenti diginitate aucta et coelestibus ditata muneribus, gratia perficiente naturam, non tam procreare ex se subolem gaudeat quam educare illam Deo . . . Constat emin matrimonii hac coniunctione, cuius Deus auctor est, perpetuam ac summam Christi Domini cum Ecclesia coniunctionem significari et arctissimam hanc viri uxorisque societatem sacramentum esse.

83. Pius IX, *Multiplices inter*, June 10, 1851, in CICF 2, No. 510; 855. Among the condemned propositions there appears one which ". . . maintains that the power with which the Church was endowed by her divine Founder, namely, to establish diriment impediments to marriage, comes to her from the secular rulers, and godlessly asserts that the Church of Christ has unwarrantedly appropriated that power."

84. CICF 2, no. 511; 858–59.

85. In the apostolic letter *Ad apostolicae*, August 22, 1851, the following propositions of I. N. Nuytz are condemned:

    "The sacrament of marriage is merely an addition to the contract, and separable from it. The sacrament itself resides only in the nuptial blessing."

    "The Church is not entitled to establish impediments diriment to marriage. This power pertains to the civil authority, which is to remove existing impediments."

    "The Tridentine canons which inflict the anathema on those who deny that the Church has the power to erect impediments diriment to marriage, either are not dogmatic, or they are not to be understood to relate to that power."

    These propositions evoke the following assessment: ". . . they hold and teach a false understanding of the nature of marriage and of the marriage bond." Cf. CICF 2, par. 3; 859.

86. On this whole affair, cf. P. Pirri, *Pio IX e Vittorio Emmanuele II dal loro carteggio privato.* I. *La laicizzazione dello Stato Sardo* (*1848–1856*) (Rome, 1944) 79*–94*, and the attached documentation.

87. P. Pirri, *Pio IX*, 103.

88. *Ibid.*, p. 117; cf. also CICF 2, no. 515; 877.

89. CICF 2, no. 515; 877: "No Catholic should or can overlook the fact that marriage is truly and in the proper sense one of the seven sacraments of the new law instituted by Jesus Christ. For this reason there can be, for the faithful, no marriage which would not be at the same time a sacrament. Among Christians, therefore, any other union between man and woman which is not a sacrament, even if contracted in accordance with civil law, is but a shameful and lethal concubinage, which the Church condemns. The sacrament may never be separated from the conjugal bond. It is, therefore, the competency of the Church to legislate with authority on all the things which, in any way whatever, pertain to marriage."

90. J. Martin, *De matrimonio et potestate ipsum dirimendi* (Lyons/Paris, 1884), 1, 56: "The words which Christ spoke through Adam, as through the image and type of himself, declare that marriage is a twofold reality, and make it such. That is, the marriage which was to be contracted across time by men and women is a foreshadowing of the divine marriage which Christ and the Church were to contract and consummate with each other once at the appointed time. In consequence, in every marriage to be rightly contracted by a man and a woman there should come to expression, and be acted out, as it were, the marriage between Christ and the Church. In a manner of speaking, the marriage between Christ and the Church is symbolically celebrated in advance in that human marriage."

91. G. Perrone, *Praelectiones theologicae* (Rome, 1838), 246–47, and n. a.

92. *Ibid.*, "in keeping with civil laws."

93. *Ibid.*, "as demanded by nature."

94. *Ibid.*, 339–40: ". . . in the very act by which it is made, the natural contract takes on the nature of a sacrament by virtue of the institution by Christ. Henceforth sacramentality remains inseparable from contract. Note carefully that sacramentality does not accrue to the natural contract already constituted in its own being. It rather springs forth and comes to fruition in the act . . . whereby the contract is made, in the very same way in which, in baptism, sacramentality springs forth from the pouring of the water."

95. *Ibid.*, 373: ". . . because the natural contract has thus been elevated, contract and sacrament come together to constitute one indivisible act." The author adds in a note: ". . . they may not be looked upon as two realities. . . . The distinction is merely conceptual: namely, between the formal concept of contract and the formal concept of contract and the formal concept of sacrament."

96. M. J. Scheeben, *Die Mysterien des Christentums* (Freiburg i. Br.: Herder, 1958), 602, n. 24; ET: *The Mysteries of Christianity* (St. Louis: B. Herder, 1946), n. 13, 608–09.

97. *Ibid.*, 602–03; ET: 610.

98. *Ibid.*, 602; ET: 608–09.

99. *Ibid.*, 593–94; ET: 601.

100. D. Palmieri, *Tractatus de matrimonio christiano* (Rome, 1880) 74.

101. A. Berlage, *System der katholischen Dogmatik* (Münster, 1864), 7, 814.

102. G. Perrone, *Praelectiones theologicae ab eodem in compendium redactae* (Brussels, 1858), 2, 474, no. 120. Perrone quotes mainly D. Carrière (1795–1864). Again according to Perrone, some German theologians need be added: cf. *Praelectiones theologicae* (Rome, 1938), 8, 352, note b.; M. Roskovány, *De matrimonio in Ecclesia Catholica* (Augsburg, 1837), vol 1, p. 37.

103. Leo XIII, *Inscrutabili*, April 21, 1878, in CICF 3, no. 573, par. 14; 114: "Godless laws, totally insensitive to the sacredness of this great sacra-

ment, have abased marriage to the level of a merely civil contract; the dignity of Christian marriage has been slighted as a consequence, and citizens make what happens to be legalized concubinage do as if it were a marriage."

104. Leo XIII, *Ci siamo*, June 1, 1879, in CICF 3, no. 577, par. 3–4; 132–33.

105. Leo XIII, *Arcanum divinae sapientiae*, February 10, 1880, (DS 3146): "Every properly contracted marriage between Christians is inherently a sacrament. Nothing is more abhorrent to the truth than to maintain that the sacrament is a sort of ornament added to the contract, or an attribute that accrues to it from without, and is separable from it at will."

106. The reference to this fact recurs constantly as well as to the fact which creates the problem. Cf. MD 127 (1976) 7–33; esp. 9–10; *Foi et sacrement de mariage: Recherches et perplexités* (Lyons: Éd. du Chalet, 1974), pp. 14–36, and 176; J. Moingt, "Le mariage des chrétiens: Autonomie et mission," *RSR* 62 (1974) 81–116.

107. See for instance, *Foi et sacrement*, 179.

108. If we understand it correctly, the position of J. M. Aubert seems to tend in this direction. Cf. "Foi et sacrement dans le mariage des baptisés incroyants," MD 104 (1970) 116–143. Between dissolubility and indissolubility, he suggests a "third way." Civil marriage "would remain at the level of the matter of the sacrament." It would not be a sacrament" (p. 140). This "capacity" is "actualized" when the obstacle, that is the lack of faith, is removed.

109. See MD 127 (1976) 30–31.

110. On these three forms, see *Foi et sacrement*, 20–23.

111. "All the same, for theologians and the magisterium a question remains to be answered, namely, whether or not there be a link between contract and sacrament." Thus, Msgr. Le Bourgeois, quoted above, 177; see also 23.

112. *Foi et sacrement*, 90–110.

113. Le Bourgeois, in *Foi et sacrement*, 177–78.

114. On this point, see MD 104 (1970) 121.

115. See *Foi et sacrement,* 52 and 67. Billuart is preferred no doubt for the simple reason that the works we are dealing with are based on secondary sources.

116. Moingt, "Le mariage chrétien," 11; the argument is formulated by Rebello.

117. *Ibid.*, 111.

118. *Ibid.*, 112.

119. *Ibid.*, 110, n. 65; also 108.

120. *Ibid.*, 112–13.

121. *Ibid.*, 107, with n. 62; 109.

122. L.-M Chauvet, MD 104 (1970) 104–05; also *Foi et sacrement*, 118–19.

123. See MD, 105 (1970) 123; also, *Foi et sacrement*, 117–22; 124–27.

124. *Foi et sacrement*, 177.

125. Strictly speaking, our problem is not to determine what relationship is between baptism, faith, and the sacrament of marriage, but whether it is possible or impossible for a marriage between baptized persons not to be a sacrament. Hence the solution offered to the first of these two problems is not necessarily decisive in terms of the second problem. Even if we grant that a determinate lack of faith prevents marriage from being validly contracted, it does not automatically follow that the baptized persons in question can marry validly and nonsacramentally. Nor does it help much to appeal to the natural right to marry, for a "natural right" connotes a capacity inherent in the human person, precisely as human. However, in the present economy of salvation, the person exists in fact only for the covenant with God in the Christ with whom we become one through baptism. If so, parting company with this economy of salvation to revert to a mere economy of the created order amounts to lapsing into nonbeing. The only alternative open to exploration is the one mentioned in proposition 3.5: namely, error and invincible ignorance. But then we are no longer at the level of Christianity but of psychology.

126. P. Lombard, *IV Sent.*, dist. 26.

127. St. Thomas Aquinas, *In IV Sent.*, dist. 26.

128. St. Thomas Aquinas, *In IV Sent.*, dist. 31, quaest. 1, a. 1, ad 1.

129. "Nothing prevents marriage from thus being traced back to two or three divine institutions: one relative to nature precisely as nature; another relative to nature precisely as fallen; a third relative to nature precisely as redeemed by Christ. And so marriage is the sacrament of innocence, in the Old Testament and in the New." Thus St. Albert the Great, *In IV Sent.*, dist. 26, a. 5, solution.

"Nature inclines to marriage, as it intends a good which does, however, vary according to the different states in which mankind finds itself. It is therefore appropriate that, in keeping with that particular good, marriage be differently instituted in the different states of mankind." Thus St. Thomas Aquinas, *In IV Sent.*, dist. 26, quaest. 2, a. 2, body. For St. Bonaventure, See *In IV Sent.*, dist. 26, a. 1, quaest. 1; Quaracchi edition, 4, 661–63.

5. INDISSOLUBILITY

1. We need not weigh down this presentation with a critical apparatus which readers can easily find in many fine recent works. How often have the same texts been quoted, commented upon, and discussed in the last fifteen years? Here we are interested less in documentation than in interpretation. The documentation can be found in the articles "Adultère" and "Mariage" in the DTC 1 (1930) 464–511 and 9 (1927) 2044–317, which retain all their value, as well as in recent publications, which likewise give rich bibliographies. Cf. particularly, P. Adnès, "Mariage et Vie Chrétienne," DS Fasc. 64–65 (Paris: Beauchesne, 1977) 355–88, and A. M.

Henry, "Mariage," *Catholicisme: Hier, Aujourd'hui, Demain,* Fasc. 34 (Paris: Letouzey et Ané, 1977) 461-500.

2. 1 Cor. 7:10-11: "To those now married . . . I give this command (though it is not mine; it is the Lord's) [cf. Mk 10:9-12 and parallels]: A wife must not separate from her husband. If she does separate, she must either remain single or become reconciled to him again. Similarly, a husband must not divorce his wife."

3. J. Masson, *Histoire des causes de divorce dans la tradition copte* ("Studia Orientalia Christiana–Collectanea") 14 (1970-71), 240-42.

4. A. Houssiau, "Le lien conjugal dans l'Eglise ancienne," AC 17 (1973) 570.

5. G. Pelland, *De Vinculo Matrimoniali apud Patres;* unpublished manuscript, 27-28.

6. Athenagoras, *Legation on Behalf of Christians,* 33 (PG 6, 965).

7. J. Masson, *Histoire des causes de divorce,* pp. 242-44.

8. W. Kelly, *Pope Gregory on Divorce and Remarriage* (Rome, 1976), 72-74; 285-86.

9. *Si quis dixerit, Ecclesiam errare, cum, docuit et docet, iuxta evangelicam et apostolicam doctrinam, propter adulterium alterius coniugum matrimonii vinculum non posse dissolvi, et utrumque, vel etiam innocentem, qui causam adulterio non dedit, non posse, altero coniuge vivente, aliud matrimonium contrahere, moecharique eum, qui dimissa adultera aliam duxerit, et eam, quae dimisso adultero alii nupserit: anathema sit* (DS 1807).

10. P. Adnès, *Histoire des conciles écuméniques,* Vol. XI (to be published).

11. The theological note "of revealed truth" could also be suggested in view of the texts of Mk, Lk, and Paul. Obviously, we would still need to explain the Matthean clause *nisi fornicationis causa.* Another difficulty even more serious is created by the interpretation given to this clause in some ancient Churches.

12. Lehman, "Unauflöslichkeit der Ehe und Pastoral für wiederverheiratete Geschiedene," IKZ 1 (1972) 364-65.

13. Ratzinger, "Zur Frage nach der Unauflöslichkeit der Ehe" in F. Heinrich and V. Eid (eds.), EE (Munich, 1972) 50-51.

6. DIVORCED AND REMARRIED CATHOLICS

1. *Evangelizzazione, matrimonio e forniglia. Magistero della Chiesa Italiana,* 1969-75, Rome, 1975, Editrice A.V.A.

2. By the same author, see D. Tettamanzi, *Il ministero coniugale. Spazio pastorale della coppia cristiana* (with an extensive bibliography) Rome, 1978, Editrice A.V.E.

3. In this study, we are considering the case of the divorced and remarried who have complete conjugal relations. This by no means excludes those who have made an effort, especially after a period of time, to live in complete continence.

4. See DC, 1977, 1011-12.

7. NEW TESTAMENT DOCTRINE OF MARRIAGE

1. The general bibliography on the subject includes the commentaries and annotated translations of the synoptic gospels and 1 Cor as well as the theologies of the New Testament.

The monographs are legion. For the period before 1959, we can depend on the literature used by J. Dupont all through his excellent book, *Marriage et divorce dans l'évangile* (Desclée de Brouwer, 1959). For this period, we may limit ourselves to recalling some French titles: F.J. Leenhardt, *L'enseignement de Jésus sur le divorce*, Les cahiers bibliques de foi et vie, no. 5 (Paris, 1938) 49–67; J. Bonsirven, *Le divorce dans le Nouveau Testament* (Paris and Tournai, 1948); J. Thomas, "Droit naturel et droit chrétien en matière d'indissolubilité du mariage," in *Collectanea moralia in honorem . . . A. Janssen* Bibliotheca Ephemeridum Theologicarum Lovaniensium," no. 23 (Louvain and Gembloux, 1948), 2 621-39; M.-F. Berrouard, "L'indissolubilité du mariage dans le Nouveau Testament," LV 4 (1952) 21–40; H. Cazelles, "Mariage," DBS 5 (1957), esp. col. 926–35. For the period 1948–59, see a very rich bibliography in J. Dupont, *Mariage*, p. 93–95.

For the period after 1959, let us quote first two of the bibliographical listings in existence: R. Metz and J. Schlick, *Mariage et divorce: International Bibliography Indexed by Computer* (Strasbourg, 1973); and A. Myre, "Dix ans d'exégèse sur le divorce dans le Nouveau Testament," in *Le divorce* (Montreal, 1973), 139–63 (covers the period 1963–72). We mention next some studies which have been helpful to us: B. K. Diderichsen, *Den markianiske skilsmisseperikope. Dens genesis og historiske placering* (Doctoral dissertation, Copenhagen, 1961; Glydendal, 1962); A Isaksson, *Marriage and Ministry in the New Temple* (Lund and Copenhagen, 1965); H. Baltensweiler, *Die Ehe im Neuen Testament* (Zürich and Stuttgart, 1967); R. Pesch, "Die neutestamentliche Weisung für die Ehe," BL 9 (1968) 208-221; H. Greeven, J. Razinger, *et al . . Theologie der Ehe* (Augsburg and Göttingen, 1969) with exegetical studies by H. Greeven, R. Schnackenburg, and others; U. Nembach, "Ehescheidung nach alttestamentlichem und jüdischem Recht," TZ 26 (1970) 251–77; B. Schaller, "Die Sprüche über Ehescheidung und Wiederheirat in der synoptischen Überlieferung," in E. Lohse (ed.), *Der Ruf Jesu und die Antwort der Gemeinde* (Göttingen, 1970), 226–46; E. Bammel, "Markus 10:11 f. und das jüdische Eherecht," ZNW 61 (1970) 263–74; T. A. G. van Eupen (ed.), *(On)ontbindbaarheit van het huwelijk* (Hilversum, 1970), with exegetical studies by B. F. M. van Iersel and J. H. A. van Tilborg; F. Neirynck, "De Jezuswoorden over echtscheiding," in V. Heylen (ed.), *Mislukt huwelijk en echtscheiding* (Louvain, 1972) 127–41) (into which Neirynck incorporates two of his previous articles); P. Benoit, *Lévangle selon saint Matthieu* BJ (Paris, 1972); A. Tosato, *Il matrimonio nel guidaismo antico e nel Nuovo Testamento* (Rome, 1976); J. A. Fitzmyer, "The Matthean Divorce Texts and Some New Palestinian Evidence," TS 37 (1976):197-226; A. Stock, "The Matthean Divorce Text," *Biblical Theology Bulletin* 8 (1978):24–33; R. Pesch, *Das Markusevangelium*, (Herder, 1977), 126–27; H. Schürmann, "Neutestamentliche Marginalien zur Frage nach der Institutionalität, Unauflösbarkeit und Sakramentalität der Ehe," in *Kirche und Bibel* (Paderborn, 1979), 409–10; P. Delhaye (ed.) *Problémes doctrinaux du Chrétien* (Coll. *Lex spiritus vitae*, 4)

(Louvain-la-Neuve, 1979). This latter work, a product of the ITC, has helpful references at the end of each chapter.

2. 1 Cor 7:10–11. Cf. Lk 16:18, but only in the hypothesis of B. K. Diderichsen mentioned below, n. 6; cf. Lk 18:29b (the word *woman* does not occur in the parallel texts); compare Lk 14:26, where *woman* occurs only in Luke.

3. In Judaism, Dt 24:1–4 became the legal text par excellence relative to divorce; but see also Dt 22:13–19; 28–29. Note, however, that Dt 24:1–4 does not deal with divorce as such. It touches on divorce only in order to stipulate that a former husband is not entitled to take back the wife he has previously divorced. The passage begins: "Supposing a man has taken a wife and consummated the marriage; but she has not pleased him and he has found some impropriety of which to accuse her; so he has made out a writ of divorce . . ."(JB).

4. The textual criticism of Mk 10:2–12 raises only minor problems, which are methodically examined by H. Zimmermann, *Neutestamentliche Methodenlehre* (Stuttgart, 1966) 107–8. The situation is different for Mk 10:12; see below, p. 223.

5. On the syntax of Mark's Gospel, see B. Rigaux, *Témoignage de l'évangile de Marc* (Desclée de Brouwer, 1965) 96–100.

6. 'Απολύειν is not, however, the verb used in the Greek version of the Old Testament. In Dt 4:1– is 'εξαποστέλλειν, which is very frequent in the whole LXX, whereas 'απολύειν is rare.

In the New Testament, 'απολύειν often occurs in the weak sense, as equivalent of *letting go* or *dismissing* (the crowds, for example). This is why it has been sometimes interpreted, at least in Lk 16:18, as meaning merely *to leave one's wife* (without divorcing her), for the sake of the kingdom, for example. Thus, B. K. Diderichsen, *Den skilsmisseperikope*, 20–47; 347. But, as J. A. Fitzmyer has recently shown, in the New Testament text on divorce (Mt 1:19 included) 'απολύειν certainly means *to divorce* in the precise legal sense we have recalled above; see "Divorce Texts," 212–13. Fitzmyer refers to hellenistic texts, and also to a text from Cave 2 of Wadi Murabba'at.

7. Similar observations in R. Bultmann, *Geschichte der synoptischen Tradition* (3rd. ed.; Göttingen, 1957) 25, ET: *The History of the Synoptic Tradition* (Oxford: Blackwell, 1963) 25–26.

We cannot agree with the suggestion of A. Loisy who maintains that, in Mk 10:3, Jesus refers to what Moses, the author of Genesis, ordains in Gn 1:27 and 2:24. See *Les évangiles synoptiques* (Ceffonds, 1908), 2, 196–97.

8. Strictly speaking, the word *prescribing* could be understood as the echo of a recommendation (suggested, perhaps, by abuses): "Do not neglect to deliver the writ of divorce before dismissing the wife, else she would risk remaining just a woman separated from her husband, and would not be entitled to remarry." See also Mt 5:31, where the text is cast in the language of obligation: "Anyone who divorces his wife must give her a writ of dismissal" (JB).

9. Κτίσις means *creation* in the sense of *created universe* that is, κοσμος,

not in the sense of *act of creating*. Compare καταβολὴ κόσμου (Mt 25:34, etc.) and 'αρχὴ κόσμοθ (Mt 24:21; Mk 18:19).

10. Thus BJ (*hardness of heart*). This translation is not perfect, but it has the advantage of being enfranchised into religious language.

11. Σκληροκαρδία occurs only three times in the LXX. However, the LXX offers many expressions with similar meaning, such as σκληροτράχηλος (Vg. *durae cervicis*), σκληρότης του λαου, etc. Fr. Delitzsch's reverse translation is *geshi lebab, duritia cordis*. In the whole New Testament, σκληροκαρδία occurs only in this passage (and in the parallel text, Mt 19:8) and in Mk 16:14, but again we find in the New Testament many expressions that convey a similar meaning. See the excellent detailed presentation of all this in Dupont, *Mariage* 19–20, with the notes.

12. The precise extent of this condemnation as understood by Mark and his readers is disputed. Did they believe that Moses had been ordered by God to mitigate the original will of the creator? If so, Moses would not be at fault, whereas pre-Christian Israel would still be stigmatized as a stubborn people. Or was Moses himself guilty of this stubbornness? In this case, he would fall under the same severe condemnation as his people. The fact that Jesus appears in the New Testament as "the new Moses" does not decide the issue, for such typology is compatible with diversities and even with contrasts. As we shall see, the dilemma becomes even more acute when it comes to deciding what Jesus himself thought in the matter.

13. See below 229–37.

14. H. Zimmermann, *Methodenlehre*, 110. Note that, although the interpretation of the Genesis texts in Mk 10:6–9 is not a rigorous exegesis, it nevertheless correctly captures the tenor of these passages. See on this some remarks in J. Thomas, "Droit naturel," 625–27.

15. A slight indication of a possible autonomy is the neuter singular ὁ ("that which"; Mk 10:9), which comes after many cases where the plural occurs. Cf. G. F. Fisher, "Mariage et divorce," VC 10 (1956) 105–20.

16. Thus R. H. Charles, *The Teaching of the New Testament on Divorce* (London, 1921), 43–61.

17. Thus J. A. Fitzmyer, "Divorce Texts," 211, refers to both classical and hellenistic Greek texts, while adverting to the silence of the LXX. On 211 he speaks of "tortuous attempts" with reference to the efforts of R. H. Charles mentioned above, n. 15.

18. This is the opinion of many authors: R. Bultmann, *Geschichte*, 25; ET: *History*, 26; F. Neirynck, *Jezuswoorden*, 140, n. 22, *etc.*

19. On this topic see M. Devisch, "La relation entre l'évangile de Marc et le document Q," in M. Sabre (ed.), *L'évangile* selon Marc (Louvain and Gembloux, 1974), 59–91. P. G. Delling has tried to reduce Mt 5:31–32 to Mk 10:11 "Das Logion Mark. X 11 im Neuen Testament," *Novum Testamentum* (1956–57) 263–74. An opposing (and better) view is in Fitzmyer, "Divorce Texts," 202-03.

20. Both μοιχάσθαι and μοιχεύειν occur with the same sense (*adulterare*, to commit adultery, *Ehebruch treiben*). The two Greek verbs occur each

a dozen times in the LXX; the second occurs especially in the Decalogue (Ex 20:13; Dt 5:18, οὐ μοιχεύσεις). In the New Testament, the first of the two verbs occurs only here (Mk 10: 11–12), as well as in Mt 19:9 (which is a parallel), and in Mk 5:32; the second verb occurs a dozen times.

The meaning is adultery precisely as distinct from fornication, πορνεία; see J. A. Fitzmyer, "Divorce Texts," 209, n. 49.

21. On the meaning of this distinction, which derives from the Old Testament, see J. Coppens, *Histoire critique des livres de l'Ancien Testament* (3rd ed.; Desclée de Brouwer, 1942) 127–30; Dupont, *Mariage*, 53, and the authors quoted there, n. 2, including those who discuss this style in the gospels; H. W. Gilmer, *the if-you Form in Israelite Law* (Missoula, Montana, 1975). The apodictic form occurs in Mt 5:32 and Lk 16:18 (πάσ ὁ . . .).

This difference is regarded as important by the exegetes of the Old Testament in view of the fact that these two modes of legislation are linked to the two contexts where they originated, and these differ widely from each other. In our texts this difference has lost some of its sharpness. It is difficult to perceive a large difference between these two formulae: "if a man . . ." and "any man who . . ." (or, "anyone who . . ."). Thus in Mk 10:11 and Mt 5:32 the expressions, which differ in the original Greek texts, are rendered the same in the BJ (*Quiconque* . . .).

22. Thus J. Staudinger, *Die Bergpredigt* (Vienna, 1957) 286, n. 1; F. Neirynck, *Jezuswoorden, passim.*

23. Our quotations are taken from J. Dupont, *Mariage*, 52 (bottom); 65; 144; 69; 144; 68; 147.

24. This is also remarked by B. Schaller, *Die Sprüche*, 244, and by F. Neirynck, *Jezuswoorden*, 135.

Very briefly, here are some other considerations: 1. The instances of Semitic syntax adduced by J. Dupont seem valid in themselves, but there are reasons to wonder whether they are as parallel to our texts as it is claimed. 2. The same observation applies to instances of words which Jesus retains but gives an entirely new meaning. 3. With regard to the concept of divorce, the hypothesis of a double meaning of that concept creates a special difficulty: it supposes that Mk 10:11 suddenly fashions a new concept, which the reader can hardly understand. This difficulty is illustrated by J. Dupont himself. After completing his inquiry on the Matthean clauses, he says in conclusion that divorce is allowed in case of misbehavior. How is the reader supposed to discern that remarriage is not allowed? The author does indeed exclude remarriage because he understands divorce to be, in this case, a simple separation, but the reader is all confused. 4. Although, taken by itself, the expression, "If anyone divorces his wife . . ." in Mk 10:11 lends itself to being read, "Suppose that . . ." does this apply in the same degree to the expression, "Anyone who divorces his wife . . ."?

25. D. Daube, *The New Testament and Rabbinic Judaism* (London, 1956) 141–50.

26. One could go even further and wonder whether in Mk 10:11–12 remarriage is not condemned chiefly in order to bring out all the perversity of

divorce itself. In the case, the connection established by Mark between vv. 2–9 and 11–12 would be as follows: Mark wishes to utilize, through the redactional link of v. 10, the two types of material–debate and sayings–which are at his disposal, and believes, in addition, that vv. 11–12 add to the preceding verses a welcome explicitness. They make it clear that, if divorce is already to be disavowed because, among other things, it entitles one to remarriage, a divorce "consummated" by this remarriage is to be disavowed all the move. This is a remarriage which even more explicitly may be labeled adultery. But this adultery is already seminally contained in divorce, which is what Mt 5:32 states: ". . . everyone who divorces his wife . . . forces her to commit adultery."

27. In order to perceive the redactional differences among the various logia relative to divorce, both these and those to be examined below, the following abbreviations may be helpful: M1, the man who divorces his wife; W1, the woman who is being dismissed by M1; M2, the man with whom W1 remarries; W2, the woman with whom M1 remarries.

28. N. Turner, "The Translation of μοιχᾶται ἐπ' αὐτήν in Mk. 10:11," *The Bible Translator* 7 (1965) 151–52.

29. 'Eὰν γυνὴ 'εξηλθη απο (του) ανδρος . . .

30. V. Taylor, *The Gospel according to St. Mark* (London, 1953) 420–21.

31. H. Zimmermann, *Methodenlehre,* 108.

32. Many authors explicitly justify the current reading, for example, J. Dupont, *Mariage,* 61–63; J. A. Fitzmyer, "Divorce Texts," 205, and the authors quoted there, n. 28.

33. J. Alonso Díaz, *Proceso de dignificación de la mujer a través de la Biblia* (Madrid, 1975) 13–14.

34. J. A. Fitzmyer, "Divorce Texts," 205, and the authors quoted, n. 29; also E. Bammel, "Markus 10:11 f.," 263–74.

35. See R. Bultmann, *Geschichte,* 39–56; ET: *History,* 39–54 ("Controversy dialogues"); note, however, Bultmann's severe criticism of the literal accuracy of the debates as recorded in the synoptics.

36. The context shows that Paul addresses himself to Christian spouses. On the importance of Paul's reference to Jesus, see a long discussion in J. Dupont, *Mariage,* 57, n. 1. See also J. K. Elliott, "Paul's Teaching on Marriage in I Corinthians," NTS 19 (1973), 219–25.

37. Ez 1:11; 23.

38. In this case, the Greek has been translated into Aramaic; see R. Le Déaut, in *Biblical Theology Bulletin* 4 (1974), 249-51; D. Daube, *New Testament,* 74; 368.

39. We shall see, at least by way of an hypothesis, that this is the case with regard to the Matthean clauses.

40. This clearly appears in what is known as the Pauline Privilege. Paul allows the converted spouse to leave the other, if he or she refuses cohabitation; cf. 1 Cor 7:11; 15–16.

41. See J. Weiss, A. Loisy, B. W. Bacon, C. G. Montefiore, B. H. Branscomb,

W. Marxen, J. Schreiber in their discussion of the matter as noted by E. Trocmé, *La formation de l'évangile selon Marc* (Paris, 1963) 115, n. 23. With regard to Mk 10:12, A. Loisy mistakenly believes that it can depend on I Cor, see *Les évangiles synoptiques*, 2, 199, n. 1.

42. See among others E. Schillebeeckx, *Jezus* (Bloemendaal, 1974), *passim;* P. M. Beaude, *Jesus oublié* (Paris, 1977), esp. 49–75; G. Vermès, *Jesus le Juif* (Desclée, 1978).

43. L. Cerfaux, *La théologie de l'Eglise suivant saint Paul* (Paris, 1965), 71–80.

44. See L. Cerfaux, "La tradition selon saint Paul," in *Recueil L. Cerfaux*, 2, 253–63.

45. Note however that the term κτίσις occurs often enough in Paul; he uses the new-creation theme to illustrate the condition of the Christian; see 2 Cor 5:17; Gal 6:15; etc.

46. Here we touch upon a major concern of the ministry of Jesus himself and the very heart of the gospel. First, the relationship of Jesus to Judaism is a sore point for the historian who searches for the Jesus of history. The way in which historians understand that relationship is a watershed between two opposite historiographies. The first and more traditional view presents a Jesus who engaged in direct confrontation with most sacred convictions of the Jews. The second maintains that this confrontation is a misinterpretation fostered by Paul, and transmitted by the evangelists and Christian tradition. The historical Jesus, we are told, was but one of many Jewish reformers. Obviously, we cannot discuss so large an issue here, but we believe that some exegetes go too far when they describe Jesus as "not different" and attribute the break with Judaism and the foundation of Christianity to Paul. From a doctrinal point of view, the stakes are high: if Jesus is not truly responsible for the origin of Christianity, its credentials are no longer very solid. Only a kind of Judeo-Christianity would accord with what Jesus of Nazareth intended.

47. See especially Mk 7:14–23 on the rules of purity, and G. Vermès, *Jésus le Juif*, 35–36.

48. Mt 5:31–32.

49. See above, 221, n. 12.

50. This is precisely the position of Irenaeus, who speaks of the Lord "who exonerates . . . Moses as his faithful servant." See the long quotation in J. Dupont, *Mariage*, 21, n.

51. J. Dupont, *Mariage*, 18–22; See also A. Loisy, *Les évangiles synoptiques*, 2:198 (Jesus "appeals from Moses to Moses").

52. J. Dupont, *Mariage*, 24–27; J. A. Fitzmyer, "Divorce Texts," 216–21.

53. W. E. Bundy, *Jesus and the First Three Gospels: An Introduction to the Synoptic Tradition* (Cambridge, Mass., 1955) 396.

54. J. Dupont, *Mariage*, 23, n. 2.

55. For a presentation of this view, see J. Dupont, *Mariage*, 38–45, and also A. Stock, "Matthean Texts," 29–33.

56. Hence the effort at recovering Jesus' original saying on the part of B. K. Diderichsen, B. M. F. van Iersel, J. H. A. van Tilborg, H. Greeven, all quoted by F. Neirynck, *Jezuswoorden*, 130–36, and of Neirynck himself.

57. This is already evidenced by the expression "church rules" (*Gemeinderegeln*) used in this connection; See R. Bultmann, *Geschichte*, 138–61; ET: *History*, 130–50.

58. The one exception is Mt 19:9. However, we should not forget that v. 9b does exist in an important manuscript tradition, the authenticity of which may well be only slightly probable, yet not entirely impossible; see Dupont, *Mariage*, 51, n. 3. But even if we admit that only Mt 19:9a is authentic, the difficulty thus created against a doubled saying is easily resolved. Often enough, Matthew improves Mark by abridging it. This is even one of the characteristics of his redactional technique. Cf. A. L. Descamps, "Redaction et christologie dans le récit matthéen de la Passion," in M Didier (ed.), *L'évangile selon Matthieu* (Gembloux, 1972), esp. 363–66.

59. Neirynck, *Jezuswoorden*, 132–33.

60. B. K. Diderichsen favors Lk 16:18, and so does Neirynck. But Diderichsen conjectures that we are dealing here with something entirely different: "A man who, in order to imitate the Christ, has left or dismissed his wife, may not marry another woman." Mark, he maintains, changes this saying by linking it to the debate (Mk 10:2–9). B. M. F. van Iersel favors Mk 10:11 (he regards v. 12 as secondary). But Jesus limited himself to defending the dismissed wife. J. H. A. van Tilborg likewise opts for Mk 10:11, but reconstructs the original form of the saying and has it mean that Jesus forbade a man to dismiss his wife in order to marry another woman. Finally, H. Greeven favors Mt 5:32 (without the clause).
    The efforts of Diderichsen, van Iersel, and van Tilborg seem motivated by the desire to solve problems of our time even at the expense of exegesis itself.

61. Neirynck, *Jezuswoorden,* 132; Fitzmyer, "Divorce Texts," 204–05.

62. Dupont. *Mariage*, 66–69.

63. Dupont, *Mariage*, 66–67, and the authors quoted there, especially 67, n. This is due especially to polygamy, which was allowed in Palestinian law; see the citation of Josephus in Dupont, *Mariage*, 67. On polygamy, see the authors quoted in Dupont, *Mariage*, 67. On polygamy, see the authors quoted in Dupont, 67, note 3, and also Greeven, *et al.*, TE, 37–39. He concludes that only the milder wording of Mt 5:32 is authentic: ". . . the man who divorces his wife *dooms her* to commit adultery." This is tantamount to forgetting the very point of the proclamation of Jesus who perhaps pushed his nonconformism as far as calling divorce adultery.

64. By many authors, among them: Fitzmyer, "Divorce Texts," 206, n. 31; Neirynck, *Jezuswoorden*, 129–41; H. Zimmermann, *Methodenlehre* 105ff., 231f; our option is for the literary dependence of Matthew on Mark; see Bultmann, *Geschichte*, 26, n. 1. On Matthew's process of composition, see Dupont, *Mariage*, 38, n.2; Descamps, *Rédaction*, 359–415.

65. Thus the silence is rather striking in Matthew 23.

66. This was the dominant tradition for a long time in Israel: R. de Vaux, *Les Institutions de l'Ancien Testament*, 3rd ed. (Paris, 1976) 1, 45–48. See J. Jeremias, *Jérusalem au temps de Jésus* (Paris, 1976) 471-92.

67. In Israel, the lewd conduct of a married woman was severely punished. It is another thing to know whether, in the time of Jesus, the rule of stoning was consistently applied. Jn 8:5 is not sufficient to prove it, even if the pericope be retained by textual criticism (see Crouzel, *L'Eglise primitive face au divorce*, (Paris, 1971) 22. The husband's infidelity was punished only if he sinned with a married woman, because he was then considered to have encroached on the right of another. See R. de Vaux, *Institutions*, 1, 62–63.

    Among the prophets (Hos 1, *etc.*) the covenant between Yahweh and his people was sometimes symbolized by marriage; in this context, to sin with a prostitute – who represented idols – also merited the name of adultery. (Jer 5:7; LXX, 'εμοιχόντο). But it does not follow that this view had penetrated the customs or feelings of the common people.

68. It is admitted today that the evangelists reinforced the impression that Jesus ceaselessly moved in the Pharisaic milieu and often in an atmosphere of hostility; they did this to explain better the break of the Church of their day with Judaism. But their emphasis was not a complete distortion of history.

69. Although its evidential value is slight, let us note that when Jesus treats the fictitious case of the woman with several husbands, he is talking about a widow, not a divorced woman (Mk 12:18–27 and parallels). Quite different is the case of the woman at the well (Jn 4:17–18), but this is situated in Samaria.

70. In any case, such was the Palestinian custom attested to by Josephus, for example (Crouzel, *Divorce*, 20). On the other hand, it is well known that the Jews of Elephantine (fifth century B.C.) allowed a woman to take the initiative in divorce. See above, 351, n. 33, and P. Grelot, *Documents araméens d'Egypte* (Paris, 1972) 195, 214, 236.

71. See especially Luke, *passim* (7:37, etc.); Jn 8:3–11. This supposition has force if we consider how constantly Jesus welcomed persons considered of little worth: lepers, insane who were possessed, children, sinners, the poor, Samaritans, women, pagans, and the like. See C. Focant, *La mort de Jésus à la lumière de sa vie et de sa résurrection*, in *La foi et le temps* (1979) 137, *etc.*

72. On the conclusions concerning its historicity, see above, 237.

73. See Lohmeyer, *Das Evangelium des Matthäus* (Göttingen, 1956) 281, n. 1; Crouzel, *Divorce*, 28.

74. In other words, if Jesus in Matthew is preparing to side with Shammai, whose rigorous doctrine was probably shared by the Pharisees, we cannot understand why there was a controversy between them and Jesus. In fact, the exception mentioned by Matthew in v. 9 – whatever its precise meaning – remains so limited that it is practically a total refusal of divorce on Jesus' part. Verse 10 confirms our exegesis; for if Jesus limited himself to the position of Shammai, we would have to suppose his disciples, who answered him by saying that it would be better then not to marry, followed Hillel, which is improbable.

75. Thus Loisy, *Synoptiques*, 2:200: "[Matthew] adds the words 'any cause whatever' with the evident intention of anticipating the addition made to the answer of Jesus 'the case of lewd conduct' . . . . " See Bultmann, *Geschichte*, 159; Neirynck, *Het evangelisch echtscheidingsverbod*, in *Collationes brugenses et gandavenses*, 4 (1958) 44–45.

76. The inversion curiously resembles Mt 15:1–9, compared to Mk 7:1–13. (Loisy, *Synoptiques*, 2:201, n. 3).

77. Let us note here that the substance of Dt 24:1 is found in Jer 3:1.

78. Lohmeyer, *Matthäus*, 282, n. 1.

79. The texts of some authors mentioned here without reference to their publications were duplicated for a colloquium held in Albano in 1977.

80. Others will be found in Loisy, *Synoptiques*, 2:200–201, and in Lohmeyer, *Matthäus*, 280–82. Curiously enough, after the author said (280) that Matthew is "literarily independent" of Mark he constantly interprets him (281–82) as if Matthew had Mark under his eyes and "was correcting" him. In our opinion, this is a good hypothesis.

81. "[Matthew] expressly presents as quotations passages from Genesis, and he gives the second entirely as the word of God, because the passage is in scripture." Loisy, *Synoptiques*, 2:201.

    On the interpretation of Gen 1:27, and 2:24 in Judaism, see Pesch, *Markus*, 2:123–24.

82. See above, pp. 219-237, n. 3 and n. 11. Recently D. R. Catchpole (quoted in Pesch, *Markus*, 2:124, n. 11a) likewise has decided in favor of the authenticity of this controversy *in vita Jesu.*

83. Mt 5:32 and 19:9 are closely parallel. Although Matthew doubtless thought of 5:32 when writing 19:9, we comment first on 19:9 because this verse concludes a pericope which we obviously should examine after its Marcan parallel. Moreover, the redactor inserted a logion which comes from Mark 10 or Matthew 19 into 5:32.

84. See above, 222–23.

85. See above, 227–28.

86. See above. Understood thus, the assertion clashes with the ideas of the Jews, for even when they considered divorce reprehensible, they never considered it as adultery against the divorced wife. Neither would divorce be an adultery against the new wife, but only against her former husband if he had not divorced her. But the precise point of the present words of Jesus is to thus overturn the ideas of the Jews.

    On 'επ' αὐτήν of Mark 10, there is a recent discussion (with N. Turner, P. Katz, B. Schaller) in R. Pesch, *Markus.* 2:125–26.

87. For the bibliography on the exception clause, see Dupont, *Mariage* (numerous indications up to 1959); P. Hoffman, *Parole de Jesus à propose du divorce*, in *Concilium*, n. 55 (1970):49–62 (with a bibliographic list); L. Ramaroson, *Une nouvelle interprétation de la clausule de Mt 19:9*, in SE 23 (1971): 247–251; H. Crouzel, *Divorce*, 11–18 (list); L. Sabourin, "The Divorce Clauses," (Mt 5:32; 19:9) BTB 2 (1972):80–86; BTB 4 (1974), 346-48.

88. BJ, 1956 ed., 1314, n. h. Dupont, *Mariage*, 96–98 cites the following in

favor of the preteritive sense for Mt 19:9: Th. Zahn, P. Dausch, W. Lauck, P. J. Arendzen, P. Benoit, E. Lohmeyer, P. Vawter.

89. See Dupont, *Mariage*, 98–99; he quotes numerous exegetes on Mt 19:9.

90. "The exception clause . . . is grammatically attached to the first subjunctive, 'if he divorces,' which it qualifies parenthetically. But the parenthesis is elliptical, it has no verb; . . . it is necessary to supply the verb 'divorce'. . . . By supplying all the terms implied, we have: 'If anyone divorces his wife, [if] this is not for lewd conduct [that he divorces her] . . .' " Dupont, *Mariage*, 102.

The correct translation of the Vulgate "*nisi ob fornicationem*," preserved in the Neo-Vulgate, undoubtedly reflects a keen sensitivity to the Greek which is particularly striking because, for the author of the ancient Vulgate, it could only create or heighten a problem in ecclesiastical discipline, in view of its divergence from the absolute assertions of Mark, Luke and Paul.

91. According to some (see B. J. Malina, "Does Πορνεία Mean *Fornication*?" NT, 14 (1972) 10–17, the Greek term could even have as wide a meaning as immodesty. In the present context one would expect μοιχεία.

92. Let us recall that in the Jewish milieu a husband cannot be called adulterous against his own wife. (Pesch, *Markus*, 2:125).

93. Bonsirven, *Divorce*, especially 7–24.

94. See the numerous authors cited by Dupont, *Mariage*, 107, n. More recently, J. Alonso Diaz, *Proceso*, 14.

95. Thus in Acts 15:20, 29; 21:25 (Dupont, *Mariage*, 111).

96. Fitzmyer, *Divorce Texts*, 213–21.

97. Dupont, *Mariage*, 114. It must be noted, however, that as competent an author as R. LeDéaut has recently suggested that the research ought to be continued on the pertinence of recourse to *zenuth*.

98. It is well known that some Greek tests, such as Mk 10:11 and parallels, often used καί to express purpose (semitism): "he who divorces his wife in order to marry another [the former only] commits adultery." In the ancient Church, "separation was forbidden because it led to adultery" (A. Houssiau, "Le lien conjugal dans l'Eglise ancienne," AC 17 (1973) 571. See Crouzel, *Divorce, passim*.

99. Dupont, *Mariage*, 115–22.

100. Dupont, *Mariage*, 136–57. For the ancient Greek fathers who considered that "Matthew's exception applied only to separation and never to remarriage," see Houssiau, "Le lien conjugal," 570.

101. Dupont, *Mariage*, 147–50.

102. Dupont, *Mariage*, 141–56. One can even suggest that although simple separation was juridically inconsistent for the Jews, it was perhaps less so in reality, for a husband who divorced his wife need not *de facto* remarry, although he had the right to do so; see above, 227.

103. *Mand.* IV, 1, 6–8; explanations in Dupont, *Mariage*, 153; commentary in Crouzel, *Divorce*, 44–53. As a matter of fact, the ancients and the moderns who favor simple separation generally attribute both the con-

cept and the exception clause itself to Jesus. They do not speak of a redactor nor of a Helleno-Christian milieu as affecting the clause. To suppose that Jesus had admitted simple separation in the case of the lewd conduct of the wife is not impossible in itself. But such a conjecture depends upon a casuistry foreign to Jesus. And casuistry there would be with double force since the hypothesis appeals not only to particular cases but also to a concept, that of simple separation, that is, to say the least, rather foreign to a Jewish milieu. Besides, the conjecture neglects literary analysis, that is, the evidence of the adventitious character of the inserted clause, such as we are going to show *sub* b. Moreover, one can no longer uphold the probability of a Proto-Matthew or Aramaic Matthew very close to the time of the discourse of Jesus in the face of such literary analysis.

104. Dupont, *Mariage,* 125, which has reference to numerous authors. The ancient Protestants and also in general the Greeks attributed the exception to Jesus himself. Again, to suppose that Jesus had permitted the deceived husband to remarry is not absolutely impossible in itself. But it would scarcely be in the style of the Master. The latter has emphasized the radicalism of his requirements, and these are little compatible with the precise exceptions in regard to principles. And then there is the evidence of literary analysis that we are going to show. Thus contemporary authors who have abandoned Jerome's exegesis refuse (with rare exceptions–see the quotation made by Dupont, *Mariage,* 129, n.1.) to attribute to Jesus the clause understood as permission to remarry in case of the lewd conduct of his wife.

    On the whole, the presence of the inserted clause *in ore Jesu* appears then to be excluded and in any case, unprovable.

105. Descamps, "Essai d'interprétation de Mt 5:17–48, see, (Berlin, 1959), 165–66.

106. See the majority of the authors cited in n. 26.

107. Dupont, *Mariage,* 147.

108. "Taken in themselves and without prejudice, Matthew's texts seem to permit complete divorce in case of adultery." (J. Thomas, *Droit naturel,* 635). The author does not accept Jerome's interpretation; such was also the opinion of G. Pouget, cited in Dupont, *Mariage,* 126, n. 2.

109. Loisy, *Synoptiques,* 1:580. W. D. Davies, *The Setting of the Sermon on the Mount* (Cambridge, 1966), 387, considers the exception clause as a sort of Christian gemara (an explanation or application) common in Matthew. Let us also observe that if Jesus had delivered the clause, its absence from Mark and Paul would be very difficult to explain.

110. R. Schnackenburg, *Die sittliche Botschaft des Neuen Testaments,* (Munich, 1954), 91.

111. See Neirynck, *Echtscheidingsverbod,* 44–46. What was said above on the grammatical analysis of the exception clause evidently remains valid.

112. One could also conjecture that Matthew attributed to Jesus, whom he deliberately placed in a unique moment of history (*unwiederholbar*), an accommodation to Jewish customs which he considered outdated in the Church. Such an explanation is purely redactional and leaves out any ec-

clesial *sitz im leben*. On the general idea of such a *historisierung* in Matthew, see G. Strecker, *Der Weg der Gerechtigkeit, Untersuchung zur Theologie des Matthäus*, 3rd, ed. (Göttingen, 1971); R. Walker, *Die Heilsgeschichte in ersten Evangelium* (Göttingen, 1967). In a contrary sense, (*enthistorisierung*), see H. Frankemölle, *Jahwebund und Kirche Christi, Studien zur Form und Traditionsgeschichte des Evangeliums nach Matthäus* (Münster, 1974).

113. The hiatus is confirmed by the fact that after Matthew used αἰτία in 19:3, with the meaning of *motive*, he used it with the entirely different meaning of *state of things* or *condition* in 19:10.

114. Article λέγω in TWNT 4:108. Other authors sharing this opinion are listed by Dupont who himself favors this solution in *Mariage*, 170–74.

115. It does not at all follow that, in itself, Mt 19:10–12 is not pre-Matthean and indeed an exact citation of a saying of Jesus from a different occasion. This idea of a "lost context" (T. W. Manson and others: discussed in Dupont, *Mariage*, 164–66) seems valid to us. It is reinforced by the fact that Mt 19:10–12 has no parallel in either Mark or Luke. The word *eunuch*, characteristic of v. 12, is nowhere else found in the gospels, nor in the New Testament except for Acts 8:27–39, where it designates a function.

116. Dupont, *Mariage*, 45–46. Our various observations on the redactional activity have not injured the substantial authenticity of the antitheses *in ore Jesus*. Indeed, they seem to echo the oral style of Jesus. It is not difficult to imagine the master saying with the tone of the prophets: "It has been said to you . . . but I, on the contrary, tell you. . . ." The problem is that the exception clause in Mt 5:32 breaks the oratorical thrust of the prophet with the qualification of a casuist. That is why strict authenticity can scarcely be extended to the clause, any more than it can to Mt 19:9. But in Mt 5:31–32, Matthew inserts a substantially authentic logion which he uses elsewhere; see Mk 10 and Mt 19.

117. Adultery is not yet committed at the time of the divorce (Dupont, *Mariage*, 74, n.) It does not seem that the fact of separation constitutes her adulterous.

118. This time the expression implied (M2 is adulterous toward W1) is not in itself contradictory in the eyes of a Jew for whom, on the contrary, such an eventuality would be normal if there had been no divorce; but as this is presupposed by the evangelist, his teaching on adultery thus becomes provocative.

119. Dupont, *Mariage*, 103–04.

120. What should be added here is that the λόγος πορνείας is perhaps a close imitation (through the intermediary of Judaism: Moore) of the Hebrew expression *ervat dabor* of Dt 24:1; it is possible, although the LXX was translated ἀσχήμον πρᾶγμα. We will not settle it, but this eventuality changes nothing of the meaning of Mt 5:32 with reference to Mt 19:9. Nevertheless, if the hypothesis is correct, it confirms the contact with Dt 24:1 and therefore the importance of divorce as the precise theme of our texts. (See Dupont, *Mariage*, 87, n. 1; Crouzel, *Divorce*, 23–29, n. 49.) On the whole, one may then read with the Vulgate and the Neovulgate: *excepta fornicationis causa*.

121. See Loisy, *Synoptiques*, 1:577–80.

122. The repeated mentioning of an adultery not followed by stoning raises a number of problems; see Dupont, *Mariage*, 105.

123. In 19:9 Matthew thought he had to safeguard the right of the husband to divorce and probably also to remarry, in the case of lewd conduct of the woman; in the same case he has, in 5:32a allowed divorce and freed the husband from all responsibility towards the new adultery which his wife will commit. But in speaking of another man marrying a divorced woman (5:32b), he does not seem to have distinguished between innocent and guilty women.

124. Dupont, *Mariage*, 46–48.

125. After μοιχεύει "M1 commits adultery" it is necessary to supply in 18a "against W1," which is quite contrary to Jewish thought.

126. Until now, we had touched the question of historicity only with respect to the clause.

127. M. Devisch, *La relation entre Marc et Q,* 59–91.

128. *See above,* 227. See also Neiryunk, *Doublets in Mark* (Louvain, 1972) *passim.*

129. Thus also Loisy, *Synoptiques*, 2:199; Neirynck, *Jezuswoorden*, 136; B. K. Diderichsen, *Den skilsmisseperikope*, 31-50; however, this last author understands the word quite otherwise (see above, 218, n. 2, and 220, n. 6). For his part, Greeven retains Mt 5:32 (without the clause) as the original form (see Neirynck, *Jezuswoorden*, 131).

130. The consensus on this second point is smaller if we take into account, for example, the opinion of Dupont, discussed above, 224–226, according to which Jesus does not condemn divorce but only remarriage.

131. Cf. 1 Cor 9:14; 1 Thes 4:15, and *ad rem*: H. von Campenhausen, *Die Begründung kirchlicher Entscheidungen beim Apostel Paulus* (Heidelberg, 1957), 21–22. For Paul, the precepts of Jesus remain those of the glorified Christ. Thus also F. Hahn, *Christologische Hoheitstitel* (Göttingen, 1974), 93. In this sense, the precepts of Jesus are then supra-historical: H. Conzelmann, *Der erste Brief an die Korinther*, (Göttingen, 1969), 44.
Another possibility to consider: not only does Paul *think* that the word of 1 Cor 7:10 comes from the terrestrial Jesus, but he was right; this is, for example, the conviction of F. Hahn, *Hoheitstitel*, 92.

132. On χωρίσθεναι, ses Dupont, *Mariage*, 142, n; Conzelmann, *Korinther*, 143, n. 5.

133. This is also the view of Conzelmann, *Korinther*, 144.

134. This is also the view of Conselmann, *Korinther,* 142 (*sie soll unverheiratet bleiben*); J. Héring, *La première epître de saint Paul aux Corinthiens*, (Neuchâtel, 1959), 52: "I enjoin her to live without remarrying, or to become reconciled to her husband."

135. Let us repeat that there are grounds, although not conclusive, for reading even the clause of Matthew in terms of this simple separation, as St. Jerome and others do. Moreover, does not 1 Cor 7:11 give us reason to admit that, even in Mark 20:2–12, Jesus condemned not the act of divorce,

but only remarriage? We think not. Mark may have remembered that the horizon of Jesus was Jewish, whereas Paul is thinking principally of converts from paganism.

136. When Paul writes "the man may not divorce his wife," does he mean that dismissal is forbidden in itself, or does he imply that divorce is forbidden because normally it ends in remarriage, which is certainly a sin? The first interpretation seems to be the obvious one.

137. On 1 Cor 7:12–16 (mixed marriages), see above, 263, *Conclusions,* 3a. For now let us limit ourselves to speaking of the words of Paul which comment on the teaching of Jesus, since the master's horizon did not include the case of mixed marriages.

138. "Jesus pronounces an unconditional and absolute condemnation of divorce" (J. Dupont, *Mariage,* 75). According to the author it is a question of remarriage, that is, of "complete divorce." Let us recall that recourse to this last expression (cf. for example, J. Thomas, *Droit naturel,* 635) itself shows the ambiguity of the word *divorce,* which we have therefore completely avoided in this essay. See above, 229.

139. We must except B. M. F. van Iersel and J. H. A. van Tilborg, in T. A. G. van Eupen (ed.), *On ontbindbaarheid,* 19, and 26–28. See Neirynck, *Jezuswoorden,* 130–32.

140. "Nowhere does Jesus say: 'Divorce is forbidden.' Jesus does make a value judgment of the act itself. . . ." (Dupont, *Mariage,* 144. However, "it is clear that Jesus does not wish to define the juridical status of bodily separation nor to formally authorize it." (68, n. 2.)

141. Although the distinction is not really relevant to this context, it is useful to recall that the real life of Jesus was "much more varied and richer in content" than what is known from history; "the historical Jesus (that is, accessible to the historian) remains poorer than . . . the terrestrial Jesus." (A. Schilson–W. Kasper, *Théologiens du Christ aujourd'hui* (Desclée, 1978. 31).

142. It hardly need be said that our philosophical anthropology does not correspond exactly to the order of creation to which Jesus refers.

143. Delimiting the scope of the historian's competence belongs in the commentary above. In some passages we did treat it, but for clarity we will summarize our remarks here.

144. Some clear examples are Mt 21:27 and parallels.

145. Besides, we often read "that in Israel, as in Mesopotamia, marriage is a purely civil act and is not sanctioned by any religious act" (de Vaux, *Institutions,* 1, 58). These statements can be understood by comparison with Christian marriage, but, taken literally, they are misleading. In a sense, nothing is purely civil in the milieu in which Jesus lived. Moreover, some texts, such as Tb 6:18, 7:11 show that marriage can be perceived as a divine blessing, calling for a feeling of thanksgiving and a prayer of petition. Although only the Vulgate version of Tb 7:15 reads "*Deus Abraham . . . conjungat vos*" (the source of the introit of the nuptial mass), it remains true that Tb develops a notion of marriage which is "Christian before its time" (BJ, 494).

146. One might say that, in the question of indissolubility, Jesus is concerned–as he is so often–about intentions, interiority, the duty of each one to assume responsibility for his acts (Mt 5:32; see also above, 230, n. 37), and to practice a loyalty that the institution cannot always respond to. In this sense, the point of view of Jesus is that of the moralist rather than the founder of a "social order." See B. Rigaux, *Le radicalisme du Règne,* in J. Dupont (ed.), *La pauverté évangélique,* (Paris. 1971), 135–73.

147. Bultmann treats the question of how Jesus unified his eschatological preaching and his moral message at the core of his being (*Theologie des Neuen Testaments,* 2nd ed. [Tübingen, 1954], 18–21). But it is immense; to resolve it clearly is to understand the historical Jesus perfectly.

148. In a sense, tradition and the magisterium have always sought to make revelation relevant, which is a fundamental concern of contemporary hermeneutics. But this raises new problems by displacing the accent more on the present than on the past, and by emphasizing the fact that all established language, even sacred, is culturally conditioned and therefore relative.

149. See above, 240, n. 80.

150. M. Goguel, *Les premiers temps de l'Eglise,* (Neuchatel-Paris, 1949), 18–19. "It was in a hellenistic milieu that Christianity had its principal development; the only one which ended in something durable." (*Ibid.,* 39) Coming from a Protestant exegete, such remarks have a particular resonance.

    Could one not apply these considerations to the oath about which one may justly raise questions in the light of Mt 5:32? If Jesus was opposed to every form of oath (Mt 5:33–37), the Church has acted otherwise and, in doing so, she surely did not feel unfaithful to her Lord. See also, above, 233, n. 51, on *historisierung.*

151. The expression is not ours, but that of E. Schillebeeckx, *Gerechtigheid en liefde,* (Bruges, 1977), 6.

152. *To decide* could never mean *that the Church define de fide* a particular interpretation of the Matthean incidental clause, since the exgetes remain hopelessly divided in their field.

153. The case of mixed marriage, absent from the horizon of Jesus, emerges, as we said, in the apostolic Church.

154. Does Paul believe that the Christian party who leaves a pagan or Jewish partner may remarry? Ambrosiaster thinks he can, but Augustine denies it and his opinion could perhaps be founded on 1 Cor 7:17–24 (each would do well to remain in his condition), 1 Cor 7:29–31 (time is short). 1 Cor 7:39–40 (death puts an end to marriage; however, the Christian widow can remarry but only with a Christian, but she will be happier, in my opinion, if she remains as she is.)

155. A number of exegetes think that here Paul permits a new marriage: for example, Conzelmann, *Korinther,* 149; Héring, *Corinthiens,* 54; Baltensweiler, *Die Ehe,* 192–93.

156. Paul has a clear concept of the universal Church, but lacks the perspective of duration.

157. The opening words of 7:1, "I come now to what you have written to me," show that Paul turns to another series of questions. This series takes up an entire chapter (7:1–40). It begins with a careful catalogue of various kinds of situations probably set forth more completely than in the query of the Corinthians, and it reveals concern of a pastor to distinguish different types of cases. Let us add that 1 Cor 7:12–17 is "relatively" long and lively and that the end speaks for itself: "such is my teaching in all the Churches."

158. Let us recall the famous passage Eph 5:22–23 which is even for those who do not admit the full authenticity of the epistle at least indirectly Pauline. Cf. 1 Tm 3:2–7.

159. See above, 229.

160. See above, 266, *Conclusions*, 2.

161. It follows that this teaching is normative, although it is not uniformly expressed. An intelligent hermeneutic of both the apostles and Jesus must be governed by the historically established tenor of their teachings, and also by the importance which these have in the very thought of the apostles and Jesus. This second insight is also grounded on exegesis, as we have already said.

162. The ancient Church regarded this teaching not as "an exceptional ideal" but as "the order of creation" relevant to all men. However, "this radicalism goes hand in hand with a great understanding of existing situations." (Houssiau, *Le lien conjugal*, 577). The problem involved is whether the gospel is to be viewed as a new law or as an ideal (*zielgebot*); this question has been treated especially by Protestants, often with reference to the Sermon on the Mount. See F. Montagnini, *Aspetti indicativi e aspetti precettivi della legge evangelica*, in *Paolo VI, predicatore del Concilio* (Brescia, 1967), 349–58 for an overview of different theories, borrowed from J. Jeremias.

163. For this reason, the Church, according to present discipline, does not claim that it has the right to touch the marriage of the nonbaptized.

164. Loisy, *Synoptiques*, 1:579–80.

165. We write "for Matthew" without forgetting that the thought of Matthew on the link between marriage and celibacy is not considered in the same light by all exegetes. On the Anglican hermeneutics of marriage, see V. Taylor, *Mark*, 421.

166. "Confrontation of the sources of the faith and the experience of Christian spouses," in V. Boulanger *et al.*, *Mariage: rêve-réalité. Essai théologique*, Montréal, 1975; "Survey of theologians on matrimonial procedures and pastoral care," in P. Hayoit, "Les procédures matrimoniales et la théologie du mariage," RTL 9 (1978): 33–58.

167. In closing let us touch on two questions which come more from hermeneutics than exegesis.

1) The moment of the completion of marriage. The texts of the New Testament are silent on this subject. The exegete can refer to the Jewish usage. The idea of a contract – if not always a written document – was a part of the betrothal rite (when the dowry was given and the penalty

agreed upon in case the contract were voided). The idea of contract, in another sense, also regulated the act of divorce, and *a fortiori* the marriage ceremony. The marriage was celebrated by festivities which lasted several days and it was consummated on the first night of this festive time. These observations, which one could surely illustrate by parallels in other cultures, involve some kind of multiplicity – at least a duality – of moments (cf. *sunoikeo* in Dt 24:1) which no doubt survives in the canonical distinction *ratum – consummatum.*

2) The distinction between indissolubility intrinsic (the conjugal bond unbreakable by the couple) and extrinsic (the bond unbreakable by competent social authority). Again, our texts are silent, but the exegete can recall that for the Jews, divorce broke the conjugal bond on the initiative of the husband alone, with no intervention from any authority. In forbidding divorce, and in any case, remarriage, Jesus then wishes explicitly to oppose all divorce and all remarriage on the part of the husband and implicitly on the part of the wife. By claiming the right to dissolve certain marriages, the Church faced new problems on which Jesus left no teaching and which it had no wish to ignore. But Paul had given the example of such dissolution. That is, perhaps he gave it, in the eyes of the exegetes who believe – in opposition to others – that Paul permits the Christian party who is persecuted by the pagan party to remarry. We must rely on this faculty of dissolution, we think, to justify Paul and the Church, and not on texts concerning the power of the keys. In these texts, *to bind and to loose* do not apply to power over the conjugal bond save perhaps virtually or remotely.

9. NATURE AND GRACE IN VATICAN II

1. See above Part II, Chapter 3.
2. According to the rules that govern a symposium, and which the ITC adopted, a first respondent follows the presentation and introduces the round table dicussion. His role is to isolate the salient points of the presentation and the questions which particularly need discussion, and also to advert to related problems. This is what we are doing here.
3. To this project we also need to relate the valuable article of Fr. de Lubac, "Petitie catéchèse sur la 'nature' et la 'grâce'," *Communio – Revue Catholique Internationale* [French Edition] 2 (1977); cf. also, *au fond de la morale*, pp. 11-23.
4. H. de Lubac, "Petite catéchèse," p. 11.
5. I am not overlooking the fact that the term *nature* is ambiguous. In my book, *Permanence du droit naturel* (2nd ed.; Louvain, 1967), I have listed some twenty usages of this word. Here I take *nature* to mean *man*, for this is the sense of the word in the theologians after Trent and in the authors who have participated in the recent debates.

   But it may help to recall that, since the time the Stoics used the term *nature* as *moral norm*, nature-as-cosmos and nature-as-logos have been confused. Today, the form this confusion takes surfaces in two very different questions: (1) Does a particular act accord with man's physiology as it happens to be? (2) If we consider what man is not only physically but also psychologically and spiritually, is a particular course of action right?

The latter thorny question still awaits an official answer, but does not involve the problem of nature and grace, or the constitution of the marriage covenant. It is nonetheless crucial in dealing with the use of marriage and conjugal life. But we shall not deal with this question here.

6. It must be stated at the outset that this theology of "nature and grace within salvation history" does not cancel out the gratuitousness of divinization, as is the case for the extreme immanentism disavowed by Pius XII (DS 3891). There would have been no contradiction if God had created man intelligent and free, but without giving him access to his friendship and to divinization. We are reflecting here on what God willed in his goodness and freedom, not on what he could or could not have willed.

7. The third proposition of Jansenius, condemned by Innocent X, says in effect: "In the state of fallen nature, freedom from constraint suffices to gain merits or demerits. Freedom from necessity is not required.–*Ad merendum et demerendum in statu naturae lapsae non requiritur in homine libertas a necessitate, sed sufficit libertas a coactione*" (DS 2003). Baius, who was condemned by Pius V, had already declared: "What we do voluntarily, we do freely even if we do it necessarily"–"*Quod voluntarie fit, etiam si necessario fiat, libere tamen fit*" (DS 1939).

8. The 25th proposition of Baius reads: "All the deeds which the pagans do are sins, and the virtues which the philosophers practice are vices"–"*Omnia opera infidelium sunt peccata, et philosophorum virtutes sunt vitia*" (DS 1925).

9. Cf. B. Bro, *Devenir Dieu* (Paris, 1978) 58 ff.

10. The same procedure was used in the nineteenth century: the Christian state is the thesis, the neutral state is the hypothesis. Once the thesis has been paid homage to, it is dropped.

11. Obviously, this hypothesis is one more proof of God's freedom. However, God's freedom disappears only if we deny this possibility. It is not affected if we realize that, in the history of salvation as it has happened, God has chosen another vocation for humanity. A parallel: theologians state that the Christ could have carried out the work of redemption by one single act of human-divine obedience, without submitting to the cross. This hypothesis, as legitimate as it no doubt is, does not cancel out the sufferings of the Lord.

12. The logic operative within the pure-nature system manages in the end to have man pursue two ultimate ends. The supernatural end is attained through grace and the theological virtues, whereas the natural end is achieved through the practice of natural virtues. J. Maritain remarks that this alleged natural end is but an invention. There is no foundation for it in revelation. See for example: *De la philosophie chrétienne* (Paris, 1933; ET: *An Essay in Christian Philosophy* [trans. E. H. Flannery; New York: Philosophical Library, 1955]); *Science et sagesse* (Paris, 1935; ET: *Science and Wisdom* [trans. B. Wall; New York: Scribner's Sons, 1940]); *Neuf leçons sur les notions premières de la philosophie morale* (Paris, 1951).

13. See R. Simon, *Morale* ("Cours de philosophie thomiste"; 11th ed.; Paris: Beauchesne, 1961) 33 ff.
14. H. de Lubac, *Surnaturel: Etudes historiques* ("Théologie" 8; Paris: Aubier, 1946); *Augustinisme et théologie moderne* (Paris: Aubier, 1965) ET: *Augustinianism and Modern Theology*, trans. L. Sheppard (New York: Herder and Herder, 1969); *Le mystère du surnaturel* (Paris: Aubier, 1965) ET: *The Mystery of the Supernatural,* trans. R. Sheed (New York: Herder and Herder, 1967); *Athéisme et sens de l'homme* (Paris: Cerf, 1968).
15. The allusion is to a book recently circulated but not commercially available.
16. Ph. Delhaye, M. Gueret, P. Tombeur, *Concilium Vaticanum II. Concordance, index, listes des fréquences, tables comparatives* (Louvain-la-Neuve, Cetedoc). Strangely, the indices in the edition of Msgr. Simon Delacroix (Ed. du Centurion), usually so valuable and precise, has no entry under *supernatural.* Note also that the French text sometimes renders the Latin *supernaturalis* by *spirituel.*
17. Note that God's freedom is being reaffirmed. We should not say, then, that God's freedom is safeguarded only in the pure-nature hypothesis.
18. The theology of the 1930s was often forced to acknowledge its own inability to answer this question. I have heard a famous professor declare that the problem had no solution. He would then fall back on limbo, which corresponds more or less to the natural end that the school to which he belonged had invented.
19. GS 2, 2 (Abbott, 200) lists concisely the three great stages through which man, the world, and nature have passed during the whole history of salvation. It speaks of the world "which the Christian sees as created and sustained by its maker's love, fallen indeed into the bondage of sin, yet emancipated now by Christ. He was crucified and rose again to break the stranglehold of personified evil, so that this world might be fashioned anew according to God's design and reach its fulfillment."

10. LITURGICAL HISTORY OF MARRIAGE

1. Lib. 1, c. 9: ed. of 1700, 2, 596–663; ed. of 1736, t. 2, col 335–402; ed. of 1763, 1783, 1788, t. 2, 122–44.
2. Tome 2, (Würzburg: Stahel, 1864) (reprinted, [Graz: Academische Druck, 1961]), p. 364-482. We will use the French translation of A. Raes, *Marriage, Its Celebration, and Its Spirituality in the Eastern Churches* (Chevetogne, 1958) (Coll. "Irénikon").
3. French translation by this title, (Paris: Ed. du Cerf, 1970) (*Lex Orandi*, 45), including some later clarifications by the author to the German edition: *Formen, Riten und religiöses Brauchtum der Eheschliessung in den christlichen Kirchen des ersten Jahrtausends* (Münster: Aschendorff, 1962) (*Liturgiewissenschaftliche Quellen und Forschungen*, 38). Hereafter referred to as Ritzer.
4. (Paris: Beauchesne, 1974) (*Theologie historique* 26).

5. Characteristic of this is canon 1100 of the Code of 1917: "Extra casum necessitatis, in matrimonii celebratione serventur ritus in libris ritualibus ab Ecclesia probatis praescripti aut laudabilibus consuetudinibus recepti."

6. Ignatius of Antioch, *Polycarp* 5, 2; trans. P. Th. Camelot, 2d. ed., (Paris: Cerf, 1951) (SC 10), 177.

7. The *Apostolic Tradition* of Hippolytus does not envision the eventual practice of marriage of the baptized, but only the catechesis of Christian marriage that must be given to catechumens and which affirms the purity of the bond of marriage: ed. B. Botte, (Münster: Aschendorff, 1963) (LQF 39), 35 and 93.

   The *Didascalia Apostolorum* is content to insist on the legitimacy of marriage, doubted by the heretics, and to invite children to marry rather early in order for them to avoid the danger of fornication: ed. H. R. Connolly, (Oxford: Clarendon, 1929), 152, 194, 202, 204.

8. II, 8 6: CCL 1, p. 393.

9. K. Ritzer, German ed., 58–67; French ed., 110–21.

10. *De pudicitia* 4, 4: CCL 2, p. 1287; *De monogamia* 11, 1–2; CCL 2, 1244.

11. III, 11, 63, 1, transl. C. Mondesert and C. Matray, (Paris: Cerf, 1970) (SC 158), 129.

12. K. Ritzer, *Formen*, German ed., 54; French ed., 106–07.

13. Ambrosiaster, *Comm. in Epist. I ad Cor. 7, 40:* PL 17, col. 238; *Comm. in Epist. 1 ad Tim 3, 12:* PL 17, col. 497; Quaest. *Novi et Veteris Testamenti,* CSEL 50, 400;

    St. Ambrose, *Epist. 19 ad Vigilium trident.*, PL 16, col. 1026: "Nam cum ipsum coniugium velamine sacerdotali et benedictione sanctificare oporteat . . . " On the *velamen,* mentioned also by Pope St. Siricius, see below.

14. The book of Tobit provides Christians not only with prayer formulas but also with spiritual and ascetical principles for marriage.

15. Formulas from the Babylonian Talmud cited by Strack-Billerbeck, *Kommentar zum neuen Testament aus Talmud und Midrash,* 1, München, 514; reprod. in K. Ritzer, French ed., 109–10; German ed., 57.

16. Lipsius-Bonnet, *Acta apostolorum apocrypha,* Leipzig, t. II, 2, 1903, 114–15.

17. Ritzer, French ed., 109–10; German ed. 57.

18. Affirmed by the *Vita Amatoris antissiodorensis,* in *Acta. Sanct.*, May 1, 52–53, of St. Avit de Vienne, Epist. 55, MGH, *Auct. Antiqui,* VI, 2, 84: a text is provided in the Latin version of the *Acta S. Thomae,* Lipsius-Bonnet, *op. cit.*

    The Bobbio Missal, ed. E. A. Lowe, London, 1920 (HBS 58), 167–68, contains a *Benedictio talami super nubentes,* of either Gallican or even Visigothic origin.

19. To tell the truth, the supplement of the Visigothic *Liber Ordium* contains an *Ordo ad thalamum benedicendum* which is a blessing of the chamber itself and not of the spouses: ed. M. Ferotin (Paris: Didot, 1904)

(Monumenta Ecclesiae liturgica 5), col. 433 (concerning the persistence of this rite in the *Manca Hispanica* after the adoption of the Roman liturgy, cf. *Sacramentaire de Vich*, ed. A. Olivar, nn. 1406–07). But the blessing of the spouses *in thalamo* is found outside of the peninsula in the liturgical books bearing marks in the Visigothic liturgy, such as the Bobbio Missal (cf. preceding note) and the Anglo-Norman books (cf. following note).

20. The benediction *in thalamo* is found in an 11th C. pontifical entitled "Pontifical of Egbert", ed. G. Greenwell (London: 1853) (*Publication of the Surtees Society* 27), 125–26, and in several other books of Anglo-Norman origin mentioned by Ritzer, German ed., 141–45; French ed., 312–17.

21. It is not easy to restore exactly the detail of the rites in the allegorical commentary of Pseudo-Georges d'Arbèle, *Expositio officiorum Ecclesiae*, transl. R. H. Connolly, CSCO 76, 142–43; but the blessing of the couple is placed after the banquet and in connection with their entrance into the chamber. The ritual preserves, after numerous other ceremonies and prayers, a *Collegatio thalami*, H. Denzinger, *op. cit.* 446–50; A. Raes, *Marriage*, 192–97.

22. Concerning the eve of the wedding, K. Ritzer, *Formen*, German ed., 81; French ed., 139; concerning what follows the signing of the contract, German ed., 62; French ed., 115.

23. "Sacerdotes, nuptiarum initia benedicentes, consecrantes et in Dei mysteriis sociantes": *Praedestinatus* (mid-fifth century), III, 31: PL 53, 670.

24. It is always difficult to date the originals of Rome sacramentaries of which we only have later copies; however, they contain *orationes* (brief forms) in which one can recognize the style of St. Leo and of St. Gelasius; the eucharistic prayer is certainly prior, the other prayers perhaps equally so.

25. Ed. L. K. Mohlberg (*Rerum ecclesiarum documenta*, principal series *Fontes* 4), nn. 1449, 1453.

26. *Hanc igitur* of the *Veronense* sacramentary 85, ed. L. K. Mohlberg (same collection, *Fontes* 1), n. 1107; of the *Reginensis* 316, *op. cit.*, n. 1447; of the *Hadrianum*, ed. J. Deshusses (*Spicilegium Friburgense* 16), n. 856.

27. *Op. cit.*, n. 1454.

28. Pliny, *Natural. hist.*, 32, 12: *ferreus anulus isque sine gemma.*

29. In Africa, according to Tertullian, *Apologeticum* 6, 4.6: "Circa feminas quidem etiam illa maiorum instituta ceciderunt, quae modestiae, quae sobrietati patrocinabantur, cum aurum nulla norat praeter unico digito, quem sponsus oppignerasset pronubo anulo", CCL 1, p. 97.

30. See for example the Byzantine rite: transl. A. Raes, 53–54; the Syrian rite, 110–11.

31. On the blessing of the dowry and its diffusion: K. Ritzer, *Formen.*, German ed., 229–31, French ed., 300–02, and especially Molin-Mutembe, *op. cit.*, 144–56.

32. Manuscript in A. Ferotin, *op. cit.*, col. 435: ". . . (mulier) dat (viro) osculum pacis, quod est verum testamentum".

33. K. Ritzer, German ed., p. 129; French ed., pp. 192–93. This rubric is no longer found in the modern euchologion.

34. *Carmen* 25, 199–232, CSEL 30, 244–45; K. Ritzer, German ed., 159; French ed., 224–25; Molin-Mutembe, 25–26.

35. Molin-Mutembe, 228–33.

36. Gregory of Nazianzus, *Letter 231*, text and transl. in the edition by P. Gallay, 2 (Coll. des Universités de France), 122–23.

37. K. Ritzer German ed., 77, 86–89; French ed., 135, 146–48.

38. Father Raès believes, in fact, that among the Chaldeans the rite of coronation in the marriage ceremony is not primitive: OCP 29, 1963, 483.

39. *Liber ordinum*, ed. Ferotin, col. 439; K. Ritzer, German ed., 191–96, 353–55; French ed., 258-63, 415–17.

40. Gregory of Nazianzus, *Letter* 193, ed. and tran. P. Gallay, *op. cit.*, 84.

41. *Barberini Euchologion 336*, 8th C.; ed. J. Goar, *Euchologion sive Rituale Graecorum*, 2d ed. (Venetiis: Javerina, 1730), p. 322; *Sinaiticus* 958, 10th C.: A. Dmitrievskij, *Opisanie liturgitseskich rukopisej*, to. 2 (Kiev: 1901), 30; etc.

42. St. John Chrysostom, *In I Tim.*, PG 62, col. 546.

43. On the *common cup* and its meaning: K. Ritzer, *op. cit.*, German edition, 135–42; French ed., 198–206.

44. I have cited a number of characteristic witnesses on the bond between marriage and the eucharistic communion in my article "The Eucharist, the Center of the Sacramental Order," in *Seminarium*, 1968, 41–44.

45. Simeon of Thessalonica, *Dialogos*, c. 282, PG 155, col. 512: "τέλος γὰρ πάσης τελετης και θειου μυστήριου πάντος σφραγὶς ἡ ἱέρα κοινωνία".

46. Traditional, it seems, in the Roman liturgy, until the end of the 11th C.; it was then removed, in favor of 1 Cor 6: 15–20, beginning with the Romano-Germanic Pontifical; the reform of St. Pius V restored it afterward in the Roman Missal.

47. In order to be complete, I point out again, besides 1 Cor 6:15–20, which is discussed in the preceding note, the pericopes 1 Cor 7: 1–14 (duties of spouses and the unmarried), which the Visigothic *Liber canonicus* proposes, and Acts 16, 13-15 (Lydia, the dealer in purple goods), which the Coptic liturgy adds to the other readings.

48. A. Raès, 131; this prayer is not in the ancient ritual.

49. The pericope from Genesis is even used as one of the readings in the Armenian rite.

50. One can also name Seth and Noah in the Armenian rite: Raès, 95, and Noah equally in the Syrian rite.

51. The pericope has a place in the Armenian liturgy: Raès, 90.

52. Syrian chant, Raès, 124.

53. Chaldean chant, Raès, 174–75.
54. For example, an Armenian hymn of the betrothed: Raès, 81.
55. Coptic prayer for the rite of betrothed: Raès, 30.
56. Armenian prayer of coronation: Raès, 84.
57. Chaldean prayer: Raès, 174.
58. Preface of the nuptial mass from the Gelasian sacramentary: "*quod generatio ad mundi edidit ornatum, regeneratio ad ecclesiae perducat augmentum.*"
59. Syrian prayer: Raès, 121.
60. Armenian prayer: Raès, 94.
61. Acclamation of the Coptic liturgy, Raès, 36; see also 60, 84, 93, 95, 181, for some more significant texts.
62. Raès, 56.
63. Rouen, ms. A 11, cited by Martène, *De antiquis Ecclesiae ritibus*, Lib. 1, c. 9, ordo 7 and reproduced by Martène in Molin–Mutembe, 304.
64. Text in the edition of E. Perels, MGH, *Epistolarum*, 4, 568-600; see also Ritzer, German ed., 340-341 (unfortunately shortened in the French ed., 420-421).
65. Session 25, December 3–4, 1563; DS 1813.
66. See Ritzer, German ed., 82, 101–104, 158, 166; French ed., 140, 163–170, 223, 229, 231.
67. Concerning all of this, see J. Dauvillier and C. de Clercq, *Marriage in Eastern Canon Law* (Paris: Recueil Sirey, 1936).
68. Molin–Mutembe, 63–73.
69. Molin–Mutembe especially 102–22.
70. Duvillier-de Clercq, 43; Ritzer, German ed. 147–50; French ed. 211–213.
71. Notably the disposition foreseen by canon 1098 of the Code of 1917.
72. This is to say that I would have difficulty in admitting the conclusions of Duval in his article "Contract and Sacrament of Marriage According to the Council of Trent" which appeared in MD 127 (1976) 34–63.

INDEX